CRIME, VIOLENCE, AND GLOBAL WARMING

CRIME, VIOLENCE, AND GLOBAL WARMING

JOHN P. CRANK
LINDA S. JACOBY

Routledge
Taylor & Francis Group

LONDON AND NEW YORK

First published 2015 by Anderson Publishing

Published 2015 by Routledge
2 Park Square, Milton Park, Abingdon, Oxon OX14 4RN

and by Routledge
711 Third Avenue, New York, NY 10017, USA

Routledge is an imprint of the Taylor & Francis Group, an informa business

Acquiring Editor: Pamela Chester
Development Editor: Ellen S. Boyne
Project Manager: Punithavathy Govindaradjane
Designer: Mark Rogers

Library of Congress Cataloging-in-Publication Data
Crank, John P., 1947-
  Crime, violence, and global warming / John P. Crank, Linda S. Jacoby.
    pages cm
  ISBN 978-0-323-26509-6
  1. Crime. 2. Violence. 3. Climate change. I. Jacoby, Linda S. II. Title.
  HV6025.C663 2015
  363.738'741–dc23

                                                    2014019378

British Library Cataloguing in Publication Data
A catalogue record for this book is available from the British Library

ISBN 978-0-323-26509-6 (pbk)

CONTENTS

INTRODUCTION

This book is about global warming and its climatic impacts on violence and crime. It is highly interpretive and inferential in our effort to peer beyond present "knowns" in anticipation of future risks. The authors faced three central challenges writing this book: (1) accurately depicting current global social and physical characteristics, (2) assessing how those characteristics will change in the future, and (3) evaluating how climatic changes will interact with those futures. This challenge is redoubled by the recognition that the present knowns are themselves often controversial. This book is consequently summative, providing our estimation of central tendencies on these topics.

Our goal is to provide important topics of discussion for policy makers, social scientists, and political leadership at all levels of governance. We also want to inform the readers of the sheer diversity of the risks, including a broad array of some quite bad outcomes, perpetuated by climate change. Any statement of risk should carry the recognition that any hypothetical climate change "outcome" is itself transitional; at this point it is not clear whether sharp curtailment of greenhouse gases will significantly slow climate change if—a very important if—major climate-induced feedbacks start kicking in. We make use of a large body of political science, criminology, earth sciences, and hydrology research to present our discussions.

This book is not intended to be politically balanced, seeking the middle ground between different rhetorical talking points of climate change and consequently inferring that different positions are somehow balanced scientifically. Indeed, one of our concerns is that efforts to find political middle ground, particularly in the form of popular media presentations, fundamentally mislead the public on a topic almost absent scientific disagreement. To draw a parallel, it is as if the field of celestial mechanics were in continued political debate and Sunday talk show controversy about whether the Earth indeed rotates around the Sun. Global warming, as Bill Nye observed, is a political controversy, not a scientific one.[1] Like the notion of human evolution, also still controversial among a large percentage of the American electorate, global warming is widely accepted in the relevant sciences. It is different from human evolution in one important way, though: Evolution reaches deeply into our past. Global warming reaches deeply into our future.

A review of the science on global warming reveals clear patterns that are taking place globally and regionally, having effects that are already well underway and already playing havoc with ecological systems. The way humans live on this planet represents a subgroup of those ecological systems, and many countries, including the US, are already experiencing impacts from warming, acknowledged or not, desired or not, and politically correct or not.

It is apparent to us that political action on climate change has not come soon enough, a view grounded in our observations of legislative resistance to prevention and planning in the face of this gathering global catastrophe. We live in an age not unlike the Renaissance, where scientific findings are adjudicated by political authority and where influential political sovereigns, backed by powerful lobbies and moneyed interests in the energy marketplace, deny the legitimacy of global warming science. It is time to prepare for a future in which our fundamental ecological relationship with the world will change. Our social compacts and nation-state structures will be altered. We should anticipate a rough ride on the way to a different world, and on arrival, a world that likely will have turned hostile to the humans that occupy it. The world our grandparents knew is over, we live in its waning shadow.

The image this book presents is one in which our future faces several potentially catastrophic risks. Security issues will be a central concern over the next 50 years, whether security is perceived in state-centric or population-centric terms. Consider the major security groupings. Intrastate security is provided by highly decentralized municipal police and, at a federal level, by national police entities. Nation-state security is provided by their militaries and bolstered by treaty and commercial interlinks. International security is provided by different international police forces, often with ties to the United Nations. Peacekeeping aims to provide external security to failed and failing states. Finally, counterinsurgency and counterterrorism is a specialized security function aimed at significant threats from small groups widely dispersed globally. These entities will need to move beyond a weakened nation-state system in the future and develop international linkages, even while bridging their own differences so that they can act effectively for the common good of citizens.

The movement of crime and security issues to the front and center of international and national policy, we think, will flow from fundamental changes in the environment of crime and violence. Powerful individual criminals with rudimentary organization, international organized crime entities, and insurgents and terrorists have undergone a fundamental change over the past 20 years and today are often conjoined, working together for common goals. Operating as unstructured, leaderless, yet highly lethal ghost presences in many countries, they seem to be undefeatable. Even in countries such as the relatively secure United States, gangs exist in all major cities and are extensively interpenetrated by international criminal groups. Importantly, global warming factors, even while undermining important state security mechanisms, play to the strength of the criminal environment. The impact of climate change on international security is likely to be substantial, with outcomes for nation-state stability and security becoming increasingly unfavorable.

This book conveys the spirit of preparedness. It is, essentially, a risk assessment of global warming from a crime and security perspective. We ask—what are the implications of global warming and what do we need to keep in mind as the planet warms? How do we prepare for battle against an enemy who seems from our limited historical perspectives to move with glacial pace, but whose strength is unassailable, whose presence is ubiquitous, and who will leave nothing on this planet untouched?

Pessimism is difficult to resist. Consider the news on no particular day—the "no particular day" below being November 20, 2012; the reader could find similar accounts on almost any other day. As we scanned the papers for information about global warming, three newsworthy items stood out. When all three are considered together, it is difficult to be optimistic and distinctly challenging even to be hopeful.

The first column below is a discussion of the growing recognition, according to its authors, that significant global warming cannot at this point in time be stopped.[2] The column noted that

> *The latest report, released Wednesday by the United Nations Environment Program, suggested that greenhouse gas emissions levels are currently around 14 percent above where they need to be by the end of the decade in order to avoid what many analysts believe could be a risky level of planetary warming.*

> *"These billions of tonnes of additional carbon dioxide in our atmosphere will remain there for centuries, causing our planet to warm further and impacting on all aspects of life on earth," said WMO Secretary-General Michel Jarraud, in a statement issued Tuesday. "Future emissions will only compound the situation."*

> *On Sunday, the World Bank issued a report suggesting that the climate could warm a full 4 degrees by the end of the century—less than 90 years from now—even if countries fulfill the modest emissions-reduction pledges they've already made.*

A 4-degree uptick in temperatures is significantly higher than what has long been deemed the maximum amount—2 degrees Celsius, or 3.6 degrees Fahrenheit—that average global temperatures could rise while still maintaining a climate similar to that in which human civilization has evolved.

Researchers have emphasized that the quantity of fossil fuels that are released into the air needs to be curtailed significantly and immediately, otherwise global warming will have catastrophic consequences.[3] Yet, it appears that we are going in the opposite direction: ramping up our use of fossil fuels to address energy issues in the face of population growth, economic progress, and the task of survival in a warmer world. The next article discusses a broad international effort to sharply increase the numbers of coal-burning plants worldwide.[4]

"Global Coal Risk Assessment: Data Analysis and Market Research," released on November 20, estimated there are currently 1,199 proposed coal plants in 59 countries. They noted that China and India together account for 76% of these plants. The United States landed seventh, with 36 proposed coal-fired power plants.

WRI's [World Resources Institute's] Ailun Yang noted, "If all of these projects are built, it would add new coal power capacity that is almost four times the current capacity of all coal-fired plants in the United States."

According to WRI, "Coal-fired power plants are the largest contributor to the greenhouse gas emissions that cause climate change." The WRI analysis, conducted in July 2012, comes as environmentalists warn that an estimated 80% of the world's proven oil, coal and natural gas reserves must remain in the ground, unburned, to avoid the release of enough carbon dioxide to warm the planet above the internationally agreed upon limit of two degrees Celsius.

The goal of increased energy from fossil fuels to meet growing needs contradicts the need to curtail fossil fuels to mitigate global warming. Yet, the expansion of energy demands is occurring in the face of recognized, extraordinarily high levels of greenhouse gases worldwide. The third article noted that, once again, the level of carbon dioxide emissions reached a new high in the world.[5] In other words, in spite of the substantial evidence showing continued increases in greenhouse gases, we continue to seek short solutions that will make the problem worse in the long-term.

GENEVA, Nov 20 (Reuters) – Atmospheric volumes of greenhouse gases blamed for climate change hit a new record in 2011, the World Meteorological Organization (WMO) said in its annual Greenhouse Gas Bulletin on Tuesday.

The volume of carbon dioxide, the primary greenhouse gas emitted by human activities, grew at a similar rate to the previous decade and reached 390.9 parts per million (ppm), 40% above the pre-industrial level, the survey said.

It has increased by an average of 2 ppm for the past 10 years.

WMO Secretary-General Michel Jarraud said the billions of tonnes of extra carbon dioxide would stay in the atmosphere for centuries, causing the planet to warm further.

Levels of methane, another long-lived greenhouse gas, have risen steadily for the past three years after levelling off for about seven years. The reasons for that evening out are unclear.

Growth in volumes of a third gas, nitrous oxide, quickened in 2011. It has a long-term climate impact that is 298 times greater than carbon dioxide.

These kinds of stories are ordinary fare for news readers, who have likely read many such stories and who may be jaded to the topic. After all, global warming does not leave an obvious signature on catastrophes. It takes a scientist to ferret out global warming effects. The public, under a relentless torrent of politically empowered, media-reinforced global warming "contrarianism," does not grasp the magnitude or significance of the changes coming in our future. Indeed, the interpretation of the three articles, when read in sequence, is that increases in climate changing gases are not only high but increasing in a nonlinear way, that the evidence of global warming is substantial, and that, globally, we are getting ready to ramp up the production of plants that will yield substantial additional quantities of greenhouse gases. We are going in the wrong direction, barreling toward a catastrophe of our own doing.

   This book is challenging for a variety of reasons. First is that many different kinds of knowledge are required to write this book. One of the difficulties with writing about global warming is trying to decide what to leave out—Climate change in some way affects practically everything. Consequently, some topics will not and cannot receive the attention they need in a relatively short book. We apologize in advance to those who have extensive expertise in some of the fields we address with too much brevity and generality.

Second, the future is, by its nature, unwritten. We don't know with certainty what will happen. Any discussion of events in the future is a tactical guess, extrapolating on current trends. Global warming is typically assessed in two ways: through modeling and through examination of prehistorical times. Inevitably, some modeling extrapolations will be wrong. Anyone who has used complex modeling techniques, even those that seem to fit historical data very well, has discovered the enormous difficulty in moving from description to prediction. Sometimes very good historical models fall apart when used to predict events. Information that predates history, though helpful, is nevertheless marked with extensive periods of unconformity from erosional processes; information may simply be unavailable. Prehistorical analyses, however, clearly show strong and clear correlations between the quantity of greenhouse gases in the atmosphere and global temperature. The challenge is not whether global warming is happening; scientifically that debate has been over for 20 years. The challenge lies in determining exactly how sensitive the climate is to CO_2 in the atmosphere.

Consequently, our goal is not to predict the future. It is to foster critical conversation as we move into unknown times and to begin to think about what is going to happen to us. If our most important state concern is to protect our citizens from risks, then we need to take into account those risks associated with global warming. This applies to businesses such as insurance, it applies to urban planning and state and county code development, and it applies to national security. Indeed, it applies to anyone who has a fiscal or budgetary responsibility to develop long-term plans to protect citizens, governments, and businesses from risks.

It should be noted that fiscal planning is not about futures already scripted, it is about future contingencies in light of possible negative outcomes. Good planners always ask "What of this?" and "What of that?" These are the sorts of questions we raise herein. We do not intend to be environmentally deterministic: Human will and creativity cannot be discounted. But, at this point, there is more than enough science about global warming to indicate the need for precautionary planning and mitigative action. With the substantial knowledge we have already amassed, to fail to act can only be described as reckless.

Third, to describe any futuristic trajectories, we must begin with a concrete and realistic description of the present and then try to figure out where we are going even without global warming figured into the mix. This is a substantial challenge because we have no particularly good reason to believe that the predominant social and political relationships that characterize the world today will similarly characterize them in the future. Many observers argue the contrary: that the future will be quite different, with or without global warming figured into the mix.

Where do our trajectories into the short-term future take us? The future moving rapidly toward us is one that has been described in terms of megacities and megadeltas populated by tens of thousands of slums housing billions of people, the emergence of feral cities, the expansion of failing states and the new dark ages, compounded by a 50% increase in the number of humans on the planet. This, some of the more astute observers of our times believe, is the human spatial and social ecology that will be us by 2050, even without global warming added. Some of the notions—the emergence of stateless, feral cities, is a bit of a reach though a true risk; others like the vast urbanization of the planet into huge favelas of poverty is inevitable and is already well underway. Mix global warming into the 2050 spatial distribution of humans on planet Earth and we begin to realize the extent to which we are in deep trouble. The future trajectories described by some of our most cogent observers take us to a collision between global warming and the largest migration of humans in history sometime around midcentury; the path through the collision is unclear, the territory on the far side of the collision is hostile, dark, and forbidding. We can no longer avoid that collision; the moment has passed. Now is the time to prepare and mitigate as best we can.

Fourth, and closely related to three, global warming is likely to have detrimental impacts on critical functional systems, especially those associated with hydrology that are already under regional stresses of one kind or other. When we talk about critical functional systems we mean both human and natural processes that are seen as essential for human well-being in specific locales. Some of those system stresses are substantial.

For instance, consider a forecast for the Great Plains area in the United States; it is anticipated that the area will have lower rates of rainfall and that what rain it receives will be in the form of less frequent but more intense storms. The American West faces the loss of snowpack that makes up the great natural reservoirs of the Rockies. That snowpack is essential for both East and West of the Rockies and contributes much of the water to the rivers that cross the plains toward the Midwest. Regional droughts will become more commonplace. It has been fancifully suggested that the era of the buffalo will return as the Great Plains become unfit for farming and ranching, and plains residents finally complete the already advanced depopulation of the area.[6] Agriculturally, this area is already under water stress. Its primary water source for ranching and farming across the region is the Ogallala aquifer. This fossil aquifer is overused across most of its substantial geography and is anticipated to be functionally depleted by the midpoint of the century.

Hence, we see a twin blow to the region: one coming from the overuse and misuse of the Ogallala, and one from global warming. The Great Plains will dry further, and its principal rivers may well run dry as the snowpack from the Rockies steadily diminishes over time. It faces the clear threat of desertification, and it faces that threat sooner rather than later. It is a region that, from mismanagement of critical water supplies, growing water needs, and global warming, is threatened with becoming altogether unusable as ranch or farmland. It is not suitable for dry farming; without a plentiful supply of groundwater agriculture, as it is now, it will be devastated. The Ogallala is not unique in this respect. Many of the major aquifers around the world are heavily stressed, and most face a similar fate. Some, like the principal aquifer under the megacity Mexico City, are already ruined.

Fifth, we must deal with a concept of crime and violence that is inconsistent with the way Western societies do the work of crime and justice. Western crime control institutions are organized around the idea that crimes are caused by human misbehavior, and they invest substantial financial and human resources into holding people punitively accountable when they misbehave. In this book, we take a sharply different tack: crimes and violence are to be attributed not to motive-driven people, but to nonmotive-propelled, nonaccountable things. Human agency—the idea that people control their decisional processes—is seen as an intervening variable, subject to the whims of earth-based physics. Temperature, for instance, is associated with higher levels of violence. More intense storms are linked to higher levels of homicides and violent crimes under some circumstances and fewer homicides and violent crimes under others. Pathogens are tied to state security failure. We think of this approach as a "big picture" approach to crime and violence. It is concerned with larger criminogenic processes, where broad contextual factors are assessed for their exogenous role in crime and violence. In the parlance of research, this is a macrosocial approach. The microsocial approach is helpful for understanding the details of a specific event, but only the macrosocial can provide the perspective that actually explains an event in a way that is policy-solvable on the scale global warming is affecting us. That is the approach we take herein, and this allows us to look at how things, not people—in this case, environmental changes in human social and geographic ecologies—are associated with crime, violence, and security.

The macrosocial approach also carries an important element not available from the microsocial perspective. If we look at a crime from a microsocial perspective, we can focus on the individual who carries out the crime and their immediate contexts, and pretty much leave it at that. However, from a macrosocial perspective, we find that people alone cannot account for crime patterns—other factors seem to be closely related to crime prevalence and likelihood.

This approach seems warranted when we look at the last 30 years of get-tough laws aimed at dealing with crime at the most immediate level—the offender. In the contemporary vernacular, we have learned over the past 30 years of intensified punishment and prisonization—in which the United States has amassed to the largest ratio of prisoners to citizens in the world—that we cannot arrest our way out of crime. Consequently, looking at broader contextual features is not only good from the perspective of studying global warming, it may be the best way forward for addressing crime generally.

Put more to the point, the microsocial approach takes us, as ordinary law-abiding citizens, off the hook by letting us blame some poor wretch for the crime she or he committed. The macrosocial approach puts us back on the hook—it is not only someone else who is at fault. We are implicated as well and a piece of the responsibility is ours. This is actually a stronger and more optimistic approach to crime control, though. If we are somehow involved in the problem, then it is within our power to fix it. So it is with global warming; for all the prophetic doom and gloom, the point of broad risk-oriented perspectives such as those embodied in this book is to try to anticipate and forestall the most severe downsides, however dark and dire they might be. At this point, we can likely no longer stop a three degree Celsius global warming and significant ocean rise; the tipping point is past, the window closed. But we can prepare, and we can try to mitigate additional, far more troubling outcomes that would occur with warming in the four degree plus Celsius range at the end of this or any century.

This book uses an interplay between two fictional characters—Clete, and Gran'ma Ruth Willis to present the future fresco with which global warming presents us. Clete, arriving at a bar named "The Apocalypse," is carrying out an oral history project in which he is attempting to understand the first century of global warming. The ideas for their conversations are derived from the book *Six Degrees: Our Future on a Hotter Planet* (Lynas, 2008), which describes the effects on the planet for each degree Celsius of heating. We chose that book because it is based on a reasonable organizing perspective of the available science and because it represents the global climatic impacts through the dawn of the twenty-second century that will occur if we essentially do nothing. It is a catastrophic forecast, as are most thorough and honest books about the long-term futures of global warming. And, thus far, what has been accomplished to stop the machinery that drives global warming is precisely nothing. We will use the oral history as a literary convenience to describe the impact of each degree of temperature change as the Earth warms through the century. Each chapter begins with an excerpt or discussion involving Clete and Ruth. The discussion is followed by a substantive review of literature and scientific research related to the topic they discuss.

Endnotes

1. "When people call these 'controversial topics,' that's misleading," he continued. "They are only controversial politically. And politics is not necessarily evidence-based." "Firebrand for science, and big man on campus: On TV and the lecture circuit, Bill Nye aims to change the world." Retrieved November 2, 2013 at http://www.nytimes.com/2013/06/18/science/bill-nye-firebrand-for-science-is-a-big-man-on-campus.html.
2. "Climate reports forecast dire future, even if action is taken." Retrieved July 11, 2013 at http://www.huffingtonpost.com/2012/11/21/climate-reports-climate-change_n_2170101.html?utm_hp_ref=climate-change.
3. "Climate change worse than we thought, likely to be 'Catastrophic rather than simply dangerous'." Retrieved January 21, 2014 at http://www.huffingtonpost.com/2013/12/31/climate-change-worse_n_4523828.html?utm_hp_ref=climate-change.
4. "Nearly 1,200 coal-fired power plants proposed globally, report finds." Retrieved December 18, 2013 at http://www.huffingtonpost.com/2012/11/20/world-coal-fired-power-plants_n_2166699.html?utm_hp_ref=climate-change.
5. "Global carbon dioxide levels hit new record in 2011, survey shows." Retrieved May 5, 2013 at http://www.huffingtonpost.com/2012/11/20/global-carbon-dioxide-levels_n_2163612.html?utm_hp_ref=mostpopular,climate-change.
6. "Buffalo commons reborn." Retrieved April 23, 2012 at http://globalwarming-arclein.blogspot.com/2009/11/buffalo-commons-reborn.html.

PROLOGUE: WELCOME TO THE APOCALYPSE

As noted in the Introduction, each chapter in this book begins with an excerpt or discussion involving Clete and Ruth.

Clete pulled up to the Apocalypse. It was rumored to be the longest-running bar in this part of the country. There was a big sign, warped and corroded, on which was written, "Welcome to the Apocalypse: Best Biker Bar in the World." Clete had been told that it was built back in 2020 and hadn't gone a day since without whisky being poured. It was founded by a scientist, Roberto (Beto) O'Hanohan-Ruiz, one of those multidisciplinary wizards who figured out what climate change *really meant* and one of the few to survive the purge unscathed.

The purge was a bad time. It began in Canada, with the burning of all library research pertaining to global warming.[1] It ended with the persecution of a number of global warming scientists in many countries and not a few lynchings—people always seemed to blame the messenger. The rest went underground. O'Hanohan saw it all coming, not just to the planet, but to its residents, human and nonhuman alike. They were in trouble deep. Then he looked at how the countries of the world were preparing for climate change. Then they say that one morning he walked out of his university office, locked the door, bought a Harley bagger, and disappeared. He showed up about 5 years later in this forlorn place, bought the bar, named it the Apocalypse, and added a grocery and hotel when people started migrating North to Canada. Yep, Clete thought, he understood people all right.

Clete had heard about an older woman there, Ruth Willis. "Gran'ma Willis" they called her. She had been around a long time, and she had traveled with O'Hanohan when she was younger. She was in her nineties, so she was around at the end of *the good time*. Clete was working on a living history project, piecing together the information about the Great Dust Desert back when it was known as the Great Plains, tracing it from *the good time* through the *great warming*. He stopped himself—we're not *through* the great warming, he reminded himself. We're *in* the great warming. He had talked to her a few times and now had the opportunity to interview her in person, in the place where her story took place. He needed to get Ruth's story.

People said that the Midwest and Great Plains were beautiful in the early 2000s, that the towns were friendly and everyone got along with everyone else. There were rivers across the Great Plains and a lot of water underground. He looked across the plains and saw only a dirt desert under a big blue sky. There was a pile of old bones off to the east, probably the last vestiges of a cattle shoot. There were antelope still and wild horses. Further south in the high country, the javelina were prospering; their numbers were growing and they were increasingly dangerous to people. They could take down a big cat, quickly. The coywolves were populating the high desert; they were pack hunters with no fear of people. Too smart to trap. Dangerous country, after the weather knocked you down, the animals would move in and pick your bones.

Clete was working on an international project at the University of Winnipeg. Winnipeg, like many cities in Canada, had undergone tremendous growth over the past half century and was itself approaching megacity status at 8 million. It sat on the edge of the Great Dust Desert but was remarkably verdant, and the temperatures were mild even into the rainy season. As the ambient crop-growing temperatures and rainfall marched steadily northward during the twenty-first century, Canada had become the one of the world's great breadbaskets. It had been hard work; at first, in the early days of *the great warming*, much of Canada was just a swampy, rocky thin-soiled wetland. Major hydrological and earth-moving projects had made the land suitable for farming and ranching on a large scale; now it was a primary food source for the megacities of the world, second only to Siberia. Winnipeg had consequently received a lot of immigration from the United States, especially from the Great Dust Desert, before they closed the border.

The desert itself was remarkable, like a living, growing thing, Clete thought. It had mostly swallowed the Great Plains and intermountain West, and was now reaching its tendrils into the Midwest, down into the thin-soiled Little Egypt area of Illinois, swallowing St. Louis, Kansas City, and Omaha. It was semiarid all the way through southern Indiana. Clete's grandparents, themselves from St. Louis, had moved ahead of the desert and relocated to Calgary in 2060. Now Clete found himself on the native soil of his grandparents, though he had never before visited it nor wanted to.

Clete was working on Midwest US oral history. His part of the project was to create a living history of the Great Plains before it was the Great Dust Desert. There was little knowledge that remained of the way ordinary people lived in that part of the country in *the good time*, and their traditions and cultures had largely disappeared. It was as if a civilization had vanished, leaving barbed wire and shotgun shell casings behind. His goal was to interview people who remembered what it was like in *the good time*, back when the United States was the place people were trying to *get to*, not *escape from*. He suspected that Gran'ma Willis was one of the few remaining people who still remembered *the good time*. The interview was a wonderful opportunity to understand a past increasingly different and unreachable.

Dust seemed to hang in the air, and there was darkness off to the West. Looked like another ripper was coming, he thought. They said that sometimes the dust storms were so bad you could choke to death. Your nose and mouth would turn black and your lungs would fill up. You would suffocate, like a bloated dead buffalo. You'd get buried alive and no one would find you. The storms could be nasty down here in the United States. They could last for two to three days. He was glad they didn't have them in Winnipeg. A bad storm, a real ripper, could gather its energy in Colorado and carry dust all the way to Chicago. Dust could even find its way to Manhattan Bay.

He got off his bike and went inside. The bike was 250 ccs, the legal limit, and provided him with good gas mileage at 60 miles to the gallon. The Apocalypse was pretty rough as bars go. The grocery, a small room on the left, was full of the usual products: a shelf for bottled water, one for hard liquor, one for toiletries, and one for canned goods. There was a locker for a few frozen goods.

The Apocalypse had a large center room with tables for gamblers and a bar to one side. There was a motel next door, with a closed sign on it and plywood covering the windows. At one time, it had done a thriving business as an overnight stop for people leaving the United States, but the migration stream had dried up. There was no one in these parts left to move.

He saw Gran'ma Willis sitting at one of the back tables. He recognized her immediately. They had previously met by *wallview*, the soft plasma folding screens that used smart-pixels to create life-sized images and could be unfolded and stretched across an entire wall. They were so realistic that a person could almost forget that the person they were talking to was a thousand miles away, especially with the microphone sensors built into the screen that followed the person around and captured and delivered the ambient background sound in multistereo. He walked back to where she was seated.

Clete. "Ms. Willis, I'm delighted to finally meet you for real at last."

Ruth. "Oh, don't call me Ms. Call me Gran'ma like everyone else. Sit down. You came down a long way to talk to me. How'd you afford the gas?"

Clete. "Scholarship. I got a gas stipend." Clete was proud of that. Very few students received gas scholarships, so almost all of them bicycled. Gas was crazy expensive at $5,000 dollars a gallon, and only purchasable with a government permit.

He smiled and looked across the table at her. "Do you actually remember much of *the good time*?"

Ruth. "Oh yea, I still remember all that stuff. I was pretty young, and the really crazy stuff didn't start until the 2020s, when I was about 15. When people finally realized that it was really happening. When they realized, it was too late to stop it. But how do you get out of the way of a catastrophe you can't see? Yep, I remember, like it was yesterday. I remember it better than last night's dreams. Most people don't have a clue about *the good time*. It wasn't all that good."

Clete took the bait. "See, that's what I want. That's exactly what I need to know. Like what?"

Ruth smiled. "I remember when the ocean was the best place to live. Everyone who could afford it lived there. I loved to go to the ocean."

How interesting, Clete thought to himself. Everyone knew how dangerous it was living next to the oceans—the crime and deterioration of all the old buildings, slums for migrants and the homeless, "homesteads for organized crime," he thought. Terrorists had carried out an attack in '76, coming down from Canada through the coastal slums that lined the ocean side of New York state and gotten to the Mayor. Her entire staff was killed. No one ever found out who the terrorists were, but there were strong suspicions that they were hired hits for an organized crime group battling for control of the harbor area. The next mayor got the picture, though: She withdrew regular police patrols from the abandoned parts of the harbor area. Clete wiped the sweat off his brow. It was late February, and the day was already heating up.

Ruth smiled. "In the late 2030s when the oceans seemed to be rising faster than expected, surprise, surprise, business stopped insuring any property that was within a half mile of the coast and below 10 feet elevation. Talk about opening a giant can of "all hell done broke loose." Millions of people had to move. So they started a resettlement program that included a government buyout of mortgages at 20 percent of the remaining balance and bought up the insurers at a dime on the dollar. All those people, yep that was millions, took major losses, but what could they do? Banks sure as hell didn't want the land. After that it just deteriorated." She laughed.

"So. You're here for the story. Me and Beto, we traveled together. I went where he went. I stayed where he stayed. We saw it all. I am still with him, you know." Clete looked away, pensive. He felt like he missed something. Ruth continued. "Let's begin back at the beginning, at the start of the great warming. We were warned."

Endnotes

1. In 2013, Canada libraries began a chaotic purge of their contents, particularly of the scientific research they contained. As one observer noted,

   Many collections such as the Maurice Lamontagne Institute Library in Mont-Joli, Quebec ended up in dumpsters while others such as Winnipeg's historic Freshwater Institute library were scavenged by citizens, scientists and local environmental consultants. Others were burned or went to landfills, say scientists.

   In all, 7 of 9 DFO (Fisheries and Oceans) regional public science libraries were "lost." Another noted that

   "The Department has claimed that all useful information from the closed libraries is available in digital form. This is simply not true. Much of the material is lost forever," reports one DFO scientist who requested not to be named.

   The decision to purge the material was made by top DSO staff, without input from the regional offices or from the public. They have been accused of reflecting what they call the anti-scientist posture of the Canadian leadership under Stephen Harper. He was quoted, just before the 2003 founding of the saying, for instance, *"We're gearing up for the biggest struggle our party has faced since you entrusted me with the leadership. I'm talking about the "battle of Kyoto" — our campaign to block the job-killing, economy-destroying Kyoto Accord."*

GLOBAL WARMING

1

THE CHALLENGES OF GLOBAL WARMING RESEARCH

Ruth: "We had a wild ride back at the beginning, me and Beto. I saw the country on the back of his bike. He would say to me, 'We've got to see this country now, before it all goes away.' He rode like we was bein' chased, and maybe we were. We had this monster storm from hell barreling down on us. But the politicians, scratch them on their fat bellies with a bit of jingle, their hearts and minds will follow. And could they sell a bill of goods! They were like, 'Do you want a job today or would you sooner have your kids go without work and food because of all these radical scientists'?"

"So, for anyone reading news or watching their TVs, you'd think that a lot of eggheads were disagreeing about what was going to happen."

Clete: "TV, do you mean liquiscreens? And did you actually read great big sheets of paper back then?"

Ruth: "You got a lot of fillin' in to do. Yep and yep. Anyway, to get back to the point, who is going to change their lives when no one can figure out what the truth is? Even when it started to happen, people did not believe it. All the way back to 2014, you could go to Norfolk and see the ocean coming up over the streets, and the pols still denied it and the people still wouldn't believe it."[1]

"We could see changes in people, too, in some places. The cities were already too hot; it was the temperature itself sometimes, all it took to make people violent. Snuff goes the power grid, snuff goes the air conditioning, everyone's pissed. Of course there's violence. They weren't violent at global warming, just angry it seemed."

This opening chapter affords us the opportunity to address two issues that are important to the topic of global warming and violence. The first is the challenge of global warming research in a hostile environment. This is important because research is at the core of the field, it is important research, and it is frequently misrepresented. We will discuss that misrepresentation, how and why research is misrepresented, and provide some suggestions on how to recognize misrepresented research. The second is a review of research focusing on what might be called the basic building block of a book on global warming and crime—is there any research that actually shows that crime and violence are related to temperature or other aspects of weather?

For a researcher, global warming is a fascinating challenge. The quality of the research produced is very high, carried out by some of the sharpest research minds in the world. Anyone playing at this level and with this crowd will quickly build and establish a reputation. Quality research that shows significant outcomes will propel one into the academic limelight quickly. Positive findings showing warming effects, especially strong findings, will publish well. Significant findings that reject predominant perspectives also publish well; such is the nature of the peer review process, and the ability to make a unique contribution is the cornerstone of reputation building. One of the many features of science wholly misunderstood by its critics is that reputations are earned, not by agreeing with everyone else's research findings, but by finding something new and different. The idea that a substantial percentage of distinguished scientists would agree on anything is remarkable.

Positive findings that are consistent with global warming, however, carry a different emotional tenor than negative ones. A positive finding has two very negative consequences that could tempt a scholar to avoid the topic altogether. For one, the researcher is finding something that is likely to mean immense hardship for many, many people in the future. If the core of one's field is doom and gloom, it is hard to stay positive. For another, the researcher is likely to come under both political and personal attack in both public and professional settings. He or she will be bitten by the very sharp teeth of politicians, lobbyists, and big businesses, and few researchers like the limelight for exactly that reason. All researchers should familiarize themselves with the adage "Politics—red of tooth and claw."[2]

From a research perspective, global warming is not a specific thing; it is an ongoing multidisciplinary work whose core structure is well known but whose contours, implications, and consequences are formative. It falls into the spectrum of problems noted by Wallerstein (1996). Their inherent nature requires multidisciplinary work, and they lack problem resolution. Problems at this scale have an additional problem and a trenchant one at that. Its advocates face harsh political counterattack. Global warming, a topic important enough to bridge the musty halls of academe and front page news, faces a hostile political agenda sharpened from the cigarette research wars: a well-organized business, lobbyist, and political constituency with one goal—create doubt with the lay public that there actually might be a global warming problem.

Section I focuses on the research dilemma faced by researchers and by the lay public as well: How do we know what respectable research is, and how can we recognize a challenge to that research when its only purpose is to create doubt? Certainly, scientists contend with each other all the time. This contention can look very much like the political doubt-creation agenda. Scientific dispute is commonplace and expected; it is at the core of the peer review process that underlays scientific assessment and publication. So we can say that we need to distinguish between two sources of contention—scientific contention that is characteristic of good science and that reflects the growth of a scientific field, and contention that is used by the doubt creators.

The doubt-creation agenda, however, is a cottage industry funded by major businesses and is recognizable for its relentless rejection of any bit of scientific research that might be used to support global warming arguments. The challenge is to recognize which is which, and a significant challenge it is, because the doubt-creation crew often uses information from scientific disputes to justify its anti–global warming agenda. This challenge is substantial; the doubt creators have substantial resources, they know how to play the doubt game, and they are in it for the long haul. Indeed, the survival of many of the businesses that fund them may depend on it.

Section II is about the most basic relationship in a book on global warming, violence, and crime: Is there any evidence that actually links crime and temperature or other aspects of weather? Historically, research on weather and crime has been largely peripheral in the field of criminology. Our field is perpetrator focused; we seem to be interested in the characteristics, or shortcomings, of people who commit crime. Adding context, especially context that is largely out of the control of humans, has simply not generated a lot of interest—at least until now. There is, however, a small body of intriguing research on the field, and with the surging interest in global warming it is likely to grow. We consequently review research on crime and temperature, and at the end of the section, we review some of the more contemporary research linking temperature and rainfall to state conflict.

Is Global Warming Research Concocted by a Bunch of Academic Anti-American Radicals? The Use and Misuse of Science in Climate Study and Forecasting

Global warming is a complex field, scientifically dense with arcane and highly technical discussions. Yet it is a field of enormous personal interest for the lay public; global warming has profound implications for their lives and for the lives of their children. It is also of financial interest to many businesses and governments; the fossil fuels that contribute to global warming are integral to technological development and routine life around the globe. Three discussions of ice melt-off and its association with global warming are presented in the information boxes below. All three were reported in July 2012. Information Box 1.1, titled "News Brief 1," describes an unusually heavy melt-off on Greenland's ice sheet.

Information Box 1.1 Rare Burst of Melting Seen in Greenland's Ice Sheet

In a scant four days, the surface of Greenland's ice sheet melted to an extent not witnessed in 30 years of satellite observations, NASA reported on Tuesday.

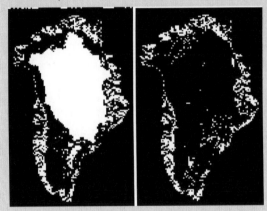

NASA

The extent of Greenland's ice sheet surface, in white, on July 8, left, and July 12, right, are based on measurements from three satellites, which pass over at different times. On average, about half of the surface of the ice sheet melts during the summer. But from July 8 to 12, the ice melt expanded from 40% of the ice sheet to 97%, according to scientists who analyzed the data from satellites deployed by NASA and India's space research institute.

"I started looking at the satellite imagery and saw something that was really unprecedented" since the advent of satellite imaging of the earth's frozen surface, or cryosphere, said Thomas L. Mote, a climate scientist at the University of Georgia who for 20 years has been studying ice changes on Greenland detected by satellite. While scientists described it as an "extreme event" not previously recorded from space, they hastened to add that it was normal in a broader historical context.

Ice core samples taken from the summit of Greenland's ice sheet that shed light on 10,000 years of its history show that a similar large-scale melting event has happened roughly every 150 years, said Lora Koenig, a glaciologist with NASA's Goddard Space Flight Center who has also studied the satellite imagery.

Source: Rare Burst of Melting Seen in Greenland's Ice Sheet. Retrieved March, 2012 at http://www.nytimes.com/2012/07/25/science/earth/rare-burst-of-melting-seen-in-greenland-ice-sheet.html?_r=0

Information Box 1.2 Seals Show Antarctic Ice Shelf Melting Slower Than Thought

The Fimbul Ice Shelf, located along eastern Antarctica in the Weddell Sea, is the sixth-largest of the 43 ice shelves on the Antarctica's perimeter. Ice shelves are thick floating platforms of ice that form where a glacier or ice sheet flows down to a coastline and onto the ocean surface. If an ice shelf is melting rapidly, the glacier may flow faster into the sea, contributing to sea level rise.

The Fimbul Ice Shelf is melting because of both its size and proximity to the East Antarctic Ice Sheet, the largest ice sheet on earth. If that ice sheet melted, the water it generated could lead to extreme changes in sea level.

Computer models had previously showed significant melting of the Fimbul Ice Shelf.

Scientists drilled several deep holes into the shelf to assess directly how quickly the ice is melting. This gave them a partial understanding of what was going on; that water there was colder than expected by previous models.

Nine male elephant seals were outfitted with sensors that measure salinity, temperature, and depth. The sensors were attached to the seals by a different research group in a separate study, but the migrating seals gathered the data needed to fill the missing blanks about the Fimbul Ice Shelf.

Past studies were based on computer models without any direct data for comparison or guidance. Those studies overestimated the water temperatures and extent of melting beneath the ice shelf, led to the misconception that the ice shelf is losing mass at a faster rate than it is gaining mass.

Source: OurAmazingPlanet Staff, (2012), "Seals Show Antarctic Ice Shelf Melting Slower Than Thought," LiveScience.com

The second news brief shares information on a novel research strategy to study melt-off in the Antarctic Ice Shelf and what it found. It is presented in Information Box 1.2.

The third news brief, in Information Box 1.3, discusses the Greenland ice melt-off and explains why it is not global warming.

The Takeaway

These three news articles share a similar theme: that the great planetary ice sheets are of considerable interest. There are also important differences in the news briefs. Those are what we call the takeaway—the points we want to make in comparing these three news briefs. They provide us with the opportunity to present, as bullet points, the uses and misuses of scientific research.

- Both of the first two briefs used scientific methods to come to their conclusions. Scientific methods have some commonalities across all fields, as shown by these two articles.
  - A scientist assesses evidence according to measuring instruments intended to assess real-world processes. This is the most integral aspect of science: It is empirical, which

Information Box 1.3 Skeptics Put the Freeze on NASA "Hot Air" About Greenland Ice

Some scientists refute NASA's claim that Greenland is experiencing "unprecedented" melting. NASA said a heat dome over the country melted whopping 97% of Greenland's ice sheet in July 2012, citing it as more evidence of the effect humankind is having on the planet.

According to glaciologists, though, it was actually to be expected.

Lora Koenig, a glaciologist and member of the research team analyzing the satellite data, said that ice cores from Summit Station indicate that melting events of this type occur about once every 150 years on average, with the last one happening in 1889.

Source: Kaplan, J.A. (2012), "Skeptics put the freeze on NASA 'hot air' about Greenland ice." See http://www.foxnews.com/scitech/2012/07/26/skeptics-put-freeze-on-nasa-hot-air-about-greenland-ice/

means that it is always based on what can be observed (even if it takes special instrumentation to observe it).

- If an idea cannot be disproven, it is not science. If it cannot be measured, it cannot be disproven and consequently is not science—it might be philosophy, political ideology, religion, or morality, and it might be a wonderful idea, but it is not science. For example, the existence of God is not disprovable. This means that he, she, and it cannot be studied scientifically. Atoms can be studied scientifically because even though we cannot see them, we can build machines that do. We have even built some machines that can remove all matter from between atoms so that we can measure what is left. It is through such machinery that we have discovered that pure empty space—space with absolutely no matter in it whatsoever—has a structure. Science is really amazing, itself an important takeaway from this.

- Nothing should be presented as "truth." All knowledge, in science, is contingent on the current level of knowledge. This has an important implication that should help the reader recognize good science—scientists never come to definitive conclusions. Findings are always, always conditional. Hence, scientists use words like consensus, probability, and significance instead of truth to indicate that, at this point, an idea has support. The word "truth" is not part of its vocabulary.

- The third news brief uses the same scientific literature to make its points. But after a careful reading of the first two briefs, it is difficult to say what the criticism is. The signature feature of the third brief is that it uses quotes that are quite accurate to make its points but that on close inspection is sharply out of context. For instance, the brief commented that NASA had called the melt-off unprecedented. If you return to the first brief, you will see that the word was used as follows: "unprecedented since the advent of satellite imaging of the earth's frozen surface." In the third news brief, the word was used to argue for the overhyping of the melt-off, taking the word and its meaning sharply out of context.

- "Global warming" is a very general category in which a large variety of scientific fields are housed. It includes disciplines that: study hydrology, ice, and glacial history, understand cloud formations, assess the history of earth's flora and fauna, develop methodologies for sophisticated statistical analyses, analyze insect migration and reproduction, study chemical reactions to a variety of important gasses under a wide variety of circumstances, assess the currents and patterns of oceans, study soil types, understand the economics of agriculture, measure celestial mechanics, study riparian areas—their viability and the limits of their ability to be fecund, and on and on. Three points from this:
  - It is unreasonable to think that all these different groups are engaged in some mass coordinated and secret conspiracy to undermine business profits, especially for the rather meager wages most scientists receive.
  - These groups are all doing their own thing, and they will inevitably develop findings that seem contradictory, and indeed are contradictory. Importantly, it is through the finding of contradictions that scientific fields grow, and all scientists pride themselves and sometimes are able to publish very well when they are able to disprove or find evidence against a theory. What they do not go out of their way to do is to agree with each other. A scientist cannot build a reputation by agreeing with everyone else; that is for textbooks. These features of science are well known to anyone working in a field that uses scientific methods, be it the physical or behavioral sciences. It also shows how amazing it is that even a small group of scientists are in agreement with regard to particular characteristics of global warming.
- Good science has a few features that you will not find in most of the bad science critiquing global warming. If the reader keeps these features in mind, she or he will be a better consumer of scientific research, and perhaps a better scientist.

- Good science tests a specific thing. The outcome of that test is always, as noted above, conditional. Scientists will state in their report exactly how they calculated that probability, using a mathematical estimate, and then they will explain what that estimate means. They stay focused on the hypothesis or the modeled set of relationships they are interested in. Pseudoscience tends not to test something but look for ways to debunk or disagree with something. In the process it often misquotes or misinterprets research, as in the example above. It does not use science but will misuse other people's findings.
- Good scientific research always identifies its shortcomings. Pseudoscience does not tend to have this quality.
- Good science does not overgeneralize its findings. In the three news briefs above, only the third article actually interpreted the Greenland melt-off in generalized terms of global warming and did so in the negative. The first news brief, which represented the side of science in our opinion, remarked on the unusualness of the event but did not generalize it to global warning.
- Good science is not rhetorical. What we mean is that it makes its point with its information and stays on point. The third article included a variety of rhetorical flourishes: It referred to NASA's claim as "nothing but a bunch of hot air," and used the comment "NASA should start distributing dictionaries to the authors of its press releases." These kinds of comments are uncharacteristic of science, but they are characteristic of the rhetorical give and take of climate science politics.

Forecasting and Global Warming

One of the generic criticisms of climate change is of the stamp "The future is unpredictable," or similarly, "we don't even know what is going to happen with the weather a week from now, let alone in a hundred years." We are generally in agreement with both of these statements: The future *is* unknowable. With that said, we want to emphasize that formalized planning and forecasting is integral to business and government alike.

The science of climate change is in significant part about forecasting. That it is about predicting future contingencies is not particularly exceptional or unusual; to the contrary, it is characteristic of modern life. All units of modern government develop forecasting and planning models of some kind. Forecasting is integral to the insurance industry; its models enable the financing of a great deal of trade and business that otherwise would not have the means to start up or to sustain operations. The mathematics of insurance are organized around what insurers consider to be strong predictive elements. International development models attempt to forecast the ability of particular changes to improve on trenchant social, medical, and economic problems in countries around the world, especially those that are "third world." Cities forecast in order to budget in anticipation of routine and unexpected problems. The notion of trying to forecast the future of the environment of the planet is not particularly odd. That there is an emphasis today on understanding climate and its changing nature is part and parcel of the broader development of forecasting systems across the public and private sectors of activity and of the sciences and social sciences today.

Forecasting and Blind Luck

We forecast, recognizing that forecasting is not so much about knowing the future but about what we need to budget for today so we can mitigate the costs of known contingencies in the future. The scientific models that we forecast with are enormously complex, and they are working with very nonnormal variables whose parameters are contingent on the behavior of other nonnormal variables. Put plainly, we don't know with any certainty quite how global warming as a climate event will take us into the future, though we have a good idea where it will take us. The first models of global warming, developed in the 1980s, continue to model contemporary trends respectably well, and we continue to flesh out the details. We can't predict the weather with accuracy over the long-term, but climate is different—it is physics based on trends over time, not precise moment to moment weather behavior, and so it is measureable and predictable. Here is the "bottom line" contingency of global warming that we face:

If we were to be *incredibly fortunate*, we would have some as-of-yet unknown thermostatic factor kick in and return temperatures to normal—and we can all get along again, that is, as best we ever really have, without having to face foundational changes in our lifestyles, our economic practices, and our energy sources. Or maybe, as some politicians suggest, all the scientists in all these different fields are engaged in some dark plot, and there is not a thing to worry about except the scientists themselves. Or perhaps, given the immense human intellect and capacity for inventiveness, we will develop solutions that not only address global warming but enable us to sustain high levels of technological and economic progress.

If, however, we become *incredibly unfortunate*, the processes of global warming could increase temperatures so much and so rapidly that the human species cannot exist in mass society at anywhere near the aggregate clustering and density we do now: most of the major cities on the planet would be swamped by rising oceans, the oceans would be toxic and too acidic for marine life as we know it today, and humans would find themselves confined to the few remaining (northerly) temperate regions where they can work and grow food. All of those contingencies are rhetorical generalizations—not very scientific, we acknowledge—and they are also hypotheticals; science is trying to work out the quite complicated details of an unknown future. But futures are, of their nature, contingently perilous; who would have known that, at the celebrations that welcomed the twentieth century, over 180 million people would be killed in wars and totalitarian regimes by its end? Yet, who would have known that we would put a man on the moon? The future is wild, dangerous, and unpredictable.

There is an old proverb and curse, purported to be Chinese and first noted by the British Ambassador to China in 1936. "May you live in interesting times." Global warming may make our times a great deal more interesting. In these interesting times, as the reader will see in our review of global warming, we're not looking very fortunate. For instance, a 2013 paper on cloud cover sought to unravel the difficult assessment of cloud impacts on global warming. The author, arguing that 4°C should be anticipated at century's end (2100) without immediate mitigation and 8°C at the end of 2200, observed that

> *Climate sceptics like to criticize climate models for getting things wrong, and we are the first to admit they are not perfect, but what we are finding is that the mistakes are being made by those models which predict less warming, not those that predict more.*[3]

Interesting times. We are not looking particularly fortunate. To the contrary, we are looking increasingly unfortunate—and increasingly like we're going to be *very unfortunate*.

Building a Link Between Climate and Crime

Global warming is directly associated in the public's mind with hotter summers and warmer winters. There are few places where citizens would not like warmer winters, although for many the notion of hotter summers is daunting. In 2012, we witnessed such a summer; the average U.S. temperature for the three months of summer broke the previous all-time high by 1.6°. We will begin this work, then, by exploring the relationship between weather and crime, particularly focusing on temperature, but also considering other aspects of weather. The most basic form of our question is: *Is there a relationship between weather and crime?*

In this section we focus on weather rather than climate. The National Oceanic and Atmospheric Administration provides the following definition of both terms:

> **Weather** *is defined as the state of the atmosphere at a given time and place, with respect to variables such as temperature, moisture, wind speed and direction, and barometric pressure.*

> **Climate** *is defined as the expected frequency of specific states of the atmosphere, ocean, and land, including variables such as temperature (land, ocean, and atmosphere), salinity (oceans), soil moisture (land), wind speed and direction (atmosphere), current strength and direction (oceans), etc. Climate encompasses the weather over different periods of time and also relates to mutual interactions between the components of the earth system (e.g., atmospheric composition, volcanic eruptions, changes in the earth's orbit around the sun, changes in the energy from the sun itself, etc.).*

We see in this discussion an issue that we raised in the introduction. We can look at the relationship between weather and particular kinds of crime, and we may find strong relationships. Does that mean that the weather "caused" the crime? Is not a particular offender or offenders responsible for a crime, regardless of the circumstances of the weather? In a legal setting, we operate in such a way that individuals are, according to rules that are often confusing and arcane, assigned full responsibility for criminal activity (see, e.g., drug schedules and their corresponding penalties.) However, if we want to understand the crime, develop plans to mitigate it, or provide adequate security, then a simple assignation of offender blame leaves us woefully unprepared.

As we will see in one of the articles we review, the relationship between crime and weather is sufficiently robust in the United States that we can forecast for increases in the number of crimes over the coming years. As cities develop long-term plans for municipal well-being, should not they take into consideration all the pertinent factors? Indeed, a major strain of criminology argues that the person is only one part of the criminal event and that we can manipulate that event in such a way as to remove criminal opportunity altogether. If we rely only on individual blame, we cannot arrive at the kind of knowledge about places that enables us to effectively address a great deal of crime today.

So the answer is, yes, weather carries part of the blame for crime. We can't put weather in prison or otherwise develop "weather" sanctions so that we get the satisfaction that it has been adequately punished for its behavior. It contributes to our understanding of crime and that contribution is important. On the other hand, we do not want to fall into the trap of environmental determinism. The environment nudges existing trends and practices. We are not environmental automatons; we can nudge back. At the end of the day, what we as humans do is up to us.

As we write this book, we believe that the environment, including the daily weather and temperature, play an underrecognized role in the production of crime and violence. At the same time, it is only a role. As we try to dissect the many ways human problems and the environment interact, we are most likely to be successful by recognizing the full interplay of all the factors, while noting throughout that the final outcomes of our hopes and designs are not up to the environment. They are up to us.

Consider a crime popularized in media accounts of gang activities—drive-by shootings. Imagine a drive-by shooting in a blinding snowstorm. How does the shooter see his or her target in a zero visibility blizzard? Invite them to the window? Will a shooter take a chance when the roads are snow or ice covered, restricting escape possibilities? Moreover, the odds that a target will be outside in a snowstorm are sharply lowered, making the lethal intent of the shooter much harder to convert into her or his desired outcome.

This does not mean that drive-by shootings will not happen in a snowstorm. One of the authors, using this metaphor in class one snowy winter's day and getting chuckles from the class by bowing to the outside blizzard to emphasize the point, read in the local newspaper the following morning that a drive-by shooting had seriously injured a young man during the blizzard. This complication of the metaphor extends to climate change processes as well. We may have some quite chilly summers and winters as we move deeper into global warming. We may see short-term reversals; this is the nature of complex systems, and it is to be expected. As we will see, the various feedbacks that potentially amplify or diminish climate change processes are challenging to model and findings can be difficult to interpret. If we take the scientific perspective, what we should look for are long-term trends, not single events.

In fact, research tends to show that there is a robust (not perfect) relationship between temperature and violent crime when we look at long-term trends (Anderson, 1987). The relationship is such that, as temperatures increase, violent crime also tends to increase. However, beyond a certain temperature, violent crimes tend to go back down (Cohn, 1990; although see Ranson,

2012). Put simply, it can be too cold or too hot to do much of anything outside where most crime tends to happen.

It should be realized that the relationship between crime and changes in weather do not take place in a neutral security setting. As patterns of crime change, one can anticipate a subsequent or delayed change in the system of crime control as well (Rotton & Cohn, 2001). What this means is that the relationship between any kind of change in crime and climate change or variation will be affected by the way the criminal justice system adapts. Weather is, arguably, the most well-known of the changes associated with global warming. Yet, there are many other kinds of changes as well. To discuss these changes, we need to review elements of global warming theory to see what kinds of changes might lead to changes in both crime and in crime control.

Cohn: Heat and Crime

Cohn (1990) provided a literature review of the relationship between environmental variables and crime. Of particular interest is her review of crime and temperatures. Generally, she found significant relationships between temperature and different categories of criminal behavior. Information Box 1.4 reviews her principal summary findings on this literature.

A positive relationship between crime and temperatures needs more than a black box explanation; what is the mechanism that explains this statistical linkage? People don't just all of a sudden freak when the temperatures warm to a certain point and then run out madly and commit a violent crime. At least we hope that is not the case. What, then, is the mechanism that underlays the relationship between violence and crime? A number of perspectives have been put forth.

1. The first one is the environmental crime perspective, particularly that aspect of environmental criminology that focuses on the way in which everyday "routine" activities create situations conducive for crime. Weather creates lifestyle opportunities for criminal behavior; warm weather enables young people to hang out outside, enjoy the night air and warm evenings, and sometimes to carry out crimes together (Cohn & Rotton, 2012). Cohn (1990) noted in this regard that

   during pleasant weather, people tend to spend more time outdoors, resulting in greater opportunities for personal interaction and increased availability of victims, as well as an increase in the number of empty (and therefore more vulnerable) dwellings.

   (Cohn, 1990, p. 51)

Information Box 1.4 Cohn: Heat and Crime

1. *Heat and collective violence.* Baron and Ransberger's (1978) examination of archival data of serious civil disorders in America between 1967 and 1971 found results that suggest a curvilinear relationship between temperature and measures of collective violence. The frequency of riots increased with ambient temperature up through about 85°F, and then decreased sharply as temperature continued to increase. Carlsmith and Anderson (1979) reanalyzing suggested that fewer riots occurred on days with temperatures over 90°F, not because such temperatures lowered the probability of people rioting, but simply because there were fewer such days. It can be concluded that collective violence tends to increase with temperature at least up to about 85°F.

2. *Heat and assaults.* Michael and Zumpe (1983) examined 16 locations around the United States for two- to four-year periods and found that the monthly mean daily temperature and the monthly mean number of assaults were significantly correlated in 14 of the 16 locations with within-jurisdiction rank-order correlations ranging from 0.58 to 0.97. An ordinary least-squares regression analysis showed significant linear relationships between temperature and assault, and there was a significant positive correlation between the dates of the temperature maxima and the dates of the assault maxima in all 16 cities. Rotton and Frey (1985) examined daily calls for police service in Dayton, Ohio, over a two-year period and found that the daily mean temperature was a significant predictor of the number of assaults ($r = 0.48$).

3. *Heat and rape.* Michael and Zumpe (1983) found significant positive correlations between the monthly mean temperature and the monthly mean number of rapes (Spearman $r = 0.64$ to 0.97) in 13 of their 16 locations. Perry and Simpson (1987) also found a significant positive correlation between the monthly average minimum temperature and the monthly rape rate ($r = 0.26$), so that the rate of rape offenses increased with temperature.

4. *Heat and domestic violence.* Rotton and Frey (1985) found that daily mean temperature was a significant predictor of the rate of domestic complaints ($r = 0.68$) in Dayton over a two-year period. They also obtained cross-lagged correlation coefficients to investigate if temperature had any delayed effect on domestic violence complaints and found that high temperature significantly tended to precede disturbance calls by one day. Michael and Zumpe (1986) found a positive linear relationship between the monthly mean temperature and the monthly number of crisis calls received by battered women's shelters in five locations around the United States over a two- to three-year period.

Moreover, Rotton and Cohn (2000) showed that weather was associated in particular with violent crimes, such as assaults. These crimes, traditionally thought of as street crimes, are consistent with the notion that weather enables lifestyles, some of which are criminogenic.

This perspective does not seem to work so well, however, to explain increases in domestic violence, which while violent are usually inside the home and consequently less vulnerable to changes in outside temperatures.

2. The second perspective is rational choice. According to this perspective, weather is one of the factors individuals take into account in order to carry out crime. When a person is

considering a crime, they will consider the likelihood of quickly carrying it out and then getting away afterward. With larger numbers of people on the streets on a warm evening, for instance, a person considering a robbery might perceive a greater likelihood for a target that pays off and the opportunity to get away easily by blending in with a crowd (Cohn & Rotton, 2000).

3. The third perspective is that environmental heat is a stress that amplifies already existing stresses, psychologically increasing the likelihood of stress-induced violent outcomes (Anderson, 1987). Anderson (2001) noted in this regard that

> *my colleagues and I believe that most heat-induced increases in aggression, including the most violent behaviors, result from distortion of the social interaction process in a hostile direction. Heat-induced discomfort makes people cranky. It increases hostile affect (e.g., feelings of anger), which in turn primes aggressive thoughts, attitudes, preparatory behaviors (e.g., fist clenching), and behavioral scripts (such as "retaliation" scripts). A minor provocation can quickly escalate, especially if both participants are affectively and cognitively primed for hostility by their heightened level of discomfort. A mild insult is more likely to provoke a severe insult in response when people are hot than when they are more comfortable. This may lead to further increases in the aggressiveness of responses and counter-responses.*

(Anderson, 2001, p. 34)

This has implications for broad effects of additional stress from generalized warming patterns such as those hypothesized by global warming. Anderson (2001) further noted that

> *using the best estimate of how much the violent-crime rate will increase for each 1°F increase in temperature (i.e., 4.48), we see that a 2°F increase in average temperature predicts an increase of about 9 more murders or assaults per 100,000 people, or more than 24,000 additional murders and assaults per year in a population of 270 million.*

(Anderson, 2001, p. 37)

The Ranson Model of Crime and Global Warming

Ranson (2012, p. 4) also looked at the relationship between crime and temperatures in the United States. He used econometric time series modeling to assess crime with "an unusually long and rich panel dataset of monthly crime rates and weather for 2,972 counties in the 49 continental states." The data covered a 50-year period from 1960 to 2009. His findings showed a robust relationship between temperature and crime for all crimes except manslaughter. Those crime categories were murder, rape, aggravated assault, simple assault, robbery, burglary, larceny, and vehicle theft. Significant nonlinear patterns were noted for the crimes of larceny and burglary. Temperature was strongly related to crime only below 40°F and disappeared above that temperature.

Ranson then used the parameters provided by this analysis to predict crime rates under conditions of global warming. To forecast future temperatures, he used estimates provided by the U.K. Hadley Centre's HadCM3 climate model and the U.S. Center for Atmospheric Research CCSM3 climate model. These models were used to forecast climate changes in each of the countries used in the first analysis. He then forecast the crime likely to happen between 2010 and 2099. He noted that overall levels of crime were expected to increase considerably. He specifically noted that:

> under the HadCM3 model, there will be an additional 35,000 murders, 216,000 cases of rape, 1.6 million aggravated assaults, 2.4 million simple assaults, 409,000 robberies, 3.1 million burglaries, 3.8 million cases of larceny, and 1.4 million auto thefts. All these changes are significant at the five percent threshold. The only case that is expected to decline is manslaughter, but the expected change is less than 1,000 cases and is not statistically different from 0.
>
> **(Ranson, 2012, p. 12)**

Ranson concluded his research with an estimate of the social costs of these additional crimes. His estimates ranged from a low estimate of 19.7-67.8 billion, depending on the analysis. He concluded that changes in crime were an important consideration in global warming research.

The research discussed above focuses on individual level outcomes associated with heat increases. Research has also looked at the way in which nations display violent tendencies when exposed to changes in weather. One of the more dramatic large scale weather events is called the El Niño/Southern Oscillation (ENSO). The ENSO is associated with inclement weather patterns; it refers to a band of unusually warm water that develops along the western coast of South America. It is associated with both droughts and flooding and can have a severe impact on agricultural states in the Americas. Fishing industries are also sometimes hard hit by the ENSO—the upwelling of warm water tends to drive fishing stocks to different areas and away from the coastal fisheries. El Niño received its name from the tendency of the coastal

Pacific waters to warm around Christmas. The ENSO is considered to be a change in the climate.

ENSO is mostly an unfavorable change, leading to hardship. It is associated with a surge of epidemic diseases in parts of Africa because of the increased rain it produces. However, in other areas, it produces drought. A Chinese famine in 1876 was one of the worst in recorded history with an estimated 13 million people killed. The famine conditions are attributed to an El Niño event that lasted from 1876 to 1877. From a climate change perspective, ENSO seems to provide the more dramatic planetary-scale weather changes predicted by global warming. Could it thereby be associated with conflict?

Hsiang and his colleagues (Hsiang, Meng, & Cane, 2011) used a quasi-experimental design comparing regions strongly affected by the ENSO—and regions only weakly affected by it. Areas strongly affected were identified as tropical South America, Africa, and much of the Asia-Pacific region. They then searched for a link between climate and armed conflicts. Analyzing data on conflicts from 1950 to 2004, they found that the risk of civil conflict doubled in the strongly affected countries during the El Niño years.

The authors also looked at conflicts globally and asserted that approximately one-fifth of the civil conflicts since 1950 could be linked to El Niño. To avoid the charge of a selection bias, he removed particular crisis-prone countries from the analysis; this did not affect the outcome. This, the authors argued, demonstrates that the stability of modern nations is closely tied to global climate patterns.

The findings, the authors asserted, display robustness, since they are able to remove some of the more extreme positive examples without affecting the outcome. However, an important consideration with this finding, and with any state-level finding, is that the specific mechanism that produced conflict is not known. One cannot conclude that, because states are more likely to engage in conflicts, then individuals in those states are also more likely to choose conflict to solve their problems. Conflicts between states are outcomes typically selected by state leaders or emergent leadership that can mount a challenge at the state level. This suggests that psychological theories cannot be used in this instance because there is no reason to think that leadership at the state level was particularly overheated. As country leaders, one would imagine that they had access to air conditioning in the routine course of their lives.

One possible explanation is based in a resource scarcity perspective (see Chapter 3). In this instance, a review of El Niño episodes suggests that these were quite hard on agrarian and fishing economies, both of which are closely tied to the seasonal routines of weather. Such countries tend to be poor and lack the kinds of reserves that would enable state support of local workers during economic downturns. A resource scarcity perspective works well when also considering the actions of state leadership because leaders may well decide, during times of particular hardship, that conflict might provide the only access to resources or that, alternatively, challenger groups would capitalize on resource scarcity events to argue that the state was unable to provide adequate resources and lacked legitimacy as a people's representative.

In another paper, Hsiang, Burke, and Miguel (2013) carried out a meta-analysis that assessed the impact of climate change on conflict at both the interpersonal and state levels. In all, they assessed 45 conflict data sets. At all levels, they found that conflict was strongly associated with changes in both temperature and rainfall.

> *Deviations from normal precipitation and mild temperatures systematically increase the risk of conflict, often substantially. This relationship is apparent across spatial scales ranging from a single building to the globe and at temporal scales ranging from an anomalous hour to an anomalous millennium. Our meta-analysis of studies that examine populations in the post-1950 era suggests that the magnitude of climate's influence on modern conflict is both substantial and highly statistically significant ($P < 0.001$). Each 1-SD change in climate toward warmer temperatures or more extreme rainfall increases the frequency of interpersonal violence by 4% and intergroup conflict by 14% (median estimates).[4]*

Similar patterns of temperature and conflict intensity were noted by Burke and his colleagues (Burke, Miguel, Satyanath, Dykema, & Lobell, 2009). The authors assessed the impact of global climate change on armed conflict in sub-Saharan Africa and found a strong relationship between civil war and temperature in Africa. The likelihood of war was significantly greater during warm years.

These results, the authors concluded, were particularly troubling when one takes into account predictions of global warming and climate change. Burke et al. (2009, p. 20674) concluded that "When combined with climate model projections of future temperature trends, this historical response to temperature suggests a roughly 54% increase in armed conflict incidence by 2030, or an additional 393,000 battle deaths if future wars are as deadly as recent wars."

Endnotes

1. "The Flood Next Time." Retrieved April 22, 2014 at http://www.nytimes.com/2014/01/14/science/earth/grappling-with-sea-level-rise-sooner-not-later.html?emc=eta1&_r=0.
2. Michael Mann, one of the coauthors of the "hockey stick" chart of global warming, has been denounced on billboards, grilled by hostile legislators, had his emails hacked and stolen, received letters laced with an anthrax-like substance, and has received death threats. He has been called the Jerry Sandusky of global warming, in reference to a college football coach charged with hiding information about sex between children and himself. "Harassment of climate scientists needs to stop." http://www.theguardian.com/commentisfree/2014/jan/09/denialist-harassment-of-climate-scientists-needs-to-stop.
3. "Solution to cloud riddle reveals hotter future: Global temperatures to rise at least 4 degrees C by 2100." Retrieved April 8, 2014 at http://www.sciencedaily.com/releases/2013/12/131231094442.htm.
4. "Quantifying the Influence of Climate on Human Conflict." Retrieved April 12, 2014 at http://www.sciencemag.org/content/341/6151/1235367.

2

WHAT IS GLOBAL WARMING?

Ruth: "Our first big trip was out West. We went to Las Vegas first, back when there was a city there. You know, Tule Springs, they call it now, for the old spring in the valley there."

"Las Vegas was one of the first American cities to collapse under the strain of warming. It depended on Lake Mead for its water. But the water was gone, except for stagnant residue in some riparian basins. All of the cities that depended on the Colorado River were gone. Even before the great warming, the region was in trouble from long-term drought conditions. Warming pushed it over the edge; it would probably have happened anyway, just not so quickly."

Ruth continued: "From Las Vegas, we traveled up Interstate 15 to Calgary. Gas stations everywhere back then. Up in Canada we could still see the remains of the great ice sheets from the last ice age. They were huge, immense, beautiful beyond words. I remember hiking up one of the mountains and looking down the other side, seeing ice as far as you could see. You just could not believe it would all go away. But Beto, he always said—don't follow your heart, follow the science."

Clete had been to the belt of cities and towns that lined the route from Calgary all the way to Alaska. The Trans-Canada highway had become the primary route for the Northern migration. It was beautiful lake country. Some of the mountains still had ice fields. But it was not for everyone: Canada had become very strict about immigration from the United States. One of the large refugee camps was now on the American side of Interstate 15. Canada now only allowed U.S. citizens in who could contribute something to the national economy; the refugee camp there had swelled to an estimated 50,000 U.S. citizens, with a few Latinos mixed in; the camps on the coasts held close to a quarter million each. Still, they were nothing like the million person camps in the Far East.

By 2035 global temperatures had already risen two degrees. What that meant, though people did not anticipate it, was that land temperatures were up about twice that amount. It turned out that one of the fastest-warming areas was Siberia, at a rate even higher. It was that high temperature over the northern land mass there, scientists thought, that initiated the first feedback: Unexpectedly large quantities of methane released from the melted permafrost. A whole village, living close to one of the large lakes that populated the region, had died overnight of methane poisoning—nearly 8,000 residents living around a lake. There was cell phone video footage of people dying. That was what spooked everyone—watching people walking along, then keeling over and dying. When the news media got hold of the story, they found that it had been happening for years and that more than 20,000 people probably had been poisoned, not to mention additional deaths in Africa. Their governments had shushed it up. That was when people finally got it. But it was too late. Even then, it was too late. Other climate feedbacks were already on the way.

Clete asked, "Do you remember the headlines when the villagers were all killed from methane?"

Ruth responded, nodding her head, "Oh yeah. That is when I finally really got it, too. I mean, you just understand better when you actually see it, and we saw the people dying on their cell phones. Now I understood at a gut level what Beto meant. Follow the science, not the heart. I remember to this day how sick I felt when I realized it was all true."[1]

Global warming is the process by which average temperature increases globally. In principle, this increase is straightforward and can be metaphorically understood. A phrase, widely used in nutrition circles, is "calories in, calories out." This means that if the number of calories a person takes in through food sources is greater than the number of calories they burn off through activities, then she or he will gain weight. The opposite is true as well: if the number of calories taken in is lower than that burned off, then a person will lose weight. So it is with the warmth that is produced by sunlight on the planet: If the quantity of energy from the sun is greater than the ability of the planet to absorb it at current levels, then the planet will heat up. Similarly, if the quantity drops faster than the ability of the planet to absorb it, the planet will cool down.

Both systems, in other words, act like a moving rheostat. They exist in a rough equilibrium, but that equilibrium shifts to a new state when inputs change. For a person, the new state can be fatal; if too few calories enter the human system, the person will die of malnutrition. For the planet, when too little solar energy strikes the planet, the planet will cool and undergo state transformations across the ecological spectrum: It is estimated that a 6°C drop shifted the planet into the cooler phase of the Eemian (the most recent) glacial age, a transformative change of the planetary surface for a seemingly small change in average global temperatures. Like the change from water to ice, small changes in temperature can lead to qualitatively different ecologies across the planet. Also, for humans, as dieters have learned, when the human body changes from one state to another, from average weight to obesity, a reversal, of course, is remarkably difficult and often simply does not happen. Such fears about qualitative, transformative changes are also associated with global warming—we know equilibrium changes will happen, but we are not clear at all on what the new equilibria will be. We reasonably fear for the survival of our lifestyles as we know them because they are so closely tied to the very processes that are causing climate change. We should be afraid: research on peak oil shows that the future availability of oil will shrink dramatically the use of automobiles for routine activities. Automobiles, and the easy availability of power from oil products, are integral to civilization in the West, and that civilization will change dramatically in the near future. Some researchers argue that peak oil passed in 2008, and the United States will face significant oil shortfalls by 2020.[2] Heightened demands for energy from global warming may actually increase the demise of oil, as its use is ramped up for increased demand.

For people, the actual relationship between calories and weight is complex, as anyone who has studied nutrition, or, more commonly, has tried to gain or lose weight, knows. Similarly, the relationship between solar energy and global average temperatures is quite complex. However, that it is complex does not mean that it is not a strong relationship. Life as we know it on this, our great, mother planet, exists because of global warming produced by the sun.

The sun alone does not explain why temperatures are what they are. Consider the moon. The moon is, for all practical matters, the same distance from the sun as the earth is. However, the moon is considerably colder on one side and hotter on the other. During its "day," the moon is about 100°C. During its "night," it is about −173°C. These temperatures are not survivable for life forms on earth, let alone humans. They are extreme for the specific reason that the moon provides no atmospheric mechanism to hold the heat at night and reflect it at day. Simply, it has no atmosphere. Consider what the earth would be like if there were no atmosphere to contain heat-trapping greenhouse gases. If we had the same energy input from the sun, continued to have the same overall quantity of oxygen and nitrogen, but did not have an atmosphere that could trap any heat, the average global temperature would be about 3°F or −16°C, which are subfreezing temperatures (Archer, 2009). These are substantially below the temperatures that would lead to "snowball earth." Because of our atmosphere, we are considerably warmer than we otherwise would be, and our planet can support life as we know it. In other words, the greenhouse effect is the source of life for our planet.[3] So, as we think about changes in the greenhouse effect, it is important to recognize that it is always present; it is not some "new" effect that was created by scientists to explain global warming. It is the source of life's continuity and survival, in the most literal sense of the term.

Greenhouse gases are one small component of the atmosphere. Currently, the composition of the atmosphere is about 78% nitrogen, 21% oxygen, and 1% other, which is predominately carbon dioxide, but includes the other greenhouse gases. That 1% makes weather possible on the planet by creating instabilities in the atmosphere. Without greenhouse gases, there would be no weather.[3]

The Ordinariness of Global Temperature Changes

Changes in the average global temperature of earth are not exceptional phenomena. To the contrary, they are routine. The world today is in its most recent "ice age"; the most current ice age began about 2.4 million years ago, at the beginning of the Pleistocene period. There have been four previous ice ages. Each of these ice ages is marked by the expansion and movement of great glacial ice sheets toward the equator, called glacial periods. The length of the glacial periods in the current ice age is about 40-100 thousand years. The interglacial periods, characterized by the melting and retreat of the great glaciers, are about 5-30 thousand years long. Glacial and interglacial periods has occurred about once every hundred thousand years over the past million years the most recent epoch.

The most recent interglacial period is called the "Holocene" and began at the end of the last glacial period, about 11 thousand years ago. Holo is Greek for wholly, and cene means recent. This event marked the end of the Pleistocene, Greek for mostly (Pleisto) and recent (cene). The Holocene and the Pleistocene are together called the Quarternary period, which refers to the last two million years of earth history. Because of human impacts on the planet, some refer to the past few centuries as the "Anthropocene," which refers to the time that humans had a significant effect on the earth's ecosystems. Some scientists extend the Anthropocene back 11 thousand years, roughly corresponding to the Holocene.

At their depth, the glacial periods are about 9°F cooler than today. The interglacials have shown temperatures up to 2° warmer than average global temperatures today. The Holocene has been favorable to human progress and development and has been called the "long summer" in a book of that name (Fagan, 2004).

The shifts between the glacial and the interglacials are correlated with the orbital pattern of the earth around the sun. The earth's rotation around the sun is slightly eccentric. It also wobbles on its axis and shifts on its tilt. Changes in these factors can alter the quantity of the sun's radiation that strikes earth. This is called radiative or solar forcing, which refers to the quantity of radiation from the sun that strikes the earth. These events also form a periodic pattern called a Milankovitch cycle, which can be studied with great precision (Archer, 2009). When this cycle is associated with minimum solar forcing, conditions are favorable for a return to glacial eras. When the cycle returns to a maximum solar forcing, conditions can lead to the interglacial periods. The point of this rather arcane discussion is that broad, global temperature changes are routine. The other point, equally important, is that what one might consider rather small, overall changes in temperature, on the magnitude of 10°F (6°C), can lead to dramatic changes in climate. Indeed, it is hypothesized that during one of the previous glacial epochs ice sheets expanded all the way to the equator, resulting in "snowball earth." This event lasted until greenhouse gases, produced by volcanic activity under the ice sheets, rekindled the global warming process.

Many critics of global warming tend to use *localizing metaphors* to describe temperature changes, for instance, a 10° warming might make for a more comfortable climate in North Dakota, a quite cold state. This tendency to conceive of the effects of global changes in temperature through localization metaphors utterly fails to capture the profound changes in climate that such changes would actually cause. The chart in Figure 2.1 shows both glacial and interglacial time, and provides a time line of the current glacial epoch and associated temperature changes.

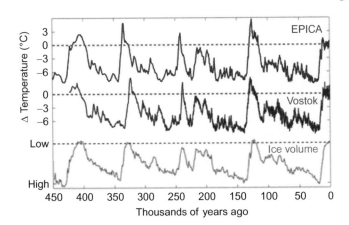

Figure 2.1 Ice age temperature changes.

These temperature estimates were taken from ice cores in Antarctica. From this chart, one can see changes from about 6°C lower than median temperatures today to temperatures about 2°C above. A drop of 10°F would put North Dakota under a mile of ice. On the other hand, the anticipated effects of global warming by the end of the century are forecast to lead to earlier and more dramatic snowmelts, longer growing seasons, more severe storms, a drop in the water table, and an increase in dangerous ticks and mosquitoes.[4]

Consider North Dakota again. It resides in a region that is anticipated to have water shortages associated with climate change. This will create a need for more effective irrigation systems. Furthermore, North Dakota relies heavily on cattle farming and the coal industry, which contribute methane and carbon dioxide disproportionately to its population. It will likely face dislocations in employment as it transitions away from its heavy reliance on greenhouse-producing gases. Favorably, though, North Dakota is well situated for wind farming, an industry that could capitalize on the state's substantial winds and wide open spaces.[5] However, the factors that change temperatures in North Dakota will be affecting all the geographies close to it and, more generally, worldwide. In other words, a seemingly innocuous—and even what might be seen as favorable—local change in North Dakota, when thoroughly examined, is indicative of broader crises that carry risks for North Dakota on a number of fronts.[6] Localizing metaphors consequently serve to sharply underestimate the impacts that will be produced by global warming.

How Do Greenhouse Gases Heat the Planet?

Greenhouse gases produce heat by taking part of the earth's energy budget, particularly that part that otherwise would be reflected back into space, and trapping it in the oceans, land, and atmosphere for an extended period. They do this because the gases reflect the heat randomly, in all directions, when reflective heat comes into contact with them. The website "green living" provides the following discussion in Information Box 2.1.[7]

Another way to visualize the concept of forcing is to think of the overall quantity of solar energy as the earth's "energy budget." That energy budget is broken down into the way the planet distributes solar energy into different purposes and outcomes. The following chart in Figure 2.2 presents a simplified model of the earth's energy budget:[8]

Information Box 2.1 The Greenhouse Effect

If you park a car outside on a sunny day, sunlight enters through the car's glass windows. That incoming sunlight warms the inside of the car when it shines on the dashboard, the car seats, the steering wheel, and other areas. But once the sunlight hits those surfaces, it loses some of its energy, and it can't shine back *out* of the car. The sunlight's energy— also called solar radiation—becomes trapped inside the car, and after an hour or two of sitting in the sun, the inside of the car becomes very warm, even on a cold winter day.

A similar process happens when sunlight shines on the earth. Some of that solar radiation is absorbed by the atmosphere and by the earth's surface, so it loses energy. Technically speaking, the powerful incoming *shortwave* solar radiation loses energy when it shines on the earth's surface and is converted into *longwave* radiation, which is weaker and can't escape through the atmosphere. That longwave solar radiation becomes trapped in the atmosphere by greenhouse gases, which get warmer and warmer as the gases absorb more and more solar radiation.

According to the U.S. Energy Information Administration, levels of greenhouse gases have increased 25% since 1850, when fossil fuels like coal and oil started to be widely burned for heating, transportation, manufacturing, and other processes. Carbon dioxide is the gas that's largely responsible for this overall increase—in the United States, roughly 82% of our greenhouse gas emissions are CO_2 from burning fossil fuels like gasoline, oil, natural gas, and coal.

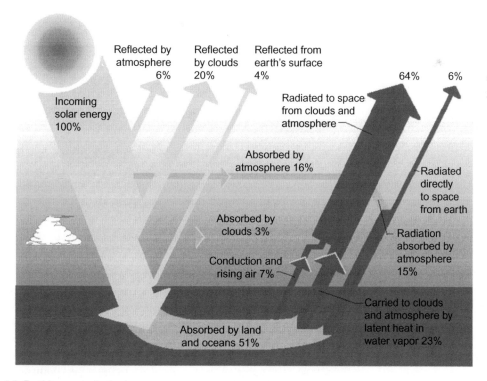

Figure 2.2 Earth's energy budget.

We see from Figure 2.2 that most of the energy from the sun, 51%, is absorbed into land and ocean, while 30% is reflected back out to space. Of that which is reflected, some will be carried into the atmosphere as water vapor, some will be absorbed as radiation in the atmosphere, and some will be lost directly to space.

The energy budget can be thought of as a thermostatic balance. That is, the average temperature, what we referred to above as the "long summer" of the Holocene, represents the heat left over from the overall solar energy that is absorbed in one way or another; by the clouds, rising air and conduction, land and ocean, and atmosphere. Anything that affects the energy budget is called a "forcing." The term "forcing" is frequently used in the research on climate change to describe the impact of various factors on global warming. The following quote identifies the two fundamental kinds of forcings:[9]

> Any changes to the Earth's climate system that affect how much energy enters or leaves the system alters Earth's radiative equilibrium and can force temperatures to rise or fall. These destabilizing influences are called climate forcings. Natural climate forcings include changes in the Sun's brightness, Milankovitch cycles (small variations in the shape of Earth's orbit and its axis of rotation that occur over thousands of years), and large volcanic eruptions that inject light-reflecting particles as high as the stratosphere. Manmade forcings include particle pollution (aerosols), which absorb and reflect incoming sunlight; deforestation, which changes how the surface reflects and absorbs sunlight; and the rising concentration of atmospheric carbon dioxide and other greenhouse gases, which decrease heat radiated to space.

Anthropogenic (human-made) forcings that are central to the global warming debate are greenhouses gases, carbon dioxide in particular. Carbon dioxide absorbs heat that is radiated by water and land surfaces. When the overall quantity of carbon dioxide in the air increases, the thermal radiation, or heat, absorbed by the atmosphere increases. The way greenhouse gases work is described below:[10]

> When greenhouse gas molecules absorb thermal infrared energy, their temperature rises. Like coals from a fire that are warm but not glowing, greenhouse gases then radiate an increased amount of thermal infrared energy in all directions. Heat radiated upward continues to encounter greenhouse gas molecules; those molecules absorb the heat, their temperature rises, and the amount of heat they radiate increases. At an altitude of roughly 5-6 kilometers, the concentration of greenhouse gases in the overlying atmosphere is so

small that heat can radiate freely to space. Because greenhouse gas molecules radiate heat in all directions, some of it spreads downward and ultimately comes back into contact with the Earth's surface, where it is absorbed. The temperature of the surface becomes warmer than it would be if it were heated only by direct solar heating. This supplemental heating of the Earth's surface by the atmosphere is the natural greenhouse effect.

What Are the Anthropogenic Sources of Greenhouse Gases?

Greenhouse gases are the drivers of global warming; the most abundant greenhouse gases in earth's atmosphere are: water vapor, carbon dioxide, methane, nitrous oxide, and ozone. The primary anthropogenic contributions to greenhouse gases are:[11]

- Burning of fossil fuels and deforestation leading to higher carbon dioxide concentrations in the air. Land use change (mainly deforestation in the tropics) account for up to one-third of total anthropogenic CO_2 emissions.
- Livestock enteric fermentation and manure management, paddy rice farming, land use and wetland changes, pipeline losses, and covered vented landfill emissions leading to higher methane atmospheric concentrations. Many of the newer style, fully vented septic systems that enhance and target the fermentation process also are sources of atmospheric methane.
- Use of chlorofluorocarbons (CFCs) in refrigeration systems, and use of CFCs and halons in fire suppression systems and manufacturing processes.
- Agricultural activities, including the use of fertilizers, that lead to higher nitrous oxide concentrations.

A more detailed review of greenhouse gases is presented in the following chart in Figure 2.3.

In Figure 2.3, titled "Annual World Greenhouse Emissions," we see the relationship between energy sectors and the production of greenhouse gases. Our research shows that coal accounts for 25% of the greenhouse gases; natural gas, 19%; and oil, 21%. Of the oil, we see that transportation accounts for 15%.[12] The chart also shows the specific economic sector that is associated with the energy sectors producing greenhouse gases. Hence, we can see in this discussion the extent to which the production of greenhouse gas is a byproduct of a great many aspects of human civilization, technology, and progress. Indeed, the economic investment in greenhouse gas producing technologies is so

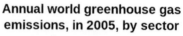

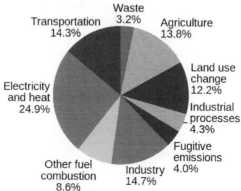

Figure 2.3 World GHG emissions flow chart. *Source*: Annual Greenhouse gas Emission, By Sector, 2005, retrieved July 7, 2014, from http://en.wikipedia.org/wiki/File:Annual_world_ greenhouse_gas_emissions,_in_2005,_by_sector.svg.

extensive that it is difficult to imagine contemporary life without it. This chart is a window on the level of resistance that business and corporate life might bring to changes that involve large-scale technological changes. Ask yourself: If we were serious about doing something about the quantity of greenhouse gases produced in modern society, what business sector would they not affect? Once we correctly frame that question, we can understand the substantial resistance that many elements of the corporate world—certainly, all those whose short-term profits rely heavily on invested technologies that are carbon dioxide producers—will wage against efforts to address global warming.

Global Warming and the Problem of Feedbacks

Current increases in global warming today are primarily caused by humans. These are the gases that we put into the air. However, one of the central issues with global warming is that feedbacks can occur that on their own will tend to increase both the rapidity and the intensity of warming. These feedbacks are especially troubling because once they are initiated, it is too late to do anything about them. Complicating this is that we do not know at precisely what temperature they will set in. The feedbacks can be thought of as the great unknowns, like fictional monsters of the deep facing ancient mariners. The difference, though, is that these monsters are real. The principal feedbacks are listed next.[13]

Carbon cycle feedbacks. There are concerns that global warming will damage many of the earth's ecosystems, leading to an increase of atmospheric CO_2 levels. These feedbacks include:

1. Methane gas, in the form of methane hydrate or sea ice and methane in the bogs of Siberia. This is of particular concern, because methane gas produces about 30 times as much heat as does carbon dioxide.

2. Rain forests, such as the immense forests in Brazil, could collapse and release their carbon stores. These forests would die and their areas would turn to desert. The water tables that the forests protect would drop sharply or simply disappear.

3. Forest fires, which add carbon to the atmosphere.

4. Warmer oceans that absorb less carbon dioxide than cooler ones. Moreover, as the oceans warm and acidify, there are concerns that they will start releasing carbon dioxide. There is about 50 times more carbon in the oceans than in the atmosphere, and the oceans serve as a powerful break on global warming. However, they serve as breaks precisely because they are absorbing heat. At unknown points, this heat will rebound into the atmosphere, contributing to the stabilization of global temperatures at levels much higher than today.

Ice-albedo feedback. Albedo is defined as the fraction of solar energy that is reflected back into space. Recall from the earth's energy budget figure above that about 4% of the sun's energy was reflected from the surface back into space. White surfaces, such as snow and ice, contribute to the albedo effect. Open water in oceans and seas, on the other hand, is dark. It absorbs heat. Both land and open water are on average less reflective than ice and thus absorb more solar radiation, in turn causing more warming. *Albedo* change contributes to what is called polar amplification. This is the process by which polar temperatures, especially those in the Northern Hemisphere, may rise twice as much as temperatures in the rest of the world.

Water vapor feedback. As atmosphere is warmed, its capacity for saturation increases. The amount of water vapor in the atmosphere will consequently tend to increase, warming the atmosphere further, enabling it to hold even more water vapor.

There are also negative feedbacks. Negative feedbacks occur when processes initiated by global warming tend to negate the warming process. These are all long-term processes. None of these feedbacks will, over the next few centuries, have a large impact on the forces in play today that are producing global warming or on the likely outcomes associated with global warming.

Le Chatelier's principle. The ocean, given time, will dissolve all the carbon dioxide humans put into the air. This is a somewhat long-term process, though. About 75% of the carbon dioxide caused by human activities will dissolve in the ocean over about three centuries. In other words, about three-fourths of the CO_2 we put in the air today will be removed in the early twenty-fourth century. However, about 25% of this will last for a very long time; the "tail" of the curve for absorption is long, geologically speaking.

Chemical weathering. Shell formation by ocean organisms, over a very long time, combs the CO_2 out of the oceans. "The complete conversion of CO_2 to limestone takes thousands to hundreds of thousands of years." In the shorter term, however, the CO_2 has an acidic impact, dissolving the shells of shelled animals.

Blackbody radiation. "As the temperature of a *black body* increases, the emission of infrared radiation back into space increases with the fourth power of its *absolute temperature* according to Stefan-Boltzmann law. This increases the amount of outgoing radiation as the Earth warms."

Secondary Feedbacks

There are also secondary feedback loops. These secondary feedbacks are described in Information Box 2.2. Almost all of these are positive feedback loops.[14]

Secondary feedbacks are important for several reasons.

1. These feedbacks are fundamentally different from anthropogenic global warming in a critical respect: We cannot do anything about them. They occur because of the heating of the planet that has already occurred, and they release greenhouse gases from anthropogenic sources.

2. The specific start-up temperature of each feedback is an unknown. That they will occur has generally been agreed on in scientific research, but when they will, that is, at what specific temperature, is not. What we know is that once they begin, they cannot be negated by mitigation efforts.

3. We do not know what the upper boundary of the negative feedbacks are, though estimates can be made. Thus, while forecasters predict a 3-5°C global increase this century, the additional increase for the next century might be considerably

Information Box 2.2 Secondary Feedback Loops

1. In a similar manner to past climatic and large-scale ecosystem changes, human-induced global warming is expected to cause a poleward shift of forest zones and thus decrease the reflectivity of the earth's surface, increase absorption of sunlight, and enhance rates of warming—a positive feedback.

2. Warming in these high-latitude regions may also result in increased rates of methane production from bogs, or peat lands. Methane is the second most important greenhouse gas. However, likely changes in soil moisture from global climatic change will also affect rates of methane emissions, but in less certain ways. Future changes in topography in these regions may also increase rates of methane release—a positive feedback.

3. Warming and associated decreases in soil moisture may bring about an increased frequency of natural fires. The burning vegetation would pump even more CO_2 into the atmosphere—a positive feedback.

4. Elevated concentrations of CO_2 have been shown to cause stunted plant transpiration, the process by which plants release water to the atmosphere. Transpiration normally acts to cool the surface; thus, the result could be even higher regional temperatures at the surface—a positive feedback (although the global implications of this are not entirely clear).

5. In soils, the CO_2 "enrichment" could lead to changing ratios among important plant nutrients and in the process lead to decreased nitrogen availability. In this case, any stimulatory effect that increased CO_2 may have on plant growth could be constrained—a positive feedback.

6. Global climatic change is expected to aggravate rates of land degradation and desertification, which in turn would result in the emission of more disturbed, windblown dust. These particles act to cool the surface, on a regional scale, by increasing atmospheric reflectivity (when the underlying surface is relatively dark)—a negative feedback.

7. As warming penetrates the ocean sediment layers it could result in the release of large amounts of methane, billions of tons of which are locked away in an icy mixture called gas hydrate that is only stable under specific conditions of high pressure and low temperatures—a positive feedback.

8. Oceanic temperature increases as a result of global warming could lead to decreased solubility of CO_2, and thus turn some regional oceanic CO_2 "sinks" into sources—a positive feedback.

greater, with estimates in the 8°C range. Upper range variability is extremely hard to assess given the nonlinear nature of the feedbacks. What we do know is that the conditions of the next few centuries are already "in the air." Much of the CO_2 being put in the air today will be in the air until the twenty-third century, and quite a bit of it for much, much longer.

4. At different times, different regional and global processes contribute different quantities of heating to global warming. In other words, global warming is not a linear phenomenon; it occurs in fits and spurts, occasionally flattening and then leaping forward again. Modeling such processes is enormously difficult.

5. We know feedbacks happen because historical records show they have happened before. Those historical patterns show that global warming can suddenly increase dramatically, with considerable warming over a relatively short time period.

6. There is no aspect of civilized life or human ecology that will be unaffected by global warming and no way to stop the feedbacks once they initiate.

How Long Will Global Warming Last?

We cannot determine how long global warming will last. What we tend to suspect is that a change in state, from one thermostatic balance to another, might happen abruptly, then level out and then happen again as we pass through various tipping points. Global warming is probably best thought of as a state change in the global temperature as reflected in the earth's energy budget. Anthropomorphic changes are likely to remain for centuries and some, for millennia. In Information Box 2.3 are four estimates of the longevity of global warming.

One of the problems with this model is that it is about the total quantity of global warming from anthropogenic sources. It does not take into account additional warming from feedback processes. For example, one of the more feared feedbacks is the release of methane from Siberia. The Western Siberia Bog alone contains about 70 billion tons of methane, about 25% of the total methane in the world. This methane will be released if and when the permafrost melts.[15] Since methane is a highly potent heat-trapping gas, there is much interest in the timing of the melting of the permafrost. Some argue that an increase of 1.5°C will trigger the melting of the permafrost. Importantly, the permafrost is already melting, tied in part to the increased heating in the polar regions. An additional 2-3° of heating is already in the pipeline from existing levels of CO_2 in the atmosphere. This is a feedback process that is likely to occur at the 2-3° point, with unknown and potentially significant impacts on global warming.

Tipping Points

A tipping point is the temperature at which a climatic change occurs that takes an ecology or a state to a new norm. It may be local or worldwide. Consider the tipping point in Information Box 2.4. The important point is that, once a tipping point is past, the old norm is gone and the ecology or state enters into a new equilibrium. The challenge of tipping points is that they represent

Information Box 2.3 How Long Will Global Warming Last?

From IPCC Fourth Assessment Report, Working Group I Executive Summary of Chapter 7

About 50% of a CO_2 increase will be removed from the atmosphere within 30 years, and a further 30% will be removed within a few centuries. The remaining 20% may stay in the atmosphere for many thousands of years.
Source: http://www.ipcc.ch/ipccreports/ar4-wg1.htm

From U.S. Greenhouse Gas Inventory Reports

Atmospheric lifetime: 50-200 years. No single lifetime can be defined for CO_2 because of the different rates of uptake by different removal processes.
Source: http://epa.gov/climatechange/emissions/usinventoryreport.html

From RealClimate Post, "How long will global warming last?"

My model indicates that about 7% of carbon released today will still be in the atmosphere in 100,000 years. I calculate a mean lifetime, from the sum of all the processes, of about 30,000 years. That's a deceptive number, because it is so strongly influenced by the immense longevity of that long tail. If one is forced to simplify reality into a single number for popular discussion, several hundred years is a sensible number to choose, because it tells three-quarters of the story, and the part of the story which applies to our own lifetimes.
Source: http://www.realclimate.org/index.php?p=134

From Susan Solomon, Senior Scientist for National Oceanographic and Atmospheric Administration

"People have imagined that if we stopped emitting carbon dioxide that the climate would be back to normal in one hundred years or two hundred years." McIbben (2011, p. 17) extending this, noted that "changes in the Earth's systems are largely irreversible for more than a thousand years after carbon emissions have stopped . . . No one is going to refreeze the Antarctic for us, or restore the pH to the oceans. . . ."

nonlinear elements and are the product of complex systems. That is, a small change in temperature will result in a sudden reorganization of several elements across a system all at once. The system moves into a new equilibrium state. It will remain there until it shifts again. We will not know when we have actually passed a tipping point until we see its consequences, and then it is too late—the new ecology or state is in the process of reorganization and the old one is simply gone.

There is substantial concern that we have crossed a critical tipping point in temperature already: that tipping point is the

Information Box 2.4 A Tipping Point of Considerable Concern: Methane Release in Siberia

Climate scientists have warned that a large portion of western Siberia is undergoing an unprecedented thaw that could dramatically increase the rate of global warming.

Researchers who have recently returned from the region found that an area of permafrost spanning a million square kilometers has started to melt for the first time since it formed 11,000 years ago at the end of the last ice age.

The area, which covers the entire sub-Arctic region of western Siberia, is the world's largest frozen peat bog. It is feared that it will release billions of tons of methane into the atmosphere as it thaws. Methane is a greenhouse gas 20 times more potent than carbon dioxide.

Scientists have identified "tipping points"—delicate thresholds where a slight rise in the earth's temperature can cause a dramatic change in the environment that itself triggers a greater increase in global temperatures.

The discovery, reported in *New Scientist*, was made by Sergei Kirpotin at Tomsk State University in western Siberia and Judith Marquand at Oxford University. The researchers found that what was until recently a barren expanse of frozen peat is turning into a landscape of mud and lakes, some more than a kilometer across. Dr. Kirpotin told the magazine the situation was probably irreversible and is undoubtedly connected to climatic warming.

Climate scientists have warned that predictions of future global temperatures would have to be revised upward.

Source: Srbin, L. (2005), "Big trouble coming from Siberia." See http://www.physicsforums.com/showthread.php?t=84838

increase of CO_2 in the air at quantities above 400 parts per million (ppm). The concern is that we are already locked in for this quantity of change. We are, by many estimates, on an irreversible course to increase global temperatures by 2°C. See the following discussion of this tipping point in Information Box 2.5.

What are some of the critical tipping points? Lynas (2008) identified the following temperatures as important milestones in the warming of the earth:

1°C increase: 350 ppm We already are at 400 ppm.

2°C: 400 ppm Current levels: this milestone was officially passed in May 2013.[16]

3°C: 450 ppm Significant feedbacks appear to kick in here. It is possible that at this threshold we will begin a process of runaway global warming.[17]

4°C: 550 ppm Concerns of dramatic releases of Siberian methane. The World Bank also has expressed the concern that there will be a catastrophic loss of crop land at this temperature.[18]

5°C: 650 ppm New territory. Aquifers for major cities are dry, climate refugees in the billions. This is a civilization-level threat.[19]

6°C: 800 ppm Last seen in Cretaceous (144-165 million years ago). This was the warmest the earth has been since the Archaen (2.5 billion years ago), and its consequences are difficult to

Information Box 2.5 A Tipping Point, Crossed

Research commissioned by *The Independent* indicates that the accumulation of greenhouse gases in the atmosphere has now crossed a threshold, set down by scientists from around the world at a conference in Britain in 2005, beyond which dangerous climate change may be unstoppable.

The danger point they predict is a rise in global mean temperatures to 2° above the level before the Industrial Revolution in the late eighteenth century.

If temperatures rise to that level, it is likely that Greenland's ice sheet will already have begun irreversible melting. This will threaten the world with a sea-level rise of several meters. They also claim that agricultural yields will have started to fall in Africa, Europe, the United States, and Russia, putting more people at risk from hunger and at risk of water shortages for both drinking and irrigation.

Tom Burke, a former government adviser on the green issues, said this means we have entered a new era of dangerous climate change.

Source: McCarthy, M. (2006), "Global warming: Passing the 'tipping point'." See http://www.independent.co.uk/environment/ global-warming-passing-the-tipping-point-466187.html

imagine, in part because the oceans were about 200 meters higher than today (the poles were melted and the oceans were shallower) and the current configuration of global geography was not in place.

What constitutes a "safe" level of parts per million, if by safe we want to maintain the current quality of life associated with the ambient climate that has characterized the Holocene? That number is likely 350 ppm, a number visible now only in our rearview mirrors. Rockstrom and his colleagues,[20] in the journal *Nature*, expressed that "above 350 ppm we threaten the ecological life-support systems that have developed in the late Quarternary period and severely challenge the viability of contemporary human societies" (pp. 472-475).

The favorable climates of the Holocene are likely to be history in the lifetimes of our children. A research project, aimed at assessing the likelihood that current trends are atypical, reconstructed regional and global temperature anomalies for the past 11,300 years using 73 globally distributed records (Marcott, Shakun, Clark, & Mix, 2013).[21] The authors found that, until two centuries ago, Holocene temperatures had been steadily declining. When current data are added, and using all the Intergovernmental Panel on Climate Change (IPCC) model projections for 2100 as comparisons, the planet will exceed the Holocene maximum by century's end. We will be in the uncharted territory of the Anthropocene, and our beneficent Holocenic climate may be lost to us.

Climate Sensitivity

The concept of tipping points is closely related to another concept: the concept of climate change sensitivity. Sensitivity is defined as the increase in earth's mean temperature due to a doubling of CO_2. This is sometimes called the Charney sensitivity. It is currently as follows:

> The equilibrium climate sensitivity is a measure of the climate system response to sustained radiative forcing. It is not a projection but is defined as the global average surface warming following a doubling of carbon dioxide concentrations. It is likely to be in the range 2°C to 4.5°C with a best estimate of about 3°C, and is very unlikely to be less than 1.5°C. Values substantially higher than 4.5°C cannot be excluded, but agreement of models with observations is not as good for those values. Water vapour changes represent the largest feedback affecting climate sensitivity and are now better understood than in the TAR. Cloud feedbacks remain the largest source of uncertainty. Panel on Climate Change (IPCC)'s Assessment Report 4 (AR4) published in 2007.[22]

The Charney sensitivity measure has been used since the early 1980s and is the standard for measuring sensitivity of global temperature to CO_2 changes. Recently, a number of critics argue that this measure substantially underestimates the sensitivity of the climate to CO_2 doubling. The central problem is that it does not take into account long-term feedbacks. Once those feedbacks are introduced, then the estimates of sensitivity change dramatically. Consider the following:

> Climate sensitivity refers to the mean-annual global temperature response to CO_2 doubling due to the radiative effects of CO_2 and associated feedbacks. The proposed range of climate sensitivity, $\sim$1.5 to 4.5°C, represents fast-feedback sensitivity that incorporates changes in atmospheric water vapor, sea ice, and cloud and aerosol distributions.[23]

In November 2013, the level of CO_2 in the air was 396 ppm. We are already substantially beyond the point where we can stop significant global warming below the 3° range, and perhaps even higher. There is simply too much CO_3 already in the pipeline, and a great deal more anticipated with the expansion of oil and coal plants and technologies. CO_2 levels in the Pliocene were about 3-4° warmer than today, with an estimated ppm of between 365 and 415 ppm. If the past is the key to the future, then we have already lost the ability to put the brakes on global warming. We are already at the level of CO_2 that will force us into a new equilibrated state.[24]

What Is the Basic Evidence for Warming?

There is a great deal of research on global warming, together with a great deal of support for the idea among global warming scientists. Duran and Kendall Zimmerman (2009) found that 97% of the climate change scientists who are actively publishing believe in global warming and that between 97% and 98% believe it is anthropogenic. In the relatively constrained space available in this book, we elect to provide only a few graphs that we think best enable the visualization of climate effects.

Chart 1: Global Surface Temperatures (Figure 2.4)

The first chart below displays patterns of global surface temperatures over time, from 1880 to 2000.[25] It shows a clear line of increase. It should be pointed out that this underestimates the changes we are likely to experience, since land temperatures, especially nighttime lows, are increasing at a much faster rate than ocean and sea temperatures.

Another way to understand this is to look at the history of global, high average temperatures.

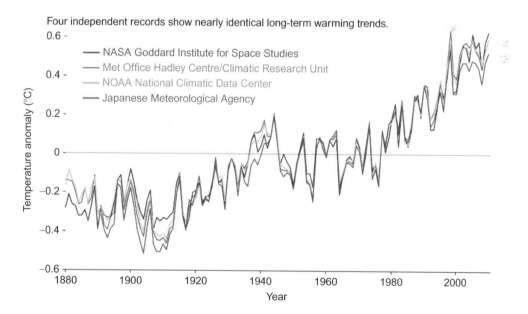

Figure 2.4 Global surface temperatures. *Credit:* NASA Earth Observatory/Robert Simmon. *Data sources:* NASA Goddard Institute for Space Studies, NOAA National Climate Data Center, Met Office Hadley Centre/Climate Research Unit, and Japanese Meterological Agency.

Many major organizations measure these annual global temperature differences, and their ranking may vary just slightly. The hottest years on record (since the start of record keeping) are listed below.[26] It shows that 8 of the 10 hottest years ever are in the twenty-first century.

1. 2010 (+1.13°F higher than the baseline) and 2005
2. 2005 tied with 2010 as the two hottest years ever
3. 2009
4. 2007
5. 2006
6. 1998
7. 2002
8. 2003
9. 2001
10. 1997

Data show that the year of 2012 was the hottest on record for the United States. As noted by the *Los Angeles Times*, May 15, 2012:

NOAA (National Oceanic and Atmospheric Administration) said that for the period from May 2011 to April 2012, the nationally averaged temperature was 55.7 degrees, 2.8 degrees higher than the 20th century average. The national average temperature for April was 55 degrees, 3.6 degrees above average.[27]

To be sure, the higher temperatures did not affect every region equally. The Pacific Northwest actually saw cooler-than-average temperatures over 2012, according to NOAA data. Much of California was also cooler than normal; Southern California had an average year. Globally, the average summer temperature tied with 2005 as the third warmest ever, at 1.15°F above the average and land surfaces at 1.85° above the average.

Chart 2: Comparison of Record Highs to Record Lows (Figure 2.5)

One way to visualize global warming is to compare record high temperatures to record lows. On any given period, average highs and lows should range around a historic average, all else being equal. However, all else is not equal. The chart below[28] from Desdemona Despair (2012) provides ratios of record highs to record lows. The last four years have shown a clear trend toward disproportionate record highs, when the average of each should be "half the pie," or 50%. According to the chart for 2012, record highs to lows were 9 to 1. Put another way, the last time the planet averaged below its twentieth century normal for an entire

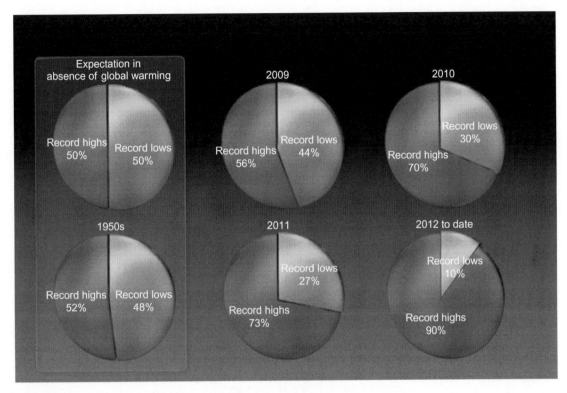

Figure 2.5 More daily record highs in United States than record lows. *Source*: 1950s data from Meehl et al.; all other from NOAA/NCDC.

month was February 1985. April makes it 326 months in a row. Sometimes the record highs are widely felt and noted, as was the record warm summer of 2011, when the United States established a new average summer temperature a full 1.6° higher than the previous record.

The message presented in these charts is clear. Global warming is not a problem that will emerge in the lives of our grandchildren, nor even our children. It is here now; its broad, sweeping changes well under way. The "long summer" of Holocene earth (Fagan, 2004) is rapidly retreating into recorded history; the new earth is arriving with summers that may not be so friendly.

Chart 3: Arctic Sea Ice Volume over Time (Figure 2.6)

One of the primary manifestations of global warming is also the quantity of ice at the poles. This is not exactly encouraging, unless, of course, you are in favor of global warming. As of September 5, the ice on the Arctic Ocean was less than 1.54 million square miles (4 million km²), a 45% reduction compared to September conditions in the 1980s and 1990s (see chart below).[29] As the authors of the chart observed,

> *New figures of modelled data from* PIOMAS *show the volume on 25 August was around 3,600 cubic kilometres. This is just one-quarter of the volume twenty years ago. This* fits with data *from the first purpose-built satellite launched to study the thickness of the Earth's polar caps showing that the rate of Arctic summer sea ice loss is 50 per cent higher than predicted.*[30]

The 2007 IPPC report suggested that by 2100 Arctic sea ice would likely exist in summer, though *at a much reduced extent.* Because many of the Arctic's climate system tipping points are significantly related to the loss of sea ice, **one might conclude optimistically that we had time to reduce greenhouse emissions and still "save the Arctic."** The 2007 IPCC-framed goal of reducing emissions 25-40% by 2020 and 80% by 2050 would "do the job" for the Arctic.

Unfortunately, the physical world didn't agree. By 2006, scientist Richard Alley *had observed* that the Arctic was already melting "100 years ahead of schedule."[31] The tipping points for the Arctic may have already been passed (Figure 2.6).

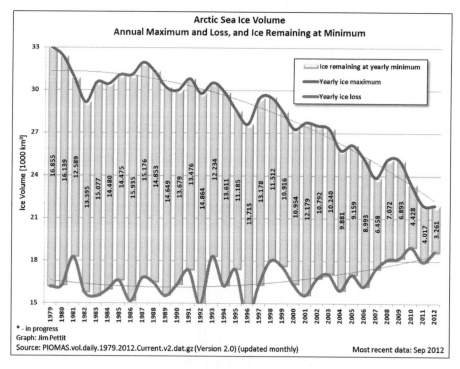

Figure 2.6 Minimum PIOMAS Arctic sea ice volume through August 25, 2012. *Graph:* L. Hamilton. *Data:* PIOMAS

How Hot Will It Get?

When we talk about warming, we are assigning an average temperature score to a quite remarkable complex of processes. A measure of central tendency is probably not the best way to conceptualize global warming. Instead, standard deviation renders a better image of present and future climate change effects. In this instance, by standard deviation we refer to weather patterns that are likely to be more severe than historical norms. When it is hot, it is likelier to be hotter. When it is cold, it is almost as likely to be colder; certainly cold can set in longer occasionally than is consistent with historical averages. Weather extremes are more likely to occur from a disruption of atmospheric flow around the earth's Northern Hemisphere; instead of fronts moving through areas and pushing others out, a weather pattern tends to sit in one place for longer periods.[32] Moreover, as we noted earlier, weather itself is a function of the quantity of greenhouse gases in the atmosphere; increase the quantity and the weather becomes more dynamic.

However, temperature has consequences, and the historical record of higher and lower temperatures shows quite different planetary landscapes and waterscapes. Increase the temperature, more water is evaporated and thermal expansion occurs, both of which push up relative ocean levels to land levels.

When we look at projected temperatures, most forecasters look forward to 2100. The reason for this selection is that the ability to predict becomes increasingly tenuous the further out in time we go. Figure 2.7 shows anticipated increases in temperature to 2200.[33]

Figure 2.7 shows estimates based on different emission standards, which is a routine way to estimate the greenhouse gas–temperature relationship. A review of this figure shows that the relationship is not linear; the rate of increase actually increases over time. Similarly, IEA chief noted that, if we continue on the current path, we should anticipate a total increase of 3.6-5.3°C, according to the National Energy Agency.[34]

Some scientists challenge the wisdom of using 2100 as an upper boundary for warming estimates. They assert that the evidence that we are going to pare back emissions is not there, and we need to assess what we might anticipate further into the future. A review of one research monograph observed that, by 2200, we might witness average global temperatures increasing by as much as 11-12°C.[35]

Scientists from Australia's University of New South Wales and Purdue University in the United States found that rising

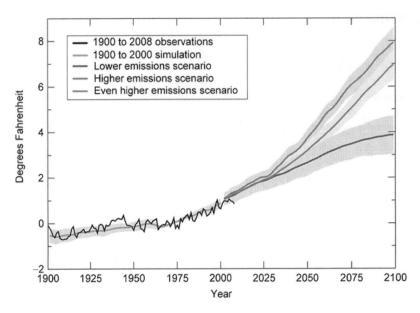

Figure 2.7 Forecast temperatures to 2200.

temperatures in some places could mean humans would be unable to adapt or survive.

"It would begin to occur with global-mean warming of about seven degrees Celsius (13 Fahrenheit), calling the habitability of some regions into question," the researchers said in a paper. "With 11-12 degrees Celsius warming, such regions would spread to encompass the majority of the human population as currently distributed. And under realistic scenarios out to 2300, we may be faced with temperature increases of 12 degrees (Celsius) or even more," Professor Tony McMichael said. "If this happens, our current worries about sea level rise, occasional heat-waves and bushfires, biodiversity loss and agricultural difficulties will pale into insignificance beside a major threat—as much as half the currently inhabited globe may simply become too hot for people to live there."

Summary

As we noted at the beginning of this chapter, global warming is not all that difficult to understand. As more carbon dioxide and other greenhouse gases are put into the air, the planet becomes warmer. However, this simple principle gets complicated very quickly when we develop mathematical models of likely outcomes based on what knowledge we have of global warming factors. For instance, the simple melting of water changes the equation, simply because melted water tends to absorb more heat than ice, which tends to reflect heat back into space. So to assess the warming effects at the poles, we have to calculate the rate of melting, and then we have to figure in differentials for the ratio of meltwater to ice.

We also have tipping points, such as the release of methane in large, uncontrollable quantities. These are the great imperfectly knowns—not unknown but still with many difficult puzzles to decipher. We know that as the earth and oceans warm, they release methane gasses. Methanes are the dark force of greenhouse gases; a rapid and large-scale release of methane has the capacity to change the heat equation very quickly, heating the planet significantly in years rather than centuries. But we don't know quite how much methane is trapped below the oceans and in the permafrosts of the world—though we have a pretty good idea—and we are not quite sure at what temperature it will be released uncontrollably—though we're starting to get a pretty good idea. It is not anticipated to be soon, but it is anticipated to occur without mitigation, initiating a process called runaway warming, a process that refers to self-induced planetary warming beyond human control.

Put simply, the long-term forecasts are considered by many researchers (including the authors) to be catastrophic. We would prefer a different, less "dire" descriptor, but we simply do not know what that word would be. It would be difficult to imagine a more troubling temperature forecast than the ones scientists are arriving at using current (2000+) research. We might have hoped that, as our research methods become more refined, we might find that the forecast is not so dire. However, the opposite is true: Forecasters are increasingly selecting the most extreme early estimates as the most likely.[36] And the number of researchers and papers supporting global warming continues to load heavily on the side of anthropogenic global warming: A review of scientific, peer reviewed research on climate change in 2014 found that, of a population frame of 2,259 peer-reviewed research papers, only one paper disagreed with human-caused global warming.[37] Finally, the most troubling of all the forecasts are those concerned with the acidification of the oceans. The earth's huge bodies of water are the primary repositories of CO_2; they absorb it, gradually lowering the overall quantity in the atmosphere. However, they become acidified in the process. Short-term acidification is already showing effects through its interference with calciferous animals to build their shells. Long-term forecasts raise the specter of dead acidified oceans, with unoptimistic consequences for terrestrial life.[38]

We certainly have not been active in efforts to respond to greenhouse emissions. One would look back to the current period—2014—and conclude that we have done precisely nothing of substance to mitigate warming. We have arguably moved backward—the North Carolina legislature, in 2012, passed a state law prohibiting scientific estimates of ocean rise related to global warming to be included in coastal planning. China and the United States are moving at an accelerated rate on coal extraction and the building of coal plants. If we were to make an analogy, it is as if we were playing Russian roulette, all the chambers were loaded, the trigger was pulled, and our best remaining hope was that the gun would misfire.

Endnotes

1. This fictional account has a basis in history. "Gas cloud kills Cameroon villagers." http://www.history.com/this-day-in-history/gas-cloud-kills-cameroon-villagers; "Thai villagers hang red shirts to repel Window Ghost, methane detectors better (Photos)." http://www.examiner.com/article/thai-villagers-hang-red-shirts-to-repel-window-ghost-methane-detectors-better; Methane, one of the spookiest of greenhouse gases, is implicated in one of the great planetary extinction events, the P-K extinction: see 5. "Methane Catastrophe (Continental Margin Methane Release)." Retrieved April 23, 2013 at http://www.killerinourmidst.com/methane%20catastrophe.html.
2. "The future of oil supply." Retrieved May 12, 2013 at http://rsta.royalsocietypublishing.org/content/372/2006/20130179.full.
3. "What If There Was No Greenhouse Effect?." Retrieved April 19, 2013 at http://www.drroyspencer.com/2009/12/what-if-there-was-no-greenhouse-effect/.
4. "North Dakota and Global Warming (Encyclopedia Entry)." Retrieved April 12, 2013 at http://www.academia.edu/167105/North_Dakota_and_Global_Warming_Encyclopedia_Entry.
5. "Ecological Footprint of Nations. 2005 Update." Retrieved May 2, 2013 at http://www.ecologicalfootprint.org/pdf/Footprint%20of%20Nations%202005.pdf.
6. "Effects of Global Warming on the State of North Dakota." Retrieved May 19, 2013 at http://www.e2.org/ext/doc/e2_northdakota.pdf;jsessionid=32AB24D39E2556A395F3A690FE5A238C.
7. Cited from "Green Living Basics." Retrieved May 5, 2013 at http://greenliving.about.com/od/greenlivingbasics/a/Greenhouse-Gas.htm.
8. "Earth's Energy Budget." Retrieved April 30, 2013 at http://asd-www.larc.nasa.gov/erbe/components2.gif.
9. "Climate Forcings and Global Warming." Retrieved May 7, 2013 at http://earthobservatory.nasa.gov/Features/EnergyBalance/page7.php.
10. "Editing Earth's energy budget." Retrieved April 1, 2013 at http://en.wikipedia.org/w/index.php?title=Earth%27s_energy_budget&action=edit&section=5.
11. "Greenhouse gas." Retrieved April 23, 2013 at http://en.wikipedia.org/wiki/Carbon_dioxide_emission.

12. "World GHG Emissions Flow Chart." Retrieved April 25, 2013 at http://www.bdarchitects.com/bd-MAP/wp-content/uploads/2011/08/world_greenhouse_gas_emissions_2000.jpg.

13. "Climate change feedback." Retrieved April 26, 2013 at http://en.wikipedia.org/wiki/Climate_change_feedback.

14. "Environmental News Index." Retrieved April 28, 2013 at http://www.andweb.demon.co.uk/environment/.

15. "Melting permafrost methane emissions: Another threat to climate change." Retrieved April 28, 2013 at http://www.terranature.org/methaneSiberia.htm.

16. "Record 400 ppm CO_2 milestone 'feels like we're moving into another era'." Retrieved May 1, 2013 at http://www.theguardian.com/environment/2013/may/14/record-400ppm-co2-carbon-emissions.

17. "Global warming: passing the 'tipping point'." Retrieved June 6, 2013 at http://www.independent.co.uk/environment/global-warming-passing-the-tipping-point-466187.html.

18. We're on pace for 4c of global warming. Here's why the world bank is terrified." Retrieved April May 2, 2013 at http://www.washingtonpost.com/blogs/wonkblog/wp/2012/11/19/were-on-pace-for-4c-of-global-warming-heres-why-the-world-bank-is-terrified/.

19. Op Cit.

20. "A safe operating space for humanity." Retrieved May 6, 2013 at http://www.nature.com/nature/journal/v461/n7263/full/461472a.html.

21. See also "Response by Marcott et al." Retrieved May 6, 2013 at http://www.realclimate.org/index.php/archives/2013/03/response-by-marcott-et-al/. As with all global warming research, challengers have been quick to find many flaws with this research. This is characteristic of all research in this field. The reader is recommended to review the online available records of the authors who consider this work fundamentally flawed as well as those who support the work. An important aside: The reader will find good scientists who disagree on fundamental principles. As noted in the text, the challenge is separating good work from that which is not. One recommendation, and even this recommendation we give with a certain caution, is to see if the scholar of interest has a record of publication in refereed journals. Such publication is respected in the sciences, having ideally been reviewed by three scholars prior to release. This is not to say that peer reviewed journals do not sometimes display scholarly biases or that they never make mistakes. It is to say that we simply do not have a better way to publish scientific guesses about the nature of things.

22. "The Rational Pessimist. Risk and the changing world of climate, resource availability and economic growth." Retrieved May 17, 2013 at http://climateandrisk.com/tag/charney-sensitivity/.

23. "From An Ancient Carbon Mystery." Mark Pagani, Ken Caldeira, David Archer, James C. Zachos. Retrieved May 18, 2013 at http://people.earth.yale.edu/earth-system-climate-sensitivity.

24. "High Earth-system climate sensitivity determined from Pliocene carbon dioxide concentrations" by Mark Pagani, Zhonghui Liu, Jonathan LaRiviere & Ana Christina Ravelo. Retrieved April 22, 2013 at http://www.nature.com/ngeo/journal/v3/n1/abs/ngeo724.html.

25. "February 2011 - Fossil fuel dependence affecting climate change." Retrieved May 25, 2013 at http://www.icsusa.org/pages/articles/2011-icsusa-articles/february-2011—fossil-fuel-dependence-affecting-climate-change.php#.Usxbw7QoKfg.

26. "What are the top ten hottest years on record?" Retrieved April 12, 2013 at http://wiki.answers.com/Q/What_are_the_top_ten_hottest_years_on_record.

27. "It really is hot in here: U.S. has warmest 12 months on record." Retrieved April 13, 2013 at http://articles.latimes.com/2012/may/15/nation/la-nn-na-hottest-year-on-record-20120515.

28. "High Times: More 2012 Record Highs than All of Last Year." Retrieved April 13, 2013 at http://www.climatecentral.org/news/more-record-highs-during-2012-so-far-than-all-of-2011-14768/.

29. "On thin ice: Time-frame to save the Arctic is melting away." Retrieved April 14, 2013 at http://reneweconomy.com.au/2012/on-thin-ice-time-frame-to-save-the-arctic-is-melting-away-88494.

30. Ibid.

31. "Little time to avoid big thaw, scientists warn." Retrieved April 15, 2013 at http://www.csmonitor.com/2006/0324/p01s03-sten.html.

32. "Weather extremes provoked by trapping of giant waves in the atmosphere." Retrieved April 15, 2013 at http://www.sciencedaily.com/releases/2013/02/130225153128.htm.

33. Figure. http://www.epa.gov/climatechange/images/science/ScenarioTemp Graph-large.jpg. Retrieved April 15, 2013 at "Climate Change." http://www.epa.gov/climatechange/.

34. "Global Warming To Rise To 3.6-5.3 Degree Celsius: IEA Report." Retrieved April 19, 2013 at http://www.rttnews.com/2133272/global-warming-to-rise-to-3-6-5-3-degree-celsius-iea-report.aspx.

35. "Earth may be too hot for humans by 2300: study." Retrieved May 2, 2013 at http://www.terradaily.com/reports/Earth_may_be_too_hot_for_humans_by_2300_study_999.html.

36. "Study Sheds Light on Effects of Clouds on Warming." Retrieved May 4, 2013 at http://www.climatecentral.org/news/study-sheds-light-on-effects-of-clouds-on-warming-16916.

37. "Scientific Consensus on Anthropogenic Global Warming: A Pie Chart." Retrieved May 5, 2013 at http://io9.com/scientific-consensus-on-anthropogenic-global-warming-a-1499762156.

38. "Researchers Find Historic Ocean Acidification Levels: 'The Next Mass Extinction May Have Already Begun." Retrieved April 23, 2013 at http://thinkprogress.org/climate/2013/10/03/2725431/unprecedented-ocean-acidification/.

3

CLIMATE CHANGE DENIAL

Clete: "Ruth, One of the things I have never really understood is the resistance to climate change. We did not really start to actually do anything about climate change until the middle part of the twenty-second century, and it was too late. Way past too late."

Ruth thought a moment and answered. "I don't think any of us will understand that. I mean, some of it is obvious; them with big money made their money off short-term profits. Their ability to see the future was crowded out by all the money coming their way. But what doesn't make sense, I guess it never will, is why so many people were going along with it, even after it was clear that we were in the thick of it."

Clete: "Do you remember when the U.S. economy crashed?"

Ruth: "Oh yeah. We were on the road then. It all fell apart around us, and fell fast, we were lucky to get home. First it seemed to be an ordinary stock market adjustment. But then the real estate market fell apart and pushed the overall market way down, kinda like in the early 2000s but worse. They were overinvested in rich coastal properties that were rapidly becoming worthless. Then oil jumped in price; we were well past peak oil, but the big producers were able to mask it until the crash and they had to sell off stock. All of a sudden big money got spooked and shifted away from the U.S. economy and toward China and Canada. Blink of an eye, thank you globalization. The market dropped 2,000 points, froze and closed. Opened the next day, dropped 3,000 more the first hour, closed again. Opened again 2 days later, dropped like a stone, closed in the first 5 minutes down another 3,000. It was like people knew the gig was up, time to pay the piper. They ran on the banks, but bank money was gone from capital flight. Government got nervous and shut down the U.S. banking system for a day. Reopened, but there was a full-blown run again the next day, and they shut the banks down for a week. That was game over. The whole thing happened in about 10 days. Just like that."

"Beto had said that every part of our livelihood was inside complex systems. One thing fails, creates pressure on the next. It fails, then the next. Then the next. Cascading failure, he called it. And he was right. But we didn't think it could happen that fast."

Clete: "So finally people realized there was a climate change problem."

Ruth: "Oh goodness no. They spun it as a banking problem; took people's minds off global warming. But times were hard everywhere after that; that was when the gangs got really strong. Let me take a break, and we can talk some more in a while."

To me, skepticism is not believing what someone tells you, investigating all the information before coming to a conclusion. Skepticism is a good thing. Global warming skepticism is not that. It's the complete opposite of that. It's coming to a preconceived conclusion and cherry-picking the information that backs up your opinion. Global warming skepticism isn't skepticism at all.[1]

(John Cook, 2010)

To plan for and mitigate global warming, countries around the world need to establish policies and economic incentives to develop low carbon technologies and shift away from current dependencies. This will be a substantial makeover of some major sectors of the economy, such as energy and transportation that currently leave a high carbon footprint. This is not happening. One of the substantial and quite effective obstacles witnessed in the United States is a powerful denialist lobby made up of wealthy corporate executives, influential political leaders, well-funded think tanks, "talk show" radio stars, and more than a few researchers with limited scientific credentials. One of their products is the very successful media image of scientific uncertainty, an image sharply contradictory to actual consensus patterns in peer research on climate change. Why?

In this chapter, we adopt a political economy perspective to explain what appears to be a striking disjunction between public perceptions and scientific consensus. We will first review the scientific consensus on global warming. We will then present the core notions of political economy, and finally we will review the specific actions in the U.S. setting that explain the way in which political economy plays out in efforts to initiate global warming policies. This discussion serves several purposes. First, it provides the opportunity to focus on those industries that are primarily responsible for the production of greenhouse gasses implicated in global warming. This is integral to this research because frequently those organizations are also the same ones that fund research and political efforts in opposition to global warming responsiveness and mitigation. Secondly, it allows us to focus on

Preventing dangerous climate change is a great investment. It will cost between one and two percent of GDP and the benefits will be between 10 and 20 percent. That's a return of 10 to 1—attractive even to a venture capitalist

(Geoffrey Heal.)

Paul Garret Professor of Public Policy and Corporate Responsibility, Columbia Business School, New York, NY; Co-organizer, U.S. Scientists and Economists' Call for Swift and Deep Cuts in Greenhouse Gas Emissions.

two of the costliest forms of crime to society; those that are perpetrated by corporations and states. Understanding the political economy of global warming brings us to the root of the problem and highlights the current issues we face, the barriers to satisfactory mitigation efforts, and the type of future that may be in store if we do not respond appropriately.

The Consensus of Scientific Work on Climate Change

Global warming is not a controversial topic in science. For those familiar with the workings of scientific research, global warming is not so much a topic as a categorical gloss, a domain term that captures many different kinds and levels of earth science topics and specializations. The word "consensus" is not the best to use to describe the way in which these scientific areas agree; a better word would be *congruence*. This means that the findings of these different fields are consistent with each other, though they cover many different fields across the earth sciences. And the congruence is quite high; these fields consistently produce research that is consistent with the hypothesis that the surface, the water, and the atmosphere of the planet is warming. The most widely cited measure of congruence is the 2013 Intergovernmental Panel on Climate Change (IPCC) report that stated that the reviewers were 95% confident that anthropogenic climate change was occurring.[2]

When we look at peer-reviewed articles in scientific journals, the congruence is even greater. One study published in 2013 assessed research papers carried out between 1991 and 2001 and found that 97.1% of them agreed with the idea of anthropogenic climate change. Importantly, this paper also found that agreement increased as time passed, with the greatest disagreement in the early years of the study and the least in the later years.[3] In a more recent study, Powell (2013) examined peer-reviewed articles in scientific journals over the period from November 12, 2012 through December 31, 2013.[4] This represented a total of 2,258 articles, written by a total of 9,136 authors. He assessed them according to one criterion—did they present evidence consistent with anthropomorphic global warming, or did they present evidence inconsistent with or contrary to anthropomorphic global warming? Of this population, he found only one paper that presented contrary findings: a publication in the journal *Herald of the Russian Academy of Sciences.* From these two research assessments, it seems that the dissensus in the scientific research about whether global warming is occurring and whether it is man-made is trivial; the already high congruence displayed at the turn of the century continues to rise.

Citizen Views of Climate Change

If climate change scientists display very high levels of congruence, we next ask whether this perception is shared by U.S. citizens. Surprisingly, citizens' views of climate change, and of their perceptions of scientific views, are quite different.

Yale University's School of Forestry and Environmental Studies and the George Mason University Center for Climate Change Communication conduct periodic polls of the perceptions of Americans regarding climate change. The survey, conducted in November 2013, displays patterns of perceptions over time. Some key results are presented in Figure 3.1.

Another important result of the survey shows that we have seen a decrease in the number of people who believe that climate change is anthropogenic (Figure 3.2). The fewer people who believe that humans are responsible, the less support we might anticipate for mitigation efforts; the evidence suggests that, to the extent that political direction is mobilized by citizens' perceptions, we will not anticipate significant climate change prevention or mitigation in the near-term future.

In addition to the decline in the number of people who believe in anthropogenic climate change, we have seen an increase in the number of people who believe that climate change is not occurring at all (see Figure 3.3). The majority of Americans still believe it is occurring, but the increase in nonbelievers is consistent with climate denialist efforts to create the public impression that scientists are divided on the topic of global warming.

How can we account for the lack of congruence between citizen and scientific views? We use a perspective called agnotology, and trace that perspective through various funders for climate change denial.

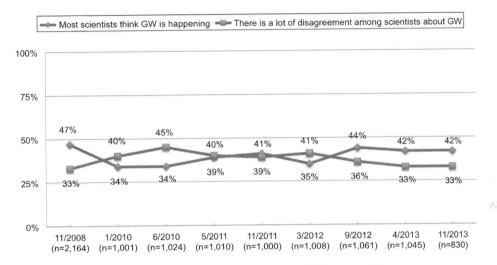

**Only four in ten Americans believe
most scientists think global warming is happening**

Figure 3.1 What Americans believe about whether scientists think global warming is happening.

Anotology: The Creation of Climate Change Controversy

Agnotology is "the study of culturally induced ignorance or doubt, particularly the publication of inaccurate or misleading scientific data."[5] This term was coined by Proctor (1995) to describe how Big Tobacco advantageously recognized that the presence of too much information could inadvertently lead to increased ignorance and confusion on any given topic. One such area is in the proffer, widely repeated in media representations, that climate change is controversial among scientists. Figure 3.1 displays the perceptions of Americans about scientific attitudes toward global warming. As noted previously, 97% of scientists worldwide agree about the presence of anthropogenic climate change.[6] A study published by Ding, Maibach, Zhao, Roser-Renouf, and Leiserowitz (2011) in the journal, *Nature Climate Change*, shows that the misperception of scientific consensus is widespread. Disbelief is consequential; it is strongly associated with beliefs about climate change and support for policy action. Hence, the ability to create the misperception that scientific dissensus exists on anthropomorphic climate change is

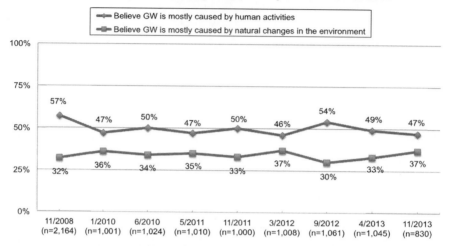

Figure 3.2 What Americans believe about whether global warming is caused by humans.

indirectly tied to political inaction that is hindering efforts to address important risks associated with global warming.

Controversy is driven by corporate entities that operate within a short-term economic profit environment. The funders of the climate change denial movement, and the organizations that promote the denial, tend to have a vested financial interest in the way in which the current economy operates. We use a perspective of political economy, which seems to be the best way to frame opposition to global warming; in this chapter that framework will entail a discussion of politics and its relationship to economic interests.

The Global Warming Denialist Movement as Political Economy

Homer-Dixon (1999) recognized that the state itself might commit crimes against people. Influential businesses will use their resources, including any leverage they might have with government officials, to acquire favorable legislation. This is one aspect of resource capture, the process by which those who already are well off are able to use their advantages to further

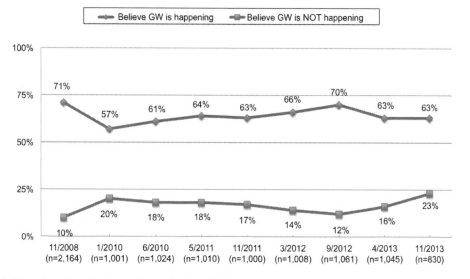

Majority of Americans believe
global warming is happening

Steady increase in the number of Americans who think it is not happening

Figure **3.3** What Americans believe about whether global warming is happening.

improve their conditions. However, in the current instance, we see legislation enacted not on behalf of corporations to place themselves favorably with regard to warming-induced scarcities, but rather to place themselves favorably through media-engineered denial mechanisms.

When resource capture is carried out by corporate actors with supportive legislation or favorable policy by the state, then the realm of inquiry is one of political economy, which is the study of the interrelationship between the economy and the state, its customs, and its laws and practices. Political economy is a widely studied field, a review of which is well beyond the current chapter. Importantly for the current research, we see the ways in which the energy sector influences governmental regulation over production and distribution of energy products such as oil. In this way, energy sector resistance to global warming is a subset of its broader efforts to stymie any kind of regulatory apparatus generally.

State and allied corporate behavior may cause harm, but it often is not a crime in that business leaders will use their influence to ensure their corporate behaviors are not brought under the criminal or civil law. Indeed, it may cause a great deal of harm and yet altogether avoid prosecution and/or punishment. Consider the Bhopal gas accident in India in 1984, in which approximately 8,000 were killed outright and another 8,000 died from related injuries later. The CEO of Union Carbide, the company that owned and operated the plant, was arrested on December 7, shortly after the accident. Six hours after the arrest he was flown out of the country on a government plane. As noted in Wiki, in 1987 "the Indian government summoned Anderson, eight other executives and two company affiliates with homicide charges to appear in Indian court. Union Carbide balked, saying the company is not under Indian jurisdiction." Seven Indian nationals were convicted of causing death by negligence and sentenced to 2 years, but were immediately released on bail. We see in this example an exceptional example of harm—ultimately over a half million individuals were compensated as were 15,310 survivors of individuals killed. Union Carbide denied all culpability. The environmental damage continues, with concerns in the current era about whether some of the toxins have leaked into the groundwater.

This example is intended to show the disjunction between law and harm; harm is an economic or physical detriment, injury, or loss to someone; law codifies the state construction of illegal behavior. The criminal law related to environmental disasters is not well positioned to label and categorize those offenses that occur as a result of laissez-faire capitalism within a global capitalist economy (Kramer & Michalowski, 2012). This notion becomes more apparent when one recognizes that the constant legislative resistance to industry regulation is better described as ongoing political efforts to undermine or altogether get rid of the laws of crime and sanctions as they apply to businesses. Hence, we see in the Bhopal incident recognition of harm and a relatively small award to each individual plaintiff, but no lasting criminal culpability in spite of the extensive number of casualties; certainly there were no penalties on the scale associated with homicide as it applies to individuals.

Kuznets Curves and Economic Ideology

Development economists sometimes argue that the benefits of development, including the development of energy gases, outweigh the costs in pollution. Although early stages of development display high costs in pollution, later stages result in increasingly lower pollution outputs. Hence, the key to dealing with industrial based pollution is to allow the free market to continue development, and eventually technologies will progressively lower pollution over the long-term. This is called the Kuznets curve.

The Kuznets curve is an inverse U and operates as follows. Pollution in a country will increase as the country industrializes and develops but only to a point. Once it reaches a threshold, its citizens will use their political influence to reduce pollution by increasing the market investment in lower polluting technologies. Overall pollution will decline (Shahbaza, Ozturkb, Afzac, & Alid, 2013). This position has been central to the World Trade Organization's support for development and globalization (Tisdale, 2001). The Kuznets curve is similarly applied to global warming in developing countries. It argues that environmental conditions in developing countries will deteriorate until an economic point, based on per capita income, is reached and then will decline. A certain amount of environmental harm is essential for economic development.

Other economists have challenged the empirical accuracy of the Kuznets curve. For instance, central to the curve is that dirty energy sources are essential for development, yet some research has suggested that dirty energy in this age is not necessary for development—clean energy can provide a developmental platform.[7] Second, research has focused only on particular pollutants; when other pollutants are studied the drop in the production of pollutants is less observable. Third is a powerful indirect cost: Developing countries will end up with a dirtier environment as industrialized and post-industrialized countries ship their polluters and waste to them, the "pollution havens" discussed in the next paragraph. Fourth, for industrialized countries, many pollutants do not act as predicted in the curve. As Homer-Dixon observed, "For any modern economy in aggregate, as wealth has increased total carbon dioxide output has increased steadily too—maybe not as fast as wealth has increased, but still significantly nonetheless. When we look at the data for carbon dioxide, we don't see anything approximating an environmental Kuznets curve."[8] Fifth, one of the central problems of globalization is that wealth creation among the wealthier countries is directly tied to wealth destruction in poorer countries, increasing global inequality at the national and subnational levels (Reinert, 2004). To adapt a widely cited economic parable, a rising tide lifts large barges but drowns small craft. It may be that wealth creation among wealthy countries is actually one of the worst things that could happen to a poor country.

Kuznets Curves and Pollution Havens

Central to the Kuznets curve is that, as societies move into post-industrial phases, their dependence on carbon-intensive technologies decreases. Consequently, in the long-term, the best strategy may be development rather than constraining regulation. However, the problem may be that, instead of actually moving to a smaller carbon footprint, they simply transfer their carbon use to other, less prosperous countries, which then become "pollution havens." Pollution havens are places—countries or regions within countries—where the regulatory laws regarding pollution are more favorable to business then their home countries.[9] The pollution haven hypothesis states that polluting industries will move from locations with environmentally stringent laws to locales that are more lax. The jurisdictions with more relaxed laws become known as "pollution havens."

In addition to moving operations to these locations, some industries export toxic goods from pollution havens to avoid regulatory oversight. This has been supported by the World Bank: Consider the internal memo dated December 12, 1991 from Lawrence H. Summers, chief economist of the World Bank.[10]

> *Just between you and me, shouldn't the World Bank be encouraging more migration of the dirty industries to the LDCs [less-developed countries]?... I think the economic logic behind dumping a load of toxic waste in the lowest wage country is impeccable and we should face up to that ... I've always thought that underpopulated countries in Africa are vastly under-polluted, their air quality is probably vastly inefficiently low compared to Los Angeles or Mexico City...The concern over an agent that causes a one in a million change in the odds of prostrate cancer is obviously going to be much higher in a country where people survive to get prostrate cancer than in a country where under 5 mortality is 200 per thousand...*

In the United States, the EPA has passed strict laws with regards to lead disposal. Spent batteries contain lead, a substance that is potentially lethal and that has a history of brain impairment among children and fetuses exposed to it. In order to dispose of lead safely, or to extract the lead for use in other products, the United States has strict regulations in place. To avoid dealing with these regulations, and to increase its profit, American companies have been exporting the spent batteries to Mexico where the regulations are far less stringent.[11] Mexico has consequently become a pollution haven, creating a lead risk for the Mexican population.

Many poor countries tend to become pollution havens for corporations that seek to avoid the stringent environmental requirements of the wealthier countries. As nations become more developed, they tend to increase their environmental awareness and concern in their own country. When this happens, they move their polluting practices to less-developed nations where environmental regulation is weak or nonexistent.[12]

Environmental Harm and Political Economy

In recent years, political economy scholars have increasingly been directing more attention to environmental harm (Michalowski & Kramer, 2006). A review of the legal issues favorable to the energy sector shows the difficulty in mounting a legal attack.

1. Legally, organizations and NGOs have focused on holding accountable the perpetrators whose organizations carry out harmful environmental acts. The challenge faced by environmentalists is that damage from global warming has not yet happened; it is in an undefined future. Consequently, it is difficult to identify a person who has standing in the courtroom due to personal harm. Yet, the evidence is clear that any postponement of mitigation or prevention is likely to sharply increase the impact of climate change on humans globally.
2. In environmental injury cases, one generally holds accountable a toxin that is dangerous to people in some way. Carbon dioxide, however, is beneficial; it is essential to the well-being of the planet. Hence, it is difficult to assert that carbon dioxide is dangerous.
3. The production of CO_2 is a byproduct of industrializing processes; an assessment of harm would take into consideration the positive benefits from the industrializing process, positive benefits that corporations and many governments outweigh over concerns about global warming.
4. In instances where we are already witness to the profound effects of extreme weather; the specific contribution attributable to global warming is not discernable; all we know is that global warming takes existing climate problems, including intense storms, and makes them worse.

Hence, one can straightforwardly see challenges to the corporate regulation of climate control. Yet, the fact that climate change will wreak economic and personal havoc and destruction, particularly on the undeveloped countries, is undeniable. Environmentalists assert that climate change carries a large number of harms, any of which might provide the grounds for litigation. White (2012) presented a description of environmental offenses, which is displayed in Information Box 3.1.

Information Box 3.1 Environmental Offenses Associated with Climate Change

Environmental Offenses (Contributing to Climate Change)

Subject of Offense	Nature of Offense
Forestry	Illegal felling of trees
Air pollution	Emissions of dark smoke
Industrial pollution	Unlicensed pollution
Illegal land clearance	Destruction of habitat and forests
Clearing native vegetation	Reducing biotic mass

Environmental Offenses (Consequences of Climate Change)

Subject of Offense	Nature of Offense
Water theft	Stealing water
Wildlife poaching	Illegal killing of animals
Illegal fishing	Diminishment of fish stocks

Associated Offenses (Civil Unrest and Criminal Activities)

Subject of Offense	Nature of Offense
Public order offenses	Food riots
Eco-terrorism	Arson, tree spiking
Trafficking	Migration and people smuggling
Violent offenses	Homicide, gang warfare

Regulatory Offenses (Arising from Policy Responses to Climate Change)

Subject of Offense	Nature of Offense
Carbon trading	Fraud
Carbon offsets	Misreporting
Illegal planting	Unauthorized use of genetically modified organisms
Collusion	Regulatory corruption

Source: White, G. (2012). Climate change and migration: Security and borders in a warming world. New York: Oxford University Press.

Factors Affecting Climate Change Policy

One of the central challenges for political economy is the transition from a high carbon to a low carbon growth climate. Mitigation of the production of CO_2 is not simply about the reduction in activity of a particular cluster of businesses: it entails the state-wide restructuring of an economy's energy sector, which is no

Information Box 3.2 Macrovariables Affecting Climate Change Policy Adaption

Why do some countries adopt ambitious climate change policies while others do not? The literature on the political economy of policymaking and reform suggests four sets of factors that are likely to be important. These relate to the international context, the structure of government, the degree of political accountability, and the characteristics of interest groups.

1. **International Context**. The making of (carbon mitigation) policy can be thought of as a two-level interaction . . . the world's governments interact strategically, each seeking to benefit from the global climate change regime while reducing its costs. Since there is no international authority with strong sanctioning power, this can be considered a "game" of voluntary contributions to a public good: climate stabilization.

2. Governments differ in the number of institutional veto players—or actors whose agreement is necessary for policies to be enacted—that they contain. The more veto players there are and the more divergent their views, the more difficult it is to change policy.

3. The motivation of these veto players depends on the degree of political accountability. In democracies, parties and individual politicians in the government have reason to take into account the views of their constituents. The more responsive the democracy. . . the more the preferences of the electorate will matter. The degree of responsiveness will depend on the electoral rules, but also on the degree of media freedom, which affects the accuracy and amount of information available to the voters. The ability of voters to extract accurate information from the media and other sources will depend on their level of education.

4. The landscape of interest groups will simply reflect the underlying economic interests in the society, associated with the inherited economic structure . . . Classic contributions to this literature suggest that the outcomes of policy will reflect the set of pressures—or bids—from competing interest groups. Even if the majority of voters do not depend on carbon-intensive industry, the carbon-intensive industry lobby can still achieve political influence disproportionate to the share of votes it can mobilize, as long as it is well organized. Thus, a strong presence of high-carbon industries may result in the effective blocking of reform.

small task. What factors seem to be associated with efforts to move to a low carbon economy? Information Box 3.2 describes four macrovariables associated with climate change policy capacity. Information is cited from the Grantham Research Institute.

An analysis of the variables discussed in Information Box 3.2 found that the most powerful drivers of policy adoption were (1) popular knowledge of climate change that is negatively associated with policy adoption and (2) the relative size of the carbon-intensive industry, which is negatively associated with policy adoption. European Union members are more likely than nonmembers to adopt policies. However, whether a country is a democracy shows no significant relationship to policy. In related research, education also does not show any significant impact on a country's position on global warming. The relative size of the carbon-based industry does; this might be considered a proxy measure or a gloss for the overall influence of the carbon industry over a state's government, mixed with the favorable opinions associated with the employment produced by carbon industries and political perceptions of the advantages of development. What this state-level analysis cannot account for is the sharp disagreement among scientific attitudes, citizen attitudes, and citizen perceptions of scientific attitudes.

Tanner and Allouche (2011) recognized the importance of subjective issues, particularly in the attitudinal domain, when assessing the political economy of global warming. They argued that structural analyses such as the one carried out by the Grantham Institute above failed to recognize how international goals are renegotiated and reconceptualized at the national and subnational level. They identified four factors that a state-level analysis of political economy should consider: Policy processes that are informed by ideology, actors, and power relations; the reinterpretation of international goals to the national and subnational level; the social construction of science and related narratives; and the political processes mediating competing claims for resources. Each of these is considered below.

1. **Policy process informed by ideology.** One of the dominant political ideologies of our time is that of the Classic Liberal society, sometimes called L-liberalism, founded on minimalist government and the economics of laissez-faire capitalism. Global warming is recognized as an immediate threat to laissez-faire capitalism: it requires international economic cooperation, substantial regulatory control, and federal control with international influence over the behavior of corporate life in the United States (Homer-Dixon, 2013) Indeed, if the role, by classic liberalism, of government is to either facilitate business or remove obstacles from business success, then notions of regulation favorable to global warming policy are inherently inconsistent with the philosophy of L-liberalism.

2. **Reinterpretation of international goals to the subnational level.** International goals associated with global warming policy are associated with the United Nations, an organization widely distrusted in the United States. A 2013 Gallup poll, for instance, found that only 35% of U.S. citizens indicated that the United Nations was doing a good job at dealing with the problems it has had to face. Moreover, public opinion polls have shown that the public is more likely to indicate that scientists are divided on the topic of global warming than that

they are in agreement (Nisbett & Myers, 2007). These findings suggest that the information obtained by U.S. citizens at the subnational level provides neither urgency nor consistency on the topic of global warming.

3. **The social construction of science**. In the United States, the way in which science is received in different areas is strongly tied to cultural understandings. This is most clearly displayed in the resistance displayed in fundamentalist groups to the teachings of the theory of evolution. Famously, the Texas Board of Education has sought repeatedly to ensure that creationism is taught together with evolutionism, while a former Texas governor, Rick Perry, "boasted as a candidate for president that his schools taught both creationism and evolution." Distrust of science, as we noted earlier, was developed as a political tactic by "Big Tobacco" when scientists first started reporting on the carcinogenic effects of cigarettes. Global warming sciences have been re-created as a liberal myth aimed at enhancing scientific incomes and stating that the scientific evidence clearly shows that there is no pattern of warming.

4. **Competing claims for resources**. The notion of competing resource claims is closely tied to the way in which power is distributed. The resource challenge is frequently framed in terms of beneficial development, often requiring industrialization processes, in balance with policies aimed at lowering carbon footprints. Hence, politically, a balance is presented as a notion of sustainability, but written into law in such a way as to "do as little harm as possible to orthodox ideas of economic development." This is a powerful corporate claim for ownership of and access to resources that conflict with global warming. Hence, in terms of politics, both in the United States and in international settings, policies aim at rapid, sustained, and long-term economic development, with more powerful groups able to capture resources and improve their already prosperous positions.

Carbon Producers and Emissions

The notion of laissez-faire capitalism suggests that the corporate carbon producers will be largely left alone by government. Yet, what we find is quite different—a great deal of the carbon emissions footprint is currently delivered by state-based corporations. An excellent article that recently appeared in *Climatic Change* provides a quantitative and historical analysis of fossil fuel production that matches emissions rates to specific

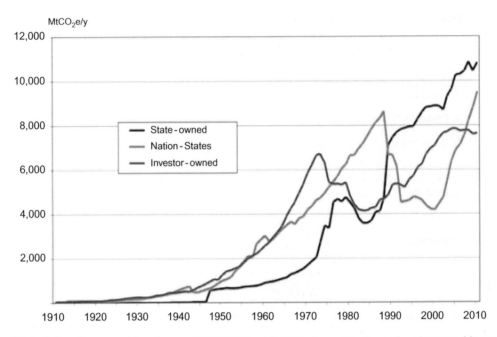

Figure 3.4 Emissions by ownership category, 1910-2010. The total historic contributions of each ownership category are nearly equal: 34.4% investor-owned, 34.1% nation-states, and 31.5% state-owned, but the proportions vary over time. Note: Left column, $MtCO_2e/y$ = million metric tons of carbon dioxide equivalent: an aggregate of greenhouse gases into a single measure, per year (Heede, 2014).

entities (Heede, 2014). Notable findings in this study are displayed in Figure 3.4.

In Figure 3.5, we see that investor-owned companies, although responsible for a good portion of emissions, are not the only players. State-owned entities and nation-states have a large stake in the carbon industry as well. It is important to note that one-half of the total of CO_2 (carbon dioxide) and MH_4 (methane) emissions from 1751 to 2010 have occurred since 1984, and just 90 companies are responsible for 60% of all anthropogenic climate change. Most of these are private or investor-owned, and produced 315 GT. Government-run industries contributed 288 GT.[13] Figure 3.5 below lists the top 10 carbon producers and their historical emission contributions.

The top producers of carbon emissions are also the top global oil producers. Their views are consistent with Tanner and Allouche's (2011) notion of resource competition. They all acknowledge climate change but at the same time seek legislative opportunity to continue to maximize the flow of oil and production of petroleum-based products. That is, they recognize the problem, but deny personal culpability and believe that the

Entity	2010 Emissions MtCO$_2$e	Cumulative 1854-2010 MtCO$_2$e	Percent of Global 1751-2010
1. Chevron, USA	423	51,096	3.52%
2. ExxonMobil, USA	655	46,672	3.22%
3. Saudi Aramco, Saudi Arabia	1,550	46,033	3.17%
4. BP, UK	554	35,837	2.47%
5. Gazprom, Russian Federation	1,371	32,136	2.22%
6. Royal Dutch/Shell, Netherlands	478	30,751	2.12%
7. National Iranian Oil Company	867	29,084	2.01%
8. Permex, Mexico	602	20,025	1.38%
9. ConocoPhillips, USA	359	16,866	1.16%
10. Petroleos de Venezuela	485	16,157	1.11%

Figure 3.5 Top ten carbon producers and their contributions. Note: MtCO$_2$e/y = million metric tons of carbon dioxide equivalent: an aggregate of greenhouse gases into a single measure. *Source:* Heede (2014).

market should decide future climate change solutions. Consider, for instance, the top three U.S. oil companies responsible for the most emissions, their stances on climate change, and their efforts to mitigate it. The information below can be found and verified through multiple sources, namely a 2012 report released by the Union of Concerned Scientists (UCS) and the annual shareholder meeting transcripts of said corporations.

Chevron Oil—Chevron's website indicates that the company acknowledges climate change and the fact that carbon emissions are largely responsible. It also provides an outline of initiatives it is reportedly taking to address the issue. Their CEO, however, has publicly stated that the government is responsible for coming up with solutions, not the companies responsible for the emissions. He also stated that the only path to global prosperity is through oil, gas, and coal. He made these statements in 2013, as his company made plans to invest $33 billion in oil and gas exploration that year.[14] Chevron continues to support anticlimate change legislation behind the scenes.

ExxonMobil—Exxon's website states that Exxon (1) recognizes climate change and cites the IPCC report and (2) agrees that changes in energy use should be addressed.[15] Their CEO, however, has also stated that (1) no one can accurately predict the degree of devastation people may face as a result of unmitigated climate change and (2) that there is no cost-effective alternative to our current energy sources. The company claims to support a carbon tax and investment in alternative energies. A review of the transcript from their annual shareholder meeting in 2013 paints a sharply different picture.[16] During that meeting, four proposals directly related to global warming mitigation, transparency, and accountability were shot down by the company's board. Two shareholders directly called the company out for paying "lip service" without backing it up with reduced emissions goals and both were disregarded. At the same time, the company's CEO discussed recent deals made with Canada and Russia. The Canadian deal will lead to the production of 700 million barrels of oil. The deals in Russia will lead to the exploration and procurement of untapped oil resources in several area seas. There was no discussion of alternative energy sources or production.

ConocoPhillips—Similar to the other two oil giants, Conoco-Phillips publicly proclaims an acknowledgement of climate change and a promise to practice mitigating efforts. Privately, however, they continue to lobby in favor of anticlimate change legislation and they have financially invested in anticlimate change politicians over climate change proponents at a ratio of 15-1.

From Production to Denial: The Climate Change Denialist Movement

With delay and obfuscation as their goals, the U.S. climate change counter-movement (CCCM) has been quite successful in recent decades. However, the key actors in this cultural and political conflict are not just the "experts" who appear in the media spotlight. The roots of climate-change denial go deeper, because individuals' efforts have been bankrolled and directed by organizations that receive sustained support from foundations and funders known for their overall commitments to conservative causes. Thus to fully understand the opposition to climate change legislation, we need to focus on the institutionalized efforts that have built and maintain[ed] this organized campaign. Just as in a theatrical show, there are stars in the spotlight. In the drama of climate change, these are often prominent contrarian scientists or conservative politicians, such as Senator James Inhofe. However, they are only the

most visible and transparent parts of a larger production.
Supporting this effort are directors, script writers, and, most
importantly, a series of producers, in the form of conservative
foundations. Clarifying the institutional dynamics of the CCCM can
aid our understanding of how anthropogenic climate change has
been turned into a controversy rather than a scientific fact in the U.S.

(Brulle, 2013)

The practices and funding of climate change denialism is central to understanding climate change resistance in the United States. By way of perspective, climate change denial has been compared to the doubt-creation strategies aimed at delegitimizing scientific research witnessed during Big Tobacco's heyday [17] (Oreskes & Conway, 2010). During that time, major tobacco companies successfully sowed enough doubt among the public, despite an increasing body of scientific research, showing the carcinogenic aspects of cigarette smoking and their lethal outcomes.[18]

The doubt creators' literature has certain features as well. They use a strategy that worked for a very long time to undercut medical science's harsh critique of cigarette smoking. The relationship between business and doubt-creation in resisting science is well documented in the work *Merchants of Doubt* (Oreskes & Conway, 2010). Doubt creation as a political tool is stated in a memo, attributed to Brown and Williamson Tobacco Products in 1969:[19]

Doubt is our product, since it is the best means of competing with
the "body of fact" that exists in the minds of the general public. It is
also the means of establishing a controversy.

Information Box 3.3 presents four elements central to the effort by the smoking industry to create doubt about the value of scientific research on smoking in the minds of Americans. The four strategies were cited from one of the Bates memos acquired from Brown and Williamson:[20] What we have done is compare them by removing the specific words related to smoking and replaced them with the language of global warming. The rest of the quote is identical.

Climate denial strategies often involve the covert movement of funding among wealthy individuals to various think tanks and philanthropic organizations (Brulle, 2013). This includes monies paid to establish and influence well-known organizations such as: Americans for Prosperity (founded by David Koch), the Competitive Enterprise Institute, the Heartland Institute, the Cato Institute (founded by the Koch brothers), the Heritage Foundation, and the Manhattan Institute. It also includes money spent on political contributions and lobbying efforts.

Information Box 3.3 Word Substitution of the Brown and Williamson Cigarette Company Memo for Global Warming

"*Objective No. 1*: To set aside in the minds of millions the false conviction that cigarette smoking causes lung cancer and other diseases; a conviction based on fanatical assumptions, fallacious rumors, unsupported claims and the unscientific statements and conjectures of publicity-seeking opportunists."

Global warming rewrite of Objective 1: To set aside in the minds of millions the false conviction that the earth is warming, causing more severe storms, coastal threats from global ice melt-off, more droughts, or more heat waves; a conviction based on fanatical assumptions, fallacious rumors, unsupported claims and the unscientific statements and conjectures of publicity-seeking opportunists.

"*Objective No. 2*: To lift the cigarette from the cancer identification as quickly as possible and restore it to its proper place of dignity and acceptance in the minds of men and women in the marketplace of American free enterprise."

Global warming rewrite of Objective 2: To lift the role of big business from some notion of global warming identification as quickly as possible and restore it to its proper place of dignity and acceptance in the minds of men and women in the marketplace of American free enterprise.

"*Objective No. 3*: To expose the incredible, unprecedented and nefarious attack against the cigarette, constituting the greatest libel and slander ever perpetrated against any product in the history of free enterprise."

Global warming rewrite of Objective 3: To expose the incredible, unprecedented and nefarious attack against big oil and coal, constituting the greatest libel and slander ever perpetrated against any product in the history of free enterprise.

"*Objective No. 4*: To unveil the insidious and developing pattern of attack against the American free enterprise system, a sinister formula that is slowly eroding American business with the cigarette obviously selected as one of the trial targets."

Global warming rewrite of Objective 4: To unveil the insidious and developing pattern of attack against the American free enterprise system, a sinister formula that is slowly eroding American business with the oil industry obviously selected as one of the trial targets.

Source: http://tobaccodocuments.org/landman/332506.html. Derived from: /bw/332506.html

Funding involves large sums of money. A report by the UCS released in 2012 titled "A Climate of Corporate Control," which provided a breakdown of dollars spent by industry and company and compared sums donated for climate change and for climate change resistance, is displayed in Figure 3.6.[21]

Charles and David Koch, better known as the Koch brothers, have been credited with much of the financial backing provided for the denial movement. Koch Industries is a multinational, private corporation that operates numerous companies in a range of

Company	Anticlimate : Proclimate Ratio	Total Political Contributions	Total Lobbying (In millions)
Murphy Oil Corporation	29 : 1	$30,000	$5.71
ConocoPhillips	15.4 : 1	$742,951	$62.71
Marathon Oil Corporation	14.7 : 1	$762,950	$43.72
Exxon Mobil Corporation	10.1 : 1	$1,556,961	$131.63
Valero Energy Corporation	9.3 : 1	$1,490,472	$4.63
Chesapeake Energy Corporation	5.3 : 1	$584,400	$5.33
Caterpillar Inc.	4.9 : 1	$990,961	$16.38
Occidental Petroleum Corporation	4.9 : 1	$689,250	$28.21
Peabody Energy Corporation	4.0 : 1	$684,283	$33.42
Denbury Resources Inc.	2.8 : 1	$34,450	$1.55
NextEra Energy, Inc.	1.9 : 1	$1,377,522	$3.20
Tesoro Corporation	1.7 : 1	$323,800	$1.26
TECO Energy, Inc.	1.6 : 1	$311,850	$14.59
DTE Energy Company	1.5 : 1	$874,678	$12.98
FirstEnergy Corporation	1.5 : 1	$828,845	$16.50
Progress Energy, Inc.	1.4 : 1	$659,051	$16.67
Xcel Energy Inc.	1.3 : 1	$626,925	$17.25
Waste Management, Inc.	1.3 : 1	$149,020	$5.58
FMC Corporation	1 : 2 : 1	$322,855	$12.43
Boeing Company	1 : 1.3	$4,517,635	$107.29
General Electric Company	1 : 1.4	$5,076,353	$189.91
Ameren Corporation	1 : 1.9	$484,900	$19.20
Applied Materials, Inc	1 : 1.9	$224,354	$6.68
Sempra Energy	1 : 2.0	$634,975	$14.06
NRG Energy, Inc.	1 : 2.7	$1,377,522	$5.74
Alcoa Inc.	1 : 2.7	$30,450	$13.82
NIKE, Inc.	1 : 3.2	$175,601	$3.24
AES Corporation	1 : 5.4	$101,504	$1.32

Key by Stock Market Sector:

■Energy □Utilities ■Industrials ■Materials ■Consumer Discretionary ■Information Technology

Total political contributions and lobbying expenditures are shown for all companies, ranked by their ratio of a:b, where "a" stands for funding to members of Congress with voting records that oppose science-based climate policy ("anticlimate") and "b" represents funding to those who support it ("proclimate"), Lobbying expenditures occurred in the 2002-2010 time frame; voting and political contribution time frames correspond to 2007-2010 for House members and 2003-2010 for senators.

Figure 3.6 Oil industry investments for and against climate change. *Source:* A climate of corporate control: How corporations have influenced the U.S. dialogue on climate science and policy. Retrieved January 27, 2014 at http://www.ucsusa.org/scientific_integrity/abuses_of_science/a-climate-ofcorporate-control.html.

industries, including petroleum, energy, chemical, asphalt, and trading. As of September 2013, the Koch brothers have an estimated combined worth of $72 billion and are reported to have spent approximately $62 million on climate denial programs and research[22,23] (Union of Concerned Scientists, 2012).

Climate Denial, Dark Money, and Pass-Through Organizations

In recent years, funders have tried to obscure their financial contributions by establishing charities through which they could anonymously donate money. These contributions provided substantial tax breaks and the appearance of anonymity and obscured the funding of research, providing it with the patina of scientific credibility.

Robert Brulle, an environmental sociologist at Drexel University, examined the funding sources for the denial movement. Among his findings, Brulle (2013) noted that since 2008, the Koch brothers sharply decreased, and ExxonMobil entirely stopped publicly funding, the denial movement. Concurrently, an exponential increase in monies donated to the denial movement through third-party pass-through foundations, such as Donors Trust, occurred (Brulle, 2013). The funders of third-parties such as Donors Trust are not publicly named. This form of concealed funding is referred to as *dark money.*

Astonishing is the indirect pattern of funding that characterizes the funding of climate denial work through pass-through organizations. The pie chart in Figure 3.7 illustrates the amount of money donated by specific foundations to climate change denial organizations from 2003 to 2010.

A relatively large piece of the pie displayed in Figure 3.7, 14% of it, belongs to Donors Trust. In 2013, an audit trail revealed that Charles Koch had indirectly been funneling millions of dollars to this organization through another third-party organization known as the Knowledge and Progress Fund. This fund is operated by the Koch family, although they do not publicly advertise that fact (Brulle, 2013). The pie chart in Figure 3.8 displays the dollar amount *received* by individual countermovement organizations. It is important to note that Donors Trust is responsible for funding the majority of these organizations. One can trace many trails through these different organizations. To consider only one, we can trace a funding trail from Koch Brothers, then to the Knowledge and Progress Fund, then to Donors Trust, and finally to FreedomWorks. FreedomWorks in turn is associated with six political action committees (PACs), which are FreedomWorks PAC, Oregon FreedomWorks

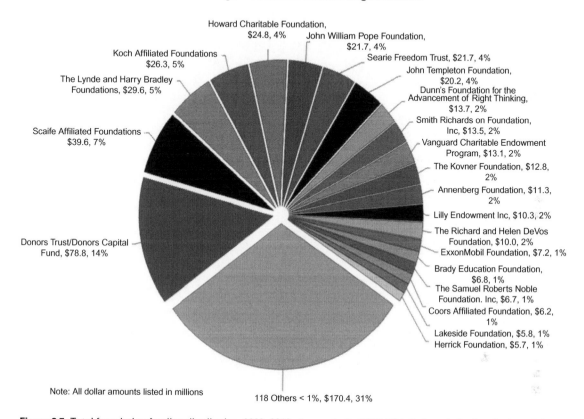

Figure 3.7 Total foundation funding distribution, 2003–2010. *Source:* Brulle (2013). With kind permission from Springer Science and Business Media.

PAC, Taxpayer Defense Fund, Citizens for PERS Reform, Judicial Integrity Coalition PAC, and League of Freedom Voters.

Taxpayer Defense Fund presents itself online as a grass-roots organization devoted to lower taxes and more freedom, is involved in the organization of conferences related to Tea Party activities, and raises political money for conservative and Tea Party candidates. All of the previous organizations can lay claim to long coattails of dark money.

Congress, Financial Incentives, and Climate Change Denial

Much of the dark money makes its way to Congress. The lobbying efforts of the fossil fuel industry are robust: 160 representatives in the 113th Congress have received over $55.5 million.[24]

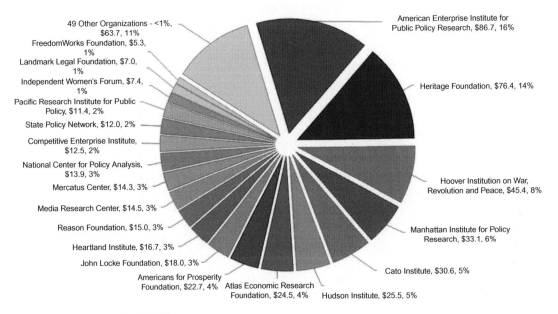

Total Foundation Recipient Income Distribution, 2003–2010
U.S. Climate Change Countermovement Organizations

Note: All dollar amounts listed in millions

Figure 3.8 Foundation recipient income, 2003–2010. *Source:* Brulle (2013). With kind permission from Springer Science and Business Media.

Though the actual influence that climate denial lobbying has over legislative decision-making can be difficult to decipher, the patterns are present. Consider the following statement made by Rep. Dana Rohrabacher (R-CA) during a town hall meeting in 2013:[25]

Just so you'll know, global warming is a total fraud and it's being designed because what you've got is you've got liberals who get elected at the local level want state government to do the work and let them make the decisions. Then, at the state level, they want the federal government to do it. And at the federal government, they want to create global government to control all of our lives.

To this statement made by Rep. Ralph Hall (R-TX) during an interview with *ScienceInsider* in 2011:[26]

I'm really more fearful of freezing. And I don't have any science to prove that. But we have a lot of science that tells us they're not basing it on real scientific facts.

Note that both of the above-mentioned representatives have served on the House Committee on Science, Space, and Technology, a committee of the House of Representatives.[27,28]

For instance, in January 2014, representative Jan Schakowsky introduced an amendment to the Electricity, Security, and Affordability Act recognizing that climate change was occurring. This bill was presented to the House Energy and Commerce Committee, a committee responsible for the oversight of environmental health and energy supply and delivery, among other things. The climate change amendment introduced by Rep. Schakowsky was voted down 24-20; most of the members of the committee are open denialists of climate change.[29]

One might ask why climate change denial is so widespread among congressional leaders. It may be that, like many citizens, legislators suffer from agnotology and simply do not know. Yet, many congress-people have used their position to openly attack climate science and the scientists and researchers who carry out this work. As we will find out in the next section, scientists are increasingly pursuing legal recourse when they are illegitimately discredited.

The Denialist Assault on Science

One of the more troubling aspects of the climate change denialist movement is its general assault and ad homonym attacks on scientists: These attacks are not only about the validity and reliability of scientific findings but about the integrity and truthfulness of the scientists carrying out the research. One such person who has been the object of repeated attacks is Michael Mann, distinguished professor of meteorology at Penn State University, who holds an M.S. degree in physics from Yale University and a Ph.D. in Geology and Geophysics from Yale.

Mann is the author of more than 160 peer-reviewed publications and two highly acclaimed books in addition to an award-winning science website related to climate change. He, along with several colleagues, developed the widely cited hockey stick graph that was showcased in Al Gore's "An Inconvenient Truth."[30] In 2009, hackers gained access to Mann's email account and stole over 1,000 private emails between Mann and other climate scientists. The incident became famously known as "climategate, in reference to the infamous Watergate incident, and the contents of the email were used to attempt to discredit Mann."[31]

In 2009 many representatives of the climate denialist movement charged Mann and his colleagues with perpetrating a fraud, publishing false research; James Stensenbrenner, U.S. congressman from Wisconsin, accused Mann of "scientific fascism."[32] The effect of these claims on public perception was immediate; within weeks public opinion about climate change changed dramatically with one poll indicating that belief in its certainty dropped 14% (Leiserowitz, Maibach, Roser-Renouf, Smith, & Dawson, 2013). A blog published at both the Competitive Enterprise Institute and the National Review compared Mann to Jerry Sandusky, the former Penn State football coach accused of covering up child abuse and accused him of molesting and torturing data.[33] Mann has since sued the publication and the institute for defamation. The case is currently pending in Washington, D.C. Superior Court. It should be observed that the Competitive Enterprise Institute, one of the primary organizations to launch these attacks, has frequently received funding from the Koch Brothers and ExxonMobil.[34,35] Several investigations of "climategate" exonerated Mann and his colleagues of all claims made against them.[36] They were found guilty of no scientific wrongdoing.

In the Virginia Supreme Court, Mann is currently battling another denialist group, now known as the Energy and Environment Legal Institute but formerly known as the American Traditions Institute. They also receive funding from the Koch brothers and ExxonMobil.[37] This group is attempting to gain access to several years' worth of Mann's emails under the Freedom of Information Act. The American Traditions Institute is heavily involved in legal and lobbying efforts to organize against wind farming in the United States, with a particular focus in Colorado.[38]

In addition to the legal challenges, Mann has received anonymous death threats.[39] Over recent years, threats against many other climate scientists have increased exponentially.[40] In order to support and provide some protection for global warming scientists, the Climate Legal Defense Fund was created in 2011 with the sole purpose of helping to protect scientists engaged in scientific-based research.[41]

Attacks against climate and environmental scientists are not limited to the United States. Since 2006, the conservative Harper government in Canada has dismissed over 2,000 scientists and researchers, shut down or cut funding for programs that monitored various environmental issues, and inexplicably closed down science libraries containing a vast collection of environmental data.[42] Over the past several years, Canadian taxpayers have contributed over $400 million to the biggest oil, gas, and pipeline companies in subsidies to encourage them to go green, but the Canadian government is, in the current era, an advocate of oil development and expansion in Canada.

Legislation and Denial: American Legislative Exchange Council

American Legislative Exchange Council (ALEC) is a think tank devoted to conservative goals. It is particularly active in climate change denial. A review of its short-term history reveals the way in which anticlimate denialists strategically use dark money organizations to resist climate change legislation.

According to their website, ALEC was founded in September 1973 as a nonpartisan association for conservative lawmakers who promote limited government, free markets, federalism, and individual liberty.[43] ALEC is an advocate of corporate-backed legislation, and they have been quite successful at it.[44] Several examples of current legislation that can be traced back to the model laws contained within ALEC's substantial library include voter identification, withdrawal from state restrictions on reduced CO_2 emissions, and detainment of suspected illegal immigrants.[45] ALEC's website includes a searchable library of their model legislation where these bills can be verified.[46] In 2011, ALEC boasted 2,200 state legislators as members and 280 corporate members.[47] Their corporate supporters include ExxonMobil and Koch Industries.[48] Some notable companies that let their membership lapse include Cola, Walmart, and Home Depot; however, Koch Industries and ExxonMobil continue to support the council.[49]

ALEC has been a tour de force in the climate change denial arena; it has successfully lobbied against EPA environmental regulations and advocated a proposal known as the Environmental Literacy Improvement Act.[50] This particular bill would require public school educators to teach climate change denial as a legitimate scientific position.[51] As of January 2013, Texas and Louisiana implemented educational standards that required the teaching of climate change denial. In addition, Tennessee, Oklahoma, Arizona, and Colorado proposed a bill to allow climate change denial in the classroom, and Utah and South Dakota passed bills that deny climate change.[52,53] Climate change scientists have expressed concern over these proposals and the curriculum that has been developed for use, stating that it will serve to confuse students rather than educate.[54]

ALEC has also been instrumental in lobbying Congress to "prohibit the EPA from regulating greenhouse gas emissions (by defunding the EPA if necessary), to impose a 2-year moratorium on any new air quality regulations, and urging the federal government to complete a study identifying all planned regulatory activity by the EPA and its impact on the economy, jobs, and American economic competitiveness."[55] By 2013, 13 states had passed similar legislation: Alaska, Iowa, Kansas, Kentucky, Michigan, Missouri, Montana, North Dakota, Pennsylvania, Texas, Utah, Virginia, and Wyoming.[56]

A Wake-Up Call: Corporate Recognition of Climate Risk

One of the general aspects of global warming is the drying out of the midcenter latitudes and the increasing wetness of the higher latitudes. This process is already well under way. Organizations whose well-being depends on traditional weather patterns are beginning to recognize and adapt to climate change, a requirement for them if they wish to survive and be competitive in a global economy. We will consider three examples below: Coca-Cola, Nike, and Munich Re.

Coca-Cola and Nike

A *New York Times* article dated January 23, 2014 brings attention to current climate change related economic threats recognized and acknowledged by Nike and Coca-Cola. These two corporations have been taking an active stance in adapting their practices to an increasingly volatile environment, one they recognized is associated with climate change factors. Coca-Cola also has installed one million coolers that now use natural refrigerants as opposed to the old hydrofluorocarbons (HFCs) that contributed to the warming of the atmosphere.[57] They are also reportedly using water conservation technologies due to the recent effect of droughts on their production capacity.[58] Nike is currently utilizing more synthetic material to break away from its historical reliance on cotton; production has been hampered by recent droughts. Nike has also begun to report the financial impacts and risks associated with climate change in its reports to the Securities and Exchange Commission (SEC).

The business community is starting to turn its attention to global warming in other ways as well. Hedge fund billionaire, Thomas Steyer, former New York mayor Michael Bloomberg, and former Treasury Secretary in the George W. Bush Administration Henry Paulson, have launched a study on the potential financial impacts of climate change. The assessment, called "Risky Business," will use models from the IPCC report and independent research to determine climate change risks to different regions of the United States and then hopefully disseminate their findings to a wide audience. In the past, Steyer has attempted to warn other wealthy business leaders of the major threat of climate change. He has referred to it as the greatest danger to the U.S. economy. The project is essentially a risk assessment that will attempt to quantify the potential economic impacts of climate change. The individuals who spearheaded the initiative have developed a website that provides a brief overview and lists the project cochairs and committee members.[59] They also posted an op-ed in the *Washington Post* on October 3, 2013, in which they made their case for the need of this assessment, specifically citing the comprehensive resilience blueprint developed by New York City in the aftermath of Hurricane Sandy.[60] The closing paragraphs of the op-ed state the following:

> *In the wake of Hurricane Sandy, New York City created a comprehensive resilience blueprint that measures climate risk across all major vulnerable areas, from the power grid to hospitals to the coastline. Our nation needs the same blueprint. It is essential that our national exposure to climate risk be understood so all Americans can make informed decisions about the future.*
>
> *We believe the Risky Business initiative will bring a critical missing piece to national conversations about climate change and help business leaders, elected officials and others make smart, well-informed, financially responsible decisions. Ignoring the potential costs could be catastrophic. That is a risk we cannot afford to take.*

The Insurance Industry and Munich Re

The insurance industry carries a particular charge—they mitigate risk by providing financial protection in the event of catastrophe. In important ways, the industry is central to modern corporate life—it enables businesses to take risks, and sometimes to act at all, in environments that are in some way financially inhospitable. One can see this in particular in the underwriting business for home mortgages; the willingness of the underwriter to assume the risk of a long-term debt—often 30 years amortized—enables the level of home ownership currently enjoyed in the United States. To do its work, it has to be able to accurately forecast the costs and likelihoods of financial risks. It cannot permit itself the luxury of ideology. After Katrina, the industry took a significant financial beating for failing to calculate into its risk the extreme damage associated with the storm.[61] It is now adapting, incorporating such risks into a broader recognition that global warming carries substantial risk both in the short- and long-term. One can see the concerns regarding global warming's impact on the industry in the following two quotes, both from principals in the reinsurance industry.[62]

"From our industry's perspective, the footprints of climate change are around us and the trend of increasing damage to property and threat to lives is clear," said Franklin Nutter, president of the Reinsurance Association of America.

Cynthia McHale, the insurance program director at Ceres, issued a more unequivocal statement: *"Our climate is changing, human activity is helping to drive the change, and the costs of these extreme weather events are going to keep ballooning* unless we break through our political paralysis, and bring down emissions that are warming our planet."

Munich Re (Refinance), one of the world's major reinsurers, has moved strongly in the recognition of global warming. In a press release in 2012, Munich Re announced its concern with global warming, stating that:[63]

Nowhere in the world is the rising number of natural catastrophes more evident than in North America. The study shows a nearly quintupled number of weather-related loss events in North America for the past three decades, compared with an increase factor of 4 in Asia, 2.5 in Africa, 2 in Europe and 1.5 in South America. Anthropogenic climate change is believed to contribute to this trend, though it influences various perils in different ways. Climate change particularly affects formation of heat-waves, droughts, intense precipitation events, and in the long run most probably also tropical cyclone intensity. The view that weather extremes are becoming more frequent and intense in various regions due to global warming is in keeping with current scientific findings, as set out in the Fourth Assessment Report of the Intergovernmental Panel on Climate Change (IPCC) as well as in the special report on weather extremes and disasters (SREX).

Corporate Life and the Flaw of Denialism

We witness, in the considerations of Munich Re, the Coca-Cola industry, and Nike, the inevitability of business recognition of climate change. The overriding theme that will further this recognition across the business community is not complicated: Any organization whose survival is based on some aspect of global ecology will have to adapt or fail to competitors that adapt. In a later chapter, we will see how a similar dynamic is motivating the U.S. military establishment to take the risks of global warming seriously. The theme can also be applied to city and state governments as well; they must adapt or fail. As we will see, the process of adaption will be daunting and not always likely to be successful.

Importantly, as large organizations such as Munich Re begin the process of adapting, they will leverage their many partners, investors, and corporate investments to adapt as well.

This applies to denialist corporate life as well. For all of their power and contemporary legislative influence, it is difficult to see how denialist global corporations can survive in the long-term. Information Box 3.4 describes the difference between organizations that look ahead to global change and those that do not. In the current era, the high carbon producers hold the advantages. But that will change. It will have to for them to survive. As so frequently noted, the central issues with global warming are not ideological, they are physical; their solutions will emerge from the science of physics, not the manipulations of attitudes. The denialist strengths in the current era—the ability to manipulate favorable trade and tax outcomes while mitigating regulation—carry portents of nonviability in the long run as their organizational cultures are increasingly out of sync with the occupational and ecological environment they inhabit and when organizations that have adapted are moving competitively against them.

Information Box 3.4 Davos 2014—World Economic Forum

Progressive Business Outgunned by the High Carbon Lobby

Nick Mabey, CEO E3G reflects on the Davos dichotomy:

Davos was a perfect demonstration of the divergent trends in the politics and business of climate change.

Perhaps the most positive sign came from the strength of statements from global companies like Unilever and Coca-Cola about the impacts climate change is having on their core businesses.

But there was a disconnect between business optimism over investing in climate solutions and the failure of low carbon business to invest in making a political impact in the debate on EU 2030 climate targets going on in Brussels at the same time.

An even clearer dissonance appeared around the risks of investment in high carbon assets. While Carbon Tracker successfully worked to socialize the idea of stranded high carbon assets into the Davos conversation, at the same time governments and fossil fuel companies were announcing new investment in exploiting coal and unconventional fossil fuel reserves.

The optimistic interpretation is that the climate conversation is being slowly reframed into the world of investment risk and business opportunity. The challenge is that those betting on a low carbon future need to organize far more successfully to shape the global politics of climate change, or we will find ourselves as outgunned by high carbon lobbies in Paris 2015, as we were in Brussels this week.

Conclusion: Laissez-Fair Capitalism, Risk, and Metabolic Rift

The danger facing the global marketplace is existential; as Homer-Dixon (2013) noted, the complexity of our social and economic systems, combined with an overreliance on marketplace solutions and substantial global inequalities, creates the risk of cascading failures and economic collapse, and ultimately violence across a world characterized by substantial inequalities. Homer-Dixon described it, in part, as a failure to understand the nature of the risks we face. The laissez-faire marketplace has worked very well for some of us individually and for some countries. But it has not worked well for others; there are large and growing global inequalities, a topic we will consider in detail in a later chapter. International processes of migration and urbanization portend a future where inequalities will be both greater and more visible, where sharply unequal populations will be living side by side.

The failure of market-based technologies to mitigate global warming at anywhere near the level at which they are needed has been conceptualized as a "metabolic rift" (see Marx, 1867; Parenti, 2011). The somewhat cumbersome term "metabolic rift" refers to a fundamental break between laissez-faire capitalism and the social and environmental ecology in which we live (Foster, 1999). This political economy is a complex system of interlocking politics, economics, norms, and cultural interpretations. In his book, *Tropic of Chaos*, award-winning writer and journalist Parenti (2011) suggested that the problem is primarily a political one, one that can be solved with a downward distribution of wealth and the political will to enforce environment-friendly legislation. Beck (1992) similarly argued that we can respond to the environmental risks created by contemporary technologies, but it will require an activist political culture.

The central problem faced by the global marketplace is how to move, and move quickly, to a low carbon footprint on a global basis. The widespread denialist advocacy, funded in significant part by some of the world's leading corporations, stands as vocal testimony that this will not happen; to the contrary, elements of it are in clear opposition to governmental climate change policy. It may be that the denialists will win the political argument; yet that will only accelerate global warming from inaction and increased carbon emissions. It would be unfortunate to see them succeed; the alternatives to a market economy are not particularly promising. One can catalog the extensive failures of a market-based economy, yet it is hard to see what could replace it. The totalitarian failures of the twentieth century show that centralized governmental change, even when initiated as advocacy for the poor, can go terribly wrong (Brzezinski, 1993). That is the challenge faced by proponents of change. The political culture must change for survival, but change to what? That question is no longer a hypothetical; it will change in the face of the looming crises posed by climate change. And we will find out if we are capable of something better than what, up to now, we have been able to achieve.

Endnotes

1. "A conversation with a genuine skeptic." Retrieved January 26, 2013 at http://news.discovery.com/earth/global-warming/a-conversation-with-a-genuine-skeptic.htm.
2. "Climate change 2013: The physical science basis." Retrieved February 1, 2014 at https://www.ipcc.ch/report/ar5/wg1/. To say that they are 95 percent confident does not mean consensus, either. Confidence, in this context, is a probabilistic term of the likelihood of an event when assessed against a null hypothesis and tells us nothing about the attitudes of the research analysts.
3. "Study: 97% agreement on manmade global warming." Retrieved September 3, 2013 at http://www.weather.com/news/science/environment/agreement-manmade-global-warming-20130516.
4. "James Lawrence Powell: Science and global warming." Retrieved March 2, 2014 at http://www.jamespowell.org/index.html.
5. "Agnotology." Retrieved February 10, 2014 at http://en.wikipedia.org/wiki/Agnotology.
6. "Scientific consensus on anthropogenic climate change." Retrieved December 18, 2013 at http://www.sciencedaily.com/releases/2013/05/130515203048.htm.
7. "Negative effects of globalization-Chemical waste and air pollution." Retrieved January 27, 2014 at http://yourknowledge.hubpages.com/hub/Negative-Effects-of-Globalization-Chemical-Waste-and-Air-Pollution.
8. "The great transformation: Climate change as cultural change." Retrieved January 10, 2014 at http://www.homerdixon.com/2009/06/08/the-great-transformation-climate-change-as-cultural-change/.
9. "Pollution haven hypothesis." Retrieved November 22, 2013 at http://en.wikipedia.org/wiki/Pollution_haven_hypothesis.
10. "Lawrence Summers: The bank memo." Retrieved February 15, 2014 at http://www.whirledbank.org/ourwords/summers.html. Summers went on to become the U.S. Treasury Secretary in the Clinton Administration as well as president of Harvard University.
11. "Lead from old U.S. batteries sent to Mexico raises risk." Retrieved November 6, 2014 at http://www.nytimes.com/2011/12/09/science/earth/recycled-battery-lead-puts-mexicans-in-danger.html?emc=eta1&_r=0.
12. It is important to point out that the research on the concept of pollution haven is not universally supportive. For instance, OEDC partner countries do not appear to participate in pollution haven seeking behavior. However, partners from Chinese sources appear to be significantly deterred by pollution taxes (Dean, Lovely and Wang, 2004).
13. "Carbon Majors: Accounting for carbon and methane emissions 1854-2010." Retrieved February 16, 2014 at http://www.climateaccountability.org/carbon_majors.html.

14. "Chevron's CEO: Affordable energy is crucial." Retrieved January 12, 2014 at http://bigstory.ap.org/article/chevrons-ceo-affordable-energy-crucial.

15. "Exxon Mobil's views and principles on policies to manage long-term risks from climate change." Retrieved February 24, 2014 at http://corporate.exxonmobil.com/en/current-issues/climate-policy/climate-policy-principles/overview.

16. "ExxonMobil Corporation CEO hosts annual shareholder meeting (Transcript)." Retrieved January 28, 2014 at http://seekingalpha.com/article/1468831-exxonmobil-corporation-ceo-hosts-annual-shareholder-meeting-transcript?

17. "Tobacco industry." Retrieved January 9, 2014 at http://en.wikipedia.org/wiki/Tobacco_companies. Big tobacco is a term typically referring to the big three tobacco companies Philip Morris USA (Altria), Reynolds American (RJR), and Lorillard. The heyday was that period in the United States up to about 1995, when several states successfully sued tobacco companies for illness and death related to carcinogenic products in cigarettes.

18. "Dealing in Doubt: The climate denial machine vs. climate science." Retrieved December 10, 2013 at http://www.greenpeace.org/usa/en/campaigns/global-warming-and-energy/polluterwatch/Dealing-in-Doubt—the-Climate-Denial-Machine-vs-Climate-Science/.

19. "Smoking and health proposal." Retrieved January 15, 2014 at http://tobaccodocuments.org/landman/332506.html.

20. An educated guess is that this document was authored by R.A. Pittman, Senior Brand Marketing Supervisor at B&W from 1968-70, with help from B&W marketing executives John Blalock, Charles I. McCarty, and Corny Muije. This assumption is based on a memo ordering the project written by J.W. Burgard, Executive Vice President of Sales and Public Relations at B&W in 1969. This memo has a Bates number adjacent to the "Smoking and Health Proposal" (Bates Number: 690010960/0961 URL: http://legacy.library.ucsf.edu/tid/sgy93f00)" From http://tobaccodocuments.org/landman/332506.html.

21. "A climate of corporate control: How corporations have influenced the U.S. dialogue on climate science and policy." Retrieved January 27, 2014 at http://www.ucsusa.org/scientific_integrity/abuses_of_science/a-climate-of-corporate-control.html.

22. "Charles Koch." Retrieved January 13, 2014 at http://www.forbes.com/profile/charles-koch/.

23. "David Koch." Retrieved January 13, 2014 at http://www.forbes.com/profile/david-koch/.

24. "The anti-science climate denier caucus." Retrieved January 13, 2014 at http://thinkprogress.org/climate-denier-caucus/.

25. "Member of congressional science committee: Global warming a fraud to create global government." Retrieved January 11, 2014 at http://www.thenation.com/blog/175697/science-committee-congressman-global-warming-fraud-create-global-government.

26. "Ralph Hall speaks out on climate change." Retrieved January 5, 2014 at http://news.sciencemag.org/2011/12/ralph-hall-speaks-out-climate-change.

27. Climate change deniers in Congress repeatedly vote down legislation that would help mitigate the issues we are facing and some continue to deny climate change's very existence (Herrnstadt & Muehlegger, 2013; McCright & Dunlap, 2011).

28. "Republicans block science laureate vote over climate change stance fear." Retrieved December 16, 2014 at http://www.theguardian.com/world/2013/sep/20/republicans-congress-science-laureate-bill-blocked.

29. "24 House Republicans just voted to deny the reality of climate change." Retrieved February 2, 2014 at http://thinkprogress.org/climate/2014/01/28/3215971/house-members-deny-climate-change/.

30. "Hockey stick." Retrieved February 2, 2014 at http://www.carbonbrief.org/profiles/hockey-stick/.

31. "What do the 'Climategate' hacked CRU emails tell us?" Retrieved January 28, 2014 at http://www.skepticalscience.com/Climategate-CRU-emails-hacked.htm.

32. "Sensenbrenner: emails are "evidence of scientific fascism." Retrieved January 9, 2014 at http://www.cejournal.net/?p=2400.

33. "Michael Mann defamation lawsuit—calling on the judge to apply the law of the case doctorine." Retrieved January 21, 2014 at http://www.climatesciencewatch.org/2014/01/14/mann-defamation-lawsuit-law-of-the-case-doctrine/.

34. "The Koch brothers take on enviro groups over mine." Retrieved December 18, 2014 at http://www.washingtonpost.com/blogs/the-fix/wp/2013/06/17/the-koch-brothers-take-on-enviro-groups-on-mine/.

35. "Anatomy of a Washington dinner: Who funds the Competitive Enterprise Institute?" Retrieved Novermber 11, 2014 at http://www.washingtonpost.com/blogs/the-fix/wp/2013/06/20/anatomy-of-a-washington-dinner-who-funds-the-competitive-enterprise-institute/.

36. "What do the 'Climategate' hacked CRU emails tell us?" Retrieved January 28, 2014 at http://www.skepticalscience.com/Climategate-CRU-emails-hacked.htm.

37. "Climate scientist wins a round for America." Retrieved January 11, 2014 at http://www.huffingtonpost.com/shawn-lawrence-otto/climate-scientist-wins-a-_b_1070426.html.

38. "Energy and environment legal institute." Retrieved January 10, 2014 at http://www.sourcewatch.org/index.php/American_Tradition_Institute.

39. "The battle over climate science." Retrieved September 2, 2013 at http://www.popsci.com/science/article/2012-06/battle-over-climate-change, http://thinkprogress.org/climate/2012/07/16/519611/what-is-the-climate-science-legal-defense-fund/.

40. "Death threats, intimidation and abuse: climate change scientist Michael E. Mann counts the cost of honesty." Retrieved January 7, 2014 at http://www.theguardian.com/science/2012/mar/03/michael-mann-climate-change-deniers.

41. "What is the Climate Science Legal Defense Fund?" Retrieved November 6, 2014 at http://thinkprogress.org/climate/2012/07/16/519611/what-is-the-climate-science-legal-defense-fund/.

42. "Research cutbacks by government alarm scientists." Retrieved January 23, 2014 at http://www.cbc.ca/news/technology/research-cutbacks-by-government-alarm-scientists-1.2490081.

43. "History." Retrieved January 8, 2014 at http://www.alec.org/about-alec/history/.

44. "Pssst...Wanna buy a law?" Retrieved December 28, 2014 at http://www.businessweek.com/magazine/pssst-wanna-buy-a-law-12012011.html#p1.

45. Ibid.

46. "Model legislation." Retrieved January 8, 2014 at http://www.alec.org/model-legislation/.

47. "ALEC facing funding crisis from donor exodus in the wake of Trayvon Martin row." Retrieved January 11, 2014 at http://www.theguardian.com/world/2013/dec/03/alec-funding-crisis-big-donors-trayvon-martin.

48. Ibid.

49. Ibid.
50. "Oklahoma, Colorado and Arizona push ALEC bill to require teaching climate change denial in schools." Retrieved December 5, 2014 at http://thinkprogress. org/climate/2013/01/31/1521401/oklahoma-colorado-arizona-alec-bill- teaching-climate-change-denial-in-schools/.
51. "Climate change skepticism seeps into science classrooms." Retrieved November 6, 2014 at http://articles.latimes.com/2012/jan/16/nation/la-na- climate-change-school-20120116.
52. Ibid.
53. "Heartland institute and ALEC partner to pollute classroom science." Retrieved February 1, 2014 at http://greenpeaceblogs.org/2012/03/30/heartland- institute-and-alec-partner-to-pollute-classroom-science/.
54. "Science educators troubled by Heartland's climate curriculum and author's credentials." Retrieved January 22, 2014 at https://insideclimatenews.org/ news/20120314/heartland-institute-climate-change-skepticism-science- education-experts-david-wojick-ipcc-kyoto-protocol?page=show.
55. "ALEC exposed: Warming up to climate change." Retrieved December 7, 2014 at http://www.prwatch.org/news/2011/07/10914/alec-exposed-warming- climate-change.
56. Ibid.
57. "Hydrofluorocarbons (HFCs)." Retrieved January 27, 2014 at http://www. thinkglobalgreen.org/HFC.html. Hydrofluorocarbons, or "super greenhouse gases," are gases used for refrigeration and air conditioning, and known as super greenhouse gases because the combined effect of their soaring use and high global warming potential could undercut the benefits expected from the reduction of other greenhouse gases such as carbon dioxide.
58. "Industry awakens to climate change." Retrieved February 1, 2014 at http:// www.nytimes.com/2014/01/24/science/earth/threat-to-bottom-line-spurs- action-on-climate.html.
59. "Risky business: The economic risks of climate change in the United States." Retrieved February 5, 2014 at http://riskybusiness.org/.
60. "We need climate-change risk assessment." Retrieved February 4, 2014 at http://www.washingtonpost.com/opinions/a-climate-change-risk- assessment/2013/10/03/d4f70e3c-2bb5-11e3-8ade-a1f23cda135e_story.html.
61. "Economic effects of hurricane Katrina." Retrieved January 22, 2014 at http:// en.wikipedia.org/wiki/Economic_effects_of_Hurricane_Katrina.
The Insurance Information Institute reports that Hurricane Katrina was the costliest disaster in the history of insurance. It said that the insurance industry paid $41.1 billion ($45.1 billion in 2009 dollars) and more than 1.7 million claims – across six states.
62. "Insurance industry: Trust us, global warming is real." Retrieved January 4, 2014 at http://www.businessinsider.com/insurance-industry-trust-us-global- warming-is-real-2012-3#ixzz20i7uLRJM.
63. "Press release: North America most affected by increase in weather-related natural catastrophes." Retrieved December 12, 2014 at http://www. munichre.com/en/media-relations/publications/press-releases/2012/2012- 10-17-press-release/index.html.

CLIMATE CHANGE AND THE RENDING OF THE SOCIAL FABRIC

This section focuses on models that attempt to address the social impacts of global warming. We are specifically interested in the tears in the social fabric—threats to state security, both local and national violence, and crime. Central to this notion is that global warming puts in play forces that have immense destructive capacity to the way humans organize and use their social geographies. In this section we will present various models that have sought to address global warming. As presented here, none of the models will be treated as true causal models; most at this point should be thought of as heuristic and didactic, suggesting directions for discussion and further development.

The challenge of global warming and crime is this: What is it about this immense global change that helps us understand local processes of individual-level crime, organized and interstate violence, and threats to state security? The two models we will consider are Homer-Dixon's (1999) model of scarcity, violence, and crime and Agnew's (2012) model presented in his work titled "Dire Forecast."

4

MODELING THE RELATIONSHIP BETWEEN GLOBAL WARMING, VIOLENCE, AND CRIME

Ruth continued. "We were so naïve back then. Well, a lot of us were. I was. We thought people would find a way to pull together, to try finally to work together to deal with this climate change monster. Beto said we had to be careful; we needed to keep a low profile. I told him that people needed his wisdom. Other people told him that, too, at least back in the beginning. He would say that people needed to cool off, then he would laugh. He said that they already knew all they needed to know. But too late was too late. And it was too late to stop it."

"'People were too selfish,' he said, 'but for all the right reasons.' They had that part of them that they just could not give up, and why should they? Those good things enabled them to create a good life for their families, for their children, and for themselves. They were not willing to trade it for some future horror story. Countries were the same way. So when they started running out of things, people started to panic. Food riots in many cities. The Sino-Israeli proxy wars in 2033 were about oil control in the Middle East. China learned what we all already knew: no one can invade the Middle East and hold territory. A country might win the war in a week or a month, but over time, terrorists would eat them alive."

"'Them that have will get,' Beto said, 'them that don't will lose.' Same with countries. Countries were going to refuse to let people in, especially the rich ones. People will be driven out of their land because they can't farm or ranch, and they will head to the cities. But the cities won't want them. No way to get out of their countries. Where were they going to go? What were they going to do? What would you do if you had kids to feed? Probably pretty much anything, I bet. Probably pretty much anything."

"I really wanted to believe that people would find a way to work through it. But as time passed it was clear that the opposite was happening. Violent times were approaching. Take a planet full of people, put it under money strains, then make all these people live next to each other, rich next to poor, nothing good could come of that. It was about to get pretty bad, everywhere."

In this chapter, we look at perspectives that allow us to tie together the broad set of phenomena that come together under the "global warming" umbrella, violence and crime. In a sense, this chapter is out of place: Because crime is at the back end of all of our models of global warming, this discussion should be toward the end of the paper. The essential causality of the model, in simplest form, is four stages: first, we must understand global warming; second, we look at the way in which planetary phenomena such as the hydrological cycles are negatively affected by global warming; then third, we look at the direct impacts on human ecologies; and fourth and finally, we look at how those changes might be associated with violence and crime. However, we believed that it was important to locate the models earlier and then throughout the book show how different aspects of violence and crime are sensible through the lens of these models. This reordering is for several reasons. First, the realist causality— what actually will likely occur—will be much more reciprocal and nonlinear than portrayed by a standard recursive model (Homer-Dixon, 2006) and will play out at very different speeds in different settings. Second, violence associated with climate change is already upon us, as shown by the excellent work on global warming by Parenti (2011). Third, the processes brought to bear by climate change are already in play; for example, extended droughts across the American High Plains will intensify water shortages already in play from overuse of the Ogallala aquifer; similarly, problems of mass migration to urban areas, organized crime, and violence are already substantial; climate change will simply make them much worse. Consequently, the models we use are models that depict real-world phenomena already in play and of which global warming is an added (though substantial) factor, and they are ones that already are in use to explain violence and crime.

Two models are presented in this chapter. These are what we call organizing perspectives. By that, we mean that they are not intended to be true causal models but are intended to give us a set of conceptual tools to help us think through the consequences of climate change. The first, *Environmental Scarcity and Violence*, enables us to think of climate change from the perspective of its impact on important resources needed for everyday life. The second, *Dire Forecast*, allows us to look at the way in which social disorganization and its accompanying strains, particularly the significant kinds of social stressors associated with climate change, will create conditions optimal to the production of crime. The order of the presentation is deliberate. The first model provides a strong discussion of one of the more important ways climate change will set particular processes in motion. The second model provides a strong discussion of how those processes will lead to crime and violence. Hence, these two models should be considered as complementary, each strengthening the other.

Model One: Environmental Scarcity and Violence

The first model is a modified conceptual model developed by Homer-Dixon (1999) to look at the impacts of resource scarcity on different kinds of violence. The model was not designed to be primarily a model for assessing the effects of global warming, but Homer-Dixon recognized that it applied to climate change circumstances. It does not address every kind of climate-related crime, but it is a useful model for looking at the complex interplay between the immediate effects of global warming and how those effects lead to violence and crime.

Figure 4.1 displays the conceptual model used to describe the relationships among global warming, crime, and violence. It is not

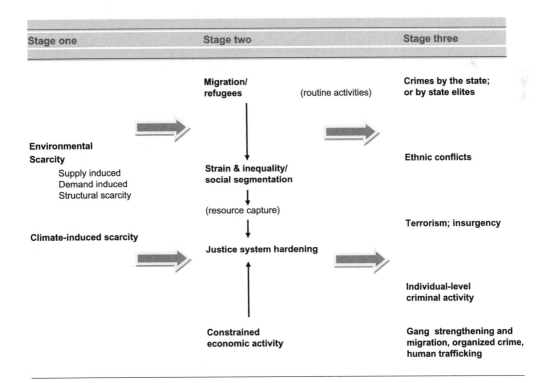

Figure 4.1 The relationship between environmental scarcity and crime. Modified from Homer-Dixon (1999).

intended to be a true "causal" model in the statistical sense, though it is intended to approximate the time ordering of events. We use it here as a heuristic model whose purpose is to allow us to trace the many different ways global warming can affect everyday life, resulting in greater levels of crime and violence.

According to this model, changes in the environment are conceptualized as kinds of scarcity. For instance, when we think about drought, the scarcity is water. Moreover, some scarcities lead to other scarcities. Heat and drought lead to the scarcity of water. The scarcity of water, in turn, leads to the loss of crops that are harvested, such as corn or soybean; the loss of ranching cattle that depend on corn; the loss of revenue for businesses than need water to manufacture their product and have to pay more; and the loss of surface water that many kinds of animals both domestic and wild depend on.

Even temperature can be framed in terms of scarcity. Think about gun crimes, especially drive-by shootings. We covered a section in which we noted the relationship between violent crime and temperature. What is the scarcity in those instances? Gun crimes require a hospitable environment to occur. One does not see many drive-by shootings in a snow storm. What is the scarcity associated with the crime of drive-by shootings? There actually are several scarcities.

1. Young people congregate, often on street corners and around bars, for the lack in part of better facilities with adult supervision where they might congregate.
2. The areas where we find such activities tend to be characterized already by inadequate jobs, few legitimate recreational outlets, and poor schools with limited after-school activities.
3. There is a significant absence of legitimate activities for gainful employment.
4. We see scarcities in poorer neighborhoods, often characterized by long-term disinvestment.
5. A lot of heat drives poor people out of their houses in the summer when they cannot afford or do not have air conditioning.
6. Lack of jobs tends to create enormous pressures on families: They tend to fall apart from the unremitting pressure of poverty. In the many one-parent households, children lack adequate supervision and easily get into trouble.

These scarcities are what we would call "social" or "economic" scarcities, and fit into stage two of our model. Crime at the community level, especially when it is sequestered by race, is closely associated with lack of access to resources across a wide spectrum of resources that are available to the more fortunate. This is the central premise of Merton's notion of anomie, and it is at the core of crime theory of social disorganization theories.

Homer-Dixon (1999, pp. 8-9) defines environmental scarcity as:

> scarcity of renewable resources, such as cropland, forests, river water, and fish stocks. This scarcity can arise . . . from depletion or degradation of the resource, from increased demand for it, and from unequal distribution. Unlike many analysts, I interpret all types of environmental depletion of damage as various forms of scarcity of renewable resources. Deforestation increases the scarcity of forest resources, water pollution increases the scarcity of clean water, and climate changes increases the scarcity of the regular patterns of rainfall and temperature on which farmers rely.

In this book, we are not looking only at renewable resources, important as they are. We also consider scarcities associated with nonrenewable resources. Klare (2002) has described the way in which violence accompanies scarcities of nonrenewable resources such as oil and coal. Oil presents itself as a scarcity of immense geopolitical importance: The Carter Doctrine established oil in the Middle East as central to the U.S. national security interests in 1973, and that national security interest has arguably contributed to our continued military investment and involvement across the region. Yet, oil may be the most important single source of global warming, and any realistic effort to address global warning must include a significant curtailment of oil use both in the United States and worldwide. At the current time, there is no remotely conceivable solution to this problem that is being discussed by the world's powers.

Environmental resources are central to the ordinary lives of most of the world's population: Homer-Dixon noted that 67% of the world's poor people are rural, and most are primarily dependent on agriculture. Most of these are small farmers, including semisubsistence farmers—they depend on what they grow to survive. Approximately 2.4 million people use fuel-wood, charcoal, straw, or cow dung as their primary energy. Over a billion people do not have access to clean drinking water. He (1999, p. 13) further noted that:

> the evidence is stark: aquifers are being overdrawn and salinized, coastal fisheries are disappearing, and steep uplands have been stripped of their forests leaving their thin soils to erode into the sea, This environmental scarcity helps generate chronic, diffuse, sub-national violence.

The Twin Dilemmas of Resource Scarcity

Important in assessing the effects of climate change-induced scarcity is the recognition that it is not occurring on a blank slate: climate change scarcity occurs on a planet in which we see already in place significant areas of environmental scarcity. All of the major threats posed by global warming do not come from new areas previously unconceived, but from existing, known, and studied problems already well established. This makes global warming particularly difficult to address—the problems it poses are with regard to issues that we have already demonstrated our inability to address effectively.

One instance of the way in which current scarcities are compounded by global warming (discussed at length later) is the scarcity of water in the Great Plains caused by the sharp draw-down of the Ogallala reservoir. Great Plains agriculture and ranching require a massive water distribution system that sits on top of the Ogallala aquifer and provides its crop and cattle abundance to citizens across the world. It is the breadbasket of the United States and the world; children in Africa starve when crops fail in the Great Plains. At current rates of use, however, it is anticipated that the Ogallala will be largely depleted by 2045 and will likely be unusable well before that.

Environmental scarcity created by an overused Ogallala is compounded by the global warming forecast for the Great Plains: the region will trend toward significant dryness, increasing periods of drought, and ultimately, desertification. In this way, a critically needed resource in the United States, water in the Great Plains, is faced with immediate scarcity issues, which may be sharply amplified by additional scarcities induced by climate change. Put simply, a two-pronged threat faces the region, each aspect of which amplifies the other. Finally, both scarcities are man-made—the drawdown of the Ogallala for corn, soybeans, and cattle ranching, and global warming through human-caused degradation of the air. And we have, thus far, failed to plan for either.

In the following section, we provide an overview of each of the elements in Figure 4.1. We will review each column, with a discussion of the elements therein.

The First Column: Scarcities

First, note on the chart that there are two categories for scarcity. The first is environmental resource scarcities, and refers to both renewable and nonrenewable resources, and the second is climate-induced scarcities.

Environmental Scarcities

Supply-induced scarcity refers to the depletion and degradation of existing resources that create a decrease in the total available resource supply. An example of this is the above-mentioned Ogallala reservoir, which is steadily degraded and salinized from overuse.

Demand-induced scarcity is a consequence of population growth in a particular area and refers to increases in the numbers of people proportional to the availability of a resource. The overpopulation of the Great Plains in the 1930s, combined with destructive agricultural techniques, led to the "dust bowl" era and collapse of farming regionally and the migration of people out of the region. Structural scarcities are caused by the misalignment of wealth and power in society or between competing countries. Structural scarcities are characteristic of colonial societies or of societies ruled by an oligarchy, an elite class, or an ethnic group. In the United States, for instance, one can see clearly the impact of the structural scarcity faced by African Americans that stems from the long history of white control of wealth. In the current era, long-term concentration of urban poverty following the Great Migration has led to the growth of a sizeable African American underclass in urban centers in the United States.

Climate-Induced Scarcities

These scarcities refer to additional scarcities that will be brought about or exacerbated by climate change. Most of this book is devoted to an elaboration of these scarcities. For instance, the increasing globalization of the planet's population is complicated by the increasing scarcity of water, which is in turn complicated by increases of temperatures associated with climate change. One can see the impacts of these temperature changes in forecasts for the Omaha region in the United States, where forecasts of drought accompany increased temperatures (Thomas, Melillo, & Peterson, 2009):

1. The time when grain seed matures is vulnerable to even small changes in temperature and is likely to change dramatically. We can anticipate, for this, decreased yields for corn, wheat, sorghum, bean, rice, cotton, and peanut crops. In 2012, we experienced severe seed failure for corn due to the drought, which stopped the seed from maturing and led to a devastating corn season.

2. Increased numbers of heavy storms may delay spring planting and contribute to root diseases, and may lead to increased soil compaction due to heavy equipment on wet

soil. Similarly, wet soil at harvest time is likely to reduce the quality of many crops.

3. Currently, invasive weeds are expanding northward. For instance, Southern soybean farmers lose about 64% of their crops to weeds, while only 22% of northern soybeans are lost to weeds. As temperatures increase, these losses will expand northward.

4. Warming allows insects and pathogens to expand into the north.

5. More insects will be able to survive over the winter, leading to a loss of control over their populations.

6. Poison ivy thrives in a high carbon dioxide environment, growing larger and producing a more toxic form of urushiol, its toxic oil.

7. Forage quality tends to decline with increases in carbon dioxide, which will affect cattle and other grazing livestock.

8. Forage availability is closely tied to water. Any drop in regular rainfall is likely to affect forage, particularly as more water is tied up in more significant storms but fewer overall rains.

9. Increases in ambient temperatures will negatively affect confined animal operations, since they will face increased energy to maintain healthy livestock.

10. Increases in heat cause animal stress, with reductions in the production of milk, weight, and reproductive capacity.

11. Nighttime recovery is essential for animals under extreme heat stress. With the nights becoming warmer faster than days, more livestock will perish.

The middle column in Chart 1 refers to the direct effects or outcomes of scarcity. They are as follows:

Migration and Refugees

Migration refers to individuals who voluntarily leave an area because it is no longer viable. Increasing sea levels will make coastal habitation nonviable: Even if someone were willing to live in a potential flood zone near an ocean, insurance options are likely to decrease or disappear altogether. Mortgages may simply become unavailable if banks will not invest in the long-term value of property. Drought in the Great Plains could make small farming and ranching livelihoods not viable. The United States has already experienced significant migration from the Great Plains to its urban centers as the family farm industry in the United States slowly collapsed over the twentieth century, and global warming is likely to reinforce this process.

Refugees are individuals who are forced off their land. African Americans in the Great Migration, for instance, represented a refugee population. Southern landholders, faced with the blight of cotton boll weevil on large cotton plantations in the rural South, reclaimed the land through mechanized labor and forced long-term itinerant workers to leave. This resulted in the largest internal migration in the history of the United States, with an estimated six million people relocating to Northern urban centers from 1920 to 1960.

Refugees and migrants may not in themselves be problematic for their new homeland. Indeed, under some circumstances, both can be quite beneficial. For instance, the United States, in the current era, faces an aging population, a condition that decreases the ratio of workers to dependent oldsters, commonly referred to as an increase in the dependency population (measured as those over 65 and under 13). This population needs financial supports and protections from the state, requiring as counterbalance a large number of working aged individuals. Paradoxically, the United States today experiences widespread resistance to Latinos entering the United States—both legal and illegal—yet desperately needs them to counterbalance an aging workforce.

Migrants and refugees alike, when not adequately anticipated, can create significant problems for their destination areas. One such problem is the illegal trade that might follow them. To describe this problem, we will briefly describe the theory of routine activities (Felson, 2002). In its simplest form, the routine activities theory asserts that routine human patterns of behavior create opportunities for routine criminal behavior. This is because most crime is opportunistic and only occurs when events are favorable for its occurrence. For instance, in large, internationally popular cities where we find many tourists, a wide variety of tourist crime emerges that follows the flow of tourists, from pickpockets to gray and black market drug and money-changing opportunities, to sexual tourism that takes advantage of the female and child slave trade. Tourists may be predator or victim or may simply create a setting where other kinds of crime flourish; for instance, illegal migrants might mimic tourist behavior to facilitate relocation.

Routine crime carries enormous potential to follow both legal and illegal migration. First of all, illegal migration may follow legal migration—this is often in the form of family members who seek to be with their relatives and significant others who have migrated. Legal migrants may share a common culture and language that is poorly understood outside their community and become vulnerable to extortion by gangs from their own country or made up of their own youth. The patterns of movement set by illegal migrants might be used by international gangs, black marketers, and terrorists, all of whom may find market opportunities by using those movements. Illegal migrants are enormously vulnerable to predation, from extortion to sexual slavery to occupational victimization by unethical employers. Hence, although migration is a complex phenomenon, under some circumstances it can create a wide variety of criminogenic opportunities.

Researchers on migration and global warming have expressed deep concerns on the future of migration. Some characterize the future as a flood, compared to the comparative trickle associated with international migration today. The urban areas of the future are simply unprepared for the enormous migration populations that they cannot avoid in the future; there is no way to avoid the enormous human migration growth that will move into populated cities, particularly in first-world countries. And that future is not far away; already some of the megacities of the world acknowledge their inability to provide security for their inhabitants.

The Middle Column: Social and Economic Factors Contributing to Crime and Violence

Scarcities do not lead directly to crime and violence. They set into play social and economic forces that in turn lead to violence. It is through these intervening factors that we can trace the consequences of global warming to more well-known factors that contribute to crime and violence. Again, we do not insist that this is a true causal model. It is symbolic, intended to show some of the general patterns that lead to violent outcomes.

The first set of intermediate factors is described as social segmentation, strain, and inequality. *Social segmentation* refers to already existing divisions between religious, ethnic, or linguistic groups and is a sociological concept. *Strain* is a criminological concept that refers to the sense of inequality felt by particular individuals because they lack opportunities for wealth available to others. When strain is accompanied by segmentation, we have groups that share a lack of participation in the goods society has to offer. *Inequality* is a relative concept referring to the wealth one has compared to another. Many sociologists and criminologists use the Gini index to measure inequality in a society, which is the ratio of individuals in the top fifth of the economic bracket in a society to those in the bottom fifth—the greater the ratio, the greater the inequality.[1]

Segmentation, strain, and inequality are associated with the unequal distribution of resources in a society. As Homer-Dixon noted and later elaborated, as resources become increasingly scarce, those who have control over them will increase their hold and those who do not will tend to experience deteriorating life quality. This process is one of resource capture, which refers to the ability of elites to capture what remains of available resources in a society and exclude others. Processes of resource capture tend to lead to increases in inequality and represent a significant threat posed by global warming.

The next category is *justice system hardening*. According to this notion, when a state is under sustained pressure, its first response is to harden, by which we mean that is becomes much more aggressive and harsh in its response to threats, through applications of the criminal law, or through the expansion of the legal system to deal with either a greater number of infractions or new infractions. This process is particularly evident in the United States today, where we witness an expansion of border interdiction efforts in response to illegal Mexican migration, an effort in many cities to use the local police to enforce federal laws against illegal or criminal migrants, and the expansion of laws designed to create a more punitive system for illegal migrants.

In the criminological and sociological literature, this variable is often conceptualized in terms of political economy, and measured in terms of inequalities stemming from differential class and economic control over state wealth. Some research, for instance, has found a substantial increase in the sheer body of law over the past 40 years in response to perceptions of increases in crime. The concept of threat is also associated with increases of state hardening, independent of actual increases in crime or violence. This means that, as powerful people perceive a threat to the state, they are likely to react harshly, whether or not the threat is actual. Even when it is, the response to the threat may be sharply exaggerated when compared to the threat itself.

The next intermediate factor is *constrained economic activity*. There are several ways that economic activity is constrained by environmental scarcities.

a. Agriculture is directly impacted by drought, particularly if no other water sources can provide an alternative.

b. Logging can produce short-term profits, but long-term losses can accrue from increased runoff due to damage to infrastructure from runoff. This increases the costs of wood for people who require it as a primary fuel source.

c. In particular, logging or other forms of forest removal can erode the soil, removing nutrients from the ground, requiring fertilizers. Homer-Dixon (1999, p. 90) cites the case of upland Indonesia, which "annually costs the country's agriculture economy nearly half a billion dollars in discounted future income."

d. Migration from rural hinterlands to cities, both legal and illegal, can have a negative impact on cities. An increase in the number of unemployed residents, whether or not they seek work, creates pressures on local governments to provide medical assistance, housing, food, gas and water, and other basic goods. At the same time it erodes the tax base while the newly arrived seek work, since they typically cannot contribute to the tax base until they are established and own taxable property. Even if all immigrants eventually find work, the lag time between arrival and work is a drain on municipal services. Moreover, the addition of people to the workforce can push down wages as competition for employment increases.

Migration can also have positive effects. For instance, the sending country may experience increased revenues from employed migrants in the new land. Additionally, migrants may fill occupational niches that are left vacant by the receiving country or region. Migration can also diffuse violence in the sending country. Hence, specific beneficial and/or negative effects of migration are highly contextualized and depend on specific local circumstances.

The Final Column: Crime and Violence

The final column shows the outputs, which refer to violence and crime. First are crimes and/or violence by *the State or State Elites*. This is a consequence of processes of resource capture, defined and described above. The mythic example of this in the United States is that of the cattle baron driving simple farmers off their land with guns and illegal land claims. Crimes by the state and state elites may be difficult to identify in that they may shift the law to criminalize previously legal practices in order to profit themselves.

Ethnic Conflicts Can Also Be a Consequence of Scarcities

This theme recognizes that in many places, current distribution of wealth is already strongly affected by ethnic imbalances. As resource scarcities increase, these conflicts are likely to increase.

Terrorism and Insurgency

Homer-Dixon (1999, p. 143) described terrorism and insurgency as a consequence of relative deprivation associated with the increasing perceptions that resources are not available to oneself:

Some groups will become increasingly frustrated and aggrieved by the widening gap between their actual level of economic achievement and the level they feel they deserve. The rate of change is key: the faster the growth of the gap, the greater the grievance. Lower status groups will likely experience the highest levels of discontent. This is because elites are anticipated to use their power to profit from scarcity in order to sustain or even improve their standard of living. As resources become increasingly scarce, non-elites will experience increasing hardships. At some point, the strength of grievances of disadvantaged groups may cross a critical threshold, and they will act violently against those groups perceived to be the agency of their economic misery.

Individual Criminal Activity

Of particular interest are the ways in which criminal activity may become emboldened or that individuals might take advantage of opportunities provided by climate scarcities. The following are perspectives that we will talk about in this book.

Routine Activities

Will changes in human living patterns, occasioned by climate change, lead to new crime opportunities? For instance, if farmers begin migrating out of areas, will their properties and equipment become more vulnerable to thieves and vandals? How do those in the process of migration themselves become vulnerable to predation? Indeed, some of the most vile predations happen to migrants and refugees stemming from their vulnerability and absence of protection in the migratory process.

Strain Theory

Recall that social strains—the tension between the wealthy and the working and unemployed classes—is a major strand of criminological theory. Strain theory, as formulated by Agnew, provides some insight into the kinds of processes facing migrants in urban areas today and in the future. The notion of strain, defined by Agnew (2012) as actual or anticipated failure to achieve positively valued goals, is a likely outcome for agricultural or ranch workers who face a declining viability from drought conditions, or for middle class homeowners who find that they can no longer insure their properties and lose their investments in them. The positively valued goal is a modest but predictable safe lifestyle, together with a significant loss of income and the "negative stimuli" of the climate change outcomes as they are personally experienced. As Agnew noted, this in itself is not enough to cause crime. One must take into consideration social supports, though those are likely to be lost during relocation. Strains are exacerbated in the face of state hardening, discouraging migrants from seeking legitimate outcomes, and by processes of resource capture, depriving individuals of their chance at a livelihood once relocated. In other words, the processes associated with population relocation under a global warming model are substantial and deeply troubling.

Social Disorganization

Social disorganization, in its earliest formulation, seems to tie nicely to the concept of climate migrants. As Shaw and McKay (1942) argued, those urban areas most characteristic of social disorganization were poor, often minority areas, and these often had unconventional norms. One can see this with regard to poor migrants, moving into an urban area with limited resources. Such areas, already with relatively high crime, are likely to experience even higher levels.[2]

Gang Strengthening and Migration, Organized Crime, and Human Trafficking

Gangs

The same factors associated with crime intensification are associated with gang strengthening. Gang strengthening may particularly be a problem for areas that lose citizens from migration, since those losses will affect the tax base, undercut the funding of security, and, at the same time, encourage individuals who do not believe that security will be adequate for their countries to join gangs.

Gangs may migrate, both across borders if they become more porous, or internally, following existing patterns of migration. Hence, any increase in factors stimulating internal and international migration is also likely to increase gang activity. Gangs bring with them a host of related problems, including coercive security practices, drug trafficking, sex trafficking, slavery, black markets for guns and other items of value, and trafficking of children. Indeed, gang growth in unsettled areas, both at the community and national levels, represent one of the most important security threats fostered by global warming and climate change.

A survey of conflict worldwide suggests that, as countries weaken or destabilize, ganglike units grow increasingly strong, and eventually can become, as in Somalia, the primary source of security in the country. Hence, countries destabilized from global warming face significant and possibly nonreversible security problems associated with gangs.

Trafficking

International human trafficking is a significant worldwide issue today. It is the fastest growing illicit business in the world and second only to drug trafficking in profits. In 2008, the United Nations estimated that 2.5 million people were being trafficked from 127 to 137 countries. In 2004 the estimated value of the trafficking enterprise was $5 billion to $9 billion.[3] It should be noted that these stats are not well studied and are likely incomplete: Some have accused the authors of pertinent reports of overestimating the extent and profits of trafficking.

Trafficking is closely tied to slavery, which is on a larger scale today than at any time in history. In particular, sex trafficking is a lucrative business, involving kidnapped girls and boys who seem to simply "disappear" from their communities and are often exported to other countries for the profits that the business of sex provides. The magnitude of the problem can be seen in Smith's (2011, p. 275) paper on sex trafficking. She noted that, since 2000, the number of sex-trafficking victims has risen while costs associated with trafficking have declined: "Coupled with the fact that trafficked sex slaves are the single most profitable type of slave, costing on average $1,895 each but generating $29,210 annually, leads to stark predictions about the likely growth in commercial sex slavery in the future."

Further, she observed that, in 2008, "12.3 million individuals were classified as forced laborers, bonded laborers or sex-trafficking victims. About 1.39 million of these individuals worked as commercial sex slaves, with women and girls comprising 98%, or 1.36 million, of this population" (Smith, 2011, p. 275).

Model Two: Agnew and Dire Forecast

Agnew's (2012) paper titled "Dire Forecast" was an effort by one of the leading criminologists to bring the issue of climate change into the U.S. criminology and criminal justice narratives. Like this book, the paper was written with a sense of urgency, recognizing that the fields of criminal justice and criminology have been too slow to take on one of the most important topics facing the globe. That paper carried many of the themes explored in more detail in this book, including the intermediate effects of global warming on migration and the formation of megacities, herein referred to both as megacities and megadeltas, which are those mega-urban locations that occupy vast riparian coastal boundaries. We have taken his examples and models, expanding on some of them. In particular, we look at opportunity theory and routine activities to provide a way of thinking about the *process of migration* itself, while strain and social disorganization are seen as providing ways of thinking about the *destinations of migration* in the megacities and megadeltas of the future.

Social Conflict and Crime

Agnew described four primary ways climate change could lead to social conflict. First, climate change increases competition over scarce resources. This is the central theme evoked by Homer-Dixon (1999) in the first part of this chapter. However, Homer-Dixon focused primarily on renewable resources. Though Agnew does not specifically refer to renewable versus fossil or nonrenewable resources, his description of resources—fresh water, food, fuel, and land—suggests that he includes both kinds of resources in his model. Second, climate change migration may lead to conflict, particularly when migrants have scarce resources, or where there are "pre-existing social divisions between migrants and those in the receiving area" (Agnew, 2012, p. 4).

Third, change will weaken states, an outcome of importance to Homer-Dixon's work. States will struggle with infrastructural maintenance, food supplies, and dealing with natural disasters. Challenger groups may use these events to assert authority or foment conflict. Fourth, conflicts can emerge between the first-world countries, which are largely responsible for causing climate change, and third-world countries, which are likely to be the primary recipients of the worst effects of climate change. Fifth, poverty in many regions will be intensified by climate change, and this may contribute to conflict at the state and local level.

Agnew focused on local violence and crime, rather than the larger-scale scenarios developed by Homer-Dixon (1999). As he noted, "It is beginning to appear that the effects of climate change are more likely to lead to small, localized conflicts, rather than to civil wars and interstate conflicts." The problem with interstate conflicts is that countries that are the hardest hit by climate change are also those who may lack the resources necessary to engage in large-scale conflicts. Agnew did not discuss the possibility that conflicts might be carried out by wealthier belligerents in order to capture the resources of third-world countries already weakened by climate change, a process Homer-Dixon (1999) refers to as resource capture.

Importantly, Agnew (2012) recognized the problematic of interstate conflicts initiated by countries already reeling from climate change problems. The resource-state destabilization-conflict linkage receives inconsistent support in the literature:

In some cases it seems sound; in others it is not supported. Simply, poor countries often cannot afford to go to war. States, to wage war against each other, need war-making capacity; armies have to be funded, air space has to be controlled, military hardware must be purchased, lodging for an army on the move has to be provided, and much, quite expensive fuel will be needed. Indeed, if conflict emerges, it may be more likely to come from states that are already well-funded and resource endowed and that seek resources or geography from weaker states before they end up in the same condition.

The prevention of state-expansion conflicts and the abeyance of empire was the purpose for the establishment of the contemporary nation-state system in the treaty of Westphalia in 1648. It is not at all clear that the system, delicately laced with its treaty-based protections from empire building and offsetting power alignments across multiple states, can survive the looming crisis. It certainly was not designed for the contemporary condition of a global hyperpower surrounded by lesser states powerful in their own right, themselves capable of unleashing regional and global annihilation. The day of empire may return, with a ferocity that only the battle for existential survival can instill. It may already be upon us. This issue will be addressed extensively in the chapter on global warming and security.

Agnew focused on crimes associated with individuals, with corporate actors, and with states acting against their own citizens. He addressed, not only on crimes as currently stated in statute, but two additional categories. First, he noted that states may themselves foment new laws that will, by definition, lead to new crimes when those laws are violated. It is not hard to imagine, for instance, that if outbound migration were to substantially increase from the coastal United States, internal states might pass laws that discourage migrants, from California for instance, settling in Oklahoma or even entering its sovereign boundaries.

Second, he focused on what he called "harms," which he described as legal acts, though causing more harm to people than state defined crimes. These harms may affect people, animals, and the environment generally (Agnew, 2012, p. 6). Homer-Dixon (1999) did not have a category associated with the term "harm" as opposed to violation of state law. The problem with the term harm is that it expands the assessment of negative personal and group outcomes to an almost unmanageable and highly subjective level. On the positive, it is important to have a way of describing violent or personally damaging outcomes that does not permit a state from legislating away the appearance of harm by making it disappear legally.

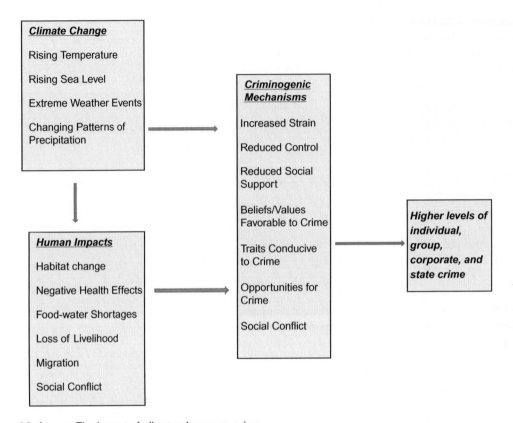

Figure 4.2 Agnew: The impact of climate change on crime.

The chart presented in Figure 4.2 is Agnew's (2012) model of the impact of climate change on crime.

Agnew (2012) discussed several ways climate change leads to crime. We will discuss each separately.

Climate-Induced Strain

Strains at the individual level lead to crime through several mechanisms: They lead to negative emotions such as anger, revenge against the source of the strain, and reduction of negative feelings through illicit drug use. Collectively, strains can reduce social control.

1. *Temperature and negative responses.* At the most straightforward causal level, increases in temperature itself can contribute to crime; this was discussed in detail in Chapter 1 of this book.

2. *Natural disasters and extreme weather events* produce a variety of strains: physical injuries, the deaths of friends and family, destruction of property, and damage to critical infrastructure necessary for activities and employment, school for children, and the like. Agnew noted that:

   As climate change proceeds, disasters will increasingly come to have these features: they will become more frequent and severe, straining the ability of individuals and governments to meet basic needs and provide security; they will more often be blamed on others, and they will more often occur in contexts of social division.

   (Agnew, 2012, p. 8)

3. *Food and freshwater shortages* can rapidly generate anger, frustration, and inequity. These in turn can lead to aggression and theft and can contribute to corporate and state crimes such as gouging. Indeed, former CIA director George Tenet once noted that water may be the most important security issue of the future.

4. *Disasters associated with climate events.* The poor are likely to pay a disproportionately high price for inequities arising from *climate disasters*. Like Homer-Dixon's notion of *resource capture*, the rich might buy land at lowered prices and employ local individuals for low wages following a disaster, thus increasing inequality and the perceptions of unfairness. This in turn can contribute to additional crimes against the rich.

5. *Forced migration.* Migration is a considerable topic in its own right. It takes on special urgency for two reasons: climate change, by many researchers, has the potential to cause levels of migration, both forced and voluntary, at levels never before seen; some assert we may experience migration in the hundreds of millions by the end of the century. Second, the United Nations has no category for climate migration, and hence climate migrants have no legal status or international protections. They, as we will see in a later chapter, are particularly vulnerable to predation. As a source of strain, Agnew (2012, p. 9) noted that:

   Migration involves the loss of home, land, close others, and often livelihood. Further, many of the migrants will settle in refugee camps and the slum areas of mega-cities in developing countries, where they are exposed to additional strains. Work and resources are scarce, living conditions are often crowded, noisy, and chaotic, and victimization is frequently high.

   Agnew noted the potential for high levels of exploitation, including border closings and genocide.

6. *Exposure to armed conflict.* Individuals who are migrating are vulnerable to others who seek to expand their territories, groups who want to increase their access to desired resources or weaken support of challenger groups.

Lower Social Control and Increased Social Disorganization

Climate change, Agnew observed, has the capability to put processes in place that would lower social control at all levels; the individual, the neighborhood or community, and societal level. These processes are listed below.

1. **Family.** The ability of the family unit to influence the behavior of members through rule making and enforcement is lessened under conditions of strain. Increased poverty will likely keep breadwinners away for unpredictable or longer times. Migration and relocation also lessen the ability of the family to influence the behavior of youth.

2. **Community or neighborhood.** The influence of communities over the stability of young people has been well established in the crime literature that consistently shows that stable communities are a positive influence on youth.

3. **The State.** Criminal justice systems are the most important state-level deterrent to crime. Historical research has strongly suggested that when the police are on strike, for instance, crime immediately escalates. In the instance of Katrina, the criminal justice system was badly damaged. The criminogenic outcomes to Katrina have been widely studied and will be discussed extensively in a later chapter. Important for the notion of control here is the recognition that disasters at the level of Katrina can effectively render hapless criminal justice systems, with regard to their ability to staff positions, their physical infrastructure essential to justice processes, and their record keeping central to tracking and reporting justice activities and individuals under jurisdiction of the courts.

4. **Stake in conformity.** Agnew noted that "Stake in conformity refers to those things that individuals and groups might jeopardize through crime. They include one's income; possessions; investments in conventional institutions such as school, work, and government; and emotional ties to conventional others" (Agnew, 2012, p. 12). Put simply, people have little to lose by engaging in crime, as Agnew noted.

5. **Fewer conventional social supports.** Social supports include those people, from friends to state-sanctioned professional

contracts, whose behavior supports conventional or legal activities and who interact with a person who might be vulnerable to criminogenic influences. Disaster research suggests that conventional supports may be fragmented in the wake of natural disasters; individuals are killed, some disappear, individuals relocate, and the places where their activities occur are destroyed.

6. **Beliefs and values favorable to crime.** As conditions deteriorate and in an environment where lawful behavior is increasingly unrewarded or capacity for punishment is forestalled, beliefs and values favorable to crime may increase. Crime may be justified for purposes of survival, to protect one's family, or as necessary violence if the criminal justice system is perceived to be broken.

7. **Increased Social Conflict.** Social conflict facilitates crime in several ways. Powerful groups will criminalize behavior that threatens their interests while decriminalizing their own self-interested behavior.

Though not developed by Agnew (2012), social conflicts can become much more intense between indigenous majorities when they take control of a country from market-controlling minority groups. This issue, developed at length by Chua (2008), happens in countries where a majority has lived in widespread poverty, where a minority has effectively controlled the economic marketplace, and where democratic (or other) reforms bring that majority suddenly into power in a country. When this happens in a country without democratic traditions or institutions, the outcomes may be genocidal, and violence of all kinds may be the result. Such violence, because it not only involves the rich against the poor but also peoples of different religions and cultures against each other, can take on the fervor of a religious conflict and result in the most brutal of acts against the other side.

The Agnew (2012) model shares many features with the Homer-Dixon model. Generally, it provides a general causal flow from global events to social and personal harmful outcomes. Both recognize that the impact of global warming is potentially destructive to social relationships. Both recognize the central role played by migration, a critical intervening factor in both models and one that is discussed in several chapters later in this book. If one were to characterize an important difference between the models, it is that Homer-Dixon (1999) seemed to have a better handle on the front end of the model. This is not surprising; Homer-Dixon's model was book length while Agnew's was a somewhat short theoretical journal article. This also shows

Homer-Dixon's training as a political scientist. Agnew more comprehensively portrayed the outcomes themselves as they relate to human harms, a weakness in the Homer-Dixon model that we have sought to develop in our revision of it in this chapter. This model shows Agnew's strengths as a criminologist. Both models, when considered with regard to their contribution to each other, reveal the importance of multidiscipline partnerships in dealing with problems of the magnitude of global warming.

Opportunities for Crime

Opportunity theory is one of the main pillars of contemporary criminology. Agnew specifically discusses *routine activities theory* (Felson, 2002): crime is "most likely when motivated offenders encounter attractive targets in the absence of capable guardians" (p. 14). Felson's central point is that, for crime to occur, all three of these elements have to come together. Humans, however, engage in broad routine activities that enable the emergence of routine crime to follow the patterns of those activities. Pickpockets, to take a simple example, are most likely to be found in areas where there are a large number of individuals, such as rich foreigners unfamiliar with local behaviors and social customs, who are milling around and not paying attention to their immediate surroundings.

Weather affects some kinds of routine activities, as discussed in Chapter 1. Drive-by shootings tend not to occur in a blizzard, for instance, because potential offenders are not motivated to search out individuals in such conditions.

Routine activities theory serves as one of the organizing perspectives of this book. Climate change fosters conditions highly favorable to crimes of opportunity. Forced migration puts victims, by the tens of thousands and, under conditions of advanced climate change, by the tens of millions into predatory environments with an absence of capable guardianship. In such environments, slavery and organized crime flourish. Keep in mind that the UN does not have a legal category that recognizes a climate migrant. Moreover, the destination for climate migrants of the future, the poverty-dense peripheries of megadeltas and megacities, may be effectively without municipal or state security, creating opportunities for organized crime, protection rackets, extortion of businesses at all levels, and easy movement of contraband such as drugs and sex slaves.

Routine Activities and Climate Change

Routine activities is a robust perspective for thinking about crime under the kinds of changes that global warming might bring. The first key element of routine activities is that crime does not occur in and only because of a motivated offender, but also requires a suitable target and the absence of capable guardians. If any one of these three components is missing, crime is not likely to occur. On the other hand, if all three elements are present, then the chances for crime increase.

Cohen and Felson (1979) argued that there will always be motivated offenders, and there will always be some targets. But targets vary in hardness—the extent to which they can be acquired—and guardians, who might serve in a variety of capacities such as moral examples or parental roles, trustworthy friends, witnesses, and agents of force, impede through force, example, or suasion of the actions of the motivated offender.

A second key element of the routine activities perspective is the notion that ordinary kinds of crime follow routine patterns of human activity. Change the routine activity, and the crime will change. These routines are some sort of patterning in human activities. For instance, that many people leave their houses in the suburbs to go to work creates large empty houses with a lot of loot in them; similarly, youth going from home to school follow corridors that tend to become criminogenic; people living in such corridors are advised to keep their yards and goods stored and locked away.

What climate change does is change the patterns of routine activities in ways that remove both formal (security agents) and informal (family and neighborhood) guardianship, providing enormous opportunities for exploitation. One of the effects of climate change is a sharp increase in migration, as some areas, due to drought or desertification, become unsuitable for farming and ranching, and as coastal areas become uninhabitable from rising seas. Migrants have limited resources at best, and often find themselves unprotected by formal security agents. At the same time traditional guardians may be absent due to family breakup and the loss of information community protections. The capacity for exploitation is great. A variety of "routine crimes" are enhanced by patterns of migration.

1. Illegal migration follows legal migration. This is not complicated—when a family member moves, others may want to join him or her. If they cannot do so legally, they may opt to do so illegally. To the extent that international

migrants cannot acquire legal entry and relocate illegally, they will contribute, in their host country, to an environment of secrecy that will complicate already existing policing and security efforts. Enforcement of migration laws tends to back-fire, leading to even greater secrecy and opportunities for organized crime, disorganized gun and drug crews seeking control of local territories, and a broad array of extortionate transactions that "protect" businesses and propertied individuals.

2. Efforts to enforce illegal migration place substantial costs on the criminal justice system. These costs include expenses on cell costs for prisons and jails, police costs, and court costs. Police departments in the current era are primarily staffed geographically, with two officers per a subunit such as a dis-trict, which are then organized into precincts. Police depart-ments are paid through municipal budgets, which in turn depend heavily on housing taxes. This also applies to city prosecution and to local jails that house misdemeanants. Any event that simultaneously increases the geography of a jurisdiction by adding districts and lowers the tax base because of uninhabitable housing will lead to a declining police presence and an increasingly understaffed criminal justice system at all local levels.

3. Migration often leads to concentrations of individuals in areas already suffering from inadequate resources, high crime, and a sinister grab-bag of other social and health problems: Legal opportunities for employment are often scant while illegal opportunities are prevalent. Mental health, physical health, and crime problems tend to intensify in such areas, creating enormous pressures for city, state, and federal services. Individuals suffering mental health issues are easily exploitable by individuals who can use them for prostitution, street corner begging, and drug muling.

4. Illegal migration carries with it the patterns that can be exploited by international gangs and international organized crime, and those entities can (1) extort illegal migrants or (2) exploit them for sex and slave trafficking.

5. Internal migration streams also carries with them opportuni-ties for gang migration, and the widening of influence of some of the stronger gangs, with the crimes that influence can generate—drugs, prostitution, covert goods, slavery, and police and court corruption.

6. Areas experiencing out-migration will see tax dollars decline to the extent that those individuals were previously contrib-uting to the tax base. This affects the presence of security in

those settings, especially the ability of municipalities to afford police. On the other hand, if only the poorest individuals leave, the area experiencing out-migration might actually benefit economically.

7. Coastal migration is likely to happen well before seas are actually "lapping at the doorstep." This is because once areas are seen as within a clear time line for flooding, mortgages are likely to disappear: Many properties may have no value over the extended life of a mortgage. This leads to a significant erosion of local tax base, increases the number of poor when propertied individuals cannot sell their houses, and, when affecting geographically homogenous areas, can lead to large suburban or urban tracts with no responsible guardianship. These areas will be ripe for gang and organized crime control, and for the occupation of these houses by squatters who cannot otherwise find a place to live. There will simply be no benefit for a police department to police areas if the properties in them become uninsurable and are in locations where no long-term development is feasible.

8. The Great Plains, facing destruction of farms and ranches both from climate change process of drought and desertification and from the currently unsustainable use of the Ogallala, also faces the prospect of losing virtually all of its population. This may lead to its sizeable geography being virtually ungovernable at the local and state levels and potentially creating uncontrollable security problems.

9. Migrants leaving coastal areas must find receiving destinations. The tendency of migrants is to stay relatively close to where one already is, barring a perceived opportunity for employment in a more distant area, or that family members or relatives live more distantly. This suggests that the areas carrying the brunt of in-migration will be in the same or nearby states or countries as those areas facing the greatest threats from rising oceans. Hence, many states will face a double burden: On the one hand they lose business income and tax base from refugees and migrants who relocate due to climate-related issues and face increased strain on municipal criminal justice and social service systems costs as those same individuals inhabit nearby urban areas.

10. Some states like California will be largely desert once one moves away from the coast. These states may face significant depopulation, undercutting the viability of state's security apparati due to loss of tax base. Relocation midstate in such areas is nonviable due to anticipated drought and desertification; simply, there will not be water licensing for new residents.

11. The presence of large numbers of migrants in receiving areas, particularly if they are poor, creates opportunities for black market merchandising and the proliferation of off-the-market goods that undercut local and regional tax bases.

12. The "target" made available by the poorest of refugees is their bodies. Women and young men are exploitable for slaving and sexual slaving, youth for conscription and war fighting, and the refugee population generally for the use of their body cavities to move contraband and to serve as human shields in state conflicts. Refugees, hence, are themselves the target, often in a setting without any guardianship and in which anyone could serve as a potential offender.

13. The relocation process is likely to contribute to extensive social disorganization in receiving areas. Many of these areas will become the megacities and megadeltas of the future, circling or banding the perimeters of core cities, and without security or other forms of protective guardianship beyond what individuals can do by working to protect each other. It is difficult to imagine what criminal opportunity would not emerge in such an environment. It is in this environment where we can anticipate to encounter many of Agnew's strains and where a rational decision maker might decide that legal or normative constraints on behavior are simply ineffective.

Endnotes

1. "GINI Index." Retrieved July 6, 2013 at http://data.worldbank.org/indicator/SI.POV.GINI.
2. Jensen, Gary F. 2003. Social Disorganization Theory. *Encyclopedia of Criminology*. Richard A. Wright (Editor). Fitzroy Dearborn Publishers.
3. "Human Trafficking." Retrieved July 6, 2013 at http://en.wikipedia.org/wiki/Human_trafficking.

5

CONSEQUENCES OF GLOBAL WARMING

Clete asked Ruth, "Was it just you and Beto? Did anyone ever travel with you?"

Ruth said, "My sister-in-law Nene traveled with us for a while. That was a wonderful time. She completely believed in what Beto did. She was actually our matchmaker." Ruth giggled, startling Clete. In that moment, she sounded just like a child.

Ruth continued, "Nene was married, and her husband joined us for a while. We were settled here when the sickness struck; that probably saved us. Well, not all of us. Nene went home to Calgary, where a lot of my family is now."

Clete: "Can you talk about the sickness a bit?"

Ruth: "The beginning of the sickness was when everything seemed to go wrong. The big cities were hit with diseases, no one knows how many died. People all over had moved to the big cities, and now they realized what a bad idea that was. The cities were starting to flood, the oceans weren't really rising all that much—not like now—but it was like, when the big storms came, the water rose quickly, like it jumped. Thing was, it didn't jump back down again; it seeped back slowly and each time less. More and more, people lost their homes. A lot of the drinking water got poisoned from the ocean salts. That was when the gangs and the terrorism started really getting bad. But the thing that really spooked us was the diseases. It wasn't that the diseases were so bad; it was that the medicines were being hoarded by the big pharmacies for resale in the rich countries.

The diseases spread like crazy in the big cities in poor countries. No one could control them. They just had to burn themselves through the population until there was no one left to infect. The rich countries, they didn't give a rat's ass about the poor people. What they didn't realize was that diseases didn't care either; they would hitch a ride on a poor person, who would carry it in his day laborer job to a rich man's house and family. Lazy disease, it will hitch a ride with anyone. Pretty soon, Mr. Rich is off on a plane and, well, you get the idea. When the diseases came to the rich countries, some of them couldn't be controlled with the drugs anymore—with all that time burning their way through poor countries, they mutated."

Clete knew the next part of the story, but he did not want to interrupt Ruth. She looked down, paused, and then continued. "So we had diseases in places that never had them before. It did not take much of a temperature change to move a lot of these diseases into higher latitudes. Lots of kids died. Especially the babies." She stopped for a second and her eyes drifted. Her voice was flat. "Two of my babies. Lots of old people died. Many cities went back to the old ways and burned the bodies in mass graves. A lot of people blamed the giant cattle farms. Some of the farms, trying to get ahead of the disease, killed off their cattle. But then the people in the cities starved instead. Lose–lose all the way around. We didn't know it then, but the human population was starting to crash. This was so far beyond what we expected. Who would have thought? The changes in the climate, they weren't that big yet. But Beto, he always saw these things coming. He said that the way we lived was too tied together. Change even one thing, it all changes. There were way too many of us for how we lived. It was coming anyway, Beto said; global warming just hurried it up. We were pretty grim after that."

There is a central problem with trying to identify the consequences of global warming. Simply, there is nothing untouched by it. Any effort to systematize the consequences will not encounter difficulty trying to find things to include. The problem is trying to decide what to leave out.

Climate change impacts are organized differently, according to a particular researcher or policymaker's particular concern.[1] Our review leads us to organize them into the following seven areas: (1) Diseases and health-related issues; (2) migration, forced migration, and refugees; (3) natural disasters; (4) drought and heat waves; (5) coastal flooding; (6) fire and wildfire; and (7) water shortages. All of these areas have direct or indirect linkages to crime and violence. Diseases, for instance, can spread in the close confines of a prison and jail, then rapidly move into civilian populations when former prisoners return to their communities. This is a particularly difficult issue for poverty-stricken areas in a city, which are also the most likely to house those returning from prisons and jails. A severely diseased population cannot field an army or maintain integrity in command ranks. Drought and heat waves create opportunities for agricultural fraud, when some farmers, facing product shortages, might develop illicit strategies to capitalize on insurance claims. In the Midwest, we have also seen that, as certain farm produce ceases to provide a viable livelihood, some farmers move on to illicit products such as marijuana. In Africa, drought has decimated cattle herds and contributed to cattle rustling and the killing of farmers.

In all of these areas, the first challenge is trying to identify where the world is today. Our estimation of risks associated with global warming depend on the accuracy of the description of the current state of affairs. We consequently will first try to sketch the predominant features of the areas, and then extrapolate into the future, looking at trends as posited by experts in the respective fields. Each area is problematic, by which we mean that each area poses fundamental problems currently and more trenchant problems in the future, with or without global warming. Global warming represents the additional stress on top of existing stressors that will amplify the consequences of these problems.

Diseases and Health Costs

All living creatures inhabit niches that are favorable to the survival of their species, whether they are in thermal vents in deep ocean trenches, burrowed under the sand in the Gobi desert, or comfortably situated inside the human body. Many of these are sensitive to even relatively small changes in temperature. Niche survival applies to insects, including disease carrying insects such as mosquitos, just as it applies to alligators and gazelles. Remove the niche, and there will be no survival. If the niche shifts, the creature will try to shift with it.

The climate change issue with pathogens is uncomplicated, though the consequences are immensely complex. As the planet warms, pathogens and the hosts that carry them tend to migrate outward from the equator. Complexity emerges when we recognize that we are already dramatically changing the environments that pathogens inhabit, and we are doing so in ways that are more in their best interests than ours, and that the pathogens are themselves mutable. Global warming is only one of several factors that may increase our pathogen risk.

Pathogens and Diseases in Contemporary Life: The Third Wave

In 2000, the National Intelligence Council released its National Intelligence Estimate on the Global Infectious Disease Threat.[2] That assessment included the following:

1. Twenty well-known diseases—including tuberculosis (TB), malaria, and cholera—have reemerged or spread geographically since 1973, often in more virulent and drug-resistant forms.

2. At least 30 previously unknown disease agents have been identified since 1973, including human immunodeficiency virus (HIV), Ebola, hepatitis C, and Nipah virus, for which no cures are available.

3. Of the seven biggest killers worldwide, TB, malaria, hepatitis, and, in particular, HIV/AIDS, continue to surge, with HIV/AIDS and TB likely to account for the overwhelming majority of deaths from infectious diseases in developing countries by 2020.

It is taken as an article of faith that medicine today is superior to any time past, to the point where the capacity to provide vaccines and medicines is global. This would seem to be an age where all the known diseases could be cured and that inroads in the most intractable could be made. Yet, this is not the case. Human ecology is changing in ways favorable to the spread of infectious diseases. This change has been called the "third wave" of infectious diseases (Brower & Chalk, 2003) and refers to the emergence of new disease strains and the re-emergence of older strains in more virulent forms. We live a fast-paced, globalized lifestyle that makes us especially vulnerable to some very nasty bugs, and they will infect and kill many of us. Brower and Chalk (2003) identified five factors that make the contemporary world particularly vulnerable to these pathogens.

1. *Globalization.* Globalization has brought people into contact with exotic and foreign animals, and in doing so we encounter new diseases. People carrying infectious diseases can move quickly across countries and continents while a disease is incubating. Overcrowded, badly ventilated aircraft provide an idealized breeding area for some viruses. In the current era, the international sexual trade may provide a most unpleasant surprise for travelers who indulge in its pleasures. The authors noted that, for instance,

   there can be little doubt that the global spread of AIDS has been encouraged by the substantial patronage of the Asian sex markets and by the equally large number of international travelers visiting such countries as Thailand, India, and the Philippines every year. (2003, p. 17).

2. *Modern medical practices.* The high and inconsistent use of antibiotics has given rise to a process called "pathogenic natural selection." This process has led directly to the development of "supergenes," pathogens that resist antibiotic treatment. Some particularly nasty bugs are becoming resistant to all antibiotics. Increasingly we see mutations among diseases such as tuberculosis that resist all treatment.

The use of invasive medical practices in hospitals provides an optimum setting for different diseases to interact, potentially developing new superstrains of diseases. Older individuals are often immune-weakened, and consequently more vulnerable to disease and as disease carriers than the host population. Hospitals, in other words, provide the opportunity for pathogens to interact and develop adaptive and new strains.

3. *Accelerating urbanization.* Life on planet Earth is increasingly urbanized. The authors noted that, in 1950, about 16% of the population of developing countries lived in cities; this increased to 40% in 2000 and was expected to reach 56% by 2030. Most of these people will live in megacities. We will discuss megacities extensively later in this book.

   The rapidity of urbanization has led to large city segments with inadequate sanitation, lack of medical treatment, roads, sewer systems, and housing, all of which are essential for physical health. This is particularly the case in the many poverty dense shantytowns that have emerged around these cities. Megacities are simply unequipped to respond with even minimal hygienic consideration to the substantial increases in the burdening and poverty stricken populations they now have.

4. *Changes in social behavioral patterns.* Slavery affects more people today than at any time in our history, and one of the particularly pernicious forms of slavery is sexual slavery. The huge international marketplace for the sex trade is an immense opportunity for the spread of lethal pathogens. In Thailand, Cambodia, and India, a thriving sex trade is associated with the rapid spread of HIV. In Mumbai, for instance, it is estimated that 75% of the 60,000 to 70,000 sex workers have contracted HIV. The spread of AIDS also is substantial in the illicit drug marketplace, where heroin users who share needles are particularly vulnerable. Users sell infected blood in order to fund their habit, thereby contributing to the spread of the disease.

5. *Global warming.* Global warming increases the range of habitats available for disease pathogens to thrive. Brower and Chalk (2003, p. 24) noted, for example, that:

   Global warming could expose millions of people for the first time to malaria, sleeping sickness, dengue fever, yellow fever, and other insect-borne illnesses. In the United States, for instance, a slight increase in overall temperature would allow the mosquitoes that carry dengue fever to survive as far north as New York City.

   Indeed, dengue fever has expanded considerably in recent years, and researchers have attributed this spread directly to changes in habitat from the effects of global warming. More broadly, the effects of global warming on disease vectors—the geographies that diseases occupy—are an immediate health concern; areas have already experienced significant changes in climate and have had to deal with their pathogenic consequences:

Instances of malaria in Madagascar, India, Ethiopia, and Peru have been attributed to sudden increases in mosquito densities resulting from higher rainfall patterns in arid and semiarid regions. Epidemics of cholera, typhoid, and dengue fever in Venezuela, Peru, and Bangladesh and plague in India have similarly been linked to major shifts in vector and infectious agent distributions caused by altered weather patterns.

(Brower & Chalk, 2003, p. 25)

Diseases are also a national security concern. As we will discuss in the second half of this chapter, diseases promote a long line of challenges to state security, undermine governmental legitimacy, and can increase the likelihood of torture, warfare, and security failure.

6. *End of life medicine and free riders.* We add a sixth vulnerability to pathogens: the way medicine is practiced. According to Brower and Chalk (2003), in 2000, the number of individuals who died from pathogenic diseases was about 170,000, twice what it was at its low point in 1980. The total cost of these diseases, according to the CDC, was about $120 billion annually. This increase stems from fundamental changes associated with urbanization. Even while human ecology undergoes change, the diseases themselves are mutating and adapting to our historically effective antigens. Even without the threat of global warming, significant disease-related issues confront us. With the added stress of global warming, these issues have the potential to be much more devastating, affecting a much larger part of the human race than previously possible.

Pathogens are not only a threat to poor countries with limited health facilities. Diseases are particularly worrying for highly advanced societies like the United States, where the medical industry is highly focused on end-of-life medicine. The extraordinary quality of end of life research and medical treatments has created the illusion that the United States has a strong public health system. It actually has virtually no functioning public health system, at least not at the federal level (Garrett, 2000). The problem faced by the end of life system is that diseases are, as Garrett observed, free riders. They do not care whether someone is insured or not. Free riders are pathogens that move into a population without adequate medical insurance and through them, spread through the

Information Box 5.1 The Livestock Revolution

From the beginning of the 1970s to the mid-1990s, consumption of meat in developing countries increased by 70 million metric tons (MMT), almost triple the increase in developed countries, and consumption of milk by 105 MMT of liquid milk equivalents (LME), more than twice the increase that occurred in developed countries. The market value of that increase in meat and milk consumption totaled approximately $155 billion (1990 US$), more than twice the market value of increased cereals consumption under the better-known "Green Revolution" in wheat, rice and maize. . . . However, the near doubling of aggregate milk consumption as food in India between the early 1980s and the late 1990s suggests that the livestock revolution goes beyond just meat and beyond China and Brazil. At 60 MMT of LME in 1996/98, Indian milk consumption amounted to 13% of the world's total and 31% of milk consumption in all developing countries. The rapid rise in livestock production in developing countries has been confronted in recent years by dwindling grazing resources for ruminant animals and a pattern of effective demand largely centered on rapidly growing megacities fueled by nonagricultural development.

seemingly protected general population. End of life medicine as we practice it in the United States provides scant protection against this kind of public health problem.

7. *Livestock revolution.* Our seventh item is the livestock revolution. About one billion people depend on livestock as a primary food source. This number is growing rapidly as the human population continues to urbanize, and the post 2000 period is sometimes referred to as the livestock revolution, with the following characteristics:[3]

   1. About two-thirds of the rural poor and one-third of the urban poor depend on livestock.
   2. Livestock provides one-fifth to one-half of the income for the poor.
   3. Livestock production is increasing rapidly in response to growth in population, income, urbanization, and changing diets; this is called the livestock revolution.

Information Box 5.1 describes the livestock revolution.[4]

The livestock revolution stems from global urbanization processes. It is characterized by large-scale ranching practices, which make it vulnerable to particular kinds of diseases, discussed in Information Box 5.2.

Pathogens

In this section, we explore the nature of pathogens. This discussion may seem somewhat aside to the field of criminal justice and criminology, but we believe it will become more important with the onset of global warming. In particular, pathogens can

Information Box 5.2 Globalization and Disease Transmission

The livestock revolution is of immense value to many developing countries for its ability to provide large quantities of food to growing cities, particularly megacities in third-world countries. However, the spread of disease associated with the revolution is emerging as a central concern.

> *Globalization is accelerating the frequency, speed and geographical scale of transboundary animal disease events (witness the current avian influenza epidemic) and facilitating the establishment of pathogens in hitherto unaffected environments. The transboundary nature of these diseases and their potential to overcome species barriers and to affect humans poses serious challenges that extend beyond the livestock sector and demand international cooperation. Endemic and "forgotten" diseases, such as tuberculosis and chronic parasitic diseases, often go unperceived, yet impair production and can affect human health.*
>
> *Source: Science and the Livestock Revolution. Retrieved June, 2014 at http://www.fao.org/ag/magazine/0511sp1.htm.*

The livestock revolution also represents dilemmas in other ways.

1. Livestock globally represent about 18% of the total greenhouse gases. This number is poised to increase sharply as livestock become increasingly central to global food sources.
2. Globalization creates problems in tracing the sources of livestock in the event of a health crisis related to livestock disease.
3. Changes in livestock production in itself are associated with the spread of diseases in novel ways. Moreover, existing diseases are evolving into new forms with potentially greater virulence. *Source: Infectious Diseases Associated with Livestock Production: Mitigating Future Risks. Retrieved August 19, 2014 at http://www.ncbi.nlm. nih.gov/pmc/articles/PMC3733682/.*
4. The revolution is occurring in areas where surveillant systems are typically inadequate or altogether lacking, contributing to the reemergence of known zoonoses in novel forms.

create devastating security problems for a nation. Their primary impact, we think, will be not so much on crime but on the criminal justice system itself. This indirectly but powerfully links pathogens to crime—any factor that undercuts the effectiveness or reach of justice systems will create opportunities for crime of all kinds, from individual opportunistic crime to more organized gang crimes. Pathogens, though at the present time appearing distant from our fields, have the capacity to become substantially important.

What pathogens are we susceptible to? Humans are richly viable host animals, host to abundant microorganisms and the occasional parasite.[5] Indeed, it is estimated that there are 342 parasites that use the human body as a host.[6] An estimated 80 viruses and other organisms live in the mouth alone. An estimated additional 80 thrive in the gut. A rough estimate is that around 200 organisms call the human body "home."[7]

Zoonoses

One kind of pathogen with which we are particularly concerned is called zoonoses. Zoonoses are diseases that are spread from animals to humans (and vice versa). Zoonoses can be very lethal—the 13 most common zoonoses are responsible for about 2.2 million human deaths every year.[8]

Because zoonoses are associated with vertebrate animals, they are most common in poor agrarian societies, particularly among poor livestock herders. The countries associated with significant zoonose problems include Nigeria, Ethiopia, and India. Zoonoses are particularly associated with poor livestock keepers, which turn out to be quite a large number of people. Consider the following statistics:

Poor livestock keepers exist everywhere, and no one is immune to a zoonose outbreak. This includes the United States, which is considered one of the four areas vulnerable to a significant zoonotic outbreak.[9] This summer, for example, a particularly severe outbreak of West Nile disease centered in Texas, and, as of August 2002, over 1,100 cases and 41 deaths were reported across the United States. It is a zoonose whose host is birds, and in the United States it is carried primarily by the American Crow and American Robin.

There are approximately 600 known zoontic diseases. Some of these are of particular concern to researchers studying the impact of global warming on pathogens. They have identified the "deadly dozen" zoonoses of particular concern for climate change, and these are listed in Information Box 5.3.[10]

Malaria

Some disease threats are not zoontic. Malaria is not zoontic; we cannot catch malaria directly from other animals (except the mosquito). However, malaria may be set to resurge onto the world stage. The World Health Organization observed that there were 216 million documented cases of malaria and that 655,000 people died from the disease in 2010.[11] By some research, a relatively small increase in global temperatures puts a much larger proportion of the planet's population at risk. The following chart in Figure 5.1, for instance, forecasts North America into Canada and Russia into Siberia to both come within malarial vectors as global warming proceeds.

The spread of malaria is contingent on a variety of factors, among which ambient temperature is only one. Sanitation and prevention, for instance with DDT, are effective ways of containing the

Information Box 5.3 Primary Zoontic Diseases

Avian influenza The virus is shed by infected birds via secretions and feces ... the movement of H5N1 from region to region is largely driven by the trade in poultry, but changes in climate such as severe winter storms and droughts ... can bring both wild and domestic bird populations into greater contact.

Babesiosis Babesia species are examples of tick-borne diseases that affect domestic animals and wildlife... In Europe and North America, the disease is becoming more common in humans.

Cholera Cholera is a water-borne diarrheal disease affecting humans mainly in the developing world. It is caused by a bacterium, Vibrio cholerae, which survives in small organisms in contaminated water sources and may also be present in raw shellfish.

Ebola Ebola hemorrhagic fever virus and its closely related cousin—the Marburg fever virus—easily kill humans, gorillas, and chimpanzees, and there is currently no known cure. We may expect to see outbreaks of these deadly diseases occurring in new locations and with more frequency.

Intestinal and external parasites Parasites are widespread throughout terrestrial and aquatic environments ... The parasites will increase in many places, infecting an increasing number of humans and animals. Many species of parasites are zoonotic, spread between wildlife and humans.

Lyme disease This disease is caused by a bacterium and is transmitted to humans through tick bites ... human-induced changes in the environment and on population patterns of species such as white-tailed deer that can carry infective ticks greatly affect the distribution of this disease.

Plague Plague, Yersinia pestis—one of the oldest infectious diseases known—still causes significant death rates in wildlife, domestic animals, and humans in certain locations. Plague is spread by rodents and their fleas and is expected to expand from global alterations in temperatures and rainfall.

Rift Valley Fever Rift Valley fever virus (RVFV) is an emerging zoonotic disease of significant public health, food security, and overall economic importance, particularly in Africa and the Middle East. People can get the virus from butchering infected livestock. Death rates for both people and livestock are high.

Sleeping sickness Also known as trypanosomiasis, this disease affects people and animals. It is caused by the protozoan, Trypanosoma brucei, and transmitted by the tsetse fly. Domestic cattle are a major source of the disease, but wildlife can be infected and maintain the disease in an area.

Tuberculosis As humans have moved cattle around the world, bovine tuberculosis has also spread. It now has a global distribution and is especially problematic in Africa, where it was introduced by European livestock in the 1800s.

Yellow fever Found in the tropical regions of Africa and parts of Central and South America, this virus is carried by mosquitoes, which will spread into new areas as changes in temperatures and precipitation levels permit. One type of the virus—jungle yellow fever—can be spread from primates to humans, and vice versa.

Source: Definitions from Wildlife Conservation Society (2008), "'Deadly dozen' reports diseases worsened by climate change." See http://www.sciencedaily.com/releases/2008/10/081007073928.htm.

spread of malaria. Also, some research suggests that malaria may actually decrease because of global warming. Corbyn (2011) observed that while global warming increases the rate at which parasites spread, it lowers their overall infectiousness.[12]

This brief discussion of malaria reminds that the role of warmer temperatures in the spread of parasitic diseases is complex and probably is not a relatively simple linear phenomenon. Corbyn's (2011) research, for instance, utilized laboratory mosquitos and was not carried out on humans, so the actual human infection rate in an uncontrolled environment is not yet known.

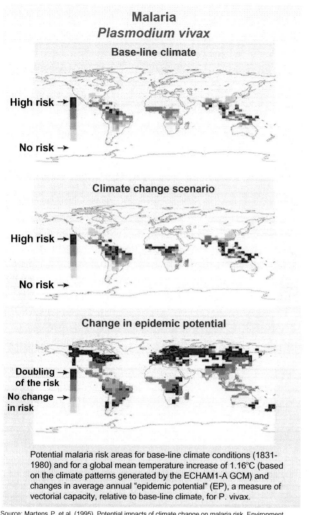

Potential malaria risk areas for base-line climate conditions (1831-1980) and for a global mean temperature increase of 1.16°C (based on the climate patterns generated by the ECHAM1-A GCM) and changes in average annual "epidemic potential" (EP), a measure of vectorial capacity, relative to base-line climate, for P. vivax.

Source: Martens, P. et al. (1995). Potential impacts of climate change on malaria risk. Environment Health Perspectives, 103(5), 458-464.

Figure 5.1 Malaria *Plasmodium vivax.*

However, this kind of research, with its potential to provide buffers to diseases associated with global warming, is essential as we move into new global ecologies that will likely fundamentally change the habitat of many parasites.

Stemming in part from the agricultural revolution, urbanization and inadequate sanitation for storage are threats, but they are not the only ones. An increase in the virulence of many diseases is associated with a decrease in the effectiveness of antibiotics, particularly penicillin. There are concerns that a time will come when antibiotics afford no protection to humans. Also, humans are constantly coming into contact with new viruses and parasites as they cut their way into areas unaccustomed to human contact. In other words, the problem of disease spread is a significant and growing problem. The additional stress from global warming is that of increasing the range of some diseases, making new populations vulnerable. Consider the chart of emerging and reemerging infectious diseases below.[13] This chart in Figure 5.2 provides the backdrop against which global warming amplifies disease threat.

The spread of disease to cattle and other livestock also creates its own crime problems. To what extent will farmers avoid reporting diseases if it costs them their livelihood? Might they kill their neighbor's cattle to protect their own? Will they be ambushed and killed by another destitute farmer and their cattle stolen? In Africa, for instance, it is reported that somewhere around 99.9% of all livestock deaths go unreported, and consequently there is virtually no way to measure the spread of infectious diseases that move through that population. Failure to report can in turn increase the impact of a disease as it is spread from the farm to the open market and its butcher stalls, and finally to the dinner table or local restaurant. Similarly, poaching can lead to the undocumented spread of disease; the spread of Ebola occurred from the poaching of bushmeat, especially simians.

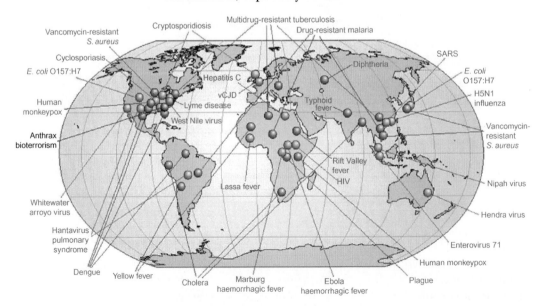

Figure 5.2 Emerging and reemerging infectious diseases. *Source:* Introduction to Emerging and Reemerging Infectious Diseases. Retrieved February 19, 2013 at http://nrse4600group9.wordpress.com/2013/02/15/introduction-to-emerging-and-reemerging-infectious-diseases/.

Disease and State Security: The Challenge of an Invisible Enemy

Can disease become a security issue at the state or international level? The role of disease in conflicts historically has been far reaching, though not as well known. Diseases have played a central role in many conflicts not ordinarily noted for their pathogenic outcomes.

Disease and War

The end of World War I, at that time called the "Great War," is popularly associated with the defeat of the Axis, a substantial military victory. However, the role of disease may have been central to its outcome. It has been observed that World War I ended, not from a desire on the part of the belligerents to end the conflict, but from the overwhelming toll the flu epidemic took on military personnel during combat operations. Indeed, the flu may have been the reason for the Allied victory. Though the flu took casualties on both sides, its impact on the Central Powers was devastating and likely contributed to their ultimate defeat.

Wikipedia noted that:[14]

> World War I did not cause the flu, but the close troop quarters and massive troop movements hastened the pandemic and probably both increased transmission and augmented mutation; it may also have increased the lethality of the virus. Some speculate the soldiers' immune systems were weakened by malnourishment, as well as the stresses of combat and chemical attacks, increasing their susceptibility. Academic Andrew Price-Smith has made the controversial argument that the virus helped tip the balance of power in the later days of the war towards the Allied cause. He provides data that the viral waves hit the Central Powers before they hit the Allied powers, and that both morbidity and mortality in Germany and Austria were considerably higher than in Britain and France.

In the United States, many battles in the Civil War were affected by the disease as well. That medical practices were inadequate for the battle injuries of that conflict has been well documented. Less well known is the tremendous toll that infectious diseases took on the North and South soldiers, particularly the more vulnerable Northerners in conflicts that took place in the South. Sartin (1993, p. 280), referring to disease as the "third army" in the war, noted that:

altogether, two-thirds of the approximately 660,000 deaths of soldiers were caused by uncontrolled infectious diseases, and epidemics played a major role in halting several major campaigns. These delays, coming at a crucial point early in the war, prolonged the fighting by as much as 2 years.

The US Civil War, it has been observed, was the last war fought before the emergence of the germ theory of disease, and a great deal of knowledge has been subsequently developed. War today is different; could a disease have such devastating effects on conflict in the modern era? Unfortunately, the answer is yes: AIDs in Africa has emerged as a significant security issue for many countries there.

AIDS and State Security

Prior to the onset of AIDs in Africa, the security implications of disease, outside historical studies, were hypothetical. This has all changed in the past 20 years as we have witnessed the tremendous toll of the epidemic in Africa and increasingly with regard to security across the developing and developed world. AIDS provides a glimpse, through the lens of its destructive impacts on state security and quality of life in Africa, of what we can anticipate and plan for on a warming planet.

The onslaught of AIDS in Africa has provided a blueprint for thinking about the way in which diseases can undermine interstate security arrangements. State security impacts that disease might have are cited in Information Box 5.4:[15]

In the globalized world, security issues affecting one area have a way of affecting others. The security issues of AIDS in Africa have created security issues for other countries, noted by Current Intelligence.[16]

1. Domestic forces are weakened or perceived as illegitimate by their home country, increasing pressures for military intervention for countries that do significant international economic or other kinds of work with them. International troops are pressured into participation in these conflicts.
2. Weak militaries may be more vulnerable to external threat, changing the balance of power in some regions. Shifts in the balance of power can change the likelihood of interstate conflict.
3. A state could become unable to adequately provide for peacekeeping operations, leaving an increased burden for outside forces such as the United States.

Information Box 5.4 AIDS and Security: Central Issues

1. *Heightened Risk of Infection*—Military personnel are at particular risk of HIV infection, with the majority of recruits between 18 and 24 years old, sexually active, and experiencing long deployments away from traditional social networks amid a military culture that promotes aggression, machismo, and risk taking.

2. *Smaller Recruitment Pool*—Recruits who are HIV-positive are seen as less suitable for military service. In response to high HIV prevalence in the general population some African militaries conduct pre-employment testing. However, testing can cause prospective recruits to self-select out of military service, shrinking the recruitment pool and reducing the overall quality of the armed forces.

3. *Loss of Experienced Personnel*—Experienced officers take decades to train and develop, making them one of the military's most valuable resources. The loss of experienced personnel to HIV/AIDS erodes African militaries of their organisational capacity and institutional knowledge.

4. *Reduction in Effectiveness*—Military personnel with AIDS are less able to complete physically demanding tasks, are more susceptible to adverse conditions during deployments, and have lower morale. Furthermore, individuals unable to perform their duties must be transferred to less demanding roles, reducing the capacity of the military to deploy homogenous units.

5. *Greater Financial Burden*—Militaries with high HIV prevalence have less financial resources available for their core functions.

6. *Reduced Peacekeeping Capacity*—HIV/AIDS weakens the ability of African armed forces to participate in regional peacekeeping operations. The epidemic undermines peacekeeping capacity in two ways. First, HIV/AIDS is making states reluctant to contribute peacekeepers. Faced with the positive correlation between peacekeeping and HIV prevalence, African states are less willing to contribute forces to peacekeeping operations. Second, ... the combination of a high HIV-prevalence among SANDF personnel and a policy of excluding HIV-positive troops from UN peacekeeping duty means that a significant portion of troops are unavailable for deployment. A 2003 RAND study reported that one South African official supposedly claimed that HIV/AIDS was the primary reason South Africa has not been more involved in the conflict in the Democratic Republic of the Congo.

4. These factors in turn contribute to international problems associated with peacekeeping and conflict with efforts to provide humanitarian assistance:

The United States' African Contingency Operations Training and Assistance programme boosts the capacity of African militaries to conduct peacekeeping and humanitarian missions on the continent. Its greatest challenge, according to one commentator, is that the HIV/AIDS epidemic is crippling the participating militaries before they can be effectively deployed. Enlarging the role of health capacity building in this and similar programmes offers a means to make friendly militaries more resistant to infectious disease, increasing their ability to provide domestic, international, and regional stability.[17]

Brower and Chalk (2003) identified human security threats posed by the spread of infectious diseases in the current era. They noted that they are concerned with "human security," as opposed to what they refer to the state-centric notion of state security. They defined "human security" as:

human security recognizes that an individual's personal preservation and protection emanate not just from safeguarding the state as a single political unit, but also from ensuring adequate access to welfare and quality of life.

Importantly, issues related to state-centric security are in important ways not different from human security; many of the kinds of security concerns that affect citizens also pose threats to the states that provide for their security. Particularly in a democracy, any threat to the citizenry is a threat to the state. However, more centric regimes face substantial issues as well, from the capacity to field an army to the ability to develop treaties and joint aid agreements with other nations. The six most significant threats, according to Brower and Chalk, are:

1. First and most important, the sheer number of individuals killed by infectious diseases far surpasses the number of individuals killed in all wars. The authors noted that:

   first and most fundamental, disease kills—far surpassing war as a threat to human life. AIDS alone is expected to have killed over 80 million people by the year 2011, while tuberculosis (TB), one of the virus's main opportunistic diseases, accounts for three million deaths every year, including 100,000 children. In general, a staggering 1,500 people die each hour from infectious ailments, the vast bulk of which are caused by just six groups of disease: HIV/ AIDS, malaria, measles, pneumonia, TB, and dysentery and other gastrointestinal disorders.

2. It undermines confidence in the states "custodial function"; that is, by failing to protect citizens from disease, the state's legitimacy can be undermined in the eyes of the public.

3. Disease can undermine the economic foundation provided by the state. Economies are adversely affected by a loss of workforce, and on a large scale such as that of AIDS in Africa, already poor states face billions in productivity loss and in healthcare infrastructure.

4. It can deeply affect a state's morale, functioning, and psyche. The authors noted that the Ebola outbreak in Uganda led the

people in the area to completely withdraw from the outside world. This in turn limits knowledge about the patterns and spread of the disease.

5. It can sharply undermine regional stability by undercutting defense force capabilities.

6. Finally, the strategic dimension of disease cannot be overlooked. This refers specifically to the use of disease as a weapon for military or terrorist purposes. The authors observed that:

> *the result (of an attack on an unprotected population) would be a massive, largely simultaneous outbreak of disease after an incubation period of only a few days. This would not only cause widespread casualties and panic, but also severely strain and possibly collapse entire public health and response capacities.*

In the current era, we fight a new battle against infectious diseases. It is not clear who will win. The diseases we fight today are not the same as the diseases we dealt with a hundred or a thousand years ago. As the authors noted, current forms of TB bear little resemblance of TB in the past century, becoming increasingly resistant to intervention and requiring daily monitoring of patients. In this battle, we fight an enemy who is capable of reproducing billions of times in one human generation—and there are thousands of different kinds of viruses among the enemy combatants. For all of our medicines and technologies, it is we who are at the disadvantage.

To look at the relationship between security and disease, we can consider the harsh lessons of AIDS. Garrett (2005), focusing on AIDS, described the Black Death as a cautionary tale. The Black Plague, raging in Europe from 1347 to 1352, utterly and irrevocably led to the redrawing of Europe by the time it had passed. By 1420 the European population was only one-third of what it had been in 1320. The Plague ushered out the Middle Ages and set the stage for the Protestant Reformation. Yet, in terms of sheer numbers, the AIDS epidemic has already surpassed the Black Death in total people killed. It has afflicted about 40 million people, killed about 20 million, and left 12 million orphans.

One of the consequences of AIDS is the predatory treatment of the orphans of AIDS. As Garrett noted (p. 47), prostitution is the crime that seems to have benefitted the most from AIDS:

> *There is striking evidence that orphaned girls as young as ten or eleven years are being forced by adult caretakers into lives of prostitution. Often described as a "victimless crime," prostitution is overlooked in many databases on the fate of children orphaned by*

HIV, but it is apparent that these girls are, themselves, the victims, as they are compelled into sexual activity with adult men, in many cases two or three decades their seniors, and are more likely to become HIV-positive than their non-orphan peers.

Garrett (2005, p. 55) concludes with the following warning:

Today, more than ever before, threats are interrelated and a threat to one is a threat to all. The mutual vulnerability of weak and strong has never been clearer . . . the security of the most affluent state can be held hostage to the ability of the poorest state to contain an emerging disease. Imagining the future shape of our modern pandemic, some two or three wave lengths ahead, is exceedingly difficult. If no effective vaccine or cure is found within the next twenty years, areas of the world that are now witnessing explosive epidemics, or are in their second or third waves of AIDS epidemics, may well be more deeply altered than Europe was following the Black Death. In Africa, for example, there are many features in place that mirror pre-plague Europe, including an enormous surplus of unskilled labor, lack of clear property rights for the bulk of the population, domination by tiny social elites, widespread warfare waged both by state and mercenary forces, and transition from dispersed agrarian to disastrously urbanized societies. Each of these factors was radically altered by the Black Death, and could well be reshaped by HIV.

Peterson and Shellman (2006) found that the prevalence of AIDS is significantly related to human rights abuses. This relationship holds when controls for urbanization and ethnic fractionalization are included in the model. The authors were interested primarily in the indirect effects of AIDS on violence through its effects on social, political, and economic breakdown. The authors looked at violence, civil conflict intensity and human rights abuses, and found that AIDS, damaged its major institutions. Moreover, both AIDS and institutional breakdown are reciprocally related to each other: AIDS increases institutional breakdown, which in turn contributes to heightened levels of AIDS. AIDS also emerged as a strong predictor of itself—increases in AIDS contributed to further increases.

AIDS, with its high rate of lethality, already the worst epidemic in human history, is a cautionary tale for the future. We are already well inside the "third wave" of diseases. A fourth wave—the onset of the next round of emergent and mutated re-emergent diseases—might occur on a warmed planet with severely eroded resources, where the vast majority of the population lives in crowded "megacity" urban settings facing deep security problems, and where medicines have lost much of their potency. The megacity and megadelta setting will be the home of 80% of the human population by 2050, with large tracts of urban poverty in zones, called periurban areas, ringing the city but outside of its security protection and sewer and water services. If one wanted to create a social and physical setting propitious for the spread of disease, one could not do better than the megacities rapidly growing in the current era—particularly in the poorest of countries—and anticipated to be the dominant form of corporate governance by the end of the century (see Chapters 7 and 8 for an extended discussion of megacities).

As we develop our understanding of diseases and their security consequences in a global warming environment, we comprehend their importance as a threat. The environments that we face and the ecologies we are developing for ourselves, even without global warming, are favorable for the emergence of pathogens, either in new forms or for existing pathogens, in more virulent forms. Add global warming and these problems become much more intense and complex—almost all megacities reside on deltas scant feet above sea level and will likely be facing extensive flooding after the midpoint of the century from rising seas. Will such areas, facing global warming, even be able to field a criminal justice system? How will even the most basic of security provisions be possible? The security threats are deep and forbidding. Clearly, this is an area where urban planning efforts will be important.

Endnotes

1. For instance, see "Is climate change already happening?" http://earthtosky. org/climate-change-categories?tmpl=component&id=39; "Physical and economic consequences of climate change in Europe." Retrieved June 12, 2013 at http://www.pnas.org/content/108/7/2678.long.
2. "National Intelligence Estimate: Global Infectious Disease Threat and its Implications for the United States." Retrieved June 16, 2013 at http://www. cfr.org/public-health-threats-and-pandemics/national-intelligence-estimate-global-infectious-disease-threat-its-implications-united-states/p18334.
3. "Mapping of poverty and likely zoonoses hotspots." Retrieved June 15, 2013 at http://www.ilri.org/node/1244.
4. "The Livestock revolution." Retrieved January 12, 2013 at http://www.fao.org/ wairdocs/lead/x6115e/x6115e03.htm.
5. Perhaps not that occasional. It is estimated that about 60 percent of the human population worldwide is infected by at least one parasite. "How many different species of human parasites are there?" Retrieved January 10, 2013 at http:// curezone.com/faq/q.asp?a=2971,999&q=188; Retrieved January 10, 2013 at "Parasites." www.curezone.com/faq/q.asp?a=4,107,999&q=186.

6. Op. Cit. "How many different species of human parasites are there?".
7. "How Many Different Species of Bacteria, Parasites, and Microorganisms Live In or On the Human Body?" Retrieved January 13, 2013 at http://www.bigsiteofamazingfacts.com/how-many-different-species-of-bacteria-parasites-and-microorganisms-live-in-or-on-the-human-body.
8. "13 Animal-to-Human Diseases Kill 2.2 Million People Each Year." Retrieved January 14, 2013 at http://www.livescience.com/21426-global-zoonoses-diseases-hotspots.html.
9. "Mapping of poverty and likely zoonoses hotspots." Retrieved January 15, 2013 at http://www.ilri.org/node/1244.
10. "The Deadly Dozen." Retrieved January 16, 2013 at http://www.wcs.org/news-and-features-main/deadly-dozen.aspx.
11. "Malaria." Retrieved January 16, 2013 at http://en.wikipedia.org/wiki/Malaria.
12. "Global Warming Wilts Malaria." Retrieved January 16, 2013 at http://www.scientificamerican.com/article.cfm?id=global-warming-wilts-malaria.
13. "Introduction to Emerging and Reemerging Infectious Diseases." Retrieved February 19, 2013 at http://nrse4600group9.wordpress.com/2013/02/15/introduction-to-emerging-and-reemerging-infectious-diseases/.
14. "Spanish Flu." Retrieved February 14, 2013 at http://en.wikipedia.org/wiki/Spanish_flu.
15. See "Infectious Diseases and U.S. National Security." Retrieved February 25, 2013 at http://www.currentintelligence.net/features/2010/7/28/infectious-diseases-and-us-national-security.html.
16. Ibid.
17. Ibid.

6

THE PROBLEMS OF WATER

Clete asked, "Do you remember this area before it became desert?"

Ruth thought for a moment. "I haven't thought about that in a long time. Yep, I remember. I suppose you want to hear about it. Well, it wasn't all that pretty then. I got the taste for the big mountains from Beto, and coming back to this flat place always bugged me. But we would take trips over to the Niobrara. That was really pretty, or down to the Platte. Platte's gone now. The sandhill cranes used to use it flying from Canada to Mexico. They made so much noise in the spring that you couldn't hear yourself think. People came from all over to see them. They're long gone, though. They went away with the river. Haven't seen a crane in 40 years. Platte's just a dry bone. Niobrara is wet three seasons. A lot of the rivers that came out of the West, they're gone."

Clete: "So all the farming went away after that."

Ruth: "No, it was already almost gone. There used to be a huge underground lake here, the Ogallala. They used it a lot, especially after it started getting warmer in the summers. Finally they drank it all up. All the way down to Texas, over to Colorado, it's gone. All that dirt farmland, it just turned to dust, and we got the Great Dust Desert. And some nasty windstorms."

Clete: "Did a lot of people live here?"

Ruth: "No, there never were a lot of people. Just a few, but enough to make all this feel like it was lived in. You can still see a lot of busted-up, old, abandoned houses here and there. You probably passed a few coming in."

Clete: "How about the cattle shoots?"

Ruth: "Oh, that was just awful. We had these huge ranches, cattle stomping around on their own crap and mud, thousands of head. Then it got dry and stayed dry. Ranchers tried to sell them but could not sell them fast enough. Finally, they took the ones left and shot 'em all. Didn't even bury them. Gas was too expensive by then to spend it on a backhoe. You can still see the bones piled up here and there, those that weren't drug off by the coywolves and wild pigs."

Good for them, Clete thought. At least something besides the lizards and red widows can live here. He said, "What was the worst thing about the water going away?"

Ruth: "You mean besides killing the land? No, I'll tell you. The sky here changed color. It's a different sky now. It is a lot brighter at night. More stars. Darker, too. In some ways, it's prettier today, but it's just wrong. When you look up at the sky, you know that it's not your world. It's like we don't belong anymore. We're just strangers here. Just passing through."

Water is astonishingly abundant in the world. Most of the surface of the planet is covered with it. It is the source of life; the origins of life itself on planet Earth are traced to the ancient seas. Water, in freshwater form, is a valued resource; humans must take in water more frequently than food in order to survive. The foundations of civilization, from Ancient Egypt to the current day, have depended upon access to abundant sources of fresh water for agriculture, without which sedentary lifestyles would be impossible. Indeed, if asked what humans are primarily made of, the answer would be water. Human males average 60% water, while females are at approximately 55% water. It has been said that the human body carries in its interior the stuff of the oceans from the dawn of the Proterozoic era, when life emerged approximately two and a half billion years ago.

Water is also a resource that appears to be affected in myriad ways by global warming. In the most general sense, a globally warmer planet will absorb more water into the air. A warmer planet is a wetter planet, all else being equal. More water also means more weather, more turbulence. Importantly, that increase will not be evenly dispersed, either geographically or seasonally. Global warming emerges as one more stressor on an already stressed environmental setting. In this chapter, we will explore some of those ways warming will affect the hydrology of different areas. Specifically, we will look at hurricanes, coastal sea-rise, drought, and water shortages. Each one of these is affected by global warming.

Water: The Fist of Climate Change

Water is the fist of climate change. We have emerged as an agrarian species, dependent on riparian basins for survival, on the economic opportunities provided by coastal cities, and in more recent times, on underground aquifers. All are in jeopardy. The hydrological challenges portended by climate change may be among the most severe of its consequences. Like a fist, they will likely hit us hard, and if the US Navy Research is correct, they are arriving on a schedule several decades faster than climate change researchers had anticipated. To the point—they are already here.

Many analysts are looking at global warming today with an eye toward the conflicts that water issues can create. The National Intelligence Assessment of global water security in 2012 warned of coming shortages, regional instabilities, conflict, and terrorism, particularly beyond the next 10 years. Those concerns are in Information Box 6.1.

Information Box 6.1 National Intelligence Assessment of Global Water Security

Global demand and supply Between now and 2040, global demand for fresh water will increase, but the supply of fresh water will not keep pace with demand absent more effective management of water resources. A major international study finds that annual global water requirements will reach 6,900 billion cubic meters (bcm) in 2030, 40% above current sustainable water supplies. Climate change will cause water shortages in many areas of the world.

River runoff ... by midcentury, annual river runoff and water availability will increase by 20-40% at high latitudes and in some wet tropical areas, and decrease by 10-30% over some dry regions at mid-latitudes and in the dry tropics, some of which are presently water-stressed areas.

Sea levels During the next few decades rising sea levels and deteriorating coastal buffers will amplify the destructive power of coastal storms, including surges and heavy precipitation. At times water flows will be severe enough to overwhelm the water control infrastructures of even developed countries, including the United States.

Drinking water From both aquifers and surface water resources almost certainly will further decline in many areas of the developing world, as water quality decreases from salt-water intrusion and industrial, biofuel, agricultural, and sanitation processes.

Global instability and risk of state failure During the next 10 years, many countries important to the United States will almost certainly experience water problems— shortages, poor water quality, or floods—that will contribute to the risk of instability and state failure, and increase regional tensions. Additionally, states will focus on addressing internal water-related social disruptions which will distract them from working with the United States on important policy objectives.

Water as a weapon The use of water as a weapon will become more common during the next 10 years with more powerful upstream nations impeding or cutting off downstream flow. Water will also be used within states to pressure populations and suppress separatist elements.

Water Terrorism Physical infrastructure, including dams, has been used as convenient and high-publicity targets by extremists, terrorists, and rogue states threatening substantial harm and will become more likely beyond the next 10 years.

There are also concerns that water conflicts are growing. The Pacific Institute has expressed their concerns over what appears to be a substantial rise in water-caused violence, according to an article reviewing water violence and interviewing its president, Peter Gleick:[1]

The Pacific Institute, which studies issues of water and global security, found a fourfold increase in violent confrontations over water over the last decade. "I think the risk of conflicts over water is growing—not shrinking—because of increased competition, because of bad management and, ultimately, because of the impacts of climate change," said Peter Gleick, president of the Pacific Institute.

The concern of substance is that water issues are already emergent and substantial. They are happening across the globe, and they are affecting all elements of hydrological studies, from violent storm intensification to global sea-rise and salinization of fresh water to increased water shortages, drought, and desertification today. These are not concerns of the future. Without the threat of climate change they were urgent. With climate change accelerants added, they provide for a bleak forecast. They will all be discussed in detail in this chapter.

Big Water and Big Winds

Big water and big winds are the marks of large hurricanes, cyclones, and typhoons: Big, cyclonic windstorms are their most recognizable, most notable characteristic, but their most lethal is big water, in the form of tidal surges. Large cyclonic storms, by any name, are to natural disasters as airplane hijackings are to terrorism: They are the sine qua non for high-profile visibility. Will they play a larger, more lethal role on a warmer planet, one with ocean waters warm enough to provide more fuel?

Cyclonic storms are difficult to predictively model for global warming research: On the one hand, the increases in temperature globally result in more moisture in the air, which research suggests will intensify storms of all kinds, and also warm the ocean water, the basic fuel of cyclones.

The Atlantic Basin seems to be showing a pattern of more severe hurricanes. Research has shown that the number of category four and five hurricanes, which represent the most severe classes of hurricane, has increased significantly since 1980, though the average number of hurricanes has remained about the same (see Curry, 2010). Shifting global and regional patterns of cool and warm water from warming on the ocean currents may offset this tendency, however, at the same time fundamentally realigning hurricane patterns in the region. The presence of El Niño and La Niña conditions, for instance, strongly influences hurricane formation, and factors affecting those two global weather patterns are important for understanding hurricane activity. There is also substantial variation in hurricane activity that may not be accounted for by the warmth of ocean water alone. Bogen, Fischer, and Jones (2010) found that many hurricanes actually intensify when they move over cooler water and that more severe hurricanes may actually intensify more. There is still much about cyclonic storms that we have to learn.

Hurricane Katrina

Often, when severe twenty-first century hurricanes are discussed, Hurricane Katrina is mentioned. Katrina was unusually severe in its impact, setting in rapid motion a series of events that both inundated New Orleans and brought storm surge devastation in the coastal areas to the East of New Orleans. The Wikipedia entry summarizing the impact of Katrina is presented in Information Box 6.2.[2]

Following Katrina, a common speculation was "Did Global Warming Cause Katrina?" This is a challenging question, because storms of similar intensity have struck the mainland United States previously and others have been more severe than Katrina. The short answer is that this is what we would predict if global warming were exerting its influence.[3] This is a quite unsatisfactory answer, though. As has been noted, the New Orleans region in the current era is particularly vulnerable to significant weather

Information Box 6.2 Hurricane Katrina: An Overview

Hurricane Katrina was the deadliest and most destructive Atlantic hurricane of the 2005 Atlantic hurricane season. It is the costliest natural disaster, as well as one of the five deadliest hurricanes, in the history of the United States. Among recorded Atlantic hurricanes, it was the sixth strongest overall. At least 1,836 people died in the actual hurricane and in the subsequent floods, making it the deadliest US hurricane since the 1928 Okeechobee hurricane; total property damage was estimated at $81 billion (2005 USD), nearly triple the damage wrought by Hurricane Andrew in 1992.

On August 29, Katrina's storm surge caused 53 different levee breaches in greater New Orleans, submerging eighty percent of the city. A June 2007 report by the American Society of Civil Engineers indicated that two-thirds of the flooding were caused by the multiple failures of the city's floodwalls. Not mentioned were the flood gates that were not closed. The storm surge also devastated the coasts of Mississippi and Alabama.

The confirmed death toll (total of direct and indirect deaths) is 1,836, mainly from Louisiana (1,577) and Mississippi (238). However, 135 people remain categorized as missing in Louisiana, and many of the deaths are indirect, but it is almost impossible to determine the exact cause of some of the fatalities.

Source: Hurricane Katrina. Retrieved July 16, 2013 at http://en.wikipedia.org/wiki/Hurricane_Katrina.

events due to "expansive lowlands (particularly in the New Orleans area), wetland loss, deforestation, rapid development, large populations of the poor, and a heavy concentration of industry."[4] It was a disaster waiting to happen.

The summer and fall of the following year 2006, moreover, was among the lowest recorded years for hurricane activity in the Atlantic basin, with no hurricanes striking the US mainland. Should we then conclude that this is what we would predict if global warming was just an anti-American scientist's end-of-days fantasy? Probably the best perspective is that we do not have the skills to relate global weather patterns to singular events, however dramatic. The evidence for global warming and consequences of global warming for cyclonic storms in the Atlantic basin, at this point in our research, have to come from the accumulation and analysis of multiple data points to build a strong statistical argument. An outlier, however dramatic, does not in itself make a theory. We must look for patterns, not single events.

Katrina and Crime

Katrina is a particularly compelling story. Citizens in the United States are infrequent witnesses of the infrastructural destruction of a major American city and the ensuing chaos and loss of governmental control. One of the lessons of Katrina, though one not frequently noted, is the extent to which the routine operation of local criminal justice systems are dependent on the municipal infrastructure. When that infrastructure fails, so does the criminal justice system. We will discuss this in detail here. The importance of this issue increases, as we will see in later chapters when coastal cities face the damage of rising seas and find they must compete for control against geographically fluid organized crime and gang control.

The collapse of the criminal justice system in New Orleans following Katrina has been widely documented (see Garrett & Tetlow, 2006). Garrett and Tetlow's narrative is particularly compelling for its record of the extent of the collapse. The level of New Orleans crime after Katrina is challenging to measure; in the period immediately following Katrina the city population dropped and the capacity to measure crime was severely hampered by reporting problems. For instance, New Orleans in 2005 had 200 homicides, for a population of about 343,000 residents. By way of comparison, Omaha, with a larger population of approximately 409,000, experiences less than one tenth as many, with about 30-35 annual homicides. In the week following Katrina, only four homicides occurred, which is not a particularly high number. However, the population had dropped substantially, and the ability to correctly identify homicides, in the face of a severely challenged justice system, may have suffered.

In the week following Katrina, the president ordered federal troops to assist in security and clean-up for New Orleans. The troops were assigned under USNORTHCOM, a military command created by President Bush to extend military authority over the continental United States. USNORTHCOM has served primarily as a first responder and as a center for communications, facilitating command and control efforts in the event of major disasters such as Katrina. However, USNORTHCOM was prohibited from making arrests: Soldiers carried rifles, but the weapons were not loaded.

Garrett and Tetlow described the city after Katrina as in a state of "undeclared martial law." After the governor ordered the evacuation of the city, military checkpoints were set up at major intersections to stop and check all traffic. The involvement of the US military was much more extensive and varied than this, however. Information Box 6.3 below, cited in the US Army website, describes

Information Box 6.3 The Army Response to Hurricane Katrina: Excerpts

The 319th Airborne Field Artillery was assigned to fix the airport. Working with airport staff, the 319th augmented the existing departure process and brought order and direction by taking responsibility for passenger manifests and security screening. Within 12 hours, 9,000 people had been evacuated through the airport. The 3rd Brigade of the 82nd Airborne worked with FEMA in search and rescue operations, providing needed manpower, equipment and standardized maps. The 56th Signal Battalion was tasked to connect commercial communications to the military communications network. The 14th Combat Support Hospital set up in downtown New Orleans to treat the injured. The 21st Chemical Company decontaminated 400 personnel, 783 vehicles, and 73 boats, and helped decontaminate both Charity and Touro hospitals. When FEMA requested that DOD take over logistics, the 13th Corps Support Command deployed from Fort Hood. Soldiers from the 82nd Airborne evacuated the Super Dome and the Convention Center, where thousands of citizens had fled for refuge when they were flooded out of their houses. The paratroopers also joined National Guard units patrolling the streets to keep order in the city.

The Army Corps of Engineers (COE) began their own operations with a three-pronged attack: drain New Orleans, mobilize military and contracting resources to close the levee breaches, and repair the pumps that keep New Orleans dry. The Engineers also helped deliver food and water. By September 2, they had delivered 1.9 million MREs, 6.7 million liters of water and 1.7 million pounds of ice. As the Title 10 troops began to draw down, the Engineers began to gear up operations: by September 15, de-water operations were 60% complete. By the end of the month, COE contractors had removed 4.3 million cubic yards of debris in Louisiana and Mississippi, carted off 120 million tons of trash, and disposed of 36 million pounds of rotting meat. By October 11, New Orleans was dry.

Source: The Army response to Hurricane Katrina. Retrieved July 18, 2013 at http://www.army.mil/article/45029/The_Army_response_to_Hurricane_Katrina/.

the various activities carried out with the use of military support:[5] It provides a sense of the extent to which a city, even in the relatively prosperous United States, loses functionality when faced with a disaster. One can see that the broad range of infrastructural problems is not limited to security. Sewer systems had to be repaired and sewage disposed of. Fresh water and food had to be provided. Rotting meat was removed—disease is always a significant possibility after catastrophe. Through all this, we see the extent to which basic municipal services, not only security, are tied to physical infrastructure. In the megacities developing across the planet today, this structure is not in place for much of their populations.

The Criminal Justice System Damage

The New Orleans Jail was damaged and uninhabitable, with the lower levels flooded and the generators having been destroyed by the flooding. The nearly 8,000 prisoners housed in the jail were evacuated in the week after Katrina, and eventually transferred to 34 facilities across Louisiana. A week after the storm, police officers recognized that they could not hold prisoners, and simply stopped making arrests. Shortly after, though, a temporary jail was set up in the Greyhound bus station, built by Angola prisoner trustees. The authors described the collapse of the criminal justice system in the following Information Box 6.4.[6]

Information Box 6.4 Katrina and the Collapse of the Criminal Justice System

Due to this institutional collapse, of the approximately 8,000 inmates transferred from New Orleans throughout the state of Louisiana, thousands served illegal sentences, thousands were released only after six months, and thousands still faced charges but have yet to see a lawyer in more than six months, and many still had not seen a lawyer a year after Katrina struck. Prosecutors worked out of their houses and in makeshift settings against a huge and growing backlog of cases. Even well after Katrina, the significant loss of tax base in New Orleans led to a significant loss of prosecutorial staff, further contributing to long-term constitutional problems. Defense counsel faced equally grave problems, often losing track altogether of defendants. Many indigent defendants were lost in the revamped emergency system. Interestingly, in spite of the substantial problems faced by the criminal justice system, there was no evidence of a crime wave or explosion of criminal activity following Katrina. There were a number of crimes specifically associated with Katrina; looting was an issue, in part a consequence of the destruction of food sources and the widespread need for basic commodities for survival. The police also faced significant issues: many simply abandoned their work. Also, four police officers were charged, five years after Katrina, with firing without provocation on six citizens on the Danziger bridge, two of whom died. None of the citizens were engaged in criminal activity.

Source: Katrina: The crime that shocked the world. Retrieved January 19, 2013 at http://www.independent.co.uk/news/world/americas/katrina-the-crime-thatshocked-the-world-2026859.html.

Katrina Migration and Crime in Destination Cities

Katrina provided some insight into the profound problems associated with migration and relocation following a major US natural disaster. In the wake of Katrina, Houston took in approximately 150,000 homeless evacuees. They were associated with a surge in crime in the city, as both criminals and as victims. Montaldo[7] described the surge in crime as follows:

> Since opening its doors to the evacuee's Houston has experienced a 5.8 percent increase in violent crime in the past 11 months. The rise in crime was predictable as the Houston population increased almost overnight changing the ratio of police officers per thousand Houstonians to 1.9 compared to 2.3 before Katrina, already down from the national average of 2.8. Calls to the police department jumped from an average of five calls on hold before Katrina to averaging 40-plus after the storm. "We used to have five calls holding, then it was 30, 40, 50, 60 calls holding or left over," said Officer John M. Trevino of the 19th District.

Montaldo considered that many of New Orleans' evacuees were good citizens, sought employment, and contributed to the city in a variety of positive ways. However, some of them were less desirable. Subsequent research, together with police records, has shown that some violent crime followed the relocation of residents to receiving cities. Montaldo observed that, in Houston, eight suspects who were evacuees were linked to nine homicides, that there was a "noticeable rise in crime among youth," public schools were experiencing fights between evacuees and residents, that parents were concerned over retaliatory crime and gangs, and that evacuees were victims or suspects in about 20% of the homicides, about double their population percentage.

One of the issues raised was whether evacuees should have been screened for criminal histories and current criminal activity. Many criminally involved individuals, as well as many gang members, relocated from New Orleans to Houston. This also contributed to a strain in city resources across the justice system, as well as additional expense associated with housing assistance and related funding for many of the evacuees. Total criminal justice system costs were around $18 million. Houston also lost about $29 million for housing assistance. After the first year post-Katrina, about two-thirds of the evacuees still required governmental assistance.

Hussey, Nikolsko-Rzhevskyy, and Pacurar (2011)[8] also noted a significant increase in crime in the receiving cities. They used an econometric model to assess crimes associated with Katrina evacuees and found substantial crime increases. The authors noted that:

> *immigration of Katrina evacuees led to a more than 13 percent increase in murder and non-negligent manslaughter, an almost 3 percent increase in robbery, and a 4.1 percent increase in motor vehicle theft. We also examine Houston, TX, home to a large number of comparatively more disadvantaged evacuees, and find dramatic increases in murder (27 percent) and aggravated assault (28 percent) coupled with increases in illegal possession of weapons (32 percent) and arson (41 percent) in areas lived by evacuees.*

Not all criminologists support the idea that evacuees were responsible for crime increases in the receiving cities. Vergano, a columnist with *USA Today*, interviewed Sean Varano about his work on overall impact of Katrina. He had found that increases in crime in the receiving cities was modest. His discussion of Katrina is presented in Information Box 6.5.[9]

The above analyses do not tend to support each other. Which is correct? Our inclination is that those showing an increase in crime are likely the most accurate, in that they have more sophisticated methodologies. The methodologies of both allowed for a garden variety of problems that trend inspections alone could not address.

Information Box 6.5 Crime Among New Orleans Evacuees

Houston received about 240,000 evacuees (a 7% population increase); San Antonio, about 30,000 (a 3% increase); and Phoenix, about 3,000 (less than a 0.5% increase). The cities were selected for the study due to their spread of evacuee impact. "Public officials and news reports suggested a criminal class was arriving in these places," Varano says. "After welcoming evacuees, Houston handles spike in crime," was a 2006 headline in The Washington Post.

"But if there was any effect, it was a modest one," Varano says, after his group weighed police crime data from the three cities to look for trends for each crime from 2004 to 2006. The study found a slight rise in murder and robbery in Houston, when adjusted for the long-term crime patterns, but no increase in other crimes (and suggested drops in rape and aggravated assaults); no effect at all in San Antonio; and another slight statistical rise in the murder rate in Phoenix. "Any increase in murder is intolerable," Varano says, but a lack of increase in crimes such as car theft and robbery, where economic motives most clearly would tempt so many displaced people, argues against a crime wave driven by evacuees, he says.

Meanwhile, "Many communities across the United States . . . also reported increases in violent crime between 2004 and 2006," notes the study, including a 30% increase in aggravated assault in cities such as Baltimore and Detroit.

Source: Report: No crime wave among Hurricane Katrina evacuees. Retrieved July 28, 2013 at http://www.usatoday.com/tech/science/columnist/vergano/2010-02-12-hurricane-katrina-crime_N.htm.

Superstorm Sandy

Katrina, however, was not the only signature outlier that has been linked to global warming in the popular media. Another storm seven years later, in 2012, was also associated with global warming. Aspects of the consequences of this storm could be more closely tied to climate change. That storm was Superstorm Sandy, so named because it was an event in which a hurricane, already named Sandy, joined with a Nor'easter to become a much more mammoth weather event. Wikipedia describes Sandy as follows:

> *Hurricane Sandy was ... the second-costliest hurricane in United States history. Sandy was a Category 3 storm at its peak intensity when it made landfall in Cuba. While it was a Category 2 storm off the coast of the Northeastern United States, the storm became the largest Atlantic hurricane on record [as measured by diameter, with winds spanning 1,100 miles (1,800 km)]. Estimates as of June 2013 assess damage to have been over $68 billion (2013 USD), a total surpassed only by Hurricane Katrina. At least 286 people were killed along the path of the storm in seven countries.*

The most devastating aspect of Superstorm Sandy was the storm surge. It was the highest ever recorded in Lower Manhattan, with the water level up to 13.88 feet above the average of the lowest low tide. The previous record was set in 1960 from Hurricane Donna (Freedman, 2012). Implicated in the intensity of the surge was the already higher levels of ocean water associated with global sea-rise generally, and with sea-rise intensification effects of the Northeast Coast. Research suggests that the sea-rise along the Eastern Seaboard is already about 15 inches above its level in 1850, a substantial increase and one that intensifies the impact of any storm that further adds to sea-rise. In this instance, Superstorm Sandy may have blown into New York on an ocean level about 15 inches higher than historic averages, potentiating its catastrophic effects. We will talk more about coastal flooding in a separate section later in this chapter.

In the wake of Superstorm Sandy, anecdotal reports described instances of looting, burglary, and robbery. These are media related reports that described instances of crime. Information Box 6.6 discusses some of these instances:[10]

That the storm provided opportunities for crime is well established. But did it lead to a crime wave? For instance, in the aftermath of Sandy, crime was reported to have dropped sharply. The New York City Police Department (NYPD) noted that homicides dropped 86% for the five days after Sandy when compared to 2011 statistics.

Information Box 6.6 Superstorm Sandy and Crime: A Routine Activities Perspective

In reports of crime following Superstorm Sandy, Lu noted that

> *Since Sandy made landfall last week, affected areas in New York and New Jersey, among other places, have been plagued with burglaries, street muggings, fights, and other crimes, reports the New York Post.*
>
> *Things have gotten so bad that police on Manhattan's Lower East Side are warning residents not to use the flashlight apps on their smartphones—for fear that the light will attract thieves and other low-lifes.*
>
> *...criminals have been lurking around ATM machines and robbing people taking out emergency money. Burglars are also waiting outside homes, knowing that cash and a well-supplied home is probably waiting. People are even pulling guns on each other in gas lines, CBS News reports.*
>
> *Along with individual victims, businesses have also been targeted by looters. While the looting of supplies like water and food may make some sense during a natural disaster, some of the reports of looting are just plain ridiculous. In one case, twin brothers allegedly stole a U-Haul truck and rammed it into a motorcycle dealership, with the apparent intent of loading up the truck with stolen motorcycles, reports the Post.*

Other crimes were associated with Superstorm Sandy. Price gouging, illegal in New York, was widely reported, for instance, "some people were selling gas on Craigslist for up to $20 a gallon." Some opportunists posed as FEMA workers or as utility crew workers to gain entry to homes in order to burglarize them. Businesses abandoned in anticipation of the hurricane were particularly vulnerable, for instance, in the Queens area, bandits broke into a drugstore and stole "thousands of pharmaceutical items."

Source: Superstorm Sandy Leads to Wave of Crime. Retrieved July 30, 2013 at http://blogs.findlaw.com/blotter/2012/11/super-storm-sandy-leads-to-wave-ofcrime.html.

Robberies also dropped 30%, assaults were down by 31%, and larceny was down 48%. Burglaries alone defied this trend, and instead crept up 3% compared to the same five days the previous year.[11]

There are two lessons that apply to Sandy from this brief review. The first is that the notion of looking at disasters from an aggregate crime perspective is likely to mislead. Rather, what disasters seem to do is rearrange the routine behaviors of people, changing the opportunity/crime equation according to highly specific local factors. Some affected areas may experience increases in crime activity; others may enjoy decreases.

The crimes anecdotally described in news outlets are consistent with routine activities. This might seem inconsistent with routine activities, since one associates weather events with disruptions of routines, not their continuity. However, one can argue that people in substantial numbers engage in predictable behaviors following a hurricane, and that some individuals will view those predictable behaviors as opportunities for crime. For instance, people are routinely advised to stock up on cash prior to a hurricane, in that banks and ATMs may not be available for an extended period after the disaster. Most people acquire money by going to their nearest ATMs, a predictable routine. Consequently, we are more likely to see robberies at ATMs as opportunists recognize this criminal opportunity. Similarly, hurricane businesses know that people stock up on sheets of plywood prior to a storm; this contributes to price gouging by lumber companies when long lines of customers form at their businesses.

The second lesson is that disasters do not inevitably bring out the worst in people. Waldman, discussing research on post-disaster social practices, suggested that the opposite may be true: Disaster victims tend to become communal, more altruistic, and more focused on self-help, aiding others than they are during normal day-to-day routines:[12]

> Researchers in disaster science have again and again debunked the idea that catastrophe causes social breakdown and releases the ugliest parts of human nature. Research from the past several decades demonstrates, as one report put it, "that panic is not a problem in disasters; that rather than helplessly awaiting outside aid, members of the public behave proactively and pro-socially to assist one another; that community residents themselves perform many critical disaster tasks, such as searching for and rescuing victims; and that both social cohesiveness and informal mechanisms of social control increase during disasters, resulting in a lower incidence of deviant behavior." People become their best selves when crisis strikes.

The long-term crime consequences of Superstorm Sandy have not been assessed; it is still too recent. The crimes associated with Katrina, and in particular with the resettlement of victims, may not have surfaced at this time. It is also important to recognize that Katrina was a much more severe storm than Sandy in terms of sheer power, loss of life, and total insurance costs.

Sandy in Haiti

There is an additional dimension to storm-related disasters that we have not yet addressed, but one that is integral to the models used in this book. The impacts of storm disasters include both short- and long-term losses of renewable resources. Such losses hit poorer countries especially hard. An example of this kind of loss is what Haiti experienced after the 2011 hurricane season. Kolbe, Puccio, and Muggah (2012), assessing the aftermath of Sandy and subsequent November (2011) flooding, noted that Haiti experienced substantial loss of crops and other food resources. The result of this was a looming food crisis, in which basic needs would be unmet. The authors made the following observations:

1. Rural households in the surveyed areas of Haiti's Ouest, Nord and Grand'Anse departments experienced severe food shortages after tropical storms hit Haiti during October and November 2012. Nearly 70% of households experienced moderate or severe hunger as measured by the USDA Food Security Scale.

2. Following the last round of tropical storms, more than two thirds (68.3%) of surveyed households lost crops from their fields. Owing to differences in crop varieties and the physical geography of farming land, this was more common in the Grand'Anse and Ouest (72.5%) than in the Nord (40.1%).

3. Postdisaster water issues are pervasive. Less than 10% of surveyed households were drinking treated water in the week after the storm. This is in addition to the fact that overflowing latrines (reported by 40% of households) may have contaminated the home's water supply.

Haiti may be more representative of the rest of the world than the United States; it, like much of the world, is heavily dependent on a local agrarian economy, with a great deal of its food supplies coming from small or personal plots of land, and water is a challenged and limited resource. Sandy inflicted significant strains on local economies: 89% of the surveyed population noted damage or loss of their cooking area, 86% noted loss of food they had planned on eating in the current month, 77% noted losses of tools for farming, 72% identified losses in crops in the field, and 80% cited losses of seeds, tubers, and roots for replanting.

Haiti, in other words, is a country where we see set in motion the scarcities that drive Homer-Dixon's model. Regardless of the well-being, altruism, or communal sentiments of the victims of the storm, the presence of these scarcities presents a crisis that they alone cannot address. The successful response to this magnitude of a natural disaster is a coordinated and effective effort from both their own government and the international community. This "demands the will of international donors, NGOs, indigenous community associations, and the Haitian government to act—rather than react—to prevent the coming food crisis" (Kolbe et al., 2012, p. 11).

Sea-Rise and Coastal Flooding

Sea-rise and coastal flooding are central concerns of global warming. Stemming from melting ice at the poles and Greenland, from the thermal expansion of ocean water, and augmented in some regions by land subsidence, sea-rise is ongoing, relentless, and inexorable. Research examining long-term patterns shows significant sea-rise globally and often at levels much higher than most would have thought. An introduction to the measurement of ocean elevations is discussed in Information Box 6.7 titled "Sea-Rise Measurement."[13] The graph provided in the information box from Church et al. (2008) shows the global mean sea level since 1870. It shows a remarkable overall rise of approximately 210 millimeters, or about 8.27 inches.

Further, the East Coast of the United States, from Cape Hatteras to Boston, is recognized as a hot spot. As Phillips (2012) noted,

> *Asbury Sallenger, an oceanographer at the USGS in St Petersburg, Florida, and his colleagues published their report today in Nature Climate Change. They analysed tide-gauge records from around North America from between 1950 and 2009, and found that the rates of sea-level rise along the northern half of the eastern seaboard—from Cape Hatteras, North Carolina, to Boston, Massachusetts—are increasing three to four times faster than rates of sea-level rise globally.*

Sea-rise is more of a problem when combined with subsidence, which is the lowering of land formations. Because of subsidence, sea-rise will affect different regions quite differently. Consider the following observation from Cynthia Rosenzweig, a climate impacts expert at NASA Goddard Institute for Space Studies:[14]

> *On average, global sea level has risen about eight inches since 1880. So, the New York rate of sea level rise of nearly one foot is higher than the global average rate. In the United States, rates of change vary. For example, Grand Isle, Louisiana near New Orleans has seen sea level increase by 23 inches since 1947 whereas Seattle, Washington, has only seen about six inches over that same period. Local factors such as land subsidence are primarily responsible for the differences.*

When Hurricane Katrina lashed New Orleans, many people wondered if the intensity of the storm was related to global warming. The question lacks a clear answer, simply because statistical analyses are not good with single cases. However, the hurricane arrived in New Orleans on an ocean nearly two feet higher than it had been 75 years earlier, according to Rosenzweig.[15] Grand Isle is only 108 miles from New Orleans. The hand of global warming in the sea-rise on which the storm came in is clear, and its future for the region bleak.

Information Box 6.7 Sea-Rise Measurement: Analysis of Global Mean Sea Level

Because the behavior of sea level is such an important signal for tracking climate change, skeptics seize on the sea level record in an effort to cast doubt on this evidence. Sea level bounces up and down slightly from year to year so it's possible to cherry-pick data falsely suggesting the overall trend is flat, falling, or linear. You can try this yourself. Starting with two closely spaced data points on the graph below, lay a straight-edge between them and notice how for a short period of time you can create almost any slope you prefer, simply by being selective about what data points you use . . . The lesson? Always look at all the data; don't be fooled by selective presentations.

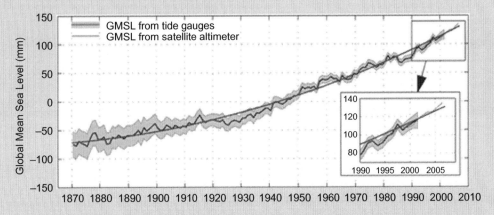

Tide gauges must take into account changes in the height of land itself caused by local geologic processes, a favorite distraction for skeptics to highlight. Not surprisingly, scientists measuring sea level with tide gauges are aware of and compensate for these factors. Confounding influences are accounted for in measurements, and while they leave some noise in the record, they cannot account for the observed upward trend.

Various technical criticisms are mounted against satellite altimeter measurements by skeptics. Indeed, deriving millimeter-level accuracy from orbit is a stunning technical feat, so it's not hard to understand why some people find such an accomplishment unbelievable. In point of fact, researchers demonstrate this height measurement technique's accuracy to be within 1 mm/year. Most importantly there is no form of residual error that could falsely produce the upward trend in observations.

As can be seen in an inset of the graph above, tide gauge and satellite altimeter measurements track each other with remarkable similarity. These two independent systems mutually support the observed trend in sea level. If an argument depends on skipping certain observations or emphasizes uncertainty while ignoring an obvious trend, that's a clue you're being steered as opposed to informed. Don't be mislead by only a carefully-selected portion of the available evidence being disclosed.

Current sea level rise is, after all, not exaggerated; in fact, the opposite case is more plausible. Observational data and changing conditions in such places as Greenland suggest if there's a real problem here it's underestimation of future sea level rise.

Source: How much is sea level rising? Retrieved August 7, 2013 at http://www.skepticalscience.com/sea-level-rise.htm.

Coastal flooding can be of two types. On the one hand, and as discussed in Katrina above, coastal flooding comes from storm surges associated with significant weather events; such events are immediate high risk events. On the other, coastal flooding can come about from ice meltoff and thermal expansion, and is a mid-to-long-term risk; it is currently low risk, but by 2050 will become more significant. Information Box 6.6 discusses sea level rise.

The issue of glacial meltoff from global warming is based on a relatively straightforward notion: Increases in temperatures worldwide will lead to greater melt-off of the world's significant glaciers, leading to a gradual rise in sea levels. To picture this, imagine that all the ice at Antarctica and Greenland melted. (The Arctic will not contribute since it is already floating on the ocean; Antarctica, on the other hand, holds about 90% of the world's fresh water, and will contribute significantly). Estimates put the sea level rise at about 215 feet, or 65 meters. This is a plausible risk, but it is also a long-term risk in the multi-century range.

How many people live in lowlands close to a coastline? A study reported in 2007 found that about 634 million people, about one-tenth of the world's population, live in a coastal setting within 30 feet of the elevation of the sea.[16] This number will skyrocket over the next 30 years, as discussed in Chapter 8. Yet, political resistance to global warming is obstructing planning, in spite of evidence that sea-rise may actually be increasing faster than anticipated.[17]

Most recently, it appears that researchers underestimated the rate of sea-rise. There is evidence that seas are rising quite a bit faster than anticipated: Researchers now suggest that the ocean on California could raise 5 feet by the end of the century, with similar increases in the New York seaboard area. This is of considerable interest to long-range coastal planners, who are advocating that coastal building should take into consideration the scenario of a 5 to 7 foot rise in coastal flooding. Unfortunately, some conservative legislators, who are opposed to the terminology of global warming, are arguing for planning in terms of current ocean levels.

The Eastern Seaboard "Hot Spot"

The Eastern Seaboard of the United States is particularly vulnerable to sea-rise associated with global warming. The area is susceptible to rise from melting ocean water, from thermal expansion factors, and for a tendency of water to "pile up" in the area.

Information Box 6.8 Global Warming Creates 600-Mile Flood "Hot Spot" Along East Coast

U.S. government researchers report that sea levels are rising much faster in the area from Cape Hatteras, North Carolina, to just north of Boston, Massachusetts, than they are in other parts of the world, putting the area in danger of flooding.

U.S. Geological Survey scientists call the 600-mile stretch a "hot spot" for rising sea levels caused by global warming.

According to their study, in this region, the Atlantic Ocean is rising at an annual rate three to four times faster than the global average since 1990.

Since 1990, sea levels have gone up globally about two inches, but in Norfolk, Virginia, the sea level has jumped a total of 4.8 inches. In Philadelphia, levels went up 3.7 inches, and in New York City, they went up 2.8 inches.

Climate change raises sea levels by melting ice sheets in Greenland and west Antarctica, and because warmer water expands.

Higher levels have been projected by computer models along parts of the East Coast because of changes in ocean currents from global warming, but this is the first study to indicate that it has already happened.

Source: Associated Press (2012), "Global warming creates 600-mile flood 'hot spot' along East Coast." See http://www.nj.com/ news/index.ssf/2012/06/global_warming_creates_600-mil.html

Information Box 6.8 summarizes the nature of the Eastern seaboard "hot spot."[18]

Freshwater Availability, Droughts, and Water Shortage

Water availability will be affected by global warming. On the one hand, global warming will increase the aggregate water available; more CO_2 means more moisture in the air, because warmer air can hold more moisture. It also means more weather, since greenhouse gases are the reason that we even have weather; without them there would be no weather.

However, changes in weather patterns will not be uniform: The general pattern forecast is for wet areas to get wetter and dry areas to get dryer. Hence, like our other section, we first begin our consideration of water from a depiction of the current status of water, how is it being used, and what is its future. After that, we can add global warming and assess its impact.

Drought in Las Vegas

In this section, we will be primarily concerned with drought and water shortage. We distinguish between the two as follows: Drought refers to changes in precipitation patterns for an extended period that depletes water supplies or is inadequate for farming.[19] Drought can cause water shortages, but they can also be caused by mismanagement and by population growth. In practice they can be closely related to each other. Consider Las Vegas, a city that grew up beside a wetland that gave the city its name—the meadows. Lake Mead, on the outskirts of the city, have enabled the dramatic growth of Las Vegas and the many surrounding towns; in 2010 the metropolitan area had an estimated population of 1,951,269. Lake Mead receives its water from the Colorado River, and that water is rationed through Lake Powell in Utah, also a substantial reservoir. Unfortunately, the region is currently in a 14-year drought, and there is no forecast end to it. As observers have considered, it might end tomorrow; it might not end for 50 years. No one knows. Currently, the lake stands at 1,106 feet above sea level, and was at 39% of its capacity in 2010. If it drops to 1075 feet, mandatory rationing for Las Vegas kicks in.

The drought is compounded by the rapid growth of the Las Vegas metropolitan area; the city itself has grown by 147% from 1990 to 2010 and 36% from 2000 to 2010.[20] The water available to Las Vegas is tightly regulated by the Colorado River Compact; there is virtually no chance that the allotment of water can be increased.

Global warming is forecast to substantially deteriorate existing water availability. Research has estimated that the Colorado River will lose from just under 10% to 45% of its capacity by midcentury. These numbers may underestimate the water shortages: The American Meteorological Association (AMA) has cautioned that decadal droughts, not planned for in the Compact, have occurred in the region's history and may amplify the effects of global warming.[21] It should be noted that not all research forecasts a drop in Colorado River flow. However, the AMA recommended that water management across the region should include in its planning a "worst case scenario" based on the imposition of megadroughts on a trendline of global warming and possible precipitation declines.

The problems faced by Las Vegas may be a precursor of the future. Unlike many metropolitan areas around the planet, the Colorado River and its attendant reservoirs are extremely tightly managed. Problems there cannot be attributed to poor management, and for the same reason, improvements in management likely cannot squeeze another drop out of the river. In a word, the region is in trouble; it faces a low though real risk of water shortages over the short-term—the next year or two—but in the mid-term (2050) the risks escalate sharply and are very high by the end of the century.

Drought Across the United States

Drought conditions are afflicting many different areas of the United States. The chart below in Figure 6.1, titled US drought area by severity, maps drought conditions as of May 2012. We chose this time line only because it was the most recent one available when we wrote this chapter; the web address in the footnotes provides regular updates to this for interested individuals. One can see that most of the United States was suffering some degree of exceptionally dry conditions, and the Southeast and Southwest exhibit large swathes in extreme and exceptional drought conditions.[22]

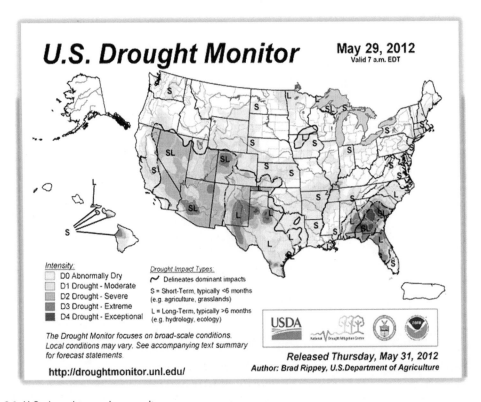

Figure 6.1 U.S. drought area by severity.

Texas in particular is suffering drought conditions and is facing the prospect of substantial losses associated with the drought. In 2011, agricultural losses were estimated at $7.62 billion, cattle sector losses at $3.23 billion, and cotton production losses at $2.2 billion.[23]

Droughts in 2011 Were Global

That the United States was experiencing drought conditions in areas central to its farming and ranching should not be taken that drought was limited to the United States. East Africa is also experiencing sustained drought conditions in many areas. As noted in Wikipedia:[24]

> Since mid-July 2011, a severe drought has been affecting the entire East Africa region. Said to be "the worst in 60 years," the drought has caused a severe food crisis across Somalia, Djibouti, Ethiopia and Kenya that threatens the livelihood of 9.5 million people. Many refugees from southern Somalia have fled to neighboring Kenya and Ethiopia, where crowded, unsanitary conditions together with severe malnutrition have led to a large number of deaths.

The drought was associated with tens of thousands of deaths. The information box titled East Africa's Drought discusses the way in which the drought was exacerbated by agriculture and freshwater mismanagement. The drought interacted with a failure to heed early warnings regarding food shortages, resulting in a human catastrophe. Information Box 6.9 summarizes the contours of the catastrophe, describing how global warming and already existing human problems interact to intensify the impact of drought.[25]

China also experienced a harsh drought at the same time. In 2011, the Yangtze River was experiencing its worst drought in 50 years.[26] China, recognizing that it needed to provide water for its urban masses at the same time as it is building its economy, has engaged in a massive water diversion program. The Three Gorges reservoir on the Yangtze was integral to that program. Drought intensified the water availability already associated with the project. It was estimated that shortages affected 4.4 million people and 3.2 million farm animals. More than 1,300 lakes have been declared dead, which means that they are no longer useable for irrigation or drinking water.

> "The primary cause of this drought is a lack of rainfall. But we can also be certain that the Three Gorges dam has had a negative impact on the water supply downstream," said Ma Jun, founder of the

Information Box 6.9 East Africa's Drought: The Avoidable Disaster

A report, titled "A Dangerous Delay," says that the deaths of tens of thousands of people during the drought in east Africa could have been avoided if the international community, donor governments, and humanitarian agencies had responded earlier and faster to warning signs that a disaster was in the making.

Figures compiled by the U.K.'s Department for International Development (DfID) suggest that between 50,000 and 100,000 people died in the 2011 Horn of Africa crisis that affected Somalia, Ethiopia, and Kenya.

The U.S. government has estimated that more than 29,000 children under the age of five died in the space of 90 days from May to July 2011. The accompanying destruction of livelihoods, livestock, and local market systems affected 13 million people, and hundreds of thousands are at continuing risk of malnutrition. The report warns,

Early warning systems in the Sahel region show that overall cereal production is 25% lower than the previous year and food prices are 40% higher than the five-year average. The last food crisis in the region, in 2010, affected 10 million people.

The report holds that although drought sparked the east Africa crisis, human factors are what turned it into a disaster:

A culture of risk aversion caused a six-month delay in the large-scale aid effort because humanitarian agencies and national governments were too slow to scale up their response to the crisis, and many donors wanted proof of a humanitarian catastrophe before acting to prevent one.

Source: Tisdall, S. (2012), "East Africa's drought: The avoidable disaster." See http://www.theguardian.com/world/2012/jan/18/east-africa-drought-disaster-report

Institute of Public and Environmental Affairs. "This is a reminder that the water in the Yangtze is not unlimited. We cannot bet everything on this river. We need to focus more on conservation."[27]

Finally, Afghanistan and England both faced severe droughts in 2011. These many examples suggest that drought in the current era is global in its reach, one exacerbated by regional mismanagement of water resources and the needs of burgeoning populations, and one that is likely to be made substantially worse by global warming. Indeed, when we add global warming forecasts to the mix, one can see that water shortages across a wide swath of the world are anticipated to increase in severity. Interestingly, an inspection of forecast water availability also shows how some areas will substantially increase their water. For some, this will be welcome news, especially as the climate warms and they develop new forms of agriculture. However, too much water, especially in the early spring, can undermine farming efforts, drowning sprouts. The following map in Figure 6.2 shows anticipated effects of climate change.[28] We can see in this map that the mid latitudes will dry out and desertify, while the polar regions will become substantially wetter.

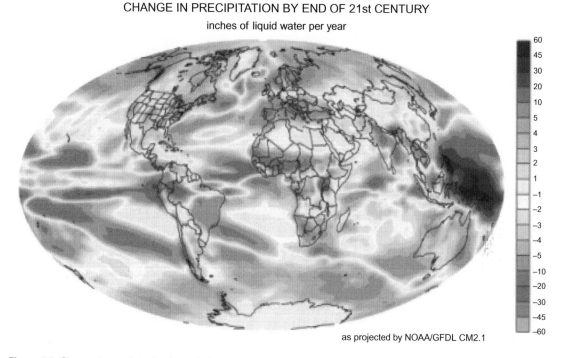

CHANGE IN PRECIPITATION BY END OF 21st CENTURY
inches of liquid water per year

as projected by NOAA/GFDL CM2.1

Figure 6.2 Change in precipitation by end of twenty-first century. *Source:* Precipitation Change in average annual temperature for the 21st century. Retrieved July 7, 2014 from http://en.wikipedia.org/wiki/File:Projected_change_in_annual_average_precipitation_for_the_21st_century,_based_on_the_SRES_A1B_emissions_scenario,_and_simulated_by_the_GFDL_CM2.1_model.png.

Water Shortages

Water is the most important resource we have, exceeded only by the air we breathe. In some countries such as the United States, water is so abundant that its citizens routinely bathe in drinkable water. In others, publicly available drinking water is difficult to find and often requires significant travel to acquire.

Already in Crisis

In any discussion of the future of water, needed is an assessment of the current state of water availability worldwide. A review of the statistics below indicates the extent to which water shortages are already in crisis for many people.

1. 780 million people lack access to an improved water source; approximately one in nine people. By improved, it is meant that some sort of water treatment insures that the water is potable.
2. Approximately 3.41 million people die from water-, sanitation-, and hygiene-related causes each year.

3. The water and sanitation crisis claims more lives through disease than any war claims through guns.
4. Approximately 1.1 billion people live without clean drinking water.
5. Approximately 2.6 billion people lack adequate **sanitation.** (2002, UNICEF/WHO JMP 2004)
6. Approximately 1.8 million people die every year from diarrheal diseases.

The World Bank has estimated that about 80 countries currently suffer water shortages.[29] The following passage summarizes water problems and attendant diseases associated with water shortages:

> *The water supply and sanitation situation around the world can only be described as abysmal. Currently, 1.5 million children under 5 die of preventable water related diseases every year (4,000 every day), around 900 million people (1 in 6) have no access to safe drinking water, and 2.6 billion (2 in 6) lack adequate sanitation. In the developing world, 90% of wastewater is dumped untreated into water bodies, spreading contamination and disease and spawning "dead zones."[30]*

Alpine Reservoirs and Their Futures

One of the significant sources of water shortages is from the loss of snowpack in a warmer world. High mountains act as alpine reservoirs, where the snowpack that accumulates in the winter provides the critically needed water for spring planting and summer crop production, for ranch animals such as cattle and sheep, and for human consumption. They represent the most important natural reservoirs on the surface of the world, feeding the rivers that fill man-made reservoirs. These reservoirs are particularly vulnerable to global warming. Information Box 6.10 reviews an article from *Nature* that considers the global impact of warming on water availability.[31]

Water Shortage and Violence in India: A Portent of Problems to Come

Water is the resource that formed the basis for modern civilization, in the great riparian valleys in Africa, particularly Egypt. As Klare (2012) has shown, it is an essential resource, and countries will fight to control it. The presence of water drives the presence of humans. And that is a problem for a world where the mid latitudes are forecast to dry from the impacts of global warming.

Information Box 6.10 The Impact of Early Snow Meltoff: A Billion Dry

Even as the ice caps melt, global warming threatens to leave a billion people high and dry, says a team of US climate scientists. If the earth warms just 1 or 2°C in coming decades, regions that depend on runoff from mountain snows for drinking water and farming will face shortages, according to a study published in the November 17 issue of the journal *Nature*.

A companion article supports the claim, showing that mountain runoff has already decreased in some regions of the world. "We found that, no surprise, less snow falls in a warmer world," said Timothy Barnett of the Scripps Institute of Oceanography in La Jolla, California. "And what snow there is melts earlier."

The two factors combine to push peak runoff from summer into spring, when reservoirs are already at capacity. "The dams get filled earlier in the year, and they can only be filled to a certain level, so there's still some flood control," Barnett said. The result: Much of the early runoff goes to waste, prompting shortages in late summer and autumn. "It's like squeezing six months of snowmelt into four," Barnett said.

To develop their climate model, which looks ahead 30 to 40 years, Barnett and Jenny Adam of the University of Washington in Seattle looked at 30 years of global precipitation records. They mapped the globe into squares and calculated how much precipitation fell in each square as rain and how much as snow. They overlaid that data onto a map of regions that depend on snow for at least 50% of their water supply, including the western United States.

"In California, Mother Nature holds the snow for us up in the Sierras," Barnett said. "It's basically a massive reservoir." Adam then researched manmade reservoirs in the target regions and found that the vast majority do not have the capacity to store the extra, early runoff. "We were surprised how many places [lacked extra capacity]," Barnett said. "[Reservoirs] were built on the assumption that . . . water availability throughout the year wouldn't change."

In addition to the western United States and Canada, hard-hit regions include parts of Europe, South America west of the Andes, and much of central Asia from northern India across to China and Russia. About one-sixth of the world's population—more than a billion people—inhabit these areas. The regions at risk also account for about a quarter of the world's economic output. "What are those people going to do?" Barnett asked. "Just sit there and be thirsty and watch their crops die?"

Source: Warming May Cause Widespread Water Shortages, Studies S. Retrieved October 13, 2013 at http://news.nationalgeographic.com/news/pf/66722603.html.

The links between water and violence are not always obvious. Yet, as Parenti (2011) has noted, patterns stand out. He described the relationship between terrorism and water as one driven by a cycle of development and denial in the political classes, and one that portended badly as the climate changed.

If one compares maps of precipitation with those of violence, a disturbing pattern emerges; where drought advances, so do Maoists . . . (The geography of drought encroachment is also the) "Red Corridor." Drought produces a chain reaction of debt, land loss, hunger, suicide, banditry, and Maoism. Why this neat correlation? The link is not natural but rather historically produced, In the years of the Naxal rise in Andhra Pradesh, drought was also intense: 1984-1985, 1986-1987, 1997-1988, 1999-2000, and 2002-2003 were all drought years.

(p. 137)

When I interviewed one of India's top climatologists, Dr. Murari Lal, he was distraught. "The political class are in total denial. They are not dealing with the issue of climate change. They think it is a rich man's problem. Nothing can get in the way of 'Shining India,' you understand? They are thinking 'development first, then address the environment."

(p. 139)

Parenti (2011) associates several factors with terrorism, and undoubtedly there are others. Climate change alone is not direct cause of any particular behavior. But the root is climate; a root that is likely to get much more powerful as the riparian areas begin to diminish their capacity in India, as the population booms and its needs increase, and as it denies the presence of a problem in order to sustain development. There is an important lesson in his work. Given the mix of climate deterioration, further development, and governmental denial, how can violence not result?

Aquifers Around the World: Stressed

Aquifers—vast underground water reservoirs—provide most of the clean fresh water in the world. Aquifers are central to the world's supply of fresh water. It is estimated that "30% of the world's fresh water resources are in the form of groundwater, whereas only 1% is on the ground surface in the form of lakes, rivers, and streams."[32] The remainder is locked up in the major ice fields in Antarctica, the Arctic, and Greenland.

Aquifers are of two kinds. Replenishable aquifers are those that receive water from another source. Replenishable aquifers are the most reliable over time, but are limited to the rate of replenishment. Many of these aquifers are stressed from overuse, and when they are depleted their use will revert to the pace of replenishment. Nonreplenishable aquifers, also called fossil aquifers, have fixed stores of water. When they are used up, all water needs dependent on them will cease.

Ogallala Aquifer

The Ogallala that lies beneath Great Plains is mostly a fossil aquifer, though a narrow band on the eastern side of the aquifer is replenished by the Missouri river. Many parts of it are already under significant stress from overuse. When it is depleted, estimated to be by 2050, a great deal of agriculture in the Great Plains will cease.

The aquifer stretches from Texas to Canada and is filled with water and rock that migrated from the Rockies during the Pleistocene. It is no longer replenished from the Rockies, and though there are some recharge effects—some movement of water back into it—mostly on the eastern side of the aquifer, it is not enough to offset the current use level. The Ogallala aquifer irrigates 13 million acres of land and provides drinking water to 80% of the region. Depletion calculations have not, for the most part, taken climate change into consideration, though it is anticipated to have a further drying impact on the Great Plains. Residents across the Great Plains face a significant midterm threat from the depletion of the aquifer. An estimated 90% of the Ogallala aquifer goes for irrigation, turning the Great Plains into one of the most productive areas in the planet.[33]

Aquifers Globally

The problems of the Ogallala are characteristic of aquifers worldwide. Information Box 6.11, "Aquifers Around the World," summarizes the central problems facing aquifers today.[34]

The challenges of current use rates globally have been widely discussed and are a central hydrological issue, particularly as the human population urbanizes. For areas that are facing drought and desertification, such as the Great Plains in the United States, the problem is serious. There is no viable future for the Ogallala. For those where water usage is already substantial and that are already in desert climates such as Las Vegas and the Sacramento Valley, already difficult problems are becoming crises.

Mexico City Aquifer

The Ogallala aquifer is actually in better condition than many of the other aquifers on which large numbers of people depend. Mexico City represents one of the aquifers in particularly depleted condition. The city itself has a storied history, originating in a large marshy lake largely controlled by the Aztec population. The original city, called Tenochtitlan, was a floating city physically constructed on the surface of the lake and connected to the shorelines by pontoon reed structures. Today, Mexico City is a megacity with an estimated population of about 25 million and is steadily growing. This substantial population have immense water and food needs. Its primary source, the Mexico City Aquifer, has been depleted since 1910. It does not have another primary

Information Box 6.11 Aquifers Around the World: In Crisis

In recent decades, the rate at which humans worldwide are pumping dry the vast underground stores of water that billions depend on has more than doubled, say scientists who have conducted an unusual global assessment of groundwater use.

These fast-shrinking subterranean reservoirs are essential to daily life and agriculture in many regions, while also sustaining streams, wetlands, and ecosystems and resisting land subsidence and salt water intrusion into fresh water supplies. Soaring global groundwater depletion bodes a potential disaster for an increasingly globalized agricultural system, says Marc Bierkens of Utrecht University in Utrecht, the Netherlands, and leader of the new study.

"If you let the population grow by extending the irrigated areas using groundwater that is not being recharged, then you will run into a wall at a certain point in time, and you will have hunger and social unrest to go with it," Bierkens warns. "That is something that you can see coming for miles."

The new assessment shows the highest rates of depletion in some of the world's major agricultural centers, including northwest India, northeastern China, northeast Pakistan, California's central valley, and the Midwestern United States.

"The rate of depletion increased almost linearly from the 1960s to the early 1990s," says Bierkens. "But then you see a sharp increase which is related to the increase of upcoming economies and population numbers, mainly in India and China."

Scientists have emphasized that the current rate of depletion is unsustainable:

...researchers from Utrecht University calculated that the rate of withdrawal of groundwater stocks jumped from about 30 cubic miles annually (126 cubic kilometers) in 1960 to about 68 cubic miles (283 cubic kilometers) in 2000, a rate they said was clearly unsustainable. The greatest rate of depletion occurred in some of the world's biggest agricultural regions, including northwest India, northeastern China, and California's central valley, according to the study, published in Geophysical Research Letters. Marc Bierkens, a professor of hydrology and lead author of the study, warned that if over-pumping of groundwater continues "you will run into a wall at a certain point in time, and you will have hunger and social unrest to go with it."

Source: Groundwater depletion rate accelerating worldwide. Retrieved October 10, 2013 at http://scienceblog.com/38936/groundwater-depletion-rateaccelerating-worldwide/.

water source, as it is located in a high mountain valley. The depletion of the city has caused several problems:[35]

1. Severe land subsidence has occurred in some parts of the city.
2. Some parts of the city are rapidly sinking. The central metropolitan area has fallen about 8.5 meters.
3. The subsidence of the city has caused quite a bit of damage to buildings and other structures.
4. The sewer system has been damaged, causing fresh and sewer water to mix.
5. More than 95% of the hazardous waste from area companies is dumped into the sewer system, creating the possibility that the aquifer could be poisoned.

6. The demand for water is increasing with the steady inflow of immigrants to the city. Not everyone in the city has daily access to water.

In the current era, about one-third of the global population depends on water from groundwater supplies. In some areas of India, the water tables have dropped as much as 70 centimeters (approximately 25 inches) and nearly 25% of India's agriculture may be threatened by groundwater depletion. China is facing problems: In areas of northern China, the water table has been dropping as fast as 1.5 meters a year for the last ten years. Groundwater depletions have led to the inability of the Yellow River in China to reach the ocean for months at a time. Many cities in North Africa and the Middle East are experiencing harsh water shortages. In Iran, villages are being evacuated because wells are running dry and there is no water supply to support resident populations. One estimate reported that the water table had dropped by 8 meters in 2001 in parts of Iran. In Yemen, on the Arabian Peninsula, the water tables have been falling on average two meters per year across the country. It has been predicted that the capital of Yemen will run out of its water supply within the next ten years.

Conclusion: How Much Fresh Water Is Left?

Fresh water is a vanishing resource. Even without global warming, human populations face a looming crisis in this once abundant resource. In two generations, the population of the planet will number nine billion. Over half will not have access to adequate water. Indeed, a majority already have impaired water sources within fifty miles of where they live.

A group of 500 scientists issued a report in 2014 issued a warning about shrinking global supplies. Information Box 6.12 presents their principal findings.[36]

Add to the issues in Information Box 6.12 the drying-out across the mid latitudes that will follow global warming, increased salinization of crops from overused aquifers, salt poisoning from cyclonic storms reaching farther inland, and one needs little imagination to comprehend the problems we face. Those who cannot obtain clean water will drink dirty water, the source of many plagues. As people concentrate in megacities, water-borne diseases will be facilitated by proximity of people who will have sharply inadequate public health services (Garrett, 1994). Access to safe drinking water may well pose a non-resolvable hydrological problem for the earth at current population levels. One cannot take

Information Box 6.12 Global Water Crisis

The world's water systems would soon reach a tipping point that "could trigger irreversible change with potentially catastrophic consequences" more than 500 water experts warned, as they called on governments to start conserving the vital resource.

1. Already, there are one billion people relying on ground water supplies that are simply not there as renewable water supplies.
2. A majority of the population—about 4.5 billion people globally—already live within 50 km of an "impaired" water resource—one that is running dry or polluted. If these trends continue, millions more will see the water on which they depend running out or so filthy that it no longer supports life.
3. The run-off from agricultural fertilisers containing nitrogen has already created more than 200 large "dead zones" in seas, near to rivermouths, where fish can no longer live.
4. Cheap technology to pump water from underground and rivers, and few restrictions on its use, has led to the over-use of scarce resources for irrigation or industrial purposes, with much of the water wasted because of poor techniques.
5. And a rapidly rising population has increased demand beyond the capability of some water resources.
6. In some areas, so much water has been pumped out from underground that salt water has rushed in to fill the gap, forcing farmers to move to other areas because the salination makes their former water sources unusable.

Source: Global majority faces water shortages 'within two generations'. Retrieved October 12, 2013 at http://www.theguardian. com/environment/2013/may/24/global-majority-water-shortages-two-generations.

comfort in these findings. They point to the importance of research and knowledge development concerning hydrological problems and solutions, if indeed there are any. They also point to the need for those concerned about international security to recognize the issue of water for the enormous security risk it might become.

Endnotes

1. "Why global water shortages pose threat of terror and war." Retrieved July 3, 2013 at http://www.theguardian.com/environment/2014/feb/09/global-water-shortages-threat-terror-war.
2. "Hurricane Katrina." Retrieved July 16, 2013 at http://en.wikipedia.org/wiki/Hurricane_Katrina.
3. "Katrina and Global Warming." Retrieved July 16, 2013 at http://www.c2es.org/science-impacts/extreme-weather/hurricane-katrina.
4. Ibid.
5. "The Army response to Hurricane Katrina." Retrieved July 18, 2013 at http://www.army.mil/article/45029/The_Army_response_to_Hurricane_Katrina/.
6. "Katrina: The crime that shocked the world." Retrieved January 19, 2013 at http://www.independent.co.uk/news/world/americas/katrina-the-crime-that-shocked-the-world-2026859.html.
7. "Crime Surge Continues in Katrina's Wake." Retrieved July 24, 2013 at http://crime.about.com/od/issues/a/katrinacrime.htm.

8. The authors cannot find a published version of this manuscript. Attached is a pdf copy of the paper. "Crime Spillovers and Hurricane Katrina." Retrieved July 26, 2013 at *https://umdrive.memphis.edu/nklrzhvs/www/papers/katrina_042010.pdf.*

9. "Report: No crime wave among Hurricane Katrina evacuees." Retrieved July 28, 2013 at http://www.usatoday.com/tech/science/columnist/vergano/2010-02-12-hurricane-katrina-crime_N.htm.

10. "Superstorm Sandy Leads to Wave of Crime." Retrieved July 30, 2013 at http://blogs.findlaw.com/blotter/2012/11/superstorm-sandy-leads-to-wave-of-crime.html.

11. "Superstorm Sandy Leads to Drop in NYC Crime Rate." Retrieved July 31, 2013 at http://www.newsmax.com/US/superstorm-sandy-nyc-crime/2012/11/06/id/462996.

12. "The Civilizing Power of Disaster." Retrieved August 5, 2013 at http://www.slate.com/articles/health_and_science/science/2012/11/looting_after_hurricane_sandy_disaster_myths_and_disaster_utopias_explained.html.

13. "How much is sea level rising?" Retrieved August 7, 2013 at http://www.skepticalscience.com/sea-level-rise.htm.

14. "Superstorm Sandy and Sea Level Rise." Retrieved August 7, 2013 at http://www.climate.gov/news-features/features/superstorm-sandy-and-sea-level-rise.

15. "More Floods Ahead: Adapting to Sea Level Rise in New York City." Retrieved August 13, 2013 at http://www.giss.nasa.gov/research/briefs/rosenzweig_03/.

16. "Study: 634 Million People at Risk from Rising Seas." Retrieved August 13, 2013 at http://www.npr.org/templates/story/story.php?storyId=9162438.

17. "Global Warming Text Was Removed From Virginia Bill on Rising Sea Levels." Retrieved August 17, 2013 at http://www.usnews.com/news/articles/2012/06/13/global-warming-text-was-removed-from-virginia-bill-on-rising-sea-levels-.

18. "Global warming creates 600-mile flood 'hot spot' along East Coast." Retrieved August 5, 2013 at http://www.nj.com/news/index.ssf/2012/06/global_warming_creates_600-mil.html.

19. "Of the many schemes for classifying droughts, the most widely used is the Palmer Drought Severity Index (PDSI), which combines temperature, precipitation, evaporation, transpiration, soil runoff and soil recharge data for a given region to produce a single negative number representing conditions there. This index serves as an estimate of soil moisture deficiency, which roughly correlates with a drought's severity, and thus, its impacts." See more at: "What is a Drought? Definition of Droughts." Retrieved August 10, 2013 at http://www.livescience.com/21469-drought-definition.html#sthash.Xx8lmgbR.dpuf.

20. "Las Vegas Population Growth and Population Statistics." Retrieved August 15, 2013 at http://www.clrsearch.com/Las-Vegas-Demographics/NV/Population-Growth-and-Population-Statistics.

21. "Understanding Uncertainties in Future Colorado River Streamflow." Retrieved August 17, 2013 at bams-d-12-00228.1-3.pdf.

22. "U.S. Drought Monitor." http://droughtmonitor.unl.edu/.

23. "A Drought of Historic Proportions." Retrieved August 19, 2013 at http://stateimpact.npr.org/texas/drought/.

24. "2011 East Africa drough." Retrieved August 21, 2013 at http://en.wikipedia.org/wiki/2011_East_Africa_drough.

25. "East Africa's drought: the avoidable disaster." Retrieved October 8, 2013 at http://www.guardian.co.uk/world/2012/jan/18/east-africa-drought-disaster-report.

26. "China crisis over Yangtze river drought forces drastic dam measures." Retrieved October 8, 2013 at http://www.guardian.co.uk/environment/2011/may/25/china-drought-crisis-yangtze-dam.

27. Ibid.

28. "Precipitation Change in average annual temperature for the 21st century." Retrieved July 7, 2014 from http://en.wikipedia.org/wiki/File:Projected_change_in_annual_average_precipitation_for_the_21st_century,_based_on_the_SRES_A1B_emissions_scenario,_and_simulated_by_the_GFDL_CM2.1_model.png.

29. "The Global Water Crisis." Retrieved October 11, 2013 at http://www.huffingtonpost.com/h-david-nahai/the-global-water-crisis_b_964576.html.

30. Ibid.

31. "Warming May Cause Widespread Water Shortages, Studies S." Retrieved October 13, 2013 at http://news.nationalgeographic.com/news/pf/66722603.html.

32. "Groundwater Depletion Rate Accelerating Worldwide." Retrieved August 22, 2013 at http://www.wrsc.org/story/groundwater-depletion-rate-accelerating-worldwide.

33. "Ogallala Aquifer." Retrieved August 23, 2013 at http://en.wikipedia.org/wiki/Ogallala_Aquifer.

34. "Groundwater depletion rate accelerating worldwide." Retrieved October 10, 2013 at http://scienceblog.com/38936/groundwater-depletion-rate-accelerating-worldwide/.

35. "Groundwater Drawdown." Retrieved October 11, 2013 at http://academic.evergreen.edu/g/grossmaz/WORMKA/.

36. "Global majority faces water shortages 'within two generations'." Retrieved October 12, 2013 at http://www.theguardian.com/environment/2013/may/24/global-majority-water-shortages-two-generations.

MIGRATION FUTURES AND MEGACITIES: A COLLISION COURSE WITH GLOBAL WARMING

In the chapters in this section, we construct as best we can an image of the present and from that extrapolate some of the broad-brush images of the future. As will be seen, that image, even without global warming, is strikingly different from the world we live in today. Our research strongly suggests that current migration and refugee population flows are likely to remain at their already high volume, as more and more people seek lives in urban settings. By the end of the century, most of the world's population will live in megacities, cities in excess of 25 million population. In turn, most of these new residents will lack basic services, including fresh water, sewer and septic systems, and municipally funded security.

7

REFUGEE MIGRATION AND SETTLEMENT AMID CLIMATE CHANGE: A PRESCRIPTION FOR VIOLENCE?

In the chapters in this section, we construct as best as we can an image of the present, and from that we extrapolate some of the broad brush images of the future. As will be seen, that image, even without global warming, is strikingly different from the world we live in today. Our research strongly suggests that current migration and refugee population flows are likely to remain at their already high volume, as more and more people seek lives in urban settings. By the end of the century, most of the world's population will live in megacities, cities with populations in excess of 25 million. In turn, most of these new residents will lack basic services, including fresh water, sewer and septic systems, and municipally funded security.

Clete: "You were on the coast for a while. But you weren't there in the '50s when it really started coming up."

Ruth: "I stayed home then. I had a big family to take care of. Kids and grandkids were still mostly here. But my sister, Nene, she was back in Calgary then. One of my grandkids, Jesse, went with her. He would travel back and forth, though the roads were dangerous."

"We talked a lot about Calgary. It had gotten to be a big city—really big. Tremendous migration into the city. But we had work, and people wanted work. Farming was incredible. The security trades were expanding everywhere, with all the crime and violence problems on the coasts. One of the new battery tech plants moved into our area, and batteries were the hot technology. With the new batteries, you could drive a car 2,000 miles, then let it recharge itself with a small energy pack overnight. We always thought, way back then, that solar power or nuclear energy was the way of the future. We were wrong. It was those silly little cheap batteries."

"In the United States, solar and wind turbines were catching. But the United States was different. It was sunny and hot; both worked good there, especially with gas so expensive. But Canada was just too wet and cloudy; with the great warming, Canada had gotten a lot more rainfall. It was too cloudy too often to get the same mileage out of solar. Batteries were the answer."

Ruth: "Jesse went over to the East Coast a few times and told us about it. It was bad there. He didn't want to go into the United States, for all the problems. All he actually wanted to do was find somewhere outside Calgary to farm and ranch. But Beto told Jesse that he needed to go see what was really going on in the rest of the world, said that it was important that Jesse and his kids know the truth about the world. Some of the family was involved in politics in Canada, and Beto said they could not make a difference unless they really understood the world. So Jesse went to New York."

"Jesse said that when he got there, his first impression was the heat. It was hot all the time, day and night. He said he could see the storm surge barriers, but they weren't as effective as they once were. The storms were too powerful, the rising oceans too high. There was no point in building more barriers, because the ocean was starting to seep around the sides. Manhattan Island was lost; it was just a matter of time. The barrier cost 20 billion dollars, but the rising seas had cost more than a trillion."

"Up and down the state, vacated coastal property had been taken over by refugees. Jesse remembered what Beto said about the gangs in Los Angeles and so steered clear of dangerous-looking areas. But he had to stop frequently to pay a toll on the roads. Local gangs controlled the roads by night and charged to use them."

"He headed North to the large refugee camp there. There were a quarter million people in it; the security in it was a joint American force from Mexico, the United States, and Canada. The three countries had cooperated when it became clear that refugees were going to crowd all the borders across the Americas. Jesse had his papers well hidden; he could not take the chance that someone would mug him and take his identification. Even with the security force present, there was a great deal of racial conflict in the camp. The gangs stirred up the conflict; it took attention away from them and helped them run the black markets. Jesse headed back to Nebraska after that, through the warm Ohio Spring, making his way to semiarid Indiana and finally to the Nebraska desert he called home."

Central to this book is the relationship between refugee relocation and violence, and how global warming contributes to migratory patterns. Migration represents one of the primary links Homer-Dixon (1999) described between global warming and violence (see Chapter 4, Figure 4.1): The relationship between environmental scarcity and crimes. Migration occurs for a variety of reasons. One of the most important ones is the loss of resources in one's homeland. Another is that one is forced off one's homeland and either physically relocated to settlement camps or set loose to find one's own way, often with minimal wealth. In turn, migration, whether forced or voluntary, creates opportunities for violence and crime of both individual and organized types.

Migrants and refugees are sometimes distinguished according to whether one voluntarily leaves one's home or one is forced to leave. In reality, the difference is often vague and unclear: People may find themselves members of a minority group in a period of religious intolerance: They might be robbed of their wealth, have their lives threatened, and then choose to "voluntarily" leave their homes. In quite a different circumstance but also prevalent in the current era, one might find his or her land to be stripped of all resources and, for survival reasons, move to more opportunistic surroundings: This is the basis for much of the population relocation to urban areas today. In both circumstances, one can make the argument that people are forced off their land and are consequently refugees, even if they voluntarily made the decision to relocate.

It is particularly difficult to separate out the concept of environmental refugee from the concept of climate refugee (see Myers, 2005; White, 2012). For instance, consider a farmer in the American Great Plains who leaves his home on the prairie and relocates to Omaha. Let's say he did so because, facing inadequate yields and inadequate water supplies from a few years of dry weather, he could not afford to maintain the farm. Is he a "climate refugee" or simply a luckless farmer, a poor businessperson taking a loss from an unfriendly shift in weather-related conditions?

A drought may drive farmers out of their areas, but this does not necessarily mean that the drought was caused by global warming. The "sodbusters" in the Northern Great Plains after the Civil War were sold a bill of goods about the capacity of the land to produce and later found out that the land lacked fertility, adequate moisture, and adequate annual rainfall. This example highlights the difficulty of placing labels on migrants. Some have recommended that the term "climate refugee" not be used at all because climate change associated with global warming is only one of the many kinds of environmental or climate problems that might be associated with a person's relocation.

Contemporary Dimensions of Refugee Populations

Refugees represent the middle column in Homer-Dixon's (1999) model. Two aspects of the model are closely tied to refugees.

First, relocation is closely tied to resource loss. People will often leave an area when the resource opportunities it provides disappear. The land may be leached of nutrient, it might be desertified from long-term drought, or any of a host of problems may make it useless as a source of resource. Ecological disasters can also ruin large swaths of land previously suitable for habitation. As we move into the future, one of the central concerns of global warming researchers is how climate changes can change weather patterns to despoil currently viable farming and ranching areas.

Secondly, resource capture processes may force individuals off of their land. Capture processes are widely romanticized in the American West movie tradition, in which bankers force poor homeowners off their land—until some white-hatted hero arrives on his golden horse to save the day. Resource capture is also witnessed in war and in ethnic cleansing, when people are forced off their land in order to survive. More important for this work is the international refugee population. The displacement of refugees implies profound international and state problems, humanitarian resettlement and security problems, and urban security issues for megacities with seam-bursting populations. Crank (2003) described the beginnings of the Great Migration, which involved the resettlement of several million African Americans in the United States in the first half of the twentieth century, in terms of resource capture and forced migration.

Migration is directly implicated in crimes of the state as well. One of the issues we deal with is the extraordinary vulnerability of refugees to violent crime, slavery, and all manner of physical abuse. At the state level, we discuss state hardening—again one of Homer-Dixon's key central-column factors linking global warming to violence—and how it enables states to act abusively and harshly against immigrants, legal and illegal.

One of the issues we have underscored throughout this book is that global warming does not occur on a blank ecological or civilizational slate. So it is with refugees—in order to reasonably consider the impact of global warming on refugees, we must first look at the current state of refugees internationally and the processes leading them to relocate. We also need to make another distinction: the distinction between refugees and internally displaced people. Internal displacements are like refugees: they were forced to relocate. However, refugees are no longer in their home country, while internal displacements are. The distinction involves many millions of people. Worldwide there are approximately 15.4 million refugees, while internal displacements numbered 27.5 million people at the end of 2010.[1] However, internal displacements will increasingly become central to refugee populations as states harden in response to global warming. Displacements will occur in two migration patterns. The first, happening now and representing the largest migration in the history of people, involves the worldwide movement of people to megacities. The second, which will become increasingly important towards the middle part of the century, will be the movement of people away from megacities as they face residential flooding from sea-rise, seawater toxification of coastal agriculture, and seawater seepage into coastal freshwater reservoirs.

How Many Refugees Are There?

Refugee populations often flee to avoid wars and war-related state conflicts. This is not surprising—most people would prefer to avoid personally lethal outcomes. The most numerous source of refugees in the world today is Afghanistan, with 3,054,709 refugees stemming from the U.S. military engagement with the Taliban and Al-Qaeda terrorists across the country. Similarly, the second highest numbers of refugees worldwide is in Iraq, with 1,683,579 refugees, stemming initially from the harsh dictatorship of Saddam Hussein, growing substantially after the subsequent military involvement of the United States from 2003-2011 and the ongoing sectarian violence in that country through the current era.

By continent, Asia has 5,715,848 refugees, Africa has 2,408,676, Europe has 1,606,639, Latin America has 373,867, and North America has 430,123 The United States has 264,574 refugees, about 60% of those in North America. Figure 7.1 displays a chart of the countries of origins for refugees in 2010.[2]

When individual countries are considered, the largest refugee populations are Columbia at 3,000,281, Iraq at 2,652,402; the Democratic Republic of the Congo at 2,555,204, Pakistan at 2,038,154, and Uganda at 2,0479,173. In addition, Syria, Nepal, Sudan, and Somalia all have in excess of one million refugees, with Iran closing in at just over 964,000.[3]

When we look at refugee populations over time, we witness a striking rise in refugees since 1960, reaching a peak in 1990 and 1991. Since then, the population of refugees has dropped steadily and seems to have leveled off. However, current levels are still substantially higher than they were in the midpart of the previous century. In 1960 there were only 1,656,664 refugees worldwide. That number rose to its height of 17,838,074 in 1992 and subsequently dropped in 2010 to 10,549,686. Although in decline since the early 1990s, the numbers in 2010 are still about six times what they were in 1960. Figure 7.2 displays the refugee population globally from 1960 to 2010.[4]

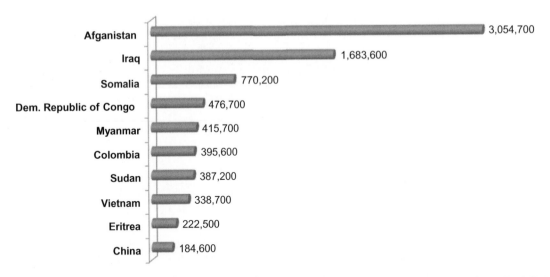

Figure 7.1 Refugees by country, worldwide. *Source:* Mapping the Foreign Born in the United States. Retrieved September 2, 2013 at http://www.cfo.gov.ph/index.php?option¼com_content&view¼article&id¼1619:mapping-the-foreign-born-in-the-united-states-part-i&catid¼165:migration-related-articles&Itemid¼901\.

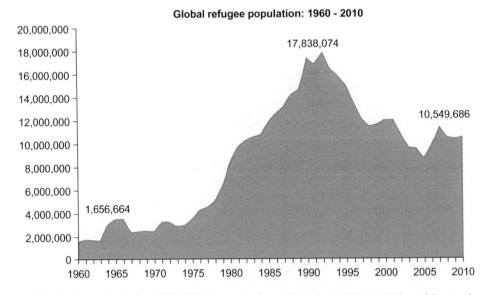

Figure 7.2 Global Refugee Population, 1960-2010. *Source:* Retrieved September 5, 2013 at http://www.johnmenadue.com/population/images/Graph1.jpg.

Climate Refugee: Real or Alarmist?

The notion that the climate will create additional refugees worldwide has been the object of a great deal of attention and substantial controversy. For instance, given that many of the world's

Information Box 7.1 A Bold Prediction

At a conference in Prague in 2005, Oxford University professor Norman Myers predicted there would be 50 million climate refugees by 2010.

"As far back as 1995 (latest date for a comprehensive assessment), these environmental refugees totalled at least 25 million people, compared with 27 million traditional refugees (people fleeing political oppression, religious persecution and ethnic troubles)," Myers said: "The environmental refugees total could well double between 1995 and 2010."

Myers's report may have been the basis for United Nations statements made in 2005.

Myers and other scientists were simply looking at climate change forecasts and counting the number of people living in areas at risk of flooding, said Stephen Castles, author of *The Age of Migration.*

It is not assured that all people threatened with environmental issues would relocate. More detailed analysis is needed to verify such a challenging forecast across so many different aspects of global warming.

Source: Ober, K. (2011), "UN embarrassed by forecast on climate refugees." See http://www.towardsrecognition.org/2011/04/news-un-embarrassed-by-forecast-on-climate-refugees/

population centers are coastally located, an increase in ocean levels could theoretically generate an enormous global refugee relocation problem. Such a forecast occurred in 2005 when the *United Nations Environment Programme* predicted that by 2010 there would be 50 million environmental refugees, in part due to island flooding.[5] This prediction is discussed in Information Box 7.1, "A Bold Prediction."[6]

Myers published his work in 2002 in *Philosophical Transactions of the Royal Society.* In a review of that document, it is not at all clear that his 2005 prediction was actually wrong. Importantly, Myers did not make absolutist statements, but couched his findings in the language of probabilities. He also described the importance of internal migration, rural-urban migration, and the impacts of droughts and chronic water shortages, not only sea-rise.

It should be pointed out that his forecast is only a problem from a specific point in time. Will it still be seen as mistaken in an additional 10 years? How about by 2050? Is the forecast simply a few years too soon, but accurate at some future point, which seems to be highly likely? Over the long view, his perspective, though derided even in scientific circles and fodder for the anti-environmental talking heads, may turn out to be surprisingly accurate. Climate policy is very time sensitive, and what looks like failure today may look like prescience tomorrow.

His predictive map is displayed in Figure 7.3.[7] It is of considerable interest, both for its prediction of likely refugee issues and for the diversity of climate-related events it encompasses.

2005 THE UN'S CLIMATE CHANGE REFUGEE MAP

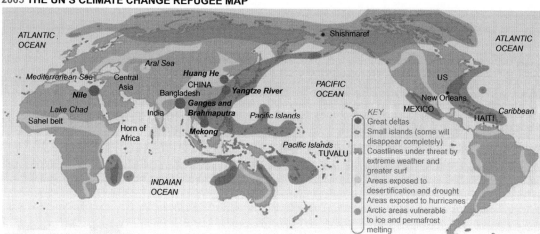

Figure 7.3 The UN's 2005 Climate Refugee Map. *Source:* Climate Refugees Map by UNEP. Retrieved September 8, 2013 at http://www.ecowalkthetalk.com/blog/2010/12/06/whither-go-climate-refugees/climaterefugees-map-by-unep/.

Figure 7.3 is helpful for many reasons. First, it highlights the important urbanized delta regions. These are regions currently seeing very high levels of migration and where the great mega-deltas (metropolis areas with populations above 10 million on low-lying coastal locations) are located. Secondly, it shows the areas prone to cyclonic storms. As was correctly pointed out by critics of the UN/Myers model, not all residents in these areas will move. But, as we discovered in 2013, failure to realize the dramatic intensification of storms associated with global warming can be catastrophic and will account for refugees at some level.

Consider, for instance, Typhoon Haiyan. It arrived in the Philippines in November 2013, with the strongest winds ever recorded for a cyclonic storm at 195 mph sustained winds and killing an estimated 6,100 people. The displaced population, a month after the typhoon, was approximately four million people.[8] These people are, at least for the short-term, living for all practical matters as refugees. Moreover, many of the coastal settlements may have to be relocated inland. The city of Tacloban is located in one of the lavender zones identified above as an area exposed to increased hurricane damage according to the map in Figure 6.4. The takeaway is that this city expected a major hurricane, and they prepared for it. But they did not expect a storm of the magnitude that actually arrived. Therein lies the danger of global warming—that such storms will yield much greater damage without recognition of the implications of climate change for such storms. And this incident also can be taken as a precursor for the ways in which significant storms will produce refugees, by whatever name or other term one wants to call them.

Other aspects of global warming displayed on the map include areas exposed to desertification and drought, areas vulnerable to permafrost melting, and areas facing coastal flooding from rising seas. This multilayered map, a summary image of dangers of global warming for areas with the possibility for producing refugees, is precisely the kind of forecast a risk analyst needs to make so that regions can begin to develop contingencies for scenarios, including worst-case scenarios.

Refugees, Crime, and Violence

Homer-Dixon (1999), in the chart in Figure 3.1, identified migration as one of the elements that led to violence. But he did not specify what that relationship was, though his discussion of specific incidents was compelling. In this section we explore that relationship.

The relationship between immigration and/or refugees and crime can be theorized in different ways. One can ask—is the question about whether migration is antecedent and causal in some way to crime, or should we be looking at the crime that happens to immigrants—or both? In this book we focus in the latter. There is simply not a lot of evidence that immigrants cause crime. There are isolated but clear exceptions to this; research discussed previously suggests that the relocation of refugees after Katrina was associated with spikes in crime in Houston. Refugee camps may also be fertile ground for terrorist recruitment of radicalized settlers, especially if the settlers there were forced off their land.[9] Although, many observers argue that the refugee-terrorist link is a fabrication of occupying forces responsible for the relocation policies. However, even in the instance of Katrina, it is not clear that the refugees were the ones causing the crime, or if instead, they were the recipients of it.

There is evidence for a reversal of this common sense causality: Findings tend to show that refugees and immigrants cause lower levels of crime than native-born populations. Lee, Martinez, and Rosenfeld (2001, p. 90) refer to this phenomenon as the "migration paradox": unexpectedly favorable social and health outcomes for immigrant groups tend to occur despite community conditions that sociologists traditionally associate with "social disorganization." They further suggest that this paradox extends to crime:

> *Although the theoretical propositions of social disorganization theory are compelling, research on the "immigration paradox" has provided support for a counterclaim that immigration stabilizes impoverished communities, increases community social control, and suppresses violent crime.*

Other research has reached similar conclusions (see Lee, 2003; Warner, 1999). Indeed, a great deal of the publicity surrounding immigrant-related crime is not data driven, but instead is a broader indication of state hardening toward immigrants, a topic we will discuss in a later chapter (see White, 2012).[10]

This research will focus instead on the opposite causality: The victimization of immigrants and refugees. Generally, there are three closely related questions regarding immigrants and/or refugees and crime: (1) What kinds of crime are happening to immigrants and refugees, (2) how does organized crime take advantage of refugee populations, and (3) how do we theoretically frame crime and refugee populations? We will begin with crime to refugees. Refugees are extraordinarily vulnerable to crime, and when people are vulnerable bad things happen to them. Looking at crime through the lens of opportunity perspective, we see how vulnerable they are. In particular, they are absent any responsible guardianship. Even the United Nations, provisionally providing peace keepers at refugee centers, are nowhere up for the task needed to protect refugees. They have an easy target—their bodies—and human bodies have value most of us are uncomfortable thinking about. And, as general and sad as it sounds, the planet is full of likely offenders. The study of refugees and crime is inevitably a study in human tragedy.

A Cautionary Tale: Refugees and Opportunity

This is a cautionary tale. If you are a leader, do not allow circumstances to unfold that lead to uncontrolled refugee flows without planning, security, and shelter on the way to and at destination points. Of all criminal opportunists, few are as vile or their deeds so horrific as those who prey on refugees. Ask yourself the following question: What does an unprotected human body have that might be of value? If it is healthy, it has organs that can be sold in an international market for a handsome profit, the rest of the body left to dessicate in the desert. If it is young and female, it can be someone's sex toy. If it is a child, then one can pay just a bit more and attain forbidden pleasures without risk of criminal liability. If it is, well, accidentally killed from overindulgence, who will know? Who will care? Maybe it is just good for target practice or to find a more effective torture. Refugees are vulnerable to genocidal impulses of cruel leadership and have been slaughtered without mercy. Even receiving population residents who are not naturally mean-spirited may find exceptions to their kindness when they see refugees settling in their areas and using their resources. All this and more can befall refugees.

Refugees, the inevitable fallout of interstate conflict, starvation, and ethnic cleansing, represent a significant problem around the world. Unlike many migrants, refugees are typically forced out of their home regions and do not have a clear destination when they leave. They only know that they have to leave. We will look at refugees in more detail later; here we will look at their linkage to crimes and violence.

Refugees sometimes face horrific crimes. These "crimes against humanity" are at times genocidal, and at many times, atrocious by any moral standard. Consider the following:

> The relocation of large numbers of people linked to widespread human rights abuses is not a new phenomenon, but they have reached unprecedented proportions since the 1994 genocide in Rwanda, which claimed as many as one million lives. In its aftermath two million Rwandese fled their country for Zaire, Tanzania, and Burundi, and set up refugee camps. These camps were the scene of widespread violence. In the worst moments of the Rwandan genocide, thousands of refugees were slaughtered, settlements were destroyed, and refugees were compelled to flee, either into the Zairian forests or toward Rwanda. The presence in the refugee camps of soldiers who had actively participated in the genocide, and who were in a position of authority over the population, was one of the main obstacles preventing the safe and voluntary return of refugees to Rwanda. Indeed, those who wished to return home were often threatened by camp leaders and pressured into changing their minds.

Information Box 7.2, "Death in the Desert," provides a personalized discussion of the evils faced by those who leave their own country and travel through Egypt in order to enter Israel in the hope of a new life. They face beatings, repeated rape, murder, prison, torture, slavery, and in some cases, are the victims of organ traffickers.

Information Box 7.2 Death in the Desert

Every year, thousands of refugees, mostly from Eritrea, Ethiopia, and Sudan, attempt the dangerous journey to Israel in search of economic prosperity and stability.

Very few make it, and the results can be seen in the morgue of the central hospital in El Arish, Egypt.

On any given day, the morgue will be crowded with the bodies of African refugees who died trying to make it to Israel.

For the past seven years, Hamdy Al-Azazy combs the desert every week, searching for corpses to ensure that they get a dignified burial.

Many refugees are enslaved, tortured, and/or raped by the Bedouin tribes of the Sinai if they are unable to come up with the money that the Bedouin try to extort from them and their families. Many remain imprisoned in camps on the Sinai Peninsula.

Interviews with refugees who have escaped or been released from the camps suggest that mistreatment and even murder are commonplace in the Bedouin camps. Al-Azazy also says that some of the refugees are forced into slave labor, often working marijuana fields that flourish all over Northern Sinai.

Source: Pleitgen, F., and M.F. Fahmy (2011), "Death in the desert: Tribesmen exploit battle to reach Israel." See http://www.cnn.com/2011/11/02/world/meast/egypt-refugees/index.html/

Migration, Organized Crime, and Sex Slavery

Migration and organized crime link together very smoothly. Migrants rarely have adequate protective security, and they are vulnerable to organized crime, especially crime that is associated with slaving practices. The brief commentary below describes how migrants become targets of a booming sex trade in Russia.[11]

High unemployment, poverty and crime have transformed Krasnodar, a city with a million-strong population, into the biggest centre for the sex trade in the North Caucasus. Official silence is letting it continue that way.

The massive illegal business has been fuelled by the influx of refugees from all over the Caucasus into what is the one of the main urban centres in southern Russia.

Most of the prostitutes are poor Russians, many of them refugees, said Viktor Mozgovoi, a high-ranking police official. Armenian and Russian criminals control the business, although Chechens and gangsters from the neighbouring region of Adygeia are also moving into the market. While the resort city of Sochi has a thriving

prostitution business in the summer months, Krasnodar, straddling
the main transportation routes, supports the trade all the
year round.

That organized crime can follow in the tracks and paths created by migrants and refugees is consistent with routine activities: Illegal organized criminal behavior flows from the opportunities created by migration. In this instance, we are dealing with two kinds of illegal behavior, but one is much more pernicious than the other. With organized crime comes slavery, which is higher in numbers worldwide today than at any time in our history. Estimates of slavery put the number globally at 29.8 million.[12]

Among slaving enterprises is the sexual trafficking of women and children. Such trafficking is highly lucrative, and individuals are available in many marketplaces for tourists who travel internationally to enjoy the trade. That the United States, a country with strong internal security forces and technologically sophisticated techniques, also has a significant population involved in sexual trafficking reveals the difficulty of dealing with this crime; an estimated 314,000 slaves are in the United States, which ranks 134 out of 162 countries for prevalence of slavery.[13]

Climate and Its Impact on Migration

Climate migration is not a new phenomenon. It has been happening for millennia. Global warming migration is new in that it is a specific subcategory of climate change that is anthropogenic in nature.

To deal with the different ways in which climate can lead to relocation, White (2012) developed a typology of climate refugees. Type 1 is in response to sudden, catastrophic change. This might be a hurricane or a nuclear disaster: The characteristic feature is that the climate is changed abruptly, although likely only on a short-term basis. As rough as disasters are, they do not necessarily lead to migration, though in the example of Tacloban discussed earlier in this chapter, they can lead to massive dislocation of populations.

Type 2 refers to instances where the damage is human induced and intentional. It is of the form of purposeful destruction. The Three Gorges Dam in China, for instance, was built to generate hydroelectric power, and resulted in the displacement of approximately 1.24 million people. This type of relocation is, as White noted, almost always coerced, and residents typically have limited time to prepare for relocation.

Type 3 refers to incremental deterioration of the environment; these may be induced by humans, but they are not intentionally destructive to the environment. Rather, environmental damage is a byproduct. In the United States, the dust bowl in the 1930s represented an incremental collapse of the ecology of farming communities due to poor agricultural practices, amplified by a prolonged drought that effectively destroyed the topmost layer of soil through erosion. Coastal flooding is another form of incremental climate change. However, how people at risk react is not known; some will stay and some will move. As White observed, even for coastal flooding situations, residents of low-lying areas might witness several seasons of inundations before seeking higher ground.

The types are not pure types but may be mixed. For instance, deforestation may be gradual, from drought, hydrological mismanagement, and poor farming practices or some combination therein, but punctuated by locally devastating forest fires. Similarly, ocean rise is a gradual process, but it is likely to be punctuated by increasingly lethal storms as the ocean level encroaches into urban settings.

Migration itself is difficult to predict; the challenge lies not only in getting global warming right on a local basis, but also then assessing the way social behavior responds to those local ecological changes. However, the ecological changes are identifiable, and they represent pressure points for migration. For instance, White's discussion of India in Information Box 7.3 shows how these various forces come together.

The Himalayan glaciers are vulnerable to melting, which puts Asia at catastrophic risk. Melting is occurring, though its pace varies substantially across regions. The most recent research we have reviewed, including the recent (2012) IPCC report, emphasizes two points: First, that the Himalayan region should not be treated as a homogenous geography.[14] Different glacial areas appear to be responding to climate changes with more sensitivity than others. In the aggregate, most areas show a decline in glacial ice volume, with many showing a substantial decline; the entire region is showing a net summative decline. A few areas, however, show increasing ice volume. Second, the effects of the meltoff on downstream populations will vary considerably by river. For instance, the Yellow River may experience an improvement in overall water flows (Immerzeel, van Beek, & Bierkens, 2010). However, others will decline:

(For) the Indus and the Brahmaputra, summer and late spring discharges are eventually expected to be reduced consistently and

Information Box 7.3 India: Climate Change and Migration

White (2012) noted that "In Western India, for example, Gujarat and Rajasthan are expected to experience water scarcity and enhanced urbanization. And storm surges in major coastal urban area such as Mumbai and Kolkata can be expected to induce migration away from the sea. Indian officials also express concerns that Himalayan glaciers will melt rapidly, initially causing flooding and then drought. The Himalayan glaciers, the 'Water Towers of Asia'—feed the Indus River, the Brahmaputra, the Mekong (which descends into Southeast Asia), the Irrawaddy in Myanmar, and the Yellow and Yangtze Rivers of China. Retired Air Marshall A.K. Singh a former commander in India's air force, foresees mass migration:

"It will be initially people fighting for food and shelter. When the migrations start, every state would want to stop the migrations from happening. Eventually, it would have to become a military conflict. Which other means do you have to resolve your border issues?"

(p. 72)

India is also in the process of securitization from Bangladesh. White further noted that

"...one sees India and Bangladesh officials in the early 00s expressing deep anxieties about Bangladesh's vulnerability to flooding. In 2003, India began construction of a 2,100 mile 'high tech' separation barrier. The officially stated (and ostensibly plausible) reason was of fear by Bangladeshi Islamists. Completed in early 2010, the fence has been fraught with tragic politics on the ground: border communities divided, property claims fenced, homes lost, and informal trade disrupted. India's efforts were supported by Washington and NATO, even as Bangladesh has been a reliable geostrategic ally. Nevertheless, as Bangladesh's vulnerability to climate change and its prospects for greater flooding have become more worrisome, being surrounded by razor wire has reified and hardened a precarious border—with Indian officials increasingly inclined to cite climate refugees, rather than an Islamist threat, as a concern."

(p. 71)

considerably around 2046 to 2065 after a period with increased flows due to accelerated glacial melt.

(Immerzeel et al., 2010)

Even with this variability, and recognizing that the Himalayas are only one component of the total water volume of the riparian watersheds, substantial numbers of people will be adversely affected: As Bostrom[15] noted, "We're not looking at a direct threat to the feeding of half a billion persons; a few millions may see actual improvement in food supply but we're left with a 'residual' of some sixty million persons whose access to food will be degraded." Importantly, access to food and water, for many of these people, is already degraded and will degrade further, promoting migration to urban areas, an outcome widely forecast across the region.

Loss of water from deglaciation is not the only climate change issue in the Himalayas. A more compelling short-term concern is lake buildup and collapsing ice dams and consequent downriver flooding, which White (2012) above called a type 1 climate change problem. Sudden outflows are called *Glacial Lake Outburst Floods* (GLOFS). They can be caused by extreme rainfall, unpredictable seismic events, or increased glacial melting.[16] Risks from GLOFS are substantial: In June 2012, the city of Kedarnath, in the Indian Himalayas, was struck with a sudden outflow, with disastrous effect. Outflow mortality was estimated at 11,600;[17] as of late October, 545 bodies had been "disposed of or cremated."[18] These events are expected to become more frequent as the Himalayas experience more meltoff in a warming future.

India also faces sea rise, with varying estimates from 0.6 meter to 1.0 meter by the end of the twenty-second century. This amount of rise would have devastating consequences for the megacities Dhaka and Kolkata.[19] Indeed, in Pakistan sea-rise is already engulfing about 80 acres daily.[20] Particularly of concern are the megadeltas across the subcontinent. A megadelta, according to Wikipedia, is a generic term given to the very large Asian river deltas, such as the Changjiang, Pearl, Red, Mekong, Irrawaddy, Ganges-Brahmaputra, and Indus. Dhaka, in Bangladesh and Kolkata, in India, are both located coastally at the confluence of these rivers in the Ganges delta. Dhaka, capitol of Bangladesh, is a megacity; the Dhaka district had a population of 18,305,671 in 2012. The city itself has the highest population density in the world.[21] Kolkata sat in the middle of an urban agglomeration of 14,112,536 in 2011. The megadeltas have several features: They are largely coastal, existing at the confluence of estuary, ocean, and river habitats, and are consequently low-lying (Kolkata, for instance, has an elevation of 5 to 30 feet). They are very vulnerable to ocean rise, violent storms including cyclones, and upriver flooding. Finally, though they have been historically agricultural areas, they are the source of a great deal of contemporary urbanization; Dhaka is forecast to reach a population of 40 million by 2050.

We can see then, across the Indian subcontinent, substantial climate stressors on current populations: Rising seas, Himalayan glacier meltoff and downriver flooding, and monsoon seasons forecast to start sooner and end later. Indeed, one would be challenged to find a place in India that will be unaffected. How many of these people will migrate, and where will they migrate to? One of the problems is that current rural-urban migration patterns, to the megacities, place more people in harm's way from rising seas. Herein lies one of the central problems faced by migrants:

The largest migration in history, about a billion people in the Indian subcontinent alone are relocating to urban areas unsustainable for human habitation. Once the land there is ruined, where *else* can they go? Upriver a few miles until it too floods? And what about the settlers already there? The coast is the end of the line.

One likely inland receiving area will be India's capitol, New Delhi, located in the north of India. The metropolitan region around New Delhi had a total population of 22.6 million in 2012, a 41% increase since 2001. However, it is by no means a safe haven, and it also already faces significant hydrological problems. It is depleting its available water sources. Eighty-six percent of Delhi's water supply comes from surface water, particularly the Yamuna River. It receives subsurface water through various wells, which are replenished from rainfall. The groundwater, however, is increasingly salinized and overexploited. It is rapidly depleting, with increasing loss of availability in different parts of the city. Delhi's groundwater level has gone down by about eight meters in the last 20 years, or about a foot a year. Delhi, in a word, is facing a water crisis. The chair of the Central Water Board for Delhi, Sushil Gupta, noted that:[22]

> in 1983, fresh groundwater was available at a depth of 10m or 33ft (1m equals 3.3ft). By 2011 it had fallen to 40m or about 132ft, with the period between 2002 and 2011 registering the most precipitous drop of 8.75m or nearly 29ft.[23]

Water tables in urban areas are declining because of the reduction in recharge areas as a result of the construction of roads, buildings, and pavements. The quality of water is deteriorating due to the mixing of sewerage water through unlined open drains, leakage from cesspits and septic drainage tanks, and contamination from industrial wastes.

Delhi, then, is no sanctuary for immigrants. Already facing significant water shortfalls, Delhi's prospects with its rapidly growing population are unfavorable. Hence, when we look across India, all of the destinations of migration are likely to be increasingly problematic or flat-out unlivable. Yet, when people are facing a coastal setting that is increasingly lashed by storms that are intensifying and dealing with a slowly but steadily rising ocean, might they migrate anyway? These kinds of questions simply cannot be answered in a precise way. All we can state with confidence is that the pressures to migrate will be enormous and that many people likely will, even though there may be nowhere to migrate.

From Subcontinent to World: Sea-Rise and Migration at +4 Celsius

The Indian subcontinent, though immense in its own, is a microcosm of the rest of the world. What will climate-related migration be when the planet averages four degrees Celsius hotter? Looking at a four degree Celsius increase, Nicholls et al. (2012) considered that:

> based on our analysis, a pragmatic estimate of sea-level rise by 2100, for a temperature rise of 4°C or more over the same time frame, is between 0.5 m and 2 m—the probability of rises at the high end is judged to be very low, but of unquantifiable probability. However, if realized, an indicative analysis shows that the impact potential is severe, with the real risk of the forced displacement of up to 187 million people over the century (up to 2.4% of global population). This is potentially avoidable by widespread upgrade of protection, albeit rather costly with up to 0.02 per cent of global domestic product needed, and much higher in certain nations.

Significant coastal displacement will occur, even if we add no further carbon in the air, due to the amount of CO_2 already in the atmosphere; indeed, there may already be enough CO_2 in the air to melt the planetary ice given time (Hansen, 2009). Without mitigation efforts, the 2012 draft of the IPCC policy-maker report cautions that "By 2100, due to climate change and development patterns and without adaptation, hundreds of millions of people will be affected by coastal flooding and displaced due to land loss (high confidence)."[24]

Myers (2002) provided regional predictions for 2050 based on climate change dynamics. Information Box 7.4 titled "Global Warming and Environmental Refugees: A 2150 Estimate" is his consideration of refugee numbers at that time.

Refugee Recognition as a UN Mandate

In the early part of the chapter, we cited numerous instances of violence committed against refugees. That the UN does not recognize climate refugees, in a time when their numbers may be on the verge of growing substantially, further puts them at risk for the worst of crimes, both individually and en masse. Though scant, UN peacekeeping forces are capable of providing some protections, and funding for water and food for refugee camps is needed for simple daily survival. Moreover, as we move more deeply into

Information Box 7.4 Global Warming and Environmental Refugees: A 2050 Estimate

Myers observed that large numbers of people will be displaced by 2050. This stems from coastal flooding, but is also associated with changes in rainfall and increasing drought in the middle latitudes. He noted that

> *Preliminary estimates indicate that the total number of people at risk of sea-level rise in Bangladesh could be 26 million, in Egypt 12 million, in China 73 million, in India 20 million, and elsewhere, including small island states, 31 million, making a total of 162 million. At the same time, at least 50 million people could be at severe risk through increased droughts and other climate dislocations.*

The consequence of this is a massive refugee crisis. In this, environmental problems ultimately may lead to conflict. Myers noted in this regard that climate refugees will stimulate political, social, and economic turmoil, all of which may be precursors to conflict. Environmental refugee problems consequently. . .

> *. . .readily become a cause of turmoil and confrontation. Leading to conflict and violence. Yet, as the problem becomes more pressing, our policy responses fall further short of measuring up to the challenge. To repeat a key point: environmental refugees have still to be officially recognized as a problem at all.*

In the wake of perceived threat to social cohesion, and national identity, refugees can become an excuse for outbreaks of ethnic tension and civil disorder, even political upheaval. This is already the case on those developed countries, where immigrant aliens increasing prove unwelcome, as with the experience of Haitians in the United States and North Africans in Europe.

Source: Myers, N. (2002). Environmental refugees: A growing phenomenon of the 21st century. Philosophical Transactions of the Royal Society, 357, 611.

the era of megacities (Chapter 8) security in the form of municipal police forces may be virtually absent in the migrant zones ringing core cities, the likely destination for most migrants. Yet, it is difficult in countries like the United States, Australia, and Canada to develop a coherent policy response to climate refugees when they are unable to develop a coherent response to global warming, or simply acknowledge it, for that matter.

A variety of entities are articulating for the development of international policy for climate refugees. These would include current climate refugees as well as those who will resettle from global warming effects. Reuveny (2008) advocated a five-step approach:[25]

1. Stimulate economic growth in LDCs (less developed countries) in order to reduce their dependence on the environment and enable investment in development and enforcement of environmental regulations and cleanup plan;
2. Promote lower population growth in LDCs in order to reduce the pressure on the environment;

3. Offset economic growth in LDCs with contraction in DCs (developed countries), keeping the rise in greenhouse gasses in check;
4. Begin adapting for climate change now in places prone to conflict and ecomigration; and
5. Fund these activities by using DCs funds, since the DCs over-reliance on fossil fuels created most of the current problem. This step could be achieved, for example, by raising taxes in DCs and investing the revenues in LDCs. [Parenthetical terms added]

Reuveny recognized that these policy proposals will not be easy. There will be problems of international collective action, and countries will try to shift their burden to others. There also is the challenge of international collective action. Reuveny expressed the concern that countries try to shift their own global warming population and economic burdens to other countries. Moreover, most countries are going in the opposite direction, fortifying their borders.

Increasingly, researchers and policy makers recognize the magnitude of the refugee problem that may stem from climate changes. There will come a time when global warming cannot be denied and when the importance of collective action on an international scale will be recognized in the highest political circles. Our hope is that such a realization occurs before it is too late, when billions of people are already on the move to escape climate change effects.

Endnotes

1. "UNHCR 2011 refugee statistics: full data." Retrieved September 3, 2013 at http://www.guardian.co.uk/news/datablog/2011/jun/20/refugee-statistics-unhcr-data.
2. "Mapping the Foreign Born in the United States." Retrieved September 2, 2013 at http://www.cfo.gov.ph/index.php?option=com_content&view=article&id=1619:mapping-the-foreign-born-in-the-united-states-part-i&catid=165:migration-related-articles&Itemid=901\.
3. "Refugees and climate change politics." Retrieved September 5, 2013 at http://thenextwavefutures.wordpress.com/2008/07/02/refugees-and-climate-change-politics/.
4. "Global Refugee Population: 1960-2010." Retrieved September 5, 2013 at http://www.johnmenadue.com/population/images/Graph1.jpg.
5. "Feared Migration Hasn't Happened: UN Embarrassed by Forecast on Climate Refugees." Retrieved September 6, 2013 at http://www.spiegel.de/international/world/feared-migration-hasn-t-happened-un-embarrassed-by-forecast-on-climate-refugees-a-757713.html.
6. Ibid. This figure shows the climate forecast model made by the UN from Norman Myers's work.

7. "Climate Refugees Map by UNEP." Retrieved September 8, 2013 at http://www.ecowalkthetalk.com/blog/2010/12/06/whither-go-climate-refugees/climate-refugees-map-by-unep/.

8. "Slow recovery in Philippines may increase storm hazards." Retrieved September 8, 2013 at http://www.bostonglobe.com/news/world/2014/01/12/philippines-faces-massive-resettlement-needs-post-typhoon-aid-comes-slowly/tdwH9886DTPbx84uyDUb8H/story.html.

9. "Palestinian refugee camps breeding ground for terrorists." Retrieved September 13, 2013 at http://rt.com/news/palestinian-refugee-camps-breeding-ground-for-terrorists/.

10. The point of this brief review is not to establish a political advocacy about crime as it is experienced among immigrants. The political advocates of all sides of this debate already have their "facts" and there is little point in trying to change someone's mind when they already know the "truth." We are simply trying to ascertain the best way to think about refugee and immigrant issues in the coming century, based on our reasoned judgment of the current life-worlds they inhabit. We think that the best overall perspective on immigrants generally is that they neither take away nor add to the crime problem in significant numbers, though the weight of evidence seems to be that they take away from crime. Consequently, the compelling question for us is, in what ways are immigrants vulnerable to victimization? For the most part, the answer to that question seems to lie in state hardening practices in response to fears about outsiders, and in the consequences of those hardening practices. Refugees, however, are especially vulnerable to victimization of all kinds, however sordid or vicious. We think that this guiding perspective is the most realistic way to anticipate resettlement problems in the future, when refugees, for all kinds of reasons including global warming, might anticipate a much more unfriendly world than the one they already inhabit, if that is possible, and experiencing that world in much larger numbers than today.

11. "Krasnodar Sex Trade Booming." Retrieved September 15, 2013 at http://iwpr.net/report-news/krasnodar-sex-trade-booming.

12. "The Global Slavery Index 2013." Retrieved September 15, 2013 at http://www.globalslaveryindex.org/findings/.

13. Ibid.

14. The 4th IPCC report in 2005 erroneously noted that the Himalayan glaciers would be melted by 2035, a figure that could not be confirmed and that was subsequently rejected by many researchers. The most recent IPCC report stops short of that prediction, though providing great detail in current levels of ice volume loss across the Himalayas.

15. "Climate Change: The Next Generation." Retrieved November 18, 2013 at http://climatechangepsychology.blogspot.com/2010/06/doug-bostrom-return-to-himalayas-fate.html.

16. "How The Hills Can Kill Again: Kedarnath calamity a proof of long ignored threat by melting Himalayan glaciers." Retrieved September 17, 2013 at http://indiatoday.intoday.in/story/uttarakhand-tragedy-floods-alarm-for-himalayan-glaciers/1/287074.html.

17. "81 pilgrims from Andhra missing in Uttarakhand." Retrieved September 17, 2013 at http://zeenews.india.com/news/andhra-pradesh/81-pilgrims-from-andhra-missing-in-uttarakhand_861198.html.

18. "15 more bodies found in Kedarnath." Retrieved September 17, 2013 at http://www.thehindu.com/news/national/other-states/15-more-bodies-found-in-kedarnath/article5285766.ece.

19. "Kolkata at risk from rising sea level." Retrieved September 19, 2013 at http://articles.timesofindia.indiatimes.com/2009-12-01/kolkata/28099932_1_sea-levels-global-warming-ipcc.

20. "Effects of Global Warming on India." Retrieved September 19, 2013 at http://en.wikipedia.org/wiki/Effects_of_global_warming_on_India.

21. "Delhi's great water fall: Capital fears riots and water shortages as groundwater level hits dangerous low." Retrieved September 20, 2013 at http://www.dailymail.co.uk/indiahome/indianews/article-2288607/Delhis-great-water-fall-Capital-fears-riots-water-shortages-groundwater-level-hits-dangerous-low.html#ixzz2jtodi16q
"The Draw of Dhaka." Retrieved September 20, 2013 at http://www.newgeography.com/content/00778-the-draw-dhaka.

22. Ibid.

23. "Delhi's great water fall: Capital fears riots and water shortages as groundwater level hits dangerous low." Retrieved September 21, 2013 at http://www.dailymail.co.uk/indiahome/indianews/article-2288607/Delhis-great-water-fall-Capital-fears-riots-water-shortages-groundwater-level-hits-dangerous-low.html#ixzz2jtodi16q.

24. IPCC (2013) Climate Change 2014 Draft (unpublished), 28 Oct. "High confidence" means that the IPCC task force, reviewing the findings, concludes that the outcome has an 80 percent chance of being correct.

25. "Ecomigration: global warming will increase environmental refugees." Retrieved September 3, 2013 at http://news.mongabay.com/2007/1128-ecomigration.html.

8

THE FUTURE OF MIGRATION: A PLANET OF MEGACITIES

Ruth continued, "By 2060, the weather seemed to stay hot all the time. We had pretty much settled here, and the rivers were still flowing through here, but they didn't flow all the time anymore. The Missouri, it is still a big strong river, but the other ones, they were on their way out."

Clete: "Did you see what was going on anywhere else?"

Ruth: "Yeah, we did, and it was our own fault. You know, we were pretty much settled at that point, but we always loved going West, so we headed out one more time. California was always beautiful—well, it used to be beautiful. So we decided to make the U.S. West Coast our second trip. We headed out on the bike on 80 through Utah. Salt Lake City was still doing pretty well, but gas was pretty scarce and extremely expensive so we had to haul a lot of our own."

Clete was curious. The intermountain West—he almost did his research there. He wanted to hear more. "Can you tell me more about Salt Lake?"

Ruth: "It was different. It was like ... well ... it was different, stronger somehow. Like it was ready for this. They were building underground reservoirs when we were there. They were making a safe zone, too. Reaching north to Boise, west to Reno. Beto said they were making a country in a country. They reached out to the reservations and built alliances with the Indians. That's why a lot of the reses have big shiny temples and lots of public works today."

"Salt Lake tried to take the land before, almost three centuries ago. But the United States stopped 'em then. Well, the United States ain't so strong now; they've got their own problems. All the troops trying to control the southern borders. The United States needs friends. Three centuries ago, the United States wouldn't negotiate. This time it did."

Clete had heard the idea batted around. The twenty-second and seventeenth centuries were in full collision around the world. The past was hammer to the present. Population crashing to seventeenth-century levels. Rebuilding cities without gas and oil. We were rewinding history and playing it forward again, but this time it was playing out differently. Religion and tribe were winning; nations were losing.

Ruth: "In Sacramento is where we saw the big changes. The city was dried out; the rivers that fed it came from the mountains and were parched.[1] The fields in the region were poisoned from ocean saltwater that somehow got in there. Most of the people had headed out to the coast, but there was nowhere to go. San Francisco? Los Angeles? They had their own problems, big time. The cities could not take care of their own citizens, with all the people moving off the coast. Criminals loved it. The city could not afford to keep all the police they were used to. So where could they go? They started heading north to Canada. Well, Canada didn't go for that. So after a few years, they closed the border."

Clete had studied the migrations in school. When you sat back and looked at it, the cities along the coast were not really that financially strapped; their budgets were only down a small percentage. But that small amount translated into significant personnel cutbacks, which in turn led to further tax base loss, and the process fed on itself. And the loss of tax base from coastal housing, especially after insurers stopped insuring the houses and businesses there, made long-term financial forecasting impossible. Fifteen percent 1 year, 20 the next, then game over. Coastal cities could not get credit ratings and couldn't pay back, and that crashed the bond market. They had to pay employees with cash, and none of them could much beyond a year. The big cities retreated to their core interiors, leaving the suburbs to fend for themselves. Some settlers just camped outside on the edge of the city; some headed for the abandoned housing along the coast; and a lot of them headed to the refugee camps at the Canadian border.

The world's population is moving into very large cities. These cities are called megacities. Any assessment of future trends must take into account this important and far-reaching development in human ecology. Global warming is occurring at the same time that human populations are clustering, and it is happening where they are clustering. When the effects of global warming are intensified, by midcentury and forward, the social and security environments that humans have created will be quite different from today. It is that global environment that we must first describe prior to assessing the influence of global warming factors. Consider the following observation from the CS Monitor:[2]

> It's a fundamental shift that may be altering the very fabric of human life, from the intimate, intricate structures of individual families to the massive, far-flung infrastructures of human civilizations. In 1950, fewer than 30% of the world's 2.5 billion inhabitants lived in urban regions. By 2050, almost 70% of the world's estimated 10 billion inhabitants—or more than the number of people living today—will be part of massive urban networks, according to the Population Division of the United Nations' Department of Economic and Social Affairs (italics added).

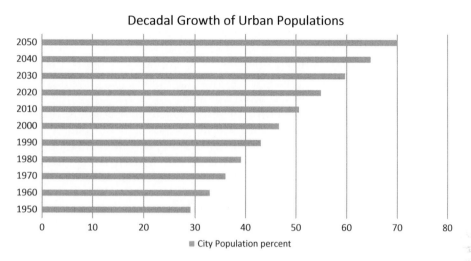

Figure 8.1 Urban growth globally. *Source:* Megacities of the world: a glimpse of how we'll live tomorrow. Retrieved September 29, 2013 at http://www.csmonitor.com/World/Global-Issues/2010/0505/Megacities-of-the-world-a-glimpse-of-how-we-ll-live-tomorrow.

These staggering statistical trends are driving the evolution of the "megacity," defined as an urban agglomeration of more than 10 million people. Sixty years ago there were only two: New York/ Newark and Tokyo. Today there are 22 such megacities—the majority in the developing countries of Asia, Africa, and Latin America—and by 2025 there will probably be 30 or more.

The chart in Figure 8.1, "Urban Growth Globally," provides a picture of the dramatic increase of urban populations around the world over time.[3] These numbers show that, from 1950 to 2050, the percent of the human population that live in cities more than doubled and by 2050 is expected to comprise 70% of the global population. These cities may not all be megacities, but they reinforce the important notion that the world's population is urbanizing, locating increasingly large numbers of people in proportionally smaller places.

Where Are People Migrating? The Global Littorals and Megadeltas

Migration is global in scope, but most migrants, whether or not they want to, likely will not come to the so-called first-world economic countries. Most cannot afford that kind of move, and in any case would be denied entry without a skill that would increase their value to the receiving country. Consequently, most urbanization will likely occur in countries already heavily urbanized, most urban populations are likely to come from within the originating country, and most resettlement will be in countries that are already poor. They will mostly end up adjacent to littoral zones. This is a significant problem; littoral zones that are today adjacent to coasts will in the future occupy contemporary coast lines, converting them to marine environments and part-marine ecosystems. They will not be habitable for people.

Countries that are the poorest, and those most vulnerable to hostile climate changes, are consequently likely to become even poorer without the substantial aid of the rich countries, those that are in fact largely responsible for global warming. Bangladesh, for instance, is likely to experience substantial population growth in its coastal areas from already-in-play forces of urbanization, and then at midcentury begin to experience the sustained effects of ocean creep into its urban centers and peripheries. The capitol of Bangladesh is Dhaka and is a megacity with a population of 13 million, including the city itself and the surrounding metropolitan area. It is located on a flood plain and is prone to monsoon flooding. The city's water table has sunk by 50 meters in the past four decades and continues to drop about 2 meters a year. The population of Dhaka has grown by 56.5% in the past decade, the highest in Bangladesh. The city is also an exemplar of the urban poor of the future. Information Box 8.1 displays a discussion of the urban poor of Dhaka (Hossain, 2008).

Dhaka does not face these problems alone. In Information Box 8.2 are a list of the fastest growing megacities in the world. None of them are in Western countries, though many of them are in the process of "Westernizing."[4]

Consider the locations of the cities in Information Box 7.2. Karachi is located on the Arabian Sea, near the Indus flood plain. It is the main seaport and financial capital of Pakistan. Shenzhen is on the Pearl River delta, next to Hong Kong, facing the South China Sea. It is southern China's major financial center and one of the busiest container ports in the world. Lagos is a major metropolitan area and largest metro area in Africa. It is an island city, located on several islands that are separated by creeks. Lagos Island, the center of commerce and the business district, is situated between Lagos Lagoon and the Atlantic. Beijing, located on the North China Plain, is about 40-60 meters above the ocean and is not threatened by rising seas. Bangkok, whose name may have derived from Bang Ko meaning island, is located on the Chao Phraya River delta, about 25 km from the Gulf of Thailand and has an average elevation of about 1.5 meters. Dhaka, located on the

Information Box 8.1 Dhaka and the Growth of the Urban Poor

Dhaka has experienced a prolific growth of slums and squatters since the independence of the country in 1971. Slums and settlements are concentrated mostly on the fringes of the city.

There is a high propensity of young people to migrate to the city of Dhaka. More than 50% of "migrant populations" in the city were less than 35 years of age. Young populations predominate in urban centers because they are usually not yet integrated into rural traditional systems and they are more likely to leave the village than the older population.

Slum dwellers have mostly settled temporarily on public or private land. They are often evicted from their settlements. For most houses, the roof is made of tin and the wall beams are constructed of bamboo. The average floor spaces of poor urban households are only 125 square feet, and even smaller in Dhaka City. Slum and squatter settlements in these areas are prone to annual flooding, and are located in low-lying areas and along canals and railway tracks.

The formation of slums is closely associated with rural-urban migration. People have migrated there from mostly rural areas. Low incomes in rural areas, river erosion of agricultural land, and job opportunities in the city are the main factors behind the migration. Urban growth is not commensurate with the economic and social development of the Dhaka City, so significant portions of the urban population are living below the poverty line. The percentage of the urban population living below the poverty line is comparatively higher in Dhaka City than other urban centers of the country. The sociopolitical and economic structures of the country are generally responsible for urban poverty and the emergence of slums in Dhaka City.

Source: Hossain, S. (2008). "Rapid urban growth and poverty in Dhaka City." Bangladesh e-Journal of Sociology, *5(1).*

Ganges delta, has already been discussed. Guangzhou-Foshan is actually two adjacent cities.

Guangzhou, formerly Canton, and Foshan are both located in the Pearl River delta. Guangzhou backs up to Baiyun Mountain, providing parts of the city with elevated protection from rising seas. The two areas are actually prefectures rather than cities per se and are separated by a tributary of the Pearl River. Shanghai, whose name derives from "on the sea," is the world's largest container port. It is on the Yangtze River delta and consists of a peninsula, China's second largest island, and a number of smaller islands located on the East China Sea. Delhi in Northern India has an average elevation of 214 meters and is not affected by sea rise. Jakarta, on the northwest coast of Java on Jakarta Bay, faces the Java Sea. Jakarta lies in a low basin whose elevation ranges from 2 to 50 meters, with an average of 8 meters.

Information Box 8.2 Fastest Growing Megacities in the World (Urban Areas with More Than 10 Million Residents)

Rank	Geography	Urban Area	Population Estimate	Growth (Decade) (%)
1	Pakistan	Karachi	20,877,000	80.5
2	China	Shenzhen	12,506,000	56.1
3	Nigeria	Lagos	12,090,000	48.2
4	China	Beijing, BJ	18,241,000	47.6
5	Thailand	Bangkok	14,544,000	45.2
6	Bangladesh	Dhaka	14,399,000	45.2
7	China	Guangzhou-Foshan	17,681,000	43.0
8	China	Shanghai	21,766,000	40.1
9	India	Delhi	22,826,000	39.2
10	Indonesia	Jakarta	26,746,000	34.6
11	Turkey	Istanbul	12,919,000	25.3

Source: Demographia World Urban Areas (2013), http://demographia.com/db-worldua.pdf.

Istanbul, in Turkey, is located on the Bosporus River. To its south is the Marmara Sea and to the north, the Black Sea. As a seaport it is at a particularly important global location: it is both the closest Asian city to Europe and the closest European city to Asia. Though located on a peninsula, Istanbul is also situated on seven hills, with its highest elevation at 288 meters.

Hence, 9 of the 11 fastest growing megacities on the planet are located in proximity to ocean-facing deltas, islands or both, and are likely to be profoundly altered, if not altogether abandoned, in the face of significant sea rise. The other two megacities, though safe from sea rise, face significant problems of water shortages from aquifer overuse and are not particularly viable as future immigration destinations.

What happens to the people who migrate to these megadeltas and megacities? Will they continue to relocate in baby steps, trying to keep a safe distance away from the encroaching ocean but still in proximity to their respective urban districts? Moreover, many of the cities are financial and industrial hubs, and any threat to them carries with it substantial economic peril both regionally and globally. It is clear that current patterns of human migration and financial investment in coastal areas, as inexorable as they seem to be, are in stark conflict with the changing global ecology of a global warming world. What options will immigrants have? Threat perspective tells us that they will not be able to leave their countries; the greater their need to relocate, the greater is likely to be the resistance from potential settler areas. Such peoples face, as Agnew (2012) observed, a truly dire future.

Megacities: Hardening or Fragmentation?

Sometime in 2012, about half the population of the planet became urban. By 2050, 80% of the population will be urban. This trend reflects movement and relocation on the part of poor populations and third-world countries worldwide; the populations of the comparatively wealthy Western countries are actually shrinking. The current rate of urbanization is dropping, but the sheer volume of it is increasing. People will move to the megacities, and they will, if humanly possible and against all odds, move to megacities in the United States and Europe. State hardening is only one outcome; state weakening and fragmentation is another. It will be recalled that Homer-Dixon (1999) emphasized that state hardening was one indication of the process of state threat and increased vulnerability; that is, state hardening was one of the first responses of a weakened state. If the state cannot harden its way out of the financial and economic pressures associated with megacity development, then it faces fragmentation and loss of border control. This is one of the likely outcomes for megacities, where security and social services for much of the newer migrant classes are financially unaffordable. This will lead to an increase in violence, which in a cyclic interaction, will further undercut the ability of the center city to exert control or economically develop the new migrant areas.

Megacities and the Modernity Lag

Why are people moving to megacities? One explanation is that the Industrial Revolution is still gaining momentum around the world. The so-called first world or postindustrialized countries have enjoyed the benefits of the Industrial Revolution, including widely perceived quality-of-life improvements, access to a wide range of goods, and life longevity. People in the rest of the world want the benefits of the revolution as well, and they find that those benefits are not available in the rural areas of the world. Information Box 8.3, titled "The Modernity Lag," describes the

Information Box 8.3 The Modernity Lag

The world's human populations want what Westerners already have: the good things in life. To achieve them, they move to cities where they hope that they can enjoy the fruits of the Industrial Revolution as it comes to their areas. The citification of the world, and the emergence of the megacity as the predominant urban form, reflects this individual desire. The following quote discusses the modernity lag.

Today, on average, 3 out of 4 people living in modern industrialized states are already building their lives within an urban area—a ratio that will jump to more than 5 in 6 by 2050. By contrast, today in the least-developed regions of the world, more than 2 out of 3 people still eke out a living in a rural area. For these people, even the slumdog existence in places like Dharavi can offer more opportunities than their villages ever could. And within these developing regions, according to UN-HABITAT, cities are gaining an average of 5 million new residents—per month.

"Most of these [urban immigrants] couldn't earn cash in their rural situations," says Chuck Redman, director of the School of Sustainability at Arizona State University in Tempe. "There's not as much of a cash economy there, but they still want cash to buy radios and mobile phones or TVs—or even send their kids to school, which costs money in many of these countries."

Call it the lag of modernity: The changes wrought by industrialization began slowly 200 years ago, accelerated through the twentieth century in the West, and now are spreading exponentially around the globe. Many observers see great promise in this urbanizing trend: The efficiencies of cities can cut energy consumption up to 20%, transportation costs for goods and labor can drop significantly, and entertainment industries can thrive when millions live together. In other words, cities are giant cash machines, the primary locus of economic growth.

Megacities face a huge challenge. The massive numbers of people moving to cities are hoping for a future they believe is not available in their current homes. Is it possible for the cities to provide support if the rural areas cannot? It is not at all clear that they can.

...as megacities evolve in the developing world, many groan under the weight of a sudden, massive, and unprecedented demand for services never seen in the West. The basic necessities of clean water, of sanitation systems to remove megatons of garbage and human waste, of transportation systems to shuttle millions of workers, not to mention the need for electrical networks, health-care facilities, and policing and security, are, simply put, creating one of the greatest logistical challenges ever seen in human history. And this is even before factoring in the challenges of climate change, terrorism, and the preservation of human dignity.

relocation of citizens to urban areas worldwide in order to seek out a better life.[5]

Davis (2006) has written extensively on the character of megacities. Most of the people who move to these areas will face a bleak future, a life with scant opportunities in massive slums beyond the social services and economic opportunities available in the core city.

Slums, according to Davis, are almost apocalyptic in their implications for inhabitants. They are populated by rural-to-urban migrants, and in the second generation their children are contributing to the population explosion in these areas.

The cities themselves will be dramatically different from the cities that were fonts of opportunity in the Western Industrial Revolution. Davis noted that "Unlike the industrial pilgrims who once flocked to Manchester, Chicago, Tokyo and the other great capitalist centers of the nineteenth and twentieth centuries, country-dwellers in the developing world today stream toward cities that hold little promise of real jobs." They bring all their possessions with them and find the only place to live is in a city's slums, squatter camps, shantytowns, or favelas typically located in the rural-urban interface to the city, also called the periurban zone. They arrive with everything they have, which often is what they have been able to hide from robbers, gangs, extortionists, and government agents. They settle in areas outside basic municipal services; they survive, but they do not thrive.[6] Their children and children's children, together with a steady stream of new immigrants, feed the massive explosion of people in periurban areas in megacities today.

These cities are not centers of opportunity unless one is a gang member, a terrorist, or a member of organized crime. Many of the periurban areas do not have sanitation, fresh water, or security. There is a juxtaposition between wealth and poverty, the business center bumping up against some of the poorest urban area in the world. Information Box 8.4, titled "Religion and Violence in the Megacity," presents Davis's dark view of the future of megacities.

Megacities, Inequality, and Crime

A United Nations report titled *State of the World Population 2007* provides a grim description of the future faced by megacities.[7] This report echoes many of the concerns Davis raised. Described as urbanization's second wave, it is responsible for *conditions that can outmatch the Dickensian squalor of the Industrial Revolution.*[8] It particularly focused on violence in the city and sought to describe the primary crime and violence concerns megacities might face. The central concern was that violence in cities was increasing, at the same time that inequality was increasing and resources for combating crime were decreasing. The findings are presented below:

Interpersonal violence. Interpersonal violence and insecurity is rising and is particularly pronounced in urban areas of poorer countries. This violence is rapidly becoming a significant security and public health issue. Data suggests that the violence is growing faster in the larger and faster-growing cities.

Information Box 8.4 Religion and Violence in the Megacity

Davis (2006) contended that megacity slums of the future will become centers for the spread of fundamental religions.

Today, religious organizations—Islamist, Hindu, Evangelical—are the single most important source of social cohesion among citydwellers in the developing world. Beyond spiritual sustenance and community, religious organizations offer social services no longer provided by the state, laws for virtuous conduct in chaotic environs, and membership in a global polity that transcends the corrupt nation-state that has excluded them. Political Islam continues to spread in power and influence from Cairo to Jakarta; the ascendance of its political parties—and their grassroots appeal—has received nervous attention from the Western media. Hindu fundamentalism, if remarked upon less often, has had an analogous trajectory in the bustees *of Delhi and Mumbai. Pentecostal sects attract new adherents at astonishing rates from Brasilia to Johannesburg, altering political and community life in ways as yet not understood.*

He concluded with an apocalyptic view of the future, one of ceaseless violence between the slums and the cities they inhabit:

Though it never becomes explicit, an air of eventual but inevitable violence hangs over this account. A "planet of the slums," in the long view, is a planet doomed to violent encounters between those living in the slums and those outside them; Davis is hardly alone in this appraisal. Inside the Pentagon, strategists "now assert," as Davis writes, "that the 'feral, failed cities' of the Third World will be the distinctive battlespace of the twenty-first century." Spurred by the recent travails of their forces in the blighted alleyways of Mogadishu, Fallujah, and Sadr City, the military's sharpest minds—who a short time ago were devising counter-insurgency tactics for the jungles of South East Asia or Central America—have turned to the challenges of "Military Operations in Urbanized Terrain"—MOUT, in Pentagonese. Davis concludes Planet of Slums *with the war planners; he leaves us with a* Blade Runner *vision of the dystopic urban future: "hornetlike helicopter gunships [stalking] enigmatic enemies in the narrow streets of the slum districts, pouring hellfire into the shanties night after night, the slums [replying each morning] with suicide bombers and eloquent explosions."*

Inequality. Day-to-day life of the urban poor is marked by social exclusion and inequality. They are often resented in cities where they relocate and become victims of crime and violence. State crime control and justice institutions are inadequate for addressing violence among the new urban poor; they end up developing their own security, often in the form of neighborhood gangs. Women are victims of both sexual and domestic violence.

Globalization of crime. Processes of globalization have aggravated inequality while simultaneously reducing the capacity of the state to take remedial action. Criminal organizations capitalize on open markets. They can expand their market base across cities and countries, creating a global criminal economy. New forms of electronic fraud and international trafficking are emerging. The drug industry is internationalizing and has a significant impact on violence and crime.

Economic impacts of violence. Violence in turn has a substantial impact on economic, political, and social organization and undercuts development efforts. The report noted, for instance, that if the Latin American region had a rate of crime like the rest of the world, its per capita gross domestic product might be a quite robust 25% higher.

Urban space and the privatization of security. Crime and violence, a consequence of the new urbanization, in turn lead to the reorganization of urban space. Security is privatized; only those who can afford to hire private security and build walls to cloister themselves from violence will do so. The privatization of security appears to be associated with violence and disrespect for human rights. Crimes of robbery, rape, and assault on poorer communities outside of privatized areas and walled communities are more severe. Walled communities also contribute to the "erosion of social capital—long-standing reciprocal trust among neighbors and community members—which is itself an effective protection against crime."

Youth and violence. The new urban demographic is also forecast to be a young demographic. A forecast for a "youth bulge" could lead to an increase in violence. Women are vulnerable to sexual violence and harassment. Young men tend to be both the recipients and cause of violent victimization and homicide. Large numbers of young contribute to gang growth and violence.

Homer-Dixon identified ways in which urban growth in the current age contributed to violence. Those ways are presented in Information Box 8.5, "Urban Growth and Violence."

Megacity Vulnerability to Global Warming

It is to the problems already faced by megacities that we look at the impacts of global warming. Geographically, almost all of them are located in areas that are particularly vulnerable to global warming effects, with enormous financial impact on those cities. Consider the map presented in Figure 8.2, "Drowning."[9]

The map in Figure 8.2 presents an estimate of flood-attributable losses from climate changes by 2050. The loss estimate, at a trillion dollars, was from an assessment of 136 cities globally. The report took into consideration subsidence (from compression from settlement and loss of ground water), storm likelihood, and sea rise. The population areas presented in Figure 8.2 only represent the top 10 cities for expenses. Importantly, most of these cities have substantial immigrant populations that are anticipated to grow substantially.

Information Box 8.5 Urban Growth and Violence

Homer-Dixon described the following factors that contributed to the rapid megacity growth and in turn are associated with megacity violence.

1950 to 1990—a fivefold increase in the rate of urban residents in developing countries. 37% of the citizens in developing countries now live in cities. By 2025, upwards of two-thirds of citizens in developing countries will live in cities.

1. Key factor for urban growth is the gap between standard of living in rural areas and perceived standard in urban areas.
2. Rural migrants tend to be young, increasing the youth demographic in urban populations in poor countries.
3. Young poor urban men are easier than others to recruit for radical political ends. Young poor families have substantial needs for social services such as education, jobs, medicine, and health care.
4. Urban violence is not only interpersonal. It includes political violence, both toward the state and by the state against challengers and communal and ethnic violence.
   a. In the 1970s, austerity measures in many countries sparked a worldwide wave of protest and violence against the state.
   b. The expansion of immense, periurban squatter settlements and slums in Africa, Asia, and Latin America was closely associated with rising crime. In these circumstances, organized crime can easily capture a foothold.

Source: Homer-Dixon, T. (1999). Environment, scarcity, and violence. Princeton, NJ: Princeton University Press.

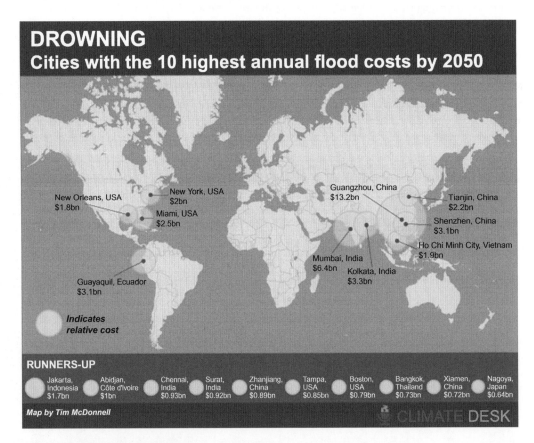

Figure 8.2 Drowning. *Source*: Hallegatte et al.

These losses should be taken in the context of municipal budgets. A significant part of a municipal budget is spent on public services—sewer, roads, security, fire prevention, and the like. These expenses have the capacity to substantially erode municipal budgets while their populations are growing. These expenses are further complicated by the geography of migration. Periurban areas tend to lack infrastructure, the investment for sewage treatment, plumbing, and fresh water, and a road system is from scratch. These areas additionally need geographically redesigned and expanded urban security. Where can these basic needs come from if a megacity is facing a steady decline in its tax base from existing shortfalls and threats to its infrastructure from rising seas?

From the discussion in this chapter; we can see that the emergent megacity populations globally face two problems, both of which are likely to get worse over time. First, it is quite challenging to see where funding for the periurban components of a criminal justice system will come from, particularly after the onset of coastal flooding from sea rise. Indeed, beyond the occasional symbolic police raid into such areas, funding for a stable security presence seems like a daunting challenge. It is a significant risk that needs to be part of long-term planning. Second, one cannot see a way that crime can be controlled. As Walker (1989) has shown in his review of analyses of U.S. cities when police went on strike, crime skyrockets immediately when a police presence is removed. Though this is only analogous to security shortcomings in megacity settings, it is difficult to imagine that crime of all kinds will not be a substantial problem.

In the next chapter, we will see that some megacities in fact seem to have a handle on crime; it is not particularly high when compared to other, smaller cities. However, others seem to have significant issues simply trying to find out what their crime problems are. The next chapter will focus specifically on the periurban areas, their characteristics, and the criminological challenges they face.

Endnotes

1. "Leading Scientists Explain How Climate Change Is Worsening California's Epic Drought." Retrieved September 28, 2013 at http://thinkprogress.org/climate/2014/01/31/3223791/climate-change-california-drought/.
2. "Megacities of the world: a glimpse of how we'll live tomorrow." Retrieved September 29, 2013 at http://www.csmonitor.com/World/Global-Issues/2010/0505/Megacities-of-the-world-a-glimpse-of-how-we-ll-live-tomorrow.
3. Ibid.

4. Westernizing, for many, is the adoption of the economic programs that facilitate the purchase of goods and products in a global economy. However, many of these areas, as Huntington noted, do not seek Western forms of religion, and resist various aspects of individualism characteristic of Western cultures. In the current era, China may be leading a trend toward Orientalism, a return to the values associated with the Orient, and away from the "permissive cornucopia" characteristic of Western culture and economic life.

5. "Megacities of the world: a glimpse of how we'll live tomorrow." Op. Cit.

6. "Our Dark Places: Mike Davis offers a grim preview of the planet's political future." Retrieved September 30, 2013 at http://www.motherjones.com/media/2006/05/our-dark-places.

7. "Social Contradictions in Growing Cities: Dialogue and Discord." Retrieved October 1, 2013 at http://www.unfpa.org/swp/2007/english/chapter_2/social_contradictions.html.

8. "Urbanization's Second Wave: A Difference of Scale." Retrieved October 2, 2013 at http://unfpa.org/swp/2007/english/chapter_1/urbanization.html.

9. "Drowning: Cities with the 10 highest annual flood costs by 2050." Retrieved October 7, 2013 at http://www.treehugger.com/climate-change/task-force-warns-time-now-prepare-future-storms.html.

9

FAVELA AND METROPOLIS: THE CRUCIBLES OF CRIME IN A MEGAURBAN ENVIRONMENT

Clete decided to follow up on the trip to California: "Did you head over to the coast from Sacramento?"

Ruth: "Oh yeah, boy was that a mistake. We really needed to find some gas, and the black market was running overtime. We knew we could find all we wanted, and we had the jingle, but, well, the coast was a mistake. Crazy, crazy."

Clete: "Do you mind talking about it?"

Ruth: "Well, it's what you're here for. Sure." She took a deep breath. "Ever see someone cut open from groin to chest? I mean, she was just there, lying in the street for a couple of days before someone bagged her and carted her off."

Clete: "Why did they do it?"

Ruth: "Did you really just ask me that? What's wrong with you? What does it matter?" Ruth stood up and walked out of the room. Clete mopped his brow; it was getting too hot for comfort, even in the shade. After a few minutes, she came back in. Her voice was emotionless. "It's still in my mind like I just saw it. The gang there wouldn't let anyone touch her; it was a warning. Our territory, *venga guardia y busca la muerte*. Cops couldn't get to her, a dead cop in a neighborhood ringed by snipers, flying gun-bots and small drone grenades—it was a trap and the cops knew it. I think it was the dogs that bothered me the most. When they bagged her, you couldn't tell what she was."

Clete felt the nausea rise in his stomach. He knew about the gangs. The big gangs had moved all through the coast and imported their violence. The powerful Mexican cartels already had people in more than a thousand U.S. cities even before the great warming. The Indonesian and Russian gangs tried to muscle in, but did not stand a chance. The American gangs learned to play fast, though. The United States was paying a vicious price for its massive prisonization experiment, and now the gangs ran the outside at will. They were tough. Maniacs. Besides, everyone seemed to want to be in a gang; it provided a plate at the table. Racial violence became increasingly common. Mayors of the major U.S. cities learned to stay out of the way. Not even the National Guard could dislodge the gangs from an urban setting, though there were some pitched battles. Welcome to Mogadishu right here at home. Some mayors survived by becoming players. When that happened, you couldn't tell the police from the gangs, except that the police got photo-ops with the mayors while they were still alive. Gang members got photo-ops with the mayors, too, but they weren't so pretty.

Urban research in the fields of criminology and criminal justice in the United States is sharply limited. Much of it is very good, focusing on critically important issues facing U.S. cities, their metropolitan areas, and the great urban underclass. Its theories are fecund and its methods increasingly focused, especially with the strong microsetting geographic turn in the recent past. It is also moving toward important policy regimes, recognizing the importance of just practices blended with programs that seek to address root causes. But it is not ready for events in the rest of the world. It shows scant interest in megacities and megadeltas, displays little curiosity about what can reasonably be called the greatest migration event in the history of the planet, and infrequently writes of favelas (although, see Villarreal & Silva, 2006), all of which increasingly represent the central tendency of social and political life on this planet.[1]

Profound changes in human ecology and predominant corporate forms are taking place globally, marked by the ascendancy of global cities over a weakened and challenged nation-state system, the massive urban influx of the desperately poor with few options beyond the economics of their own bodies, the globalization and accumulation of vast wealth of the criminal enterprise, and the increasing blend of crime, business, and terrorism in advantageous urban geographies. Add global warming to the mix, and challenges to the survival of the nation-state system seem overwhelming.

Our fields of research in criminology and criminal justice, focused on the accurate depiction of the immediate, the well-defined, and the highly focused, tend to avoid the messy imprecision associated with broad trends and their implications for the future. Further, research on events in the United States does not provide a sensibility of what is going on internationally in the important arenas of crime globalization, megacity and megadelta urbanization, and the increasing overlap of terrorism and illicit goods marketeering. Indeed, the difference between crime and justice in the United States and much of the rest of the world is not of degree but of kind; our research here will not advance our knowledge elsewhere.

Consider the following quote:

Since the early 1990's global illicit trade has embarked on a great mutation. It is the same mutation as that of international terrorist organizations like Al Qaeda or Islamic Jihad ... The world's first unmistakable glimpse of this transformation came on September 11, 2001. Politicians would later say that on that day "the world changed." It might be more apt to say that on that day something about the world was revealed.

(Naim, 2005, p. 7)

We emphasize the word "revealed" in this quote. Almost all of us have traded in the global illicit marketplace; it is hard to avoid. Many of us have purchased knock-offs made in sweatshops employing a labor force that works under conditions that mimic chattel slavery. Much of the available music purchased online is illegally downloaded and repackaged in the image of legal outlets. Change handed out to street urchins sometimes goes back to middlemen who use it to buy working corners for female slaves to offer their personal favors. Many of the lower priced computers, and some of the more expensive ones as well, blend in parts illegally purchased or produced and reproduced, then refabricated or disguised as a legal product. Pornography is pervasive on the internet and supplies funds for sexual slavery, especially of children. Inexpensive medicines are available from seemingly legal online pharmacies that are fronts for illicit medical drug enterprises. None of these are innocent purchases. They happen daily by the millions and they feed a criminal underground that accounts for nearly a tenth of the world's economic gross product. Products in the illicit marketplace, moreover, sometimes fund international terrorism. Indeed, one of the profound changes in the globalized, fast paced, incredibly wealthy—and illicit— economy is its meshing with terrorism, jihadism, and insurgency. That is what was revealed on September 11, 2001. And that is why this line of research and discussion is important to the fields of criminology and criminal justice.

The U.S. criminal justice system is also complicit in the booming illicit marketplace, even when it is not directly corrupted. Citizens are routinely exiled from legal employment by virtue of their placement of an "x" in a box on an employment form asking about previous arrests. To the extent that they are motivated to have a family, maintain a livelihood, and enjoy the good things in life, their occupational choices are provided only by the illicit marketplace. Every time someone is released from prison, whatever their high hopes, they likely will find their occupational opportunities limited to the criminal or drug underground. Thus the state sabotages itself. Whatever the justification for sending someone to prison—and those justifications may be substantial—the economic and security fallout is immense and long-term, though rarely considered seriously.

The globalization of illicit enterprises, facilitated by massive arms sales and the proliferation of drugs, is occurring against a backdrop of megaurban growth fed by the largest migration in human history (Naim, 2005). The dynamic of urbanization carries with it violence, ranging from the street crimes of opportunistic individuals to organized insurgency intended to destabilize a region or state. Moreover, the violence in urban areas is fundamentally different than in rural areas; one infrequently finds street gangs defending turf in rural areas, though it does happen. The opposite seems to be true as well; one infrequently finds street gangs NOT defending their turf in the favelas of large metropolitan areas. Moreover, the rate of urban growth in many cities around the world is explosive, and carries with it portents of violence and individual suffering only now being studied and understood.

Many of the very large and densely populated urban areas are located on the megadeltas of the world. These urban areas are on a collision course with global warming and the rising seas it will bring; in the clash between rapidly growing littoral populations and global warming, global warming wins hands down. Physics trumps demography. Beyond that collision, the black market with its substantial flexibility of operations has substantial advantages over the legal market, as we will discuss. For these reasons, megaurban perspectives on crime and violence should occupy a prominent role in efforts to understand the larger urban impacts of global warming.

Violence Correlates in the Burgeoning Metropolis

The urban framework we will look at is *Crime and violence in an urbanizing world*. Brennan-Galvin (2002), in this synthetic work, provides a glimpse of the present and near-term future of cities and their metropolitan environments, both in terms of the social/economic problems they face and the kinds of crime and violence to which they are vulnerable. We will add material to her discussion, but the core elements of her model of megaurban futures provides a thoughtful and helpful perspective on future urban issues.

We focus on metropolitan areas because of their enormous importance in understanding future issues facing human residents of a hothouse world. We use the term *metropolitan area* because it provides a better sense of the sheer congestion of the human race that a focus on "city" does not. For instance, in the United States today, there are 51 or 52 metropolitan areas with over a million population,[2] though only about 6 cities can boast that population. We will use the terms metropolitan area, megacity and megadelta interchangeably, in that many people writing about megacities are actually referring to high growth metropolitan areas.

The urban factors that Brennan-Galvin discusses pertain to metropolitan areas over a million population. According to population projections, by 2050 an additional 28 metropolitan areas with over a million population will be in the United States, and six megacities—metropolitan areas with over 10 million residents—will also be in the United States.[3] This is a small number compared to the rest of the world, though.[4] In 2030 China is forecast to have 221 cities over a million population.[5] Globally, we can anticipate 70 megacities by 2050. The UN projects that in the next 30 years the global population will increase from 7 to 9 billion—and almost all of that growth is anticipated to be in urban populations.

When we consider the ratio of urban to rural residents, we can see the striking growth of cities. In 1990, less than 40% of the global population lived in a city. By 2010, more than half of all people live in a city. By 2030, 6 out of every 10 people will live in a city, and by 2050, this proportion will increase to 7 out of 10 people, 70%.[6] In terms of sheer numbers, we see two patterns—first are the tremendous absolute numbers of people cities will absorb, and second, these new city dwellers will almost all be in metropolitan areas in already poor countries:

In all human history we have reached 3.5 billion of urban settlers and in the next 30 years we are going to have 3 billion more . . . . Imagine the changing rate—what we have done in all human history, we nearly will do in the next 30 to 40 years of history. With 96 percent of the growth of cities expected in poorer developing countries . . . there are going to be huge demands on land, resources and services for urban residents.[7]

Metropolitan areas are also centers for the expansion of criminal syndicates and the internationalization of criminal activities. One of the ways we see this is in the relationship of local gangs to international organized crime. For instance, a homicide from a gang retaliation in Omaha, Nebraska may appear to have little to do with terrorism in Southeast Asia. However, the retaliation may involve individuals involved in the sales of heroin, a product most likely from Mexico, but also possibly from Afghanistan. Each of those drug sales increases the reach of major cartels who do an astonishingly lucrative business in spite of worldwide efforts to suppress it. Some of these drug sales are laundered through other enterprises or help finance terrorism. The sales of opium through Karachi is sponsored in part by Al-Qaeda terrorists who seek funds in exchange for drugs manufactured from poppy fields in Afghanistan. In other words, the international urban linkages that connect different kinds of illicit enterprises has tendrils across the American urban landscape and affects our poorest urban areas with particular virulence. Put differently, one of the major problems with the poorest inner cities in the United States is not that they are economically disengaged but just the opposite; they are densely engaged, just with the wrong economies. Brennan-Galvin (2002) captured the globalization and urbanization of crime in Information Box 9.1.[8]

Violence Crucibles

One of the central challenges of crime in the metropolis is its quite high spatial and temporal correlation with poverty and other measures of the geography of human misery. These measures of misery are reciprocally related, a problem that increases their policy complexity.[9] Many criminologists, for instance, describe crime causation in terms of root causes, by which is meant measures of social and economic disadvantage. However, crime, once it is in place, itself becomes a "root cause" in the sense that economic development and investment is unlikely to occur without first addressing crime.

Our interest here are places where economic and social disadvantages, as well as crime, tend to concentrate, what Crank, Murray, Sundermeier, and Irlbeck (2011) called *hot zones*. In Brazil, the word used to describe such areas is *favelas*, which refer to temporary structures on large land tracts on the outskirts of a city. These areas may hold up to a million residents. We will use the term "favela" generically in that the concept applies to conditions faced in some areas in megaurban cities globally, particularly in the periurban zones discussed in the previous chapter. These areas tend to grow rapidly, sometimes too rapidly for the emplacement of typical features of the municipal environment—streets, sewers, or electricity. They also tend to lack

Information Box 9.1 Brennan-Galvin: The Urbanization and Internationalization of Crime

According to Ellen Brennan-Galvin, just about every major city in the developing world has seen an increase in international criminal activity—as a source or transit zone for illegal contraband or produce, a venue for money laundering or illicit financial transactions, or a base of operations for criminal organizations with global networks. Many major cities serve all three purposes for international criminal operations.

Allowing the drug trade to flourish are factors such as globalization, the liberalization of international markets, and the suppression of borders. Crime associated with drug production and drug possession tends to have a significant positive correlation with the homicide rate in a given city, consistent with the fact that the illegal drug trade is usually accompanied by violent disputes for market share among different networks of producers and distributors. At the local level, organized criminal groups linked to global networks, including mafia groups and drug cartels, tend to become involved in other profitable illegal activities such as gambling, prostitution, and extortion rackets. These, in turn, tend to involve corruption of local government officials.

As crime has become increasingly international in scope, its financial aspects have grown more complex due to rapid advances in technology and the globalization of the financial services industry. Drug syndicates, for example, generate large amounts of cash that, pass through legitimate international banking or commercial channels. Money laundering poses serious national and international security threats. It provides the fuel for drug cartels, terrorists, illegal arms dealers, corrupt public officials, and others to operate and expand their criminal enterprises, and can undermine the legitimate private sector in emerging markets because front companies have a competitive advantage over legitimate firms. Ultimately, laundered money moves into global financial systems, where it can weaken national economies and currencies.

Source: Brennan-Galvin, E. (2002). Crime and violence in an urbanizing world. Journal of International Affairs, 56(1).

municipally provided security and are vulnerable to geographical control by organized crime syndicates, gangs, and terrorists alike.

We use the term "violence crucibles" to describe specific urban areas in which there are concentrations of poverty, unemployment, crime, and mental and physical health problems, all of which are knitted together in seemingly intractable ways, and in which the only economic opportunities within the areas are illicit. The notion of crucible is used to suggest that all these problems are so tightly bound that one cannot reasonably separate them into cause and effect relationships. From a policy perspective, any effort to address the problems in violence crucibles is likely to fail unless it comprehensively addresses them all. These violence crucibles contain a mix of disease, mental health problems, family instability and absent parents, malnutrition and childhood poverty, absence of sewer infrastructure, absence of fresh water, gang conflict, organized crime, alcohol and other drug problems, and rapid growth, fear, and anxiety.[10]

Violence crucibles are important urban domains, not only for contemporary criminology and urban policy planning, but for the way they may interact with climate change. In important ways the illicit economies facilitated by violence crucibles may be more flexible and adaptable in a global warming environment than licit economies, discussed later in this chapter.

Kilcullen (2013) captures the geography of violence crucibles with his description of periurban areas around megacities. Unlike "hot spot" crime zones in the United States, periurban zones often lack even elementary municipal infrastructure such as houses, streets, and the like. Because they are the product of rapid, unplanned urbanization, they tend to suffer from extensive environmental degradation, a lack of access to energy of all types, hunger and disease. Many depend on scavenged lumber and trash products for cooking fires. Security tends to default to local gang or warlord control. Finally, many of these periurban zones are in coastal cities, providing access to and opportunities for international criminal activity such as smuggling of goods, drugs, and people, piracy, and extortion of licit shipping goods. Below are the elements of violence crucibles in the emergent megaurban setting.

Poverty

Poverty, already integral to the megaurban areas in the current era, looks to be one of the most important features of their future as well. One cannot say that poverty causes crime; however, urban areas where there is concentrated poverty are also areas high in crime and violence. Certainly, this should not be surprising; areas where legitimate opportunities for success are unavailable become areas where illegitimate opportunities can flourish without competition for resources or labor. Brennan-Galvin (2002, p. 132), in this regard, noted that "murder and violence are often clustered in specific delinquency areas with high concentrations of prostitution, street crime, and drug dealing, low-income housing, unemployment, single-parent families and school desertion."

The extent of poverty in urban areas globally is already dismal. The Wilson National Center for Scholars described global urban poverty as follows:

One billion people—one-third of the world's urban population— currently live in slums (UN-HABITAT 2006). In cities across the globe, hundreds of millions of people exist in desperate poverty without access to adequate shelter, clean water, and basic sanitation. Overcrowding and environmental degradation make the urban poor particularly vulnerable to the spread of disease. Insecurity permeates all aspects of life for slum dwellers. Without land title or tenure, they face the constant threat of eviction. Crime and violence are concentrated in city slums, disproportionately affecting the urban poor.[11]

Global poverty has become an urban phenomenon. In the year 2002, 746 million people in urban areas were living on less than $2.00 a day (Ravallion 2007, 16). The absolute number of urban poor has increased in the last fifteen to twenty years at a rate faster than in rural areas. Rapid urban growth has made Asia home to the largest share of the world's slum dwellers (Halfani 2007).... In the last fifteen years the number of slum dwellers has almost doubled in sub-Saharan Africa, where 72% of the urban population lives in slums (UN-HABITAT 2006, 11).[12]

The urban impoverished occupy a great deal of the demographic landscape of the world's cities. Consider this description of Sao Paolo:

Close to a third of São Paulo's 11 million people—in a metropolitan region of almost 20 million—live in slum-like conditions. There are some 1,600 favelas (private or public lands that began as squatter settlements), 1,100 "irregular" land subdivisions (developed without legally recognized land titles), and 1,900 cortiços (tenement houses, usually overcrowded and in precarious state of repair).[13]

Poverty experienced in many places, moreover, is much more severe than what we find in the United States. In Haiti, for instance, 61 percent of the population earns less than 1.25 American dollars per day.[14] In Liberia, the number jumps to 84% of the population, and 19 of 20 of its citizens (94.88%) earn less than 2 dollars a day.[15]

Money intake is an abstraction of poverty; its concrete expression lies in the living conditions faced by the urban poor. The following quote provides some insight into what poverty means:

In one part of Kibera slum in Nairobi, Kenya, there is one latrine per 4,000 people—many people have to resort to so-called flying toilets, using plastic bags to dispose of waste. Kibera is more than 80 times more densely populated than Birmingham. These plastic bags are thrown onto public rubbish heaps which are often not collected, creating serious public health risks.[16]

The measurement of the crime-poverty link is particularly difficult in such areas; the actual population of these areas is rarely known, only estimated. Official birth records for many of the new urban are absent. Security, in the form of local police, can be an unaffordable megaurban luxury, so there is no point in reporting a crime. Moreover, retaliation is a significant concern. Consequently, crime is difficult to measure with any accuracy.

Income Inequality

Income inequality is closely related to poverty. Increasingly, the wealthy in the new cities live inside fenced compounds and protect themselves with private security. The only contact the rich have with the urban poor is through the occasional opportunity to hire labor, or in a reversal of roles in the illicit marketplace, through robbery, extortion, kidnapping, and home invasion.[17] The urban rich in cities like Sao Paolo are increasingly using helicopters for their daily traffic to avoid traffic and crime: Traffic jams of up to 130 miles have been reported,[18] which themselves can be criminogenic; helicopters represent an improvement in security for those who can afford them.

What is new about income inequality in the megacity is the close juxtaposition of the rich and poor; large urban tracts of extreme squalor can reside adjacent to securitized compounds whose residents include the very wealthy. All the poor have to do to acquire a deep sense of unfairness and inequality is stand in their front door and look outside. Brennan-Galvin suggested that a Robin Hood economic model explained many of the attitudes toward organized crime—such groups brought income back into poor neighborhoods,[19] even though they also generated fear and anxiety.

Rapidity of Growth

Research in the United States has found that the rapidity of growth contributes to violence and crime: Called the boom town phenomenon, rapidly growing areas were two to three times as likely to experience crime as comparable areas with stable populations (Freudenburg, 1984). Rapidity of growth has been noted internationally as well.[20] Gaviria and Pages (1999) found that, on average, an increase of 1% point in the rate of population growth in a number of Latin American cities increased the probability of crime victimization by almost 1.5%, suggesting that rapid urban growth might diminish the effectiveness of law enforcement institutions.

Size

Is the size of a city related to violence? Clearly, a number of violent phenomena are fundamentally urban, such as gangs and street violence. Crime and violence are not obviously a function of city size, however, as some of the world's largest cities, such as Tokyo and Shanghai, are among the safest. Research conducted in Latin America by Fajnzylber and others (2000) found that homicide rates were not significantly related to city size, but crime in general (as measured by victimization) did appear to be related to city size, possibly because larger cities have lower probabilities of arrest. Conducting a large public opinion survey in a number of Latin American cities, Gaviria and Pages (1999, p. 17) found that a household in a city of more than 1 million inhabitants was almost twice as likely to be victimized as a household in a city of less than 20,000 inhabitants, though additional increments in population showed no additional increase in the probability of victimization.

Density

In research in the United States, density is widely associated with violence, though it tends to be used as a control variable in order to assess other factors such as ethnicity and poverty. Harries (2006) noted that both property and violent crimes and were moderately associated with density. Harries found no evidence for the proposition that more dense settings provide for natural surveillance, thereby lowering crime. However, in research in Irvington, Texas, Li and Rainwater found that density and multi-family housing was unrelated to crime but socioeconomic status was.[21] It is likely that density is not itself causal to crime but is associated to crime by the nature of the physical structure of the space inhabited, which may or may not create opportunities for violence and crime.

Age Structure

This is consistently associated with crime and violence. This is a problem for many developing countries where the population of males between 15 and 24 years of age is exceptionally large. Of particular concern is that this population is increasingly facing bleak employment prospects in many urban areas. In developing countries, Gaviria and Pages (1999) noted that 700 million young people would be entering the labor force in developing countries. There are already about 70 million unemployed youth, who have about double the unemployment rate as adults. This is an explosive mix; a large unemployment bubble for youth is rapidly approaching and the jobs simply are not there to absorb them.

Rural-to-Urban Migration

The migration of rural populations to urban settings, noted above as the second urban migration, is one of the signature events of the end of the twenty-first century and into the twenty-second century. How will this in and of itself affect them? Some research has suggested that individuals, removed from their rural settings, would become isolated in a metropolis and vulnerable to violence and extremist influences. Other research, however, suggested that violence occurred later, after migrants were settled. An aspect of this is the second generation phenomenon—first generation migrants bring the stability of their culture and customs with them, but their children, adapting to city life, are able to participate in an urban environment and take advantage of their parent's lack of knowledge about the law, the language, and their inability to participate in mainstream activities. Able to avoid oversight, they were prone to trouble, especially in the form of gangs. Hence, the rural-urban-crime link was a delayed one, set back a generation but nevertheless was an important aspect of the migration-crime nexus. The second generation phenomenon is consistent with opportunity theory. Young people, socialized into urban life, are able to avoid their parent's more traditional authority and take advantage of whatever opportunities they find, including illicit opportunities. This is particularly the case when children can avoid the traditional authority structures that their parents experienced as youth.

One of the most significant challenges of rural to urban relocation is the lack of property ownership. New urban residents often find themselves in the role of "squatters," occupying property owned by businesses, absentee landlords, or formerly rural land that is absorbed into the rapid growth of the metropolis. This migration outcome seems to correlate with some kinds of crime opportunities, discussed in Information Box 9.2.

The discussion in the information box below suggests that efforts to understand settler or destination region crime should consider the kinds of opportunities and physical structures that such in-migration creates. Importantly, in this research, the structure of criminal opportunity was different for each of the three kinds of neighborhoods studied. That is, destination opportunity structures are endogenous intervening variables. More troubling, however, is that organized crime groups can themselves seize the areas in which new residents find themselves, buying off or

Information Box 9.2 Crime and Violence Among Neighborhoods in Eltik, Turkey

A research project in Turkey examined resettlement and squatter crime and violence in an urbanized area outside of Ankara. Erdoğan, Gedík, and Dŭzgŭn (2010) assessed urbanization variables and crime among three populations in Eltik: A planned neighborhood for new residents, a squatter neighborhood, and an in-transition neighborhood. The squatter, termed "*Gecekondu*" is described as follows: "...literally means 'built overnight' and the type of *gecekondu* housing that is referred to in this paper is *early stage gecekondu*, i.e., pre-1980..." The planned neighborhoods are areas that have developed as *planned* settlements or were transformed into *planned* settlements. The in-transition areas are peripheral areas, comprising *early stage gecekondu (built overnight)* housing but is being transformed through improvement plans. These conditions, characteristic of rapid in-migration and then squatter settlement on already owned lands, are characteristic of much of the megacity growth in the current era. Two important kinds of findings came from this research. First, crime was actually rather low in the squatter areas, when compared to the other areas.

> Even though people living in these squatter areas are economically worse off, at least for the study period as the majority did not benefit from the rent of gecekondu transformation, the sense of community they experience and their feeling of belonging to a place and being a part of the community likely prevents them from exposure to high incident rates, despite some fragmentations between the different ethnic/religious groups. The second reason for the low incident rates may be because such areas do not provide opportunities for incidents (p. 545).

Planned areas actually had the highest levels of crime. As the authors explained:

> the planned areas, with more heterogeneous and mixed land uses and higher densities of population and places for different Routine Activities of targets, have an increased likelihood of occurrence of the three conditions for incidents (motivated offender, suitable target and lack of crime suppressor) [34] in these places. The low level of neighborhood relations, the high concentration of people of mixed origin and the low sense of community also contribute to this likelihood (p. 544).

The other finding is somewhat technical but of importance to this paper: In order to best assess the relationships between specific geographic areas and crime, one needs to look at micro settings where crime is highly diversified. However, where crime is predictable and somewhat homogenous, larger geographic areas provide an accurate picture. This means, in practice, that the immediate organization of space is a powerful predictor of crime and that routine activities and related opportunity perspectives enable effective conceptualization of crime patterns.

intimidating responsible guardians, and bringing into neighborhoods illicit opportunities that such groups provide.

Intense Competition for Limited Resources

In urban areas, land can be a scarce resource, competitively sought by different groups, licit and illicit. In many places one sees the practice of land grabbing; acquiring land by any means possible to convert into housing for new residents. Land grabbing is reminiscent of the old West mythos in the United States: if

Information Box 9.3 Land Grabbing in Karachi

"There is continuous battle over various segments of land in Karachi, Pakistan, between various groups of people who I would not say are given sanction by any one political party; but who as a strategy align themselves with political parties," Rehman explained. "And police and of course all the government departments and the elected members are all partners in this. Because the money involved is so much, that overnight you can earn so much more."

It's a strategic mix of politics, crime and business. Once a political party's thugs steal land, it's divided and illegally sold to others. And that creates an instant—beholden—constituency.

This phenomenon of "land-grabbing" exploits the weakness of state institutions, as well as the ever-increasing demand for housing not met by the government. About half of Karachi's estimated 17 million people live this way, dependent on one private group or another.

"It could be housing, transport, drinking water, even electricity," said Haris Gazdar, a political economist at the Collective for Social Science Research in Karachi. "Most of all, all of these activities are underpinned by informal systems of contract enforcement. So contracts were then enforced by private people, sometimes in collusion with government officials who had all kinds of side deals with them. So you had a situation where the private use of violence was legitimate."

Add to the mix a massive influx of arms to Karachi during the Soviet War in neighboring Afghanistan during the 1980s, creating what is referred to locally as the "Kalashnikov culture."

Source: Urban Violence and Land Grabbing in Karachi. Retrieved November 29, 2013 at http://pri.org/stories/2012-01-18/urban-violence-and-land-grabbingkarachi.

the owner of a large cattle ranch has acquired too many cattle for his spread, he manipulates the bank to steal a neighbor's property for the water and food sources it provides. Land grabbing, however, is very much a contemporary practice. A description of land grabbing in Karachi[22] is presented in the Information Box 9.3, "Land Grabbing in Karachi."

Local municipal governments may also engage in the practice, giving urban land to favorite individuals in payment for patronage or for a percentage of the cut in a business resale. These land grabs have often occurred without prior notice, without compensation to the current landholder, and with inadequate time to appeal or even to remove one's belongings. Patronage land grabbing in Kenya has been associated with mass forced evictions and deterioration in the landscape as public spaces such as parks, playgrounds and even public toilets. Finally, as Apiyo noted, the level of violence during land grab evictions is very high.[23]

Land grabbing, as a criminal enterprise, becomes more popular as property values increase during periods of large-scale in-migration. Organized crime land grabbing is apparent in Mumbai, where criminal organizations have capitalized on the high levels of in-migration and subsequent squatter zones to develop large areas for private and commercial use. The central government,

Information Box 9.4 Organized Crime and Property Development

In the mid-1990s, Mumbai's large, increasingly global organized crime groups emerged alongside a broader set of actors to gain greater influence in the property development industry. Their activities were supported by Mumbai's strict regulatory context, which limited opportunities to develop property through purely legal means. But rather than being passively affected by regulations, Mumbai's OCGs appear to be shaping this context, pressing for the continuance of certain restrictive barriers on legal development. Meanwhile, the involvement of both OCGs and local goondas in land politics has helped support the state's efforts to clear land and pursue its own development objectives. Amidst a slew of state-sponsored urban renewal schemes, initiated to bolster Mumbai's global standing, newly supportive relations between the state and OCGs appear to be reshaping the city's development context.

High land prices, paired with the government's nontransparent land use laws and opportunities for corruption, have helped facilitate the entrance of OCGs into this area of investment. . . . The city's major OCGs have effectively utilized violence, threats, and bribes to secure permits and overcome regulatory barriers, where non-criminal developers may otherwise be halted. Just as restrictions on alcohol production facilitated the emergence of Mumbai's "liquor mafias," and tariffs and regulations on imported gold and consumer items supported their transition to "smuggling mafias," land use regulations have helped create Mumbai's "development mafias." As they have grown powerful in part because of their formal political connections, these groups have sought to retain the regulatory structure on which much of their economic activity depends.

Source: Weinstein, L. (2008). Mumbai's development mafias: Globalization, organized crime and land development. International Journal of Urban and Regional Research, 32(1), 23–39.

seeking World Bank investment and support, has "looked the other way" as organized crime groups, internationalized through involvement in the drug trade, have taken control of large areas for development. The relationship between land grabbing, illicit land marketing and international development is discussed in Information Box 9.4 titled "Organized Crime and Property Development" (Weinstein, 2008).

The various examples of land grabbing above show how land in much of the world has qualities dramatically different from the relatively straightforward concept of fixed acreage for personal ownership in Western societies. Land, in these examples is a public good, contested by different groups, and rarely on more than temporary loan, a scarce resource barely controlled by the individuals who live on it.

Crime: Urban Gangs and Illicit Markets

Gang influences in the new urban megacity represent substantial criminogenic influences. Their potential for criminal infiltration into legal as well as illegal markets in a hot house world should not be underestimated: climate change facilitates their activities just as it undermines the legal marketplace for goods.

Urban Gangs—A Measure of State Power

The topic of urban gangs is expansive and the research on it is dense, and an adequate treatment is substantially beyond this brief discussion. However, they cannot be neglected, gangs, correctly understood, stand to increase their reach substantially from climate change.

By correctly understood, what we mean is that there are different ways of defining gangs, almost all of which are controversial. We present them herein as *that corporate entity that contests the state's authority to secure the public urban space not immediately under state control.* By immediately, at that specific moment is meant. Police departments, for instance, often deal with gangs through repetitive raiding practices, carrying out operations and then leaving the area once the operation is over. During the operation the state controls the territory; when the operation is over the territory reverts to gang control (Crank et al., 2011). Seen in this way, specific urban geographies are a limited resource, and entities both licit and illicit compete for it. The primary intrastate entities who compete for control are local gangs and municipal police; international gangs and federal police organizations are frequently involved as well.

When the state is strong in a particular urban area, gang members are involved in minor crime and social activity, and their behavior is often seen in terms of youthful indiscretion, which is pretty much all there is to it. Any effort to use gang influence to assert security control over urban territory and the enterprises in that territory is quickly countered by the power of the state. As state control over its physical geography begins to recede, gangs become more powerful, marketing drugs and guns and becoming organized criminal enterprises. At this level they contest each other for control, and they become involved in serious crime—extortion, home invasion, revenge killings and assassinations, kidnapping, and the like.

When the state is weak, gangs internationalize, working directly with organized international crime elements, actively contributing to the underground marketplace, and controlling large swathes of urban territory. With further loss of control, at the level of state failure, gangs and insurgency become one and the same thing, with strong paramilitary groups seeking direct control over state lands. The state itself may come under organized criminal control—a gangster state—the final step of gang control. Seen in this way, gangs are a function of the absence of authority and power of the state in everyday life.

We are not saying here that this model represents a linear or historical progression under which gangs grow. Every corporate form works out its particular structures and activities according to the dynamics of the social environment it finds itself in. What we are saying is that these different models represent a way to think about encroachments on state authority and on likely gang responses under such conditions.

In the current age, the state's ability to control its turf appears to be receding around much of the world, opening its geographies for competition from a wide variety of groups (Myers, 2002; Romig, Backus, & Baker, 2010; Smith, 2007a). The model that seems to be emerging in the megaurban and megadelta municipal setting is one in which a municipal authority controls the inner cities, the periurban spaces are controlled by gangs and illicit marketplaces, and where the rural areas become irrelevant except for illicit pipelines, for their resources, and for the production of goods for urban areas (Kilcullen, 2013; Naim, 2012). These state-level events are discussed in Chapter 10, where we transition away from this focus on cities to turn our gaze to nation-states and violence associated with global warming.

The Geographic Plasticity of Illicit Markets

One way to think about licit economic enterprises—banks, business centers, insurance groups, hospitals, and the like—is that they are heavily tied to physical infrastructures—buildings, in a word. They can move, but movement is expensive. Even more tied to physical structures is the work of the criminal justice system. Police departments have headquarters with elaborate office structures and assigned geographic zones, jails require heavily in-built physical space, and courts require large structures with substantial security protections.

Illicit markets and organized crime enterprises do not tend to rely on investiture into fixed structures—they are geographically plastic, capable of rapidly moving from one place to another as needs, or the pressures of the police, dictate. Economic enterprises have a great deal of wealth tied up in physical structures, and damage to those structures, if extensive enough, can wreak havoc on local economies. Indeed, in extreme cases they can substantially undermine the global economy, which is what happened with the Al-Qaeda attacks known as the "September 11 attacks." The damage to fixed economic structures—the twin towers of the World Trade Center—was enormous, an enormity magnified by its impact on Wall Street. According to one reference, "the City of New York lost $95 billion in jobs, lost taxes, damage to infrastructure, and clean-up costs; the insurance industry took a $40 billion hit. And the loss of air traffic revenue they estimate at $10 billion."[24] The Dow Jones average closed immediately following the attacks, and when it reopened several days later the market suffered its greatest one day loss, dropping 684 points. The final tally, including the attacks on the Pentagon, has been estimated by the Institute for the Analysis of Global Security at $2 trillion;[25] one can arguably add to that cost the long-term economic and political impact of two wars—a huge success for a terrorist attack carried out by a small band of individuals operating out of rural Afghanistan. The central point is that a great deal of the licit economy is tied up in physical structures. In the age of globalization, vast sums are remarkably liquid, and a nation's wealth can move internationally in moments. However, significant parts of those immense sums are tied up in physical infrastructure, and when that infrastructure is coastal, it is vulnerable. Much of that structure in fact is moving or already has moved to the great megadeltas of the planet, especially in China and the Far East. Coastal megadeltas are, consequently, a critical economic weakness of global warming: vulnerable to the twin problems of coastal flooding and sea-rise. The wealthier they are, the more vulnerable they are.

Make no mistake. Illicit and licit markets are in competition with each other (see Naim's 2002 excellent treatment of this topic). Because illicit markets are fluid, they have an economic advantage over licit markets in the age of global warming. And this means that organized crime groups and gangs will have opportunities to substantially increase their reach into the legal marketplace.

The Street Model of Illicit Markets and Global Warming

Illicit economies do not need to be invested in physical structures. Consider a typical extortion—a gang controls a particularly active street used by local and international travelers to purchase local goods. Such streets are commonplace in all the major port cities of the world, and they are often lined with stalls promoting knock-off black market goods such as CD's and clothing (Kilcullen, 2013; Naim, 2002). Vendor spaces are not free. Gangs can charge a small extortion fee to allow a vendor to use a particular space, on top of any rental fee charged by the city's local business district.

This extortionate model is global and reveals three dimensions of the illicit economy. First is the vendor, whose income stems from his or her sales and who needs the black market income to survive. Second are the assembly plants that make the knock-off goods that are globally purchased.[26] Third is the gang that controls the space and profit from the enterprises in it. The gang controls the terrain and may negotiate its control with the legitimate authority of the city, or may simply threaten the local vendors.

This extortionate street economy needs no fixed structures to carry out its work, beyond a stall to keep products in and a tin roof to protect goods from monsoon rains. The entire economic market can relocate as needed, and it is consequently impervious to global warming sea-rise. Even the maquiladoras can relocate by moving their minimal goods—sewing machines, supplies and cloth—to any abandoned structure and start from scratch with little financial loss.

Global Reach of Gangs

The reach of gangs is global and international. Even in high security countries like the United States, the power of gangs to reach inside the country is remarkable. In the United States, it has been reported in 2010 that at least 1,000 cities had at least one of four Mexican drug cartel members present and active.[27] Drug gangs are creating no-go areas in Great Britain where the police have no effective control.[28] Gangs in the United States, working with Mexican drug cartels, are increasingly involved in crimes not traditionally associated with gang activities, moving into new markets, and branching internationally. The 2011 National Gang Drug Threat Assessment, conducted by the FBI noted that:

1. Gangs are responsible for an average of 48% of violent crime in most jurisdictions and up to 90% in several others, according to NGIC analysis. Major cities and suburban areas experience the most gang-related violence.

2. Aggressive recruitment of juveniles and immigrants, alliances and conflict between gangs, the release of incarcerated gang members from prison, advancements in technology and communication, and Mexican Drug Trafficking Organization (MDTO) involvement in drug distribution have resulted in gang expansion and violence in a number of jurisdictions.

3. Gangs are increasingly engaging in nontraditional gang-related crime, such as alien smuggling, human trafficking, and prostitution. Gangs are also engaging in white-collar crime such as counterfeiting, identity theft, and mortgage fraud, primarily due to the high profitability and much lower visibility

and risk of detection and punishment than drug and weapons trafficking.

4. U.S.-based gangs have established strong working relationships with Central American and MDTOs to perpetrate illicit cross-border activity, as well as with some organized crime groups in some regions of the United States. U.S.-based gangs and MDTOs are establishing wide-reaching drug networks; assisting in the smuggling of drugs, weapons, and illegal immigrants along the southwest border; and serving as enforcers for MDTO interests on the U.S. side of the border.

The business of gangs is territory, and the best business in that territory may be illicit drugs. The supply of heroin in the Americas seems largely impervious to interdiction. According to the U.S. Office of Drugs and Crime (2011), 40 tons of heroin was available in the Americas in 2009. Of that, 25 tons were purchased across the Americas, where the lions share, 21 tons, went to the United States. Only 3.5 tons were interdicted. These numbers are estimated, but if they are accurate, the unsold or leftover quantity in the Americas was actually greater than the amount interdicted. The sources for U.S. heroin are Mexico, South America with an emphasis on Colombia, and Afghanistan. Afghanistan provided nearly all the heroin for Canada, 87%, brought in from India, Pakistan, and Africa[29] (U.S. Office on Drugs and Crime, 2011).

The heroin market, like the streets of any major city dense with stalls for knock-off sales, is plastic. For all its immense wealth, it needs no permanent structures to facilitate its activities. The opium fields in Afghanistan, however, are vulnerable to global warming: Afghanistan is anticipated to lose much of its arable land to climate change. On the other hand, research has suggested that the potency of poppies might increase substantially in a warmer world with more CO_2 in it.[30]

Understood this way, illicit markets are more resilient to global warming than are licit markets. They are adaptable to the coastal areas where licit markets face the existential challenge of flooded physical infrastructures. Gangs and their marketplaces in urban settings look well situated for growth in a warming world.

Summary: Violence Crucibles in a Flooded World

Kilcullen (2013) observed that there are four "megatrends" that characterize the emerging megacities: rapid population growth, accelerating urbanization, littoralization, and increasing connectedness. Littoralization refers to the increasing relocation of human populations to coastal megacities. Considered together in the emerging megacities and megadeltas; these create the conditions for a "conflict climate" in which, he asserts, will account for a great deal of future conflict, from interpersonal violence to war. To these trends one should add the physics of global warming. An assessment of risk would take into account the following considerations:

1. Warming will generate sea-rise, which will be a midterm threat (20-40 years in the future) to these coastal megacities. By 2050 megacities will hold somewhere between 70% and 80% of the world's population. End of the century risk assessments should prepare for substantial infrastructure loss to cities in littoral areas and the impact that will have on its tax base, and their ability to fund security and social services.

2. Sea-rise will increase the access of major tropical storms to population centers. This already constitutes an immediate threat, as was likely witnessed in Hurricane Katrina in 2005, which arrived in New Orleans on a sea that was 23 inches higher in 2005 than in 1950, a consequence of both rising seas and sinking land. Increasingly warm ocean waters are anticipated to increase the ferocity of storms. The 2013 typhoon Haiyan, which struck the Philippines with the fastest ever recorded wind speeds of 195 sustained miles an hour, may be a portent of the future.

3. Storms and rising seas will push saltwater inland, ruining large tracts of agricultural land. Breadbasket areas adjacent to populated littorals, such as the Sacramento (CA) delta region, are particularly vulnerable, with substantial loss of cropland for food and supplies needed by adjacent cities.

4. Rising sea waters will tend to salinate freshwater sources of drinking water, both riparian and aquifer, already overwhelmed by megacity consumption.

5. The financial impact of these aspects of warming on megacities will be substantial. One of the significant costs is anticipated to be in their capacity to deliver basic services, since service delivery requires property tax revenue and more valuable ocean front properties will be steadily encroached by rising seas. Municipal services include the criminal justice system, itself an expensive component of municipal governance. Put simply, the geographic area that the city can secure is likely to shrink at the same time that its population is growing and expanding outward.

6. Gangs and organized crime will likely fill in those areas where cities abandon municipal operations. These areas include coastlines where property values have collapsed, where many properties have become uninsurable at any cost, and the periurban regions, noted by Kilcullen (2013), that surround many cities.

7. The coast, which will be the area most vulnerable to flooding and loss of value, nevertheless provides the primary access to international markets, both licit and illicit. Crime syndicates may consequently have even better access to international markets than they already do, though rapidly advancing drone technologies can offset this because of their ability to track open water activity.

8. Licit markets are tied to physical structures, while illicit markets are plastic, moving according to opportunity. The municipal shortfalls associated with global warming should benefit illicit markets, while at the same time proving expensive and perhaps unprofitable for licit market competition.

In sum, these factors suggest that global warming will be a significant accelerant to the formation and intensification of urban violence crucibles. Indeed, it is difficult to imagine a set of factors that can offset crime crucible growth. Planning, at the municipal level, will need to adapt to population growth, large areas of impoverished citizens in dense *favelas*[31] and sharply expanded need for services precisely at a time when its capacity to invest in such services is curtailed by the financial impact of global warming. Failure to prepare will create fertile soil for the expansion of already quite healthy illicit marketplaces and for the contestation and control of municipal spaces from gangs, organized crime, and terrorists. Indeed, it may be that the primary belligerents for the control of a city's periurban geography in the future will not be municipal authority itself, which might be reduced to an incidental player—occasionally conducting symbolic raids to sustain the illusion of control—but will in actuality be among organized crime groups and powerful local gangs.

Endnotes

1. Parag Khanna, an international relations scholar, asserts that the twenty-first century "will not be dominated by America or China, Brazil or India, but by the city." In his view, "cities rather than states are becoming the islands of governance on which the future world order will be built. . . ." ". . . by 2030 an estimated 5 billion of the world's population (which is estimated to be 8.1 billion at that time) will live in cities, about 2 billion of those (40%) will live in slums. The ratio of slum dwellers to elite (and middle class) will be variable throughout the world, and within mega-cities, but in some regions it will be stark. . . . Urbanization and favelazation (the development of vast tracts of slums) promise to be increasingly synonymous. As a result slums/*desakotas*/ *favelas* are likely to become important nodes in the embryonic megapolises of the future . . . Parts of these slums will be 'lawless zones' or 'failed communities' where extreme violence will fester; others will be vibrant incubators of innovation." "Command of the Cities: Towards a Theory of Urban Strategy."

Retrieved November 10, 2013 at http://smallwarsjournal.com/jrnl/art/command-of-the-cities-towards-a-theory-of-urban-strategy.

2. "Largest Cities in the United States." Retrieved November 11, 2013 at http://www.currentresults.com/Weather-Extremes/US/largest-cities-list.php.
3. "Projection: Metropolitan areas in 2050." Retrieved November 11, 2013 at http://www.skyscrapercity.com/showthread.php?p=96840879.
4. "New population estimates put 52 areas above 1 million." Retrieved November 11, 2013 at http://www.bizjournals.com/bizjournals/on-numbers/scott-thomas/2013/03/new-population-estimates-put-52-areas.html.
5. "In twenty years, China will have 221 cities of over 1 million people." Retrieved November 14, 2013 at http://io9.com/5614523/in-twenty-years-china-will-have-221-cities-of-over-1-million-people.
6. "Urban population growth." Retrieved November 14, 2013 at http://www.who.int/gho/urban_health/situation_trends/urban_population_growth_text/en/.
7. "UN predicts near doubling of city dwellers by 2050." Retrieved November 15, 2013 at http://abcnews.go.com/US/wireStory/predicts-doubling-city-dwellers-2050-21155452.
8. "Crime and violence in an urbanizing world." Retrieved November 21, 2013 at http://www.thefreelibrary.com/Crime+and+violence+in+an+urbanizing+world.-a094337333.
9. For instance, one of the challenges for policy makers is to bring in businesses, which will bring money into such an area, begin the processes of upscaling and investment, and gradually improve the economic plight of residents. However, businesses are not going to move into an area that they consider risky for robbery or other street crime. High levels of such crime, however, are associated with "root causes," among them lack of employment. Hence, in this example one can see the reciprocal relationship between lack of investment and crime.
10. "Several of the most harmful and socially destructive changes in Latin American cities that have sparked most discussion and concern are the acceleration of a climate of fear, both in terms of physical and psychological well-being . . . and an attendant reduction in the quality of public life, neighborliness, and community cooperation" (Davis, 2006).
11. "Global Urban Poverty: Setting the Agenda." Retrieved November 22, 2013 at www.wilsoncenter.org/sites/default/files/GlobalPoverty.pdf.
12. Ibid.
13. Ibid.
14. "List of countries by percentage of population living in poverty." Retrieved November 22, 2013 at http://en.wikipedia.org/wiki/List_of_countries_by_percentage_of_population_living_in_poverty.
15. Ibid.
16. "Cities are on the brink of disaster as urban poverty around the world ignored." Retrieved November 23, 2013 at http://www.careinternational.org.uk/news-and-press/press-release-archive-2006/1012-cities-are-on-the-brink-of-disaster-as-urban-poverty-around-the-world-ignored.
17. "Brazil 2013 Crime and Safety Report: São Paulo." Retrieved November 25, 2013 at https://www.osac.gov/Pages/ContentReportDetails.aspx?cid=13521.
18. "High above Sao Paulo's choked streets, the rich cruise a new highway." Retrieved November 25, 2013 at http://www.theguardian.com/world/2008/jun/20/brazil.
19. Cited from Mayra Buvinic and Andrew R. Morrison, "Living in a More Violent World," Foreign Policy 118 (Spring 2000).
20. Gaviria and Pages found that, on average, an increase of one percentage point in the rate of population growth in a number of Latin American cities increased the probability of crime victimization by almost 1.5%, suggesting that rapid

urban growth might diminish the effectiveness of law enforcement institutions. A. Gaviria and C. Pages, Patterns of Crime Victimization in Latin America (Washington, DC: Inter-American Development Bank, 2000).

21. "The Real Picture of Land-Use Density and Crime: A GIS Application." Retrieved November 28, 2013 at http://proceedings.esri.com/library/userconf/proc00/professional/papers/PAP508/p508.htm.

22. "Urban Violence and Land Grabbing in Karachi." Retrieved November 29, 2013 at http://pri.org/stories/2012-01-18/urban-violence-and-land-grabbing-karachi.

23. "'Land Grabbing' and Evictions in Kenya." Retrieved November 29, 2013 at http://ww2.unhabitat.org/mdg/documents/africa/Vol4_No1_land_grabbing_and_evictions.doc.

24. "World Trade Center anniversary: What did 9/11 really cost?" Retrieved December 2, 2013 at http://www.significancemagazine.org/details/webexclusive/1340691/World-Trade-Centre-anniversary–What-did-911-really-cost.html.

25. Ibid.

26. According to the Counterfeiting Intelligence Bureau (CIB) of the International Chamber of Commerce (ICC), counterfeit goods make up 5 to 7% of world trade. A report by the Organization for Economic Co-operation and Development (OECD) states that up to $200 billion of international trade could have been for counterfeit and pirated goods in 2005 and around $250 billion in 2007. Cited from "counterfeit consumer goods" in Wikipedia.

27. "Mexican Drug Cartels Have Infiltrated All Of These US Cities." Retrieved December 3, 2013 at http://www.businessinsider.com/this-graphic-shows-what-mexican-cartels-and-drugs-come-to-your-town-2012-7.

28. "UN: drug gangs controlling parts of British cities." Retrieved December 3, 2013 at http://www.telegraph.co.uk/news/uknews/law-and-order/9110374/UN-drug-gangs-controlling-parts-of-British-cities.html.

29. National Gang Threat Assessment – Emerging Trends (FBI, 2011). Retrieved December 4, 2011 at http://www.fbi.gov/stats-services/publications/2011-national-gang-threat-assessment.

30. "Warming World, Potent Poppies: Rising carbon dioxide levels lead to higher concentrations of opiates in poppies." Retrieved December 5, 2013 at http://scienceline.org/2009/08/environment-ortlip-poppies-opium-climate-change/.

31. A cluster of jerry-built shacks lying on the outskirts of a city; the word is Brazilian, whose roots may be from the word for honeycomb. Favelas, a consequence of rapid immigration to urban areas by the very poor and destitute, is characteristic of periurban areas globally (Kilcullen, 2013).

GLOBAL WARMING AND INTERNATIONAL SECURITY: THE NATION-STATE SYSTEM AND STATE CHALLENGERS

10

STATES AND THEIR CHALLENGERS

Clete: "I'd like to go back and run through this idea about the past replaying itself, but differently this time. What was Beto thinking about?"

Ruth: "That was a theme that he really worked on later in his life. We talked about it a lot in the 2070s, when warming was really becoming destructive. He said that there were points in history when the world changed. One was the Treaty of Westphalia. After the Treaty, everything shifted. It did not end all the wars, that was for sure. But it created enough peace for the Enlightenment to get going. The almost magical discovery of the old manuscript *On the Nature of Things*, in 1417,[1] might have been the most important discovery in the world and was another point where everything changed. It was the coming together of the ideas in Lucretius' poem, together with the Peace of Westphalia in 1648, that created the political and scientific environment for the Enlightenment, modern science, and European and U.S. global domination for the next several centuries. Beto was big on the power of ideas. He said, what if we replayed history and the treaty never happened? What if the state system never developed, but was overpowered by the church and by the tribal-like relationships among the royalty of England and France? But we still had the knowledge?"

"In Europe, the 30-Years War would have continued decimating the continent. It is unlikely that Europe would have ever become as strong as it could have been. The United States would be a Portuguese- or Spanish-speaking country. Spain had strong Arabic roots, and the United States would be more Arabic in its language, and maybe in its mentality, than it is today. It would still be a powerhouse, but not so big or so fast. Remember, it was the twentieth century's wars that made the United States the world's top power. What if they did not happen?"

"Familial relationships in tribal form, Beto said, are the forever form of government. Extended families—tribes—create an impenetrable environment of followers; everyone knows everyone else. We would have seen a lot more of that around the world and especially in Europe. The center of powers would shift from states to cities, controllable by a small elite, like Mexico, with strong family relationships determining leadership. Just imagine going back five centuries and erasing state boundaries. The cities are still there, the knowledge is still there. Where does that roll forward to? That is what we are discovering today. A lot of nations were not up for the stresses of global warming or for much else as it turned out. The cities were, although they took a vicious beating and are considerably smaller today. States have nominal control of their land, but powerful city lords and nonstate actors, criminals, and organized crime groups are really in control of much of it. Each wants a piece of the pie—control the pie and you control destiny."

Political commentators, students of global warming, and blog enthusiasts have commented on the impact of climate change on "civilization." This discussion goes something like, "Global warming will bring about the end of human civilization as we know it." But what is it about global warming that could destroy civilization, and what is the thing called "civilization as we know it" that would be destroyed?

Let us consider one particularly troubling aspect of global warming: sea-rise. A survey of 90 sea-level experts from 18 countries provided their research-derived median estimates of sea-rise, taking into account glacial meltoff, warming expansion, and elevational trends of land adjacent to the oceans of the world (Horton, Rahmstorf, Engelhart, & Kemp, 2014). These researchers considered that, if climate mitigation were prompt and sufficiently wide reaching, there would be a likely rise of 40-60 centimeters by 2100 and 60-100 centimeters by the year 2200. With unmitigated warming—that is, if we do nothing—the likely range is 70-120 centimeters by 2100 and 2-3 meters by the year 2200. Is that enough to destroy civilization?

Note that the estimates of sea-rise were median scores. The distribution of sea-rise estimates was not normal, but was sharply skewed to the upward end. About a dozen researchers had substantially higher estimates if countries carried out no mitigation, with one expressing concern for a 46-foot increase by 2,200. Would that quantity of sea-rise be the end of "civilization as we know it"? Financially, it would wreak havoc on the world's economy while rather rapidly drowning the most populated cities. However, "civilization as we know it" is in many places not all that advanced or so full of glittering household baubles as it is in Western countries, certainly not the industrial magic of indoor plumbing and air conditioning that citizens in the West take for granted. For some, "civilization as we know it" would certainly take a hard hit. For others, "civilization as we know it" would continue being the wretched place it already is, without plumbing, fresh water, adequate food, sanitation, real floors, or preventive health services. But what is it? The question is too large to answer.

In this chapter, we are going to look at a more focused entity than civilization—the nation-state. The two related questions we ask in this chapter are: Under what conditions are nation-states threatened and weakened? and How will global warming mitigate or intensify those conditions? Nation-states, though still a broad topic, have been the object of considerable empirical research, including research into state security and violence. We cannot say if the collapse of the nation-state system is civilization ending, but before we prognosticate on the impact of global warming on nation-states we need to first discuss their condition and likely futures first.

There are some writers who argue that the nation system has outlived its usefulness and is in the process of replacement by regionalized economic zones (Ohmae, 1995). Others have expressed darker warnings of the emergence of ungovernable feral cities actively weakening a state's control (Kilcullen, 2013). Still others have asserted that the nation-state system has never been all that strong and that the predominant model of nation-states, the Westphalian model, is Euro-centric. And others have talked about a return to the "forever" form of corporate life, the tribe (Smith, 2007b). This chapter enables us to briefly explore some of these ideas. In this chapter, we will look at (1) war and warlike conflicts, (2) the problems of weak and failing states, and (3) the effects of climate change on nation-state viability and interstate relations.

War and Megadeath

The first threats to nation-state stability we consider are war and warlike conflicts.[2] We approach the study of warlike conflicts with the same logic we approach other topics such as hydrology, renewable resources, demographics, and urbanism. To present a picture of the future of conflicts, we need to first assess the current state and likely future of conflicts, and then we can stir into our assessment the additional impacts of global warming. Generally, our summary position is that global warming, instead of bringing us together, is more likely to be an accelerant of interstate conflict and terrorism, and our reasoning is provided throughout this chapter.

In the most general sense, we might ask: Given that people seem so ill suited for peace during the comparatively mild climate of the current holocenic age, is it reasonable to expect that people will do any better when faced with the ecologically destructive conditions of global warming? The relationship between conflict and global warming, to be sure, is more complicated than suggested by that flippant question. But first, we begin by considering patterns of conflict in the world today; how much there is, and where it is, and what factors might affect future conflicts.

The National Defense Council Foundation in 2001 identified 59 "conflict zones" in the world and also placed 121 countries on its "watch list" as areas that carried potential to become conflict zones.[3] Figure 10.1, Map of world conflicts, shows world conflicts that spanned the period from 1997 to 2001.[4] Note that these conflicts were identified before the commencement of the wars on terror, on Iraq, and on Afghanistan.

Figure 10.1 is an inventory of global conflicts, and two features are noteworthy. First, conflicts are disproportionately carried out in poor countries. Westernized countries displayed almost no conflict. This does not mean they should be considered less belligerent; we have seen the United States, for instance, heavily involved in Iraq, Somalia, and Afghanistan. Moreover, the United States is the leading arms merchant for the planet, providing more military armament than any other country (Klare, 2002).

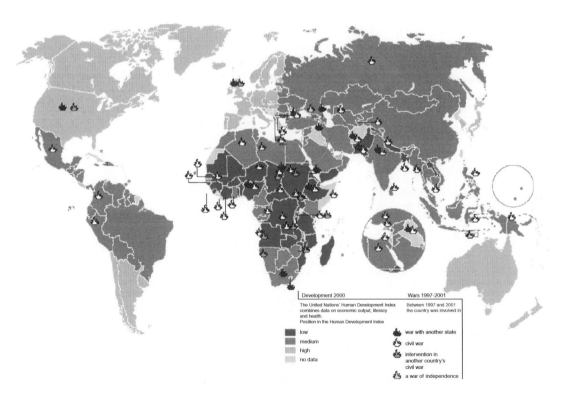

Figure 10.1 Map of world conflicts. *Source*: Myriad Editions Limited. www.MyriadEditions.com from *The Atlas of War and Peace* by Don Smith, published by Earthscan, www.earthscan.co.uk.

According to the Congressional Research Service, the U.S.'s total arms sales in 2011 added to $66.2 billion, followed by Russia at $4.8 billion, less than a tenth of the U.S. sales.[5] U.S. arms sales are particularly active in the Middle East, having provided arms to major belligerents in the region such as Saudi Arabia, Israel, Egypt, Libya, and Iraq, among others.

The second feature is that there is a great deal of ongoing conflict worldwide. Wikipedia lists 12 ongoing conflicts in 2013 in which more than 1,000 people have been killed annually, with an additional 30 conflicts in which fewer than one thousand are killed annually. The largest of these, Afghanistan, has resulted in about 1.5 to 2 million killed, followed by Somalia and Colombia, each with about a half million killed. Some of the countries with less than a thousand killed have in the past had much more significant numbers. For instance, the Lord's Resistance Army insurgency in Africa lists about one-half million killed, according to high-end estimates. And some recent conflicts are no longer listed in 2013; these include Iraq, which according to the "Costs of War" project had about 180,000 killed, including 134,000 civilians.

Wars, intrastate conflicts, and genocidal state (and nonstate actor) policies have taken a fearsome toll in human life. Brzezinski (1993) referred to the twentieth century as the *century of megadeath*.[6] He asserted that twentieth-century wars "extinguished no less than approximately 87,000,000 lives, with the numbers of wounded, maimed, or otherwise afflicted being beyond estimate." He added to this another 80,000,000 individuals killed not in actual combat, but because of doctrinal hatred and passions. Of this latter figure, some 60,000,000 were killed in the effort to build communism in the twentieth century, "making communism the most costly human failure in all of history." Brzezinski arrived a cumulative toll of about 167,000,000 human beings killed by wars and genocide. Though acknowledging progress in the sciences and medicines, he concluded that "this (technological) progress, unfortunately, was not matched on the moral level—with politics representing the twentieth century's greatest failure."

Factors Associated with Warlike Conflicts

Research on the topic of conflict is dense with explanations, many of them quite thoughtful and thorough. Indeed, one might conclude from the abundant literature on the topic that it is not conflict but its absence—peace—that needs explaining. We will touch upon a few of those explanations in an effort to identify some of the more significant factors that seem to be associated with conflicts.

Nonrenewable Resources

Conflict is associated with the availability of and access to nonrenewable resources. Nonrenewables may be the most valuable global resource and include oil, gas, coal, water, and minerals. Klare, assessing the distribution of conflict and its proximity to these nonrenewable resources, observed that *"Resource wars will become, in the years ahead, the most distinctive feature of the global security environment"* (Klare, 2002, p. 213). This is because, on the one hand, security interests worldwide are being determined by increasingly scarce resource assess. On the other, American security interests, since the Cold War, have been determined by economic considerations. As we move into climate change, resource wars may well intensify, with resources in areas like the Antarctic openly contested by the major powers (Klare, 2012).

Three factors have elevated the importance of nonrenewable resources to a security concern. First, there is an insatiable demand for oil, the most important of the nonrenewable resources. Second, there is a looming risk of shortages. No one, for instance, can say when the world will run out of oil; but many observers have noted that oil reserves are already at the point where demand exceeds availability. Third, these resources often sit in areas where they can be contested. Iraq's oil, for instance, sits in areas internally that are disputed by major religious divisions. Pipelines are vulnerable in ways that oil is not—they extend over thousands of miles, vulnerable in their entire lengths to terrorism and insurgency.

Resource protectionism has hence become, for the United States, a component of international military and economic policy, stemming from the Carter Doctrine in 1980. It is involved in resource contests across the Middle East with Russia and increasingly with China. The importance of oil as a factor in the United States's invasion of Iraq in 2001 is not clear but indisputable nevertheless: The oil ministry was the first of the ministries to be occupied by U.S. troops. Hence, just as Homer-Dixon (1999) argued with regard to renewable resource scarcities, Klare (2002) asserted that nonrenewables are becoming scarcer while demand is growing. Both authors asserted that the likelihood of conflict is increased as their scarcity becomes more prevalent.

Rapid Democratization and Economic Liberalization

Democracy and economic liberalism are widely touted as the panacea for conflicts: Liberalized countries are less likely to go to war with countries with whom they do business, and democracy ensures that a democratic majority is, through their leadership, consulted before engaging in a war. Chua (2008) argued that such a perspective failed when dealing with countries that have market-dominant minorities. Such countries, when they undergo democratization, may inadvertently create conflict. This is because market-dominant minorities, when they lose power, tend to find new democratic regimes acting against them, sometimes violently.

Market-dominant minorities are "ethnic minorities who, for widely varying reasons, tend under market conditions to dominate economically, often to a startling extent, the 'indigenous' majorities around them" (Chua, 2003, p. 6). They include the Chinese in Burma, Bolivia and other countries with Amerindian majorities and white minorities; Jews in Post-Communist Russia; and the English in postcolonial Africa. These minority groups, capitalizing on the immense wealth made available by an international free market, have become immensely wealthy—or in the case of the British who were previously wealthy—and occupy broad influence over the governance of their respective countries. When those countries enact democratic reforms, the political power of the majority ethnic group—who often were living in abject poverty—is suddenly increased as they become the political majority. They use the democratic reforms to act harshly and sometimes violently against their former elite. These revenge actions can include such nondemocratic outcomes as land seizures and ethnic cleansing.

Culture and Religion

Huntington, in *A Clash of Civilizations*, asserted that future conflicts would be along the fault lines separating civilizations and would arise between peoples belonging to different cultures. A "civilizational paradigm" was needed to meaningfully develop policy about international relations in the current era. At the heart of civilizations was a common culture:[7]

Civilizations, Huntington asserted, are defined in terms of six elements. First, civilizations are plural, an idea different from the old notion of civilization versus barbarism. Second, civilizations are cultural entities, identified at their center by religion, and then by family and tribal relationships. Third, they are comprehensive, attempting to provide regulation or meaning for all aspects of life. Fourth, civilizations tend to be very long-lived. They are mortal—no civilization lasts forever—but they have the capacity to endure. Fifth, they are not only political entities. Finally, scholars tend to agree on the boundaries and identities of modern civilizations.[8] These are the Sinic (the common culture shared by China and Chinese communities across the Southeast), Japanese, Hindu (core of the Indian civilization), Orthodox Christian (primarily in Russia), Western, Latin American, and African (still in the process of forming a civilizational identity).

Future conflicts were most likely to be "fault line wars," defined as "communal conflicts between states or groups from different civilizations" (p. 252). The Soviet-Afghan war of 1979-1989 was a fault line war, as were conflicts that involved the United States in Iraq, Afghanistan, and Somalia. In all of these, Huntington described a set of values pitted against another set. The values may themselves not be the primary reason for the conflict, but their presence is an accelerant: they tend to intensify the conflicts and make peace-finding more difficult.

The Growth of the Vulnerable State

Aside from the immediately debilitating and destructive impact of war, a variety of other factors have been associated with state debilitation. To consider this, we will start with the concept of the state itself—where did the modern political entity of a state come from?

The history of statecraft and nation-state stability is often associated with the Treaty of Westphalia in 1648. The treaty ended the 30-Years War and is associated with the emergence of the modern nation-state, the end of the Middle Ages and beginnings of the Age of Reason, and the subsequent (occasional) peace among European nations. More importantly, the principles of the treaty are principles of statecraft and, according to some, provide the central model for modern definitions of the nation-state.

The nation-state is the predominant corporate form for governance today. States create the world's currencies that are integral in all global and regional economies. Because they manufacture money, they enable businesses to transact across sharply different cultures and societies. Their standing armies and mass destruction weapons are capable, in some cases, of annihilation on a global scale. They try to provide security for their citizens and control the interior spaces of their countries. In a sentence, the state is the central organizing concept in the world of politics and governance.

As Williams (2008) observed, nation-states today face emergent threats, some of which are substantial. The challenge faced by countries was that nonstate actors were increasingly adept at circumventing borders for their purposes, typically illegal and

sometimes violent. These actors, in the current era of globalization, were much more powerful, and posed much more of a threat,
than was recognized. He decried what he referred to as "state-
centric" ways of thinking, arguing that the presumption that the
nation-state is the best and only way to govern is so normative
that alternatives are frequently seen as "heretical, irrelevant, or
misguided" (49). One needed to recognize that the nation-state
system was not immutable and should not be taken for granted.
It was being undermined by challenger groups and international
problems that, if not recognized and countered, could fundamentally undermine the state system and lead to a new "dark age"
where the state has lost its central role as a governing form.

The arc of history, Williams (2008) suggested, represented a
trend away from the stability of the Westphalian nation-state system that reached its zenith in the middle twentieth century. The
current era, he argued, was more like the Middle Ages, in which
nation-states had yet to emerge as primary political entities and
contended with church and regent for power. Countries are vulnerable to a wide variety of threats discussed below.

1. **Loss of control and privatization of core state functions.** Loss
   of core state functions is not necessarily wrested by force; at
   times they are given away. This is particularly evident in the
   United States. Several contemporary mechanisms reveal processes that lead to voluntary abandonment of core functions.
2. **Permeable borders**. Borders for most countries are fluid and
   permeable, even though no boundary marks the limits of a
   state's sphere of control. Inside that boundary, states in principle exercise absolute authority as provided by their constitu-
   tions; that authority disappears on the other side of that
   boundary. Borders, for precisely that reason, offer enormous,
   highly lucrative opportunities for corruption. One of the
   authors of this book recalls repeatedly placing a few local cur-
   rency bills in a passport to facilitate passage through the
   aduana (border office) when traveling across Central America.
   With the heightened movement of goods internationally from
   globalization, together with the lowered restrictions on international trade, it has become easy to move illicit goods across
   borders.
   a. *Privatization*: Strong states such as the United States have
      privatized many of their core functions, including military
      and international security, its prison system, its many reg-
      ulatory functions, its internal antiterrorism and surveil-
      lance operations, and many elements of its internal safety
      net. Private contractors operate as a vast and highly decen-
      tralized shadow government, mostly unknown to ordinary

citizens and only partly bound by the regulatory laws that govern many state institutions.

b. *State to private sector migration of personnel*: Former state executives in a variety of fields join the staffs of major corporations, working with them to undermine the regulatory influence and taxes they cede to states. Lobbyists exert a great deal of influence in Washington and are often the only individuals legislators meet prior to making decisions on important laws.

c. *Policy influence*: Large businesses can force states to compete with each other for employment opportunities, worksites, and resources. Exxon, the largest corporation in the world, had a market valuation of approximately $278.8 billion in 2000, after its merger with Mobil. In 2014, its market value was nearly twice that, estimated at $486.429 billion.[9] It has used its wealth to exercise broad influence against global warming action by supporting groups such as the Koch brothers and Heartland Institute. It has been tied financially to several researchers who publish on the topic of global warming denial.[10]

We see in this example how large business can direct its substantial resources in ways that can create threats to the security of even powerful states (the United States, in this instance) by undercutting its ability to respond to climate change. One of the central problems with private contractors is that they are largely uncontrollable and highly decentralized, a problem recognized by General Petraeus when, as Commander in Afghanistan, he sought to increase the authority of the government to control its activities.[11] We see in these examples that the process of contracting governance limits the state's ability to control the distribution of its resources—security, social services, environmental protections, and other publicly regulated goods, and can act directly against the interests of the state.

3. **Contested property rights**. The newly urbanized areas surrounding many of the emergent megacities, described previously as periurban areas (Kilcullen, 2012), tend to be owned by large property holders but are overwhelmed by slum tenants, who vie with them for authority and control in a setting largely beyond municipal support and security. In rural settings, several countries in the world today are attempting to buy large swathes of land for agriculture in anticipation of large future populations in their own countries. Many of these purchases occur in Africa, and some have involved tracts larger than a million acres; in one astonishing agreement, the

Democratic Republic of the Congo promised 7 million acres to a Chinese firm, ZTE Corporation, for a palm oil plantation (Klare, 2012). However, the governments who sell the land often fail to acknowledge or mention the landholders already resident on the land, residents who in turn do not acknowledge the government's authority to sell the land. This leads to conflict of local residents with the government agents who arrive to facilitate agricultural endeavors.

4. **Inequality and marginalization.** In many countries, the rich and the poor exist side by side, inflaming tensions. As Chua (2008) noted, economic frictions between rich and poor, when they involve different ethnic groups, can be explosive and lead to open conflict. Moreover, the empowerment of marginalized groups through democratic elections may backfire, leading to revenge, increased violence, and, in extreme cases, ethnic cleansing. Globally, inequality is down but only slightly; by way of example, the richest 300 people in the world have more wealth than the bottom three billion, with an estimated total value of 3.7 trillion dollars in 2014.[12] Indeed, the World Economic Forum in 2014 asserted that the gap between rich and poor was the single most important risk facing the world.[13]

5. **Multiple and fragmented loyalties.** The emergence of identity politics has reshaped many areas of the earth. The tribal forms, what have been called the "first and forever form of social organization," are central political entities in many of the worlds, most troubled regions—the Balkans, Middle East, South Asia, the Caucasus, and Africa. When tribal entities associated with these countries engage in terrorism, Williams (2008) stated that they can inspire fierce loyalties. They also are very difficult for counterterrorists and counterinsurgents to penetrate because of the close-knit familial identities of the members. The gradual relinquishment of colonial authority in Africa has led to the reemergence of previous loyalties that are not state based, but are associated with violent conflict across the continent.

6. **The spread of geographical and social "no go" areas.** These are areas where the rule of law no longer exists. In North Mexico, the state finds its authority contested and sometimes overwhelmed by the drug gangs that control a great deal of the territory there and where police and other public officials are routinely murdered. In Peru, the Sendero Luminoso is resurgent, and the government has little control or influence beyond the capital of Lima. In the peripheries of the megacities and megadeltas, centralized or state security is largely absent due to a lack of resources to fund police. Even in prosperous countries, the poverty areas of many cities are contested by the

police and gangs, with the police controlling largely through raiding strategies, leaving the gangs to exert controls when they withdraw. The United States has been in the enviable position of witnessing substantial drops in crimes in its major cities, but with the long-term disinvestment in governance characteristic of many municipalities, it is unclear how long this trend can continue.

7. **Globalization of trade.** Globalization has a variety of aspects that limit the power of the state. Globalization ensures that the world's masses have the cheapest products available. Competition among businesses is extremely keen. Wages suffer, and local efforts to participate in the global economy ensure that locals will receive the minimum wages available—more and more that minimum being a calculus based on the international availability of a cheap labor pool. It is unclear, in this kind of environment, how an economically viable middle class, with the traditional labor protections and occupational-based stabilities, can survive in existing markets and emerge in new ones. The central problem here is that the middle class provides a great deal of the tax base for state security efforts, and its loss substantially undercuts a state's ability to pay for relatively expensive security. Because large business can successfully relocate globally, it can shelter its taxes so that it does not contribute to state welfare while at the same time absorbing a state's resources. In other words, in the current global environment, large businesses need to be recognized as significant and powerful challengers to state sovereignty.

Globalization of trade has also emerged as a significant challenge to the ability to control borders. Consider containerized cargo, one of the emergent forms for moving commerce internationally. In 2010, China—the largest user of containerized trade, exported 31.3 million tons of containerized cargo. The United States, second to China, exported 11.2 million tons the same year.[14] Inspecting the vast volume of trade carried by containers is challenging. The TSA in the United States inspects about 6% of containerized cargo; the other 94% represents cargo that has been previously screened.[15]

Containerized cargo, because of its immense volume, provides opportunities to covertly carry illicit merchandise, mixed in with legal products. Consequently, cargo screeners are a focal point of efforts to move illicit cargo. Consider the following example. Dar es Salaam Port (Tanzania) personnel failed to use the three screening platforms available to scan cargo. Two operational platforms were broken, but a third functional scanner was not installed. The Tanzania Transport Minister suggested that the screening platforms would have identified illicit cargo, thereby undercutting the ability of screeners to take graft: "TPA and other verification agencies do not want scanners because they reduce their ability to manipulate data at the port, hence making it extremely difficult for them to cheat." He noted that cash transactions were occurring openly when he toured the port.

8. **Globalization of communications.** The Internet, combined with the cell phone, enables relatively local actors to challenge state-level interests and do so effectively. Indeed, cell phones enable a level of contra-secure activity and organization not previously available. As noted by Kilcullen,[16] over 6 billion people—1.5 billion more than have access to fresh water—own cell phones. Cell phones specifically, and other forms of Internet media as well, are accelerants on the ability of challenger groups to organize rapidly and coherently against states while at the same time tracking state behavior itself. Information Box 10.1, Mass Communication, Crime and Conflict, describes various ways that global communications contribute to local crime, organized international crime, and terrorism.

9. **Reinforcing dynamics**. Many of the international dynamics discussed above are mutually reinforcing. Internationally, one increasingly finds terrorist organizations working closely with organized crime, a commonplace that was virtually unheard of 20 years ago (Kilcullen, 2012). No-go areas in Northern Mexico, controlled by powerful gangs, when combined with porous borders in the United States, allow both for the presence of large quantities of Mexican heroin and marijuana and for the organizing presence of Mexican cartel members in cities in the United States. Porous borders work the other direction as well, where cartels are able to acquire large quantities of weapons in the United States and transport them to Mexico, funded directly from drug sales.[17]

The nine risks listed above are a threat to the sovereign authority of the state. Williams (2008, p. x) expressed the concern that these risks could lead to a tipping point, which he described as an:

abrupt, non-linear shift from the New Middle Ages to the New Dark Age. This will be characterized by the spread of disorder from the zone of weak states and feral cities in the developing world to the countries of the developed world. When one adds the strains coming from global warming and environmental degradation, the diminution of cheaply available natural resources, and the proliferation of weapons of mass destruction, the challenges will be formidable and perhaps overwhelming.

Information Box 10.1 Mass Communication, Crime, and Conflict

The following represent only a few of the many creative ways that modern technology has internationalized or otherwise been used to stymie security efforts across different kinds of jurisdictional borders.

1. In Tunisia and Egypt, participants in the urban revolutions coordinated their efforts online to battle riot police. Kilcullen.

2. In Lybia, fighters used skype to plan attacks.

3. The rebels in Syria used remote controlled maching guns installed in homemade tanks. They used Gameboy consoles with flatscreen TVs to drive the tanks.

4. Nigerien terrorists used prepaid, unattributable cell phone numbers to kidnap and coordinate the movement of two French nationals in 2011. Because of this, Niger sought to have cell phone cut off for one third of its population, all those with unattributable numbers. Niger cuts off third of mobile phones to stop crime. Retrieved Jan 5, 2014 from http://www.france24.com/en/20131127-niger-cuts-off-third-mobile-phonesstop-crime.

5. Criminals can use Facebook to monitor their neighbors and plan burglaries during vacations. Vacation Alert: How criminals use Facebook. Retrieved Jan 12 2014 from http://tech.ca.msn.com/photogallery.aspx?cp-documentid¼25643186&page¼1

6. Gangs, like organized crime rings, have taken to the Internet as a facilitator in sending messages to associates throughout the United States and other countries—including deported gang members, deliver threats, assert territorial boundaries that used to be scrawled as graffiti across buildings, fences, and signs, brag, and conduct 'business'. Gang business includes drug trafficking, human trafficking, prostitution, weapons trafficking, smuggling illegal aliens across borders, murder, theft, fraud, armed robbery, auto theft home invasions, gang rapes, and more (Source FBI 2009) http://ilookbothways.com/2010/06/14/gangs-use-of-the-internet-and-cell-phones/.

7. The use of prepaid cell phones to commit crimes by inmates in prison in many countries, enables untraceable activity. Cell Phones Being Used to Commit Crimes Behind Bars. Retrieved January 18, 2014 from http://www.ktvb.com/news/politics/Cell-phones-being-used-to-commit-crimes-from-behind-bars138087593.html.

8. In Mexico, it has been noted that around 700 criminal entities were using unattributable cell phones to arrange extortion and kidnap ransom payments. Catching Criminals: Mexico to Fingerprint Prepaid Cell Phone Users. Retrieved January 19, 2014 from http://technews.tmcnet.com/fixed-mobile-convergence/topics/mobilecommunications/articles/50468-catching-criminals-mexico-fingerprint-prepaid-cell-phone-owners.htm.

9. Cell phone microphones can be activated from a distance, turning them into an eavesdropping device.

10. Some cell phones are being circulated that already have viruses in them that, when the phone is activated, send user information and passwords to remote sources.

11. Bulletproof hosting services are created by a host who provides an Internet protocol addresses and computer servers, constructed in a way that protects criminal users' anonymity. Three Alleged International Cyber Criminals Responsible for Creating and Distributing Virus That Infected Over One Million Computers and Caused Tens of Millions of Dollars in Losses Charged in Manhattan Federal Court. Retrieved February 11, 2014 from http://www.fbi.gov/newyork/press-releases/2013/three-alleged-international-cyber-criminals-responsible-for-creating-and-distributing-virus-that-infected-over-onemillion-computers-and-caused-tens-of-millions-of-dollars-in-losses-charged-in-manhattan-federal-court.

12. Gang members may have several prepaid phones and calling cards to ensure their calls are untraceable for any communications about criminal activities, and easily disposable. They use encrypted internet technologies like VoiceOverIP (VoIP) on products like Skype on their mobile phones or computers to avoid wiretapping—making it nearly impossible for law enforcement to track their actions or crimes. Gangs use cell phones' cameras and video to document crimes or collect information for future crimes, and use GPS coordinate attacks and crimes, as well as surreptitiously

monitor those they think might be ratting them out. They use cell phones to assist in robberies, for extortion, as evidence of accomplished hits, to arrange drug deals, set up transactions, prostitute girls and boys, commit identity theft, and more. Gangs have been known to place a member inside a bank, (or near an ATM, or any other place that cash is transacted) to take photos of likely victims and watch to see who withdraws large sums, then send it to another gang member sitting outside the banks to identify the victim to follow and rob.

The Failing State and the Emergence of the Feral City

Two contemporary terms have entered the discourse of security: The failing state and the feral city.

Failing States

The notion of state failure has been in the political science literature for nearly 30 years, but is generally not present in research in the fields of criminology and criminal justice; the feral city is a twenty-second century term. A failing state is defined as follows:[18]

Common indicators include a state whose central government is so weak or ineffective that it has little practical control over much of its territory; non-provision of public services; widespread corruption and criminality; refugees and involuntary movement of populations; sharp economic decline.

The Failed States Index is an index of state health developed by "Fund For Peace" and published annually in Foreign Policy. In 2012, the index included 177 states for assessment.[19] Of these, 33 were classified as "alert" (the highest category of failed state), 92 as "warning," 39 as "moderate," and 13 as "sustainable (the lowest category)." The map in Figure 10.2 is a list of states by their scores on the state stability index.

The assessment of state vulnerabilities has become central to security since the end of the Cold War. From a security perspective, state stability presents a fundamentally different conflict perspective than did the primary conflicts of the twentieth century: The Cold War between the U.S. and the Soviet Union; WWI; and WWII. The world has steadily declined in the numbers of interstate conflicts, though the reasons for that are unclear (although, see Pinker, 2011).[20] However, a new security concern, that of failed states, is regions where organized crime, violence, gangs, drugs, and terrorism can foment. In U.S. security, weak states is considered one of the primary reasons for the emergence of terrorist organizations such as Al-Qaeda and their ability to launch attacks

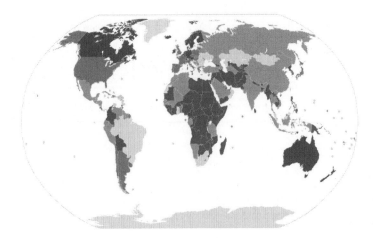

Critical
In danger
Borderline
Stable
Most stable

Figure 10.2 States by their scores on the state stability index. *Source:* Failed State Index. Retrieved January 15, 2014 at http://en.wikipedia.org/wiki/Failed_state.

globally from relatively isolated countries. The effectiveness of nonstate actors to stymie the armies of even the strongest of international states is witnessed in the Afghanistan conflict, the longest war in U.S. history and one without winners. Hence, one of the primary characteristics and principal security concerns of state failure is the ability of nonstate actors to contest states for territorial control. Such groups have proven capable of using contested spaces to launch attacks internationally.

Failing states pose complex policy questions. Should neighboring states intervene? If so, then how do we legitimize intervention, which is an aggressive act and a violation of the UN charter? If we fail to intervene, are we abandoning human rights issues in that country and implicitly encouraging criminal states and terrorists? Should we provide military support to preferred belligerents, knowing that such support will increase the likelihood of civil war? Should we provide only economic supports, which may simply end up in the hands of the most powerful nonstate actors and on the black market? All of the alternatives pose risks to international security. As noted by the Fund for Peace:

> *The important point is that weak and failing states represent a new class of conflict, not isolated events. Approximately 2 billion people live in countries that run a significant risk of collapse. These insecure and unstable states are breeding grounds for terrorism, organized crime, weapons proliferation, humanitarian emergencies, environmental degradation, and political extremism—threats that will affect everyone.* [21]

Feral Cities

One of the entities that is moving into the void left by state collapse is the "feral city." The notion of the feral city was initially proposed as an "ideal type," one that did not exist in pure form, but that represented the direction of many modern megacities and megadeltas. Norton (2003, p. 97) described the feral city as follows:

Imagine a great metropolis covering hundreds of square miles. Once a vital component of a national economy, this sprawling urban environment is now a vast collection of blighted buildings, an immense petri dish of both ancient and new diseases, a territory where the rule of law as long been replaced by near anarchy ... Yet, this city would still be globally connected. It would possess at least a modicum of commercial linkages, and some of inhabitants would have access to the world's most modern communication and computing technologies. It would, in effect, be a feral city.

The feral city is so named for two characteristics. First, it tends to occur in a weak or failing state, and the only security available to it is the security it provides for itself. It is typically described as an entity with weakly centralized authority, torn with competing warlords for power. However, there is no reason it could not have a strong mayor and strong central authority; the central aspect of its ferine nature is its independence from state control. It is absent any social safety net and is periodically overwhelmed with diseases. Secondly, it sits on an immense urban landscape, the megacity, and many of the outer areas of the city are altogether beyond either city or state control. It is feral in the sense that it has become an entity beyond state control, in charge of its own destiny. It is, for all practical matters, a stateless city.

Feral cities, like failing states, pose enormous security challenges. As Norton further observed, the vast size and structural complexity of such a city would "offer nearly perfect protection from overhead sensors, whether satellites or unmanned aerial vehicles." The city's citizens are easily recruitable for terrorism or to maintain an intelligence network (Norton, 2003, p. 99). Indeed, from a terrorist perspective, one of the primary differences between failing states and feral cities may be only the relative geographic reach of each. However, feral cities offer guerillas and terrorists advantages the countryside does not—the ability to hide in plain sight in the streaming populations of large cities and megacities, a wealth of targets, and access to recruits.

Such cities may represent the dominant corporate form in the future. In the current era, only Mogadishu (Somalia) is described as a "true" feral city (Kilcullen, 2013). The overwhelming growth features of megacities today and into the future will render large parts of them fundamentally ungovernable. One should keep in mind that in the next 30 or so years, many people may move into the world's urban areas—about three billion—as were alive in 1960. Many of these most populous urban areas are better understood as megadeltas for their coastal orientation, and hence are major global transshipment ports for all manner of cargo, licit and illicit. The terrorist danger is substantial: "a terrorist group in a feral city with access to world markets, especially if it can directly ship material by air or sea, might launch an all but untraceable attack from its urban haven" (Norton, 2003, p. 101). Moreover, urban environments are especially difficult areas for outside forces to invade when there is a dedicated belligerent that can use the built environment to offset advantages in military superiority.

Global warming poses an immediate and long-term financial and existential threat to the megadeltas and will undermine efforts of emergent feral cities to develop strong centers capable of exercising security across their jurisdictions. Many weak states and coastal urbanized zones will wither under the economic impacts of global warming, rendering them even more ungovernable than they would be otherwise. The greatest threat to states, Norton concluded, will come from the proliferation of weapons of mass destruction available in many of the poorer countries as these countries weaken and are challenged by nonstate actors, who would include feral city inhabitants. The security challenge, already well underway, is to identify, locate, and neutralize all known weapons of mass destruction.

Conclusion: The Geopolitical Context for Climate Change in a Violent World

We have argued throughout this class that context is important. Context carries the weight of history and human action, and in this case, the weight of histories of grievances of peoples against each other. The twentieth century was the first century of megadeath, with estimates of 250 wars and war-related deaths ranging as high as 187 million deaths worldwide (Hobsbawm, 1984). The terrorist attacks on the World Trade Center and Pentagon in 2001, described by President Bush as the first war of the twenty-first century, was not: There was immense competition for that title by all the other countries already deeply engaged in every kind of conflict imaginable. That such an utterance could be spoken during a major foreign policy speech by a U.S. President in 2001 reveals the extent to which political leadership is out of touch with global conflicts and their causes and, by implication, how unprepared we are for dealing with them. Against a backdrop of world violence and megadeath, what is amazing is not that the United States should become the object of the violent attack now known as 9/11 and usher in the Afghan War, but that the American people could have been so astonishingly unaware of international violence out of which this attack emerged.

The lesson we take from this is that we live in a violent world, shaped in part by events and players beyond our control and in part by events of our own doing. How do we step back from our violent dispositions and begin the process of dialogue, if the future of the human race hangs in the balance? That is an important question. Unfortunately, there is scant evidence that we, as a people united through shared ancestry, can rise to the challenge.

Endnotes

1. See Stephen Greenblatt, (2011) *The Swerve: How the World Became Modern.* New York: W.W. Norton & Co.
2. By war and warlike conflicts we are referring to wars between states, terrorism, and insurgencies. The important feature of conflict we are considering in this chapter is that at least one nation-state is involved.
3. "World Conflict List 2012." Retrieved December 18, 2013 at http://ndcf.dyndns. org/ndcf/Conflict_List/World2002/2002conflictlist.htm.
4. "Zur Lage der Welt 2010." Retrieved December 19, 2013 at http://nomenom. blogspot.com/2011/01/die-lage-der-welt-2010.html.
5. "U.S. Arms Sales Tripled In 2011 To $66.3 Billion: Report." Retrieved December 20, 2013 at http://www.huffingtonpost.com/2012/08/27/us-arms-sales-2011_ n_1833602.html
6. "A review of *Out of Control: Global Turmoil on the Eve of the Twenty-First Century.* By Zbigniew Brzezinski." Retrieved December 22, 2013 at http:// www.billmuehlenberg.com/1993/11/19/a-review-of-out-of-control-global-turmoil-on-the-eve-of-the-twenty-first-century-by-zbigniew-brzezinski/.
7. "The Clash of Civilizations and the Remaking of World Order." Retrieved December 22, 2013 at http://www.leaderu.com/ftissues/ft9705/reviews/ bacevich.html.
8. A map of Huntington's civilizations can be found at the following web address: http://en.wikipedia.org/wiki/The_Clash_of_Civilizations, Retrieved December 22, 2013.
9. "Exxon Net Worth." Retrieved January 4, 2014 at http://www.getnetworth.com/ exxon-net-worth/.
10. "ExxonMobil is also connected to nine of the top ten authors of climate change denial papers. Wei Hook Soon, an astrophysicist with the Harvard-Smithsonian Center for Astrophysics has co-authored several papers repudiating climate change. His work has been highly criticized by climate scientists for content and for his funding by the American Petroleum Institute, including ExxonMobil. Soon has also received funding from the Koch Foundation, a charity of the Koch Industries, an oil and gas conglomerate." "ExxonMobil, climate change deniers and global warming–follow the money." Retrieved January 4, 2014 at http://www.examiner.com/article/exxonmobil-climate-change-deniers-and-global-warming-follow-the-money.
11. "Petraeus issues Afghan contracting guidance." Retrieved January 6, 2014 at http://www.marinecorpstimes.com/article/20100913/NEWS/9130308/ Petraeus-issues-Afghan-contracting-guidance.

12. "Top 300 Billionaires Worth $3.7 Trillion; An Increase of $500." Retrieved January 7, 2014 at http://iacknowledge.net/top-300-billionaires-worth-3-7-trillion-an-increase-of-500-billion/.

13. "World Economic Forum warns of dangers in growing inequality." Retrieved January 7, 2014 at http://www.reuters.com/article/2014/01/17/us-davos-risks-idusbrea0f0h920140117.

14. "World Shipping Council: Trade Statistics." Retrieved January 8, 2014 at http://www.worldshipping.org/about-the-industry/global-trade/trade-statistics.

15. "The 5 Percent Myth vs. US Customs and Border Protection Reality." Retrieved January 10, 2014 at http://www.itintl.com/the-5-percent-myth-vs-us-customs-and-border-protection-reality.html.

16. Nairobi Foreshadows Tomorrow's Urban Conflicts. David Kilcullen, The Financial Times, 1 October 2013. Retrieved January 11, 2014 at http://www.ft.com/cms/s/0/17d09b3e-2606-11e3-8ef6-00144feab7de.html#ixzz2lmvwSq5o.

17. "More than 70% of 29,284 firearms submitted to the U.S. Department of Alcohol, Tobacco, Firearms and Explosives for tracing by the Mexican government during 2009 and 2010 originated in the United States, according to the report. The report, released Monday, is the latest element in a debate over how large a role the United States plays in arming the ruthless Mexican drug cartels that are responsible for more than 34,000 killings since 2006." "Report: Many weapons used by Mexican drug gangs originate in U.S." Retrieved January 14, 2014 at http://www.cnn.com/2011/US/06/14/mexico.guns/index.html.

18. "Failed State Index." Retrieved January 15, 2014 at http://en.wikipedia.org/wiki/Failed_state.

19. The Failed States Index assesses the following state characteristics:
Social
Mounting demographic pressures.
Massive displacement of refugees, creating severe humanitarian emergencies.
Widespread vengeance-seeking group grievance.
Chronic and sustained human flight.
Economic
Uneven economic development along group lines.
Severe economic decline.
Political
Criminalization and/or delegitimization of the state.
Deterioration of public services.
Suspension or arbitrary application of law; widespread human rights abuses.
Security apparatus operating as a "state within a state."
Rise of factionalized elites.
Intervention of external political agents.

20. "Violence Vanquished" (2011). Retrieved January 1, 2014 at http://online.wsj.com/article/SB10001424053111904106704576583203589408180.html.

21. "Failed States Index FAQ." Retrieved January 1, 2014 at http://ffp.statesindex.org/faq#5.

11

SECURITY ISSUES AND GLOBAL WARMING

Ruth: "Your turn. Tell me about Canada."

Clete: "You've seen some of it, but a lot has changed since then. In 2015 Canada did one small thing; it staffed a security zone in the Arctic Circle, with the support of the United States, Russia, and China."

Ruth: "China?"

Clete: "China's a player. You cannot deal them out, and they had a big maritime fleet for commerce. Routes through the Arctic could save them a lot of money. Anyway, that security force enabled Canada, over time, to get a piece of the pie for the mineral discoveries made across the Arctic Circle. They also made a lot of money from the trade that went through the Arctic. By 2030, the Arctic was completely ice-free, and the commerce through there boomed. Canada became a rich country."

"We took some of that profit and invested it in land-works. By 2050, the winters were a lot milder, but the soil up here was pretty ratty, thin, and wet, not really suitable for crops. We brought in thousands of day laborers from the United States to work for us. Completely reworked the land, made it into an agricultural mecca. Back then we welcomed U.S. citizens as heroes when they came across the border by the bus-full; it sure is different now."

"But it was the maritime fleet that made Canada a world power. All through the first half of the century, piracy became more and more prevalent. With our Arctic connections and our heavy ships, we could provide escorts for a cut of the profit. We designed the Escort Fleet, heavily armored and powerfully gunned. Some of the big cities in the Far East went totally over to organized crime, became piracy centers. The Canadian-Indonesian littoral wars established Canada as a world maritime power, with the Chinese coastal cities our primary benefactors."

Ruth: "Why wasn't this China's war?"

Clete: "The northern provinces in China were deep in water crisis, and they were breaking away. The big coastal cities were too busy fighting insurgents from the North. Terrorism had become daily fare. And the cities were regularly getting raiding parties from the pirate criminals. You gotta keep in mind, the state system was on the ropes in most of the world at that time, though the cities were strong. China's northern border was up for grabs. Canada offered to take charge of the seas. China had a good maritime force, but they were designed for commerce, with only a smaller, specialized force for combat. Canada had the best. China was glad to let Canada fight the wars for it."

Ruth: "What about Australia? Did they help?"

Clete: "They were already fried by then. Done totally, stick a fork in 'em. They couldn't help themselves, let alone anyone else."

The previous chapter focused on the problems faced by nation-states and the emergence of megacities as primary players on the world stage. This chapter looks at the security implications of that environment in a climate change setting. This chapter extends some of the principal findings from the previous chapter, particularly with regard to the increasing power of nonstate actors.

As in previous chapters, the first task it to assess predominant issues and problems within a particular domain, in this chapter, international security. The first question is, what are the principal security issues faced by the United States globally, and second, where are those problems going? We focus in particular on the steadily increasing empowerment of nonstate actors. Then we assess ways in which global warming might affect that security environment; alternatively, we look at the additional risk to that environment created by climate change.

The Empowerment of Nonstate Actors

That powerful nonstate actors have emerged to challenge states is recognized in the literature on emerging issues in state security. As Robb (2007, pp. 16-17) observed, the nation-state system, as the corporate model for the organization of territory, has only been dominant in Western societies for about three and a half centuries and, for much of the world, considerably less. Its heyday has come and gone. In the current era, even a small force can successfully challenge a state. We are approaching the time when even a single individual can. Consider the following comment from Robb:

> . . .states have extended their reach to control the economy, personal rights, borders, resources, security, laws infrastructure, education, and health of their citizens. . . That control is coming to an end. The culprits are globalization and the internet. This new environment is sweeping aside state power in ways that no army could. States are losing control of their borders, economics, finances, people, and communications. To further complicate matters, a new competitive

*force is emerging in this vacuum of state power. Nonstate actors in
the form of terrorists, crime syndicates, gang, and networked tribes
are stepping into the bready to lay claim to areas one in the sole
control of states. It is this conflict, the war between states and
nonstates, that is the basis for the first epochal or long war of this
century.*

Nor are states particularly effective at fighting guerilla wars. For
example, for all its vaunted strength, the U.S. military machinery
is mired in an unwinnable conflict against opponents in Afghanistan who ride on horseback and in Subarus, and the United States
is engaged in the longest war in its history. The winnability problem may not be due to some quirk of the U.S. military; it might
reside in the nature of the conflict itself. The problem, Robb
(2007, pp. 28-29) suggested, is that when a strong belligerent fights
a weak one, the strong one becomes weak. The problem is that
military superiority can win battles but it cannot, over the long-
term, hold terrain. Thus, the British lost the United States, the
United States lost Vietnam, the Soviet Union lost Afghanistan,
and the French lost Vietnam and Algeria. Indeed, the United
States has had a dismal record of conflicts since the Second World
War, winning none outright. Robb, discussing Crevald, a military
historian, observed that:

*Crevald realized that whenever a state takes on a guerilla
movement, it will lose. The reason is that when the strong are seen
beating the weak (knocking down doors, roughing up people of
interest, and shooting ragtag guerillas) they are considered to be
barbarians. This view, amplified by the media, will eventually eat
away at the state's ability to maintain moral cohesion and
drastically damage its global image. As the state's soldiers continue
to fight weak foes, they will eventually become as ill-disciplined and
vicious as the people they are fighting, due to frustration and mirror
imaging. For the state, it will likely not only lose the war but also in
the process destroy the effectiveness of its army.*

The tool that asymmetrically weak belligerents have is "systems disruption." It is the sophisticated and interlocked nature
of our modern technologies that make us particularly vulnerable.
By systems disruption is meant that, for a fairly modest price, a
small enemy can do enormous economic and psychological damage to a large enemy. The 9/11 attacks are the hallmark of systems
disruption; for approximately $50,000, Al-Qaeda cost the U.S.
economy an estimated $50 billion, about a $1 million to $1 return
on investment. That was a highly symbolic attack; the danger to a
state lies in a small enemy essentially "bleeding the state dry" by

attacks on essential infrastructures such as energy, transportation, utilities, and the like. A stateless enemy has no system to disrupt. A large standing army, major weapons systems, and air superiority such as the United States has, with its immense lethality capability against the military might of any state in the world, are only of limited value in the conflicts of the twenty-second century. As conflicts move into megacities and megadeltas, U.S. military superiority will be even further offset by asymmetries of urban conflict (Kilcullen, 2013).

Terrorism, Guerillas, and Transnational Crime

Terrorists and guerillas have changed over time, adapting to a changing landscape. Today, these groups view themselves to be engaged in global conflict, and their weapons are technology, globalization, and morality. They are referred to as fourth generation guerillas, the term taken from fourth generation wars, those fought at the end of the twenty-first and beginning of the twenty-second century.[1] One of the targets of the fourth generation guerillas is international businesses, especially those with military connections. As noted in the previous chapter, the United States extensively outsources much of its security. Outsourced security organizations tend to operate locally according to their own dynamics and outside of command control, and they are consequently both vulnerable to guerilla attacks and limitedly responsible to the chain of command. Robb, commenting on this vulnerability in the second Iraq–United States conflict, observed that

> *Although they may seem haphazard, the endless series of hostage dramas and assaults on contractors in Iraq form a pattern. They are aimed at the fault lines in the outsourced service market. The pattern is quickly being copied by a rapidly proliferating number of groups that swarm on these soft edges. (2007, pp. 55-56)*

We used the word vulnerabilities to emphasize the decentralization and consequent multiplication of targets that private corporations offer. Not only can they undermine "unity of command," they are vulnerable to attack without the communications, the rapid mobilization, and full spectrum response available to combat units.

Modern terrorist networks are difficult to defeat because of the nature of their organization. As Robb (2007, p. 136) noted, a state, engaged against such an enemy, is fighting a "thousand tiny armies." They tend to have a sparse operational network with connections typically through brief face-to-face meetings. The administrative network behind them may be substantial, but it is scattered and thin in any one place, lacking formal hierarchy. Informal leadership relationships control operations and can quickly transition from one person to another. Moreover, many of the leaders, as well as the players, will be unknowns.

These networks tend to be horizontal, rather than the vertical command structures associated with more conventional forces. They are not vulnerable to leadership assassination, since they are formally leaderless. They also take advantage of globalization. They are "wired, educated, and globally mobile. They build complex supply chains, benefit from global money flows, travel globally, innovate with technology, and attack shrewdly" (Robb, 2007, p. 146).

Transnational crime can develop alongside insurgent and terrorist networks, and organized international criminals tend to have organizations and operational styles similar to insurgents. This is because they tend to use the same geographic pipelines, make use of the same underground contacts, face the same problem of survivability in the face of state repression, and both need economic resources for success. One of the lessons of the modern era is that, increasingly, organized crime and terrorism today are extensively overlapped. This is an important change from the twentieth century, when they were typically seen as functionally different entities, both in terms of their activities and goals. Almost half of the governments identified by the U.S. State Department as terrorist organizations, for example, are also involved in drug smuggling (Robb, 2007). They consequently develop similar horizontal structures, use similar networks, and take advantage of the same security weaknesses within and between nation-states.

Transnational crime thrives because it can provide desired, and sometimes essential, goods that are prohibited by states. It can provide drugs, undocumented workers, weapons, intellectual property rip-offs, and money for insurgents. These provisions in turn can be further used to undermine states. Drugs enhance the reach of local gangs and are the lifeblood of underground economies. Weapons are fuel for conflicts ranging from local gang beefs to proxy wars. Weapons needs are self-fulfilling; they enable levels of conflict to escalate, further increasing the demand for weapons. Undocumented workers provide slave labor, sex workers, and child sex slaves and are fed by the surging populations of unemployed and migrants who provide large quantities of cheap labor in the international marketplace. Property rip-offs flood online purchasing and buying, transitioning seamlessly between illicit and licit marketplaces such as online shopping networks.

The international reach of transnational crime is immense. By some estimates, the "black marketplace" occupies up to 10% of the total world trade. Moreover, it is growing at a rate estimated to be about seven times as fast as the legal global marketplace (Robb, 2007). It thrives because it satisfies individual needs prohibited by licit markets in states, because states are not strong enough to shut them down, and because it may provide goods much cheaper than licit markets. Their growth is further evidence of the contemporary vulnerability of the state system to regulate goods. The four important features of transnational crime are virtually the same as fourth generation insurgency: (1) its rapid growth, (2) its huge reach, (3) its decentralized and horizontal organizational structures, and (4) its increasing integration with other nonstate actors. Robb's central conclusion is that state security, as it currently exists, lacks the mobility and fluidity to effectively suppress transnational crime. Transnational crime groups have emerged on the world stage as important challengers to state authority.

Transnational crime and terrorism work together various ways. The following ways have been cited (Rollins & Wyler, 2013):

1. **Expand skill base.** Partnerships are a force multiplier, enhancing the strengths of both. Specialized skills can be obtained that enhance functionality and success. This kind of partnering, for the expansion of resources, may lead to a dependency of the terrorist organization on criminal transactions, increasing the vulnerabilities that international security agents can exploit.

2. **Shared tactics.** Tactics may be appropriated from one group to another. In spite of ideological differences, operational tactics are often the same for both groups. These include acts of violence, for-profit criminal activity, money laundering, stealth when crossing borders, illegal weapons acquisition, and the corruption of public officials.

3. **Organizational evolution.** Criminal groups may evolve politically; conversely, political terrorists may gravitate toward criminal for-profit enterprises.

The integration of terrorists and transnational crime is in part the result of successes the international community has had in combating terrorism. Terrorists in many cases have lost other sources of funding; state sponsorship is increasingly difficult to obtain with the focus of counterterror experts on closing off financial funding opportunities. This alliance is increasingly one of necessity for terrorists in the current era. Transnational criminals may not want the additional exposure that they receive by affiliating with terrorists. However, the force multiplier for successful collaborations is a significant state threat in many

Information Box 11.1 Farah: Terrorism, Transnational Crime, and Criminalized States in Latin America

The emergence of new hybrid state and nonstate transnational criminal and terrorist franchises in Latin American poses a tier-one security threat for the United States … (Their) activities are carried out with the support of regional and extraregional state actors whose leadership is deeply enmeshed in criminal activities, yielding billions of dollars in illicit revenues every year in the regions, and trillions globally. Leaders of these organizations share a publicly articulated doctrine to employ asymmetric warfare against the United States and its allies that explicitly endorses the use of WMD as a legitimate tactic.

The threat centers around an improbably alliance of groups that often seem to have irreconcilable world views and ideologies; e.g., Iran, a conservative Islamist theocracy and primary state sponsor of Hezbollah and the Bolivarian alliance espousing twenty-first century socialism, led by Venezuela's Hugo Chavez. Such alliances, in turn, offer material and political support to the Marxist Revolutionary Armed Forces of Colombia (FARC). This group … produces more than two-thirds of the world's cocaine and is rapidly strengthening its ties to Mexican cartels.

Such illicit forces in Latin American within criminalized states have begun using tactical operations centers as a means of pursuing their view of statecraft. That brings new elements to the "dangerous spaces" where nonstate actors intersect with regions characterized by weak sovereignty and alternative governance systems. This new dynamic fundamentally alters the structure underpinning global order.

The traditional state/nonstate dichotomy is no longer useful for an adequate illumination of these problems. Similarly, the historic divide between transnational organized crime and terrorism is becoming increasingly irrelevant (pp. xii-xiii).

Source: Farah, D. (2012). Transnational organized crime, terrorism, and criminalized states in Latin America: An emerging tier-one national security priority. Carlisle Barracks, PA: U.S. Army War College, Strategic Studies Institute. http://strategicstudiesinstitute.army.mil/pubs/display.cfm?pubID=1117.

places: As Robb noted, it is surprisingly easy to buy off some governments.

The emergence of specific groups and their impact as a "tier one" security threat has been documented by Farah (2012) and is noted in Information Box 11.1.

Geographic Black Holes, Pipelines, and Criminalized States

Nonstate actors act within black holes and through pipelines. A black hole is a geographic area where the state governs ineffectively or weakly, and where the nonstate actors can carry out activities in pursuit of their illicit goals (Korteweg & Ehrhardt, 2005).

As Farah (2012) noted, such players can move in, not only where the state is truly weak, but also where there is "a perception on the part of the local population that the state poses a threat to their communities, livelihoods, or interests." Gangs represent that perception; they are viable, even in seemingly strong states, where the community views the state as a threat. Geographic holes can extend to criminalized states; some states have the work of organized crime as their primary business. The republic of Transnistria, one of the breakaway republics from the former Soviet Union, is run by former Russian Secret Police and is known as "Europe's Black Hole" for its trafficking in weapons.

Black Holes

Black holes are areas that are beyond the control of a state or city's security or constabulary forces. These challenges proliferate in cities, and their challenges to security are discussed below.

1. We have emphasized the security problems of megacities with high levels of migration. These already pose a significant security issue from the perspective of migrants, many of whom will live in geographies beyond a megacity's ability to provide social or security supports. The municipal challenges to megacities and megadeltas were documented above in the section on feral cities. Even nonferal cities will—already have—significant tracts that are impoverished and suffer from lack of development.

2. Megadeltas will likely have a citizenry in a quasi-permanent state of mobility, as they move inland and uphill from encroaching seas. These will likely be the poorest of citizens who already are outside most of a city's ability to provide supports, largely located in violence crucibles. If they have to move inland from rising seas they can anticipate conflict from other groups who are already living in preferred or inland areas or from the property owners of the land on which they settle. It is difficult to imagine some of the megadeltas not being in a permanent state of internal violent conflict.

3. Violence crucibles of megadeltas will increasingly be "no-man's land" and under the control of nonstate actors. Unless delta cities wall themselves off from their coastlines, they will be victimized by forays into the city itself in the form of terrorism, kidnapping, extortion, drug sales, and human trafficking.

4. Many conflicts around the world today have a strong ethnic component (see Chua, 2002). These conflicts are likely to relocate to megacities as they surpass states to become the primary corporate political entity with the vast bulk of the human population.

5. Cities will contribute to further global warming. They will need enormous quantities of energy to sustain their populations, especially their businesses. They contribute to deforestation

in two ways. On the one hand, they need the agribusiness from large-scale cattle farming and crop growing sources. If one were to look at a cattle farming ranch today, one would see thousands of cattle on an acreage whose surface is a mix of crap and mud. On the other hand, they may clear land around the city itself to take away hiding places for criminal gangs.[2] Third, the ozone produced by smog decreases the ability of surrounding vegetation to absorb carbon.[3] Fourth, poverty areas in megacities have residents who rely on coal or open fires for fuel for cooking and warmth (Miskel & Liotta, 2006).

6. Municipal authorities are vulnerable to corrupt opportunities, particularly for cities facing budget challenges and shortfalls. For instance, it has been observed that the police in Mexico City are "officers by morning, thieves by afternoon." The corruption of the criminal justice system by nonstate illicit marketeers creates new pipelines that open the door for terrorism. Global warming will exacerbate the financial challenges because of damage to infrastructure and increased service population needs, stimulating an environment of municipal corruption.

7. Violence crucibles will be breeding grounds for gangs and for recruitment of terrorists. In turn, legitimate entrepreneurs in these areas may relocate, contributing to the loss of legitimate revenue, declining property values, and the expansion of illicit enterprise. In this way, black holes feed off themselves and will expand proportionally to their abilities to undercut the city's tax base.

8. Conflicts will occur among populations separated by a millennium of technology. Populations in the twenty-second century, walled off in inner cities, will live alongside populations who are effectively still living in the twelfth century, lacking access to clean drinking water, having limited supplies of coal and wood for fuel, wearing clothing gleaned from open pit trash dumps, and having no electricity beyond what they can occasionally pilfer from batteries. Such living arrangements will likely breed strong emotions and hostile sentiments among the poor.

Geographic Pipelines

Pipelines are emergent spaces that are used by nonstate actors as conduits for the movement of goods and people. They include both physical and virtual (web-based) conduits that can be used to "move products, money, weapons, personnel, and goods." In many places, pipelines are traditional smuggling routes, riparian or coastal locations, urban places, and other out of the way routes that have a long historical use as pipelines. Many of them lie adjacent to or close by existing routes for goods (Farah, 2012, pp. 29-30).

A good metaphor for a pipeline network is the human blood distribution system. The system is designed to take a product to every aspect of the larger body—the planet, in this case—that needs the product. Where the state has weak security the pipeline is robust; in weakly controlled areas in strong states, pipelines spider out through a multiplicity of small, highly decentralized routes. Also, like the flow of blood, if a pipeline is shut down, another one will grow to replace it and the overall system will be unaffected. The metaphor breaks down in one important regard, though. The center of the human blood supply is the heart. A pipeline has no heart. It is decentralized, carried out by a multiplicity of replaceable actors.

Criminalized States

The security demands of the future tend to focus on urban settings (see Kilcullen, 2013), leaving the rural countryside untended. Rural areas can be ripe for the acquisition by and competition among nonstate actors. Afghanistan, a country with the presence of a multinational force led by a very strong state, is nevertheless the largest poppy producing country in the world and seems to be able to move heroin globally at will. Indeed, opium production has risen steadily since the U.S. invasion in 2001. In 2007, Afghanistan's poppy/opium export value was estimated at about $4 billion, with "a quarter being earned by opium farmers and the rest going to district officials, insurgents, warlords, and drug traffickers."[4]

A focus on nonstate actors can overlook one of the most influential players in the illicit marketplace—criminal states. Manea (2013), writing about the concept of the collapsing state, observed that

> The notion that the state is weakening and collapsing might not be really appropriate for many parts of the world where the state has always been defined as a mafia bazaar. You take over the state so you can issue exceptions from law enforcement to your friends, so that you and your friends can make money.[5]

Africa, she suggested, should not be thought of as a state in the Weberian sense, where the "raison d'etre is to deliver public goods to citizens in exchange for legitimacy and sustainability."

> Many areas in the world, Africa being the prime example, have had a different notion of the state, one much closer to the medieval conceptualization where the purpose of the state and the purpose of

power competition for controlling the state apparatus is to make money for oneself.[6]

States such as these can themselves serve both as black hole for the orchestration and movement of illicit goods and people. Guinea-Bissau, Conakry, Liberia, and Sierra Leon are weak states whose functions are largely controlled by transnational organized crime, and are an integral asset to the movement of cocaine across Africa and into Europe. Iran, on the other hand, is a strong state that is also a sponsor and exporter of terrorism across the Middle East. Farah, in this regard, noted that

The emergence of criminalized, strongly anti-American governments in the Western hemisphere, in alliance with Iran and other states that sponsor terrorist organizations and who consider the United States to be the great Satan, now represent a tier-one threat to the security of the U.S. homeland.

(Farah, 2012, p. iv)

Into a Warmer, Vulnerable Future

Global warming, combined with the massive migration of the planet's human population to highly vulnerable megadeltas and megacities, fundamentally changes the state-nonstate competitive environment. Almost all the changes brought by global warming favor the nonstate actors over state-based ones. There are some very powerful exceptions to this; the United States is geographically isolated and militarily strong when compared to the rest of the world, and it has control over its resources directly or indirectly through international contract or coercive relationships.[7] Such exceptions will be isolated in an increasingly hostile world.

The changes in lower riparian basins and coastline regions will create a favorable environment for criminal pipeline development. Nation-states will experience boundary shrinkage and competition with a rising ocean. Property values in these areas will likely collapse well before the land is drowned under a rising sea. The emergence of long areas of economically unviable coast and riparian areas will increase their availability for pipelines.

Coastal cities, many already reeling from uncontrolled population growth through the first half of the twenty-second century will have an additional security burden that they likely cannot take on. It does not take a lot of imagination to foresee large swaths of coastline largely under the control of nonstate actors, the growth of gangs in expanding violence crucibles even in strong states, an expansion of closed-in staging grounds for terrorist attacks, and the movement of drugs smoothly from coast to inner city, all of these activities adjacent to and accessible to major urban areas globally.

Security's Fast Forward: The U.S. Navy in the Arctic

Given the security challenges anticipated by global warming, it seems astonishing that the United States does not seem to prepare for them; an examination of congressional attitudes shows open resistance by a sizeable number of politicians in the face of very, very strong evidence. Oklahoma Republican Senator Jim Inhofe published a book titled *The Greatest Hoax*, in which he aggressively rejected all aspects of the science of global warming. The U.S. Congress proceeds in a peculiar way indeed, which is particularly troubling given the immense contribution its country provides to the causes of global warming. The denial of global warming, by one of its major nation-state contributors, foments additional security risks to the United States through the harm done by climate change to poorer countries, who bear the brunt of climate change consequences and who can do nothing about them. Indeed, global warming terrorism blowback against the United States should enter the lexicon of security risks for the U.S. security establishment.

The U.S. military establishment is proceeding in a direction sharply different from its government. It is moving briskly ahead, carrying out its own research, utilizing academic researchers at its military and war colleges, and displaying the important recognition that global warming may be an existential threat to the United States. Indeed, many of the articles we use in this paper have been taken from military-related journals and interviews. Make no mistake—U.S. military institutions are in the global forefront of adaptation to climate change.

The U.S. Navy may be moving the most rapidly of the military branches in efforts to sort out the security dimensions of global warming. Reasonably, this is not surprising; the Navy deploys in maritime environments and has to be able to rapidly adapt to even small changes in the world's oceans and seas, should a security threat to the United States emerge. Such a security threat has emerged, and it is directly tied to global warming: the rapid melt-off of summer Arctic ice and the opening of a channel across the Arctic. The Navy has been critical of existing global warming research but not for contrarian reasons. It has asserted that current warming models are underestimating the pace of melt-off.

Information Box 11.2 U.S. Navy: Predictions of Ice-Free Arctic Summers

An ongoing U.S. Department of Energy-backed research project led by a U.S. Navy scientist predicts that the Arctic could lose its summer sea ice cover as early as 2016—84 years ahead of conventional model projections. The project, based out of the U.S. Naval Postgraduate School's Department of Oceanography, uses complex modeling techniques that make its projections more accurate than others. A paper by principal investigator Professor Wieslaw Maslowski in the *Annual Review of Earth and Planetary Sciences* sets out some of the findings so far of the research project:

> *Given the estimated trend and the volume estimate for October–November of 2007 at less than 9,000 km³, one can project that at this rate it would take only 9 more years or until 2016 ± 3 years to reach a nearly ice-free Arctic Ocean in summer. Regardless of high uncertainty associated with such an estimate, it does provide a lower bound of the time range for projections of seasonal sea ice cover.*

The paper is highly critical of global climate models (GCMs) and even the majority of regional models, noting that "many Arctic climatic processes that are omitted from, or poorly represented in, most current-generation GCMs. . .do not account for important feedbacks among various system components." There is therefore "a great need for improved understanding and model representation of physical processes and interactions specific to polar regions that currently might not be fully accounted for or are missing in GCMs."

Such Arctic changes "could have significant ramifications for global sea level, the ocean thermohaline circulation and heat budget, ecosystems, native communities, natural resource exploration, and commercial transportation."

Source: US Navy predicts summer ice free Arctic by 2016. Retrieved October 14, 2013 at http://www.theguardian.com/environment/earth-insight/2013/dec/09/usnavy-arctic-sea-ice-2016-melt.

This is presented in Information Box 11.2 titled "U.S. Navy: Predictions of Ice-Free Summers."[8]

We can trace significant Navy interest in Arctic warming since 2009, when the Vice Chief for Naval Operations issued a memorandum providing a "roadmap." At that time, the Navy was responding to ice-free summers by the 2030s, before it moved up the time line to the mid-teens. Its roadmap included outreach to the scientific community: They list the following organizations to work with to develop knowledge valuable to security interests:

1. National Science Foundation (NSF); National Academy of Science; National Research Council; U.S. Arctic Research Commission; Naval Post-Graduate School Naval War College; National Defense University; Office of Naval Research (ONR)

2. Strategic Environmental Research and Development Program; U.S. Army Corps of Engineers (USACE) Cold Regions Research Lab (CRREL); University of Washington's Applied Physics Lab Polar Science Center; University of Colorado, Boulder; University of California, Los Angeles; Pennsylvania State University; Wood Hole Oceanographic Institution

3. University of Alaska, Fairbanks' International Arctic Research Center; University of New Hampshire; NASA's Jet Propulsion Laboratory; NOAA's National Snow and Ice Data Center, National Climatic Data Center, National Weather Service, National Ocean Service, Climate

We see in the roadmap the recognition of the critical importance of merging U.S. security with the scientific community, together with a plan to carry out that knowledge merger.

Why is the Navy particularly interested in the Arctic region? Ice-free passage in this region represents a fundamental change and immense opportunities in global economics as well as new dangers in global security.

New Commerce from Ice-Free Passage

The Northern Sea Route skirts the United States along the Alaskan coast and Russia across Siberia. It is of immense value: Russian President Putin has repeatedly recognized the development of the Arctic region in speeches.[9]

Rosneft, an oil company in which Russia is the majority partner, has indicated that it will pay a trillion dollars for the development of the Northern Shelf along Siberia. ExxonMobile is in a partnership, investing $200,000 in a Russian research center; this partnership suggests the immense potential value of Arctic opportunities. There are also values in the route itself, independent of the available resources. In 2009, two Belugan ice-strengthened, heavy-lift haul vessels became the first Western haul vessels to transit the Northern Sea Route, although with some Russian assistance. The president of Beluga Shipping noted that the voyage saved each of the vessels about 300,000 euros (414,000 U.S. $). By 2012, 46 cargo vessels made the passage, about 80% of which carried a cargo of oil.

China is also interested in maritime passage. About half of China's gross domestic product (GDP) is related to international shipping, and the opening of the Northern Sea Route would be 6,400 km shorter than the widely used route through the Suez Canal. Sharp increases in the costs of insurance could also be mitigated if a route was found where piracy was not a concern.[10] China also is investing in resource exploration across the region. It is financing a major international mining project at Greenland's Isua iron-ore field and is partnering with Russia's Rosneft to increase the quantity of oil brought from Russian oilfields to the Chinese mainland. Moreover, China is moving to establish research entities in the region in order to better understand climate change. It now considers itself to be an "Arctic stakeholder."[11]

Emergent Security Concerns

Security issues also loom in the open waters of the Arctic. Smuggling has been raised as a possibility:

Sometime in the not-so-distant future, a ship loaded with cocaine could set sail from Colombia to South East Asia and take the Arctic route to avoid inspections at one or more of the choke points. Human traffickers in Bangladesh could smuggle girls up through the Bering Straights and into Western Europe. Gangsters could ship fissile material needed to construct nuclear weapons out of Russia to Burma, avoiding the harassment that they might encounter by using other maritime routes.[12]

Increased trade, especially through restricted areas, or "choke points," created opportunities for extortion and corruption; small towns tended to emerge along trade routes so that cargo can be offloaded, repairs made, and ships refueled. Illicit opportunities can emerge in these places as informal costs of doing maritime business, from port "tariffs" to piracy.

Terrorism is also a possibility, though a distant one. There are, simply, very few targets of value in the region. However, eco-terrorism is a concern: An attack on an oil rig, in the relatively confined space of the Arctic region, could be catastrophic in terms of spillage on Arctic ecosystems. The capacity for clean-up or capping such a disaster is not technologically present in the region.[13]

Finally, it is not clear that, in spite of pronouncements to the contrary, countries in the region will not militarize for the purposes of displaying a strong maritime presence and protecting their interests. In an assessment of international security in the Arctic under conditions of global warming, Huebert, Exner-Pirot, Lajeunesse, and Gulledge (2012) evaluated three hypotheses regarding international arctic security. The first, that there was no emerging security environment, they discounted. The second hypothesized that the security environment would herald a cooperative period and multilateral alliance building. The third hypothesized that the new environment would be "a recipe for competition and potential conflict."

The authors found that, generally speaking, interested countries voiced cooperation, the need for alliances, and a willingness to work together. However, their actions suggested unilateral military buildups across the region. Five of their principal findings indicated that the Arctic was in a period of rapid militarization. The first finding was that there was unprecedented national attention to the arctic region. Second, environmental security was a central concern. However, the countries all indicated that they lacked the capacity for a constabulary presence, and one was needed to provide environmental protections. Third, although all countries evinced a desire for cooperation, the rule or maritime law, and peace, in practice they were fortifying their military presence with the intent to protect and provide for national security. Fourth, countries were remilitarizing and modernizing their forces across the region. Fifth, non-Arctic states are seeking roles in the region. Both France and China have indicated a desire for a presence in the Arctic. In sum, international activities in the Arctic represent the first global militarized response to a changing environment, in which global warming is clearly seen as the cause of the changes.

This brief review of U.S. military preparedness for global warming is both heartening and disheartening. It is heartening in that the military establishment appears to be moving in a direction diametrically opposed to the U.S. legislature, mired as it is in nonaction and negative oratory. It is also heartening that there is recognition of the economic and strategic benefits of multilateralism. It is disheartening in that the pattern of action is one of military buildup for defense and the counterpositioning of interested countries as they also build up their military might in the Arctic region. Yet it is at the same time essential; military alignment and preparedness, done smartly, will be increasingly important for the destabilizations of the future, particularly when global warming is stirred into the mix. The buildup of forces in the region is clear acknowledgment, by an inherently conservative set of military institutions, that global warming is a force already on us.

Endnotes

1. "The Changing Face of War: Into the Fourth Generation." Retrieved January 19, 2014 at http://globalguerrillas.typepad.com/lind/the-changing-face-of-war-into-the-fourth-generation.html; see also "Global Guerillas." Retrieved January 19, 2014 at http://globalguerrillas.typepad.com/globalguerrillas/2004/05/4gw_fourth_gene.html.
2. Discussing Nairobi, Liskel and Liotta (2006: 47) noted that "Topping a ridge, we looked at a minor depression to his neighborhood. He proudly declared that he loved to watch eagles soar up and down the valley during the day. Yet across on the other slope the entire hillside had been deforested. His explanation was clear: "This makes gangs moving up from the slums on raids far more noticeable."

3. The gas enters plants through respiratory pores, called stomata, in the leaves. It then produces byproducts that crimp efficiency in photosynthesis, leaving a plant that is weak and undersized. "Smog To Accelerate Global Warming." Retrieved January 20, 2014 at http://www.terradaily.com/reports/Smog_To_Accelerate_Global_Warming_999.html.

4. "Opium production in Afghanistan." Retrieved January 21, 2014 at http://en.wikipedia.org/wiki/Opium_Production_in_Afghanistan.

5. "Gangs, Slums, Megacities and the Utility of Population-Centric COIN." Retrieved October 12, 2013 at http://smallwarsjournal.com/jrnl/art/gangs-slums-megacities-and-the-utility-of-population-centric-coin.

6. Ibid.

7. The US also has a citizenry tolerant of high levels of surveillance and prisonization, allowing the government to closely surveille and screen its populations for potential threats and to act on those perceived threats with very strong criminal sanctions.

8. "US Navy predicts summer ice free Arctic by 2016." Retrieved October 14, 2013 at http://www.theguardian.com/environment/earth-insight/2013/dec/09/us-navy-arctic-sea-ice-2016-melt.

9. "The value of the Northern Sea Route and the development of the Arctic Shelf." Retrieved October 15, 2013 at http://www.arctic-info.com/FederalMonitoringMedia/Page/the-value-of-the-northern-sea-route-and-the-development-of-the-arctic-shelf--federal-media-monitoring--december-17-23--2012.

10. "China and the Arctic: An Element of an Evolving Global Strategy." Retrieved October 16, 2013 at http://www.sldinfo.com/china-and-the-arctic-an-element-of-an-evolving-global-strategy/.

11. "China's Arctic strategy: Since gaining Arctic Council observer status, China has been quick to move on its interests." Retrieved October 16, 2013 at http://thediplomat.com/2013/06/chinas-arctic-strategy/.

12. "Arctic Security: Changing Paradigms for the 21st Century (Part One)." Retrieved October 17, 2013 at http://sofrep.com/30308/arctic-security-changing-paradigms-21st-century-part-one/.

13. "Arctic Security: Changing Paradigms for the 21st Century (Part Two)." Retrieved October 17, 2013 at http://sofrep.com/30315/arctic-security-changing-paradigms-21st-century-part-two/.

12

CONCLUSION: WHITHER THE SOCIAL CONTRACT?

Clete: "Do you mind talking about Beto? What happened to him?"

Ruth: "Here." She stood up slowly, stiff. "Let's take a walk, I'll show you."

They walked outside the building, around the back, where a small cemetery was located. "This one here is Beto," Ruth said, walking over to one of the graves. "He just got old and died. Like all of us. But he died in peace. He did what he could, and we all knew it. He will always be in my heart."

Clete: "Who are the others?"

Ruth: "Two are my kids, died of the diseases. They were very young. Some of the others were strangers who just couldn't make their way any farther. This is their final home. We thought it was the respectable thing to do to give them a good burial."

Clete: "Your kids—are there others? Do you mind my asking?"

Ruth: "I have two others who moved back to be with my sister in Calgary. They went into politics. They have Beto's vision. They have good hearts. I have visited them a few times, but I have not seen them in 10 years at least. I have seen their kids and their kids' kids. One is about 16. He will be special, I just know it. He will get into politics, too; he is gonna change things."

Clete: "I hope you're right." Clete thought about the toxic oceans. That was a big deal; if they got much worse, it would be the end of them all. Planet killer, that one was.

Ruth gave him a look, and again he thought he missed something. She said, "You have to have hope. Even Beto knew that. It keeps us going. Some way we will work through this. We will find a way." She paused. "Do we have any more to talk about? You're welcome to spend the night."

Clete: "I appreciate that, and I will take you up on that kind offer." He put away his notepad. "Now maybe I could find a tall beer and we can just relax and talk...."

This book has presented a dark image of our futures as they apply to our most basic social contract: our ability to get along with each other. Our history suggests that we do not play well together. Our political response to global warming, the primary marker of a government's willingness to invest its resources in a significant problem, is abysmal. Yet, a substantial part of the population recognizes the immediacy of the threat of climate change and they recognize the change it will bring. Fortunately, this part of the population also has the skills and knowledge to address and mitigate the problems. Their presence gives us hope.

We have sought to address an elemental and important aspect of global warming; its socially destabilizing influences, and the ways in which those destabilizing influences can lead to violence and crime. The topic is difficult even to grasp intellectually; trying to ascertain the impacts of global warming on crime and violence is trying to foresee the interactions of two complex, nonlinear systems: one physical and based in earth sciences; the other criminological, rooted in research on crime, opportunity, and social disorganization. The topic is justified, not because we can produce hard findings about the interactions of these systems, but because it is so important. All the big picture items, however, can be translated in terms of local risks affecting cities and businesses and can be accordingly built into long-term planning. It is already too late to stop many of the effects: the oceans are going to rise, and they will likely rise 2 meters by the end of the century regardless what we do at this point. But it is not too late to prepare, and it is not too late to stop the effects from being as bad as they could be. As bad as 2 meters will be, it is minor compared to a rise of an additional 5-10 meters another century in the future.

The social contract, a central element of moral philosophy in the Age of Enlightenment, sought to answer the question—under what conditions should each person voluntarily give up some of his or her freedom to the state? In 1762, when Rousseau wrote a book of that title, the global population was about 864 million people.[1] In 2050, the population is expected to exceed nine billion people. It is not clear that notions of social contract, conceived when the population was less than one-tenth of its 2050 estimates, can survive. Whither the social contract when the state itself becomes an empirical question? How can migrations be governed when they involve a billion people? What are the states' responsibilities to the billions trapped in megadeltas as the seas inexorably rise? Do the prosperous states, those directly responsible for climate change, help or will they abandon their responsibilities? As we move more deeply into the era of climate change, one in which we will have largely used critically important global resources and one in which most of us are crowded and poor as never before, with astonishing levels of income inequality faced by the bottom two billion people... Is this where the social contract has brought us? Is this the best we can do?

This line of reasoning may seem inappropriate for a social scientist. It rings too much of moral advocacy. But on this one this time, with this much at stake, no one can sit on the uninvolved sidelines. On this one, there are no sidelines.

Our principal findings and recommendations are below. Here, though, we conclude on a moral note. The way ahead is dire indeed, as Agnew (2012) observed. We will find a way through, though, because we are very good at muddling through problems. Our remaining option is limited to mitigation, and at this point in time, even mitigation is an unfashionable and unlikely political goal. But the role of science is to continue to do science, to publish and get into print, and to make knowledge available, believing and knowing that at some point, the voice of science will become the strong voice.

Principal Findings and Recommendations

This book has, on each substantive topic, asked three questions: (1) What is the current state of the risk, (2) what are the central developments for the risk in the coming years, and (3) how will global warming affect those risks? From that approach, we can identify the following principal findings. These findings are organized from flow chart 3.1, the adapted Homer-Dixon model of resource scarcity and violence (see Figure 4.1, p. 91).

We also provide recommendations for the fields of criminology and criminal justice following those findings. Our views of crime and recommendations are closely aligned with Agnew's (2012). However, we emphasized throughout the way how changes in routine activities, particularly as they are associated with migration, created opportunities for crime and violence. We also strongly agreed with the way in which global warming, in the context of existing global factors, might lead to social disorganization on a level not previously seen. Our consideration of favelas and violence crucibles paralleled social disorganization perspectives, although there is research asserting that the level of disorganization in favelas is not as great as it might appear to an outsider. To the point, it is not that people are socially disorganized per se, but that traditional patterns of social disorganization are overwhelmed by contemporary megacity forces.

    I. Aspects of global warming.

        1. Most analyses of global warming locate temperature increases at about 4°C by the end of the century, though the top-end estimates have been increasing due to nonmitigation and underestimates of climate sensitivity. Lacking is a full analysis of the additional warming beyond the end of the current century; those who have carried out this research tend to find substantial additional increases.

2. Positive trends in mitigation efforts are almost nonexistent. Because of that, many contemporary analyses of climate change across the earth sciences are finding that the pace of warming is tracking at the upper end of early estimates. In one research program involving analyses of sea ice sponsored by the U.S. Navy, estimates of effects have been moved up by 100 years.

3. The central problems associated with climate change outlined in this book are changes in disease vectors, melting ice and increased elevation of the oceans and seas, the desertification of already dry regions, heat waves and water shortages, and increasingly severe storms. Each one of these lead to shifts in resource availability and each generates security risks.

4. Droughts associated with global warming will leave many cities in the midlatitudes uninhabitable at today's population levels, especially those already in desert climates and suffering water shortages. There will be exceptions to this; the semipermanence of El Niño's effects, anticipated in tomorrow's hot house world, will increase rainfalls in some areas substantially.

II. Resource scarcities.

5. Global warming is occurring on a tableau in which resource use is already maximized and in which the population is already facing shortfalls. Aquifers for major cities, for instance, face a triple threat: many already are depleting too rapidly for long-term viability, in-migrating populations will add additional strains to those water resources, and global warming will further increase refugee populations and increase the needs for fresh water.

6. Global resources are being realigned. Both renewable and nonrenewable resources face significant shortfalls. The world today runs on oil, from its military institutions to its material working environment that relies heavily on transportation. From either declining oil stocks or from mitigation efforts, this will end. Current global levels of food production are not sustainable in a hot house world and will be insufficient to feed citizens in the megadeltas in the future.

7. Rising seas have the potential to affect the business, municipal, and criminal justice infrastructure of major port cities and megadeltas. This impact can negatively impact the overall wealth of the business community, undercut the municipal funding for security and social services, and directly affect the operations of local criminal justice systems.

8. Increasing scarcities, associated both with already occurring shortfalls of scarce renewables and nonrenewables, are driving migration. Migration pressures are likely to be amplified as the impacts of climate change set in.

III. Migration.

9. We are currently experiencing the greatest migration in the history of the human race, and approximately 80% of the human population will be urbanized by 2050. Although the rate of migration has diminished somewhat, the quantity of people migrating is at its highest in the current era.

10. Most of that urban population is relocating to the megadeltas of the world and most will be in poor countries. The populations of the megadeltas, by current trends, appear likely to peak at the same time that global sea-rise begins to significantly take hold. Urban inland megacities are already suffering from water shortages and consequently provide no respite from migrants who, at some point, are likely to stream out of coastal areas.

11. Not all at risk for becoming refugees or migrants will do so. From this, we should not minimize the importance of recognizing the potential for very large relocation populations. The lesson of Typhoon Haiyan is that, even if populations do not migrate away from damaged coastlines, they may well remain as substantial relocation populations with substantial resource (food, water, sanitation, housing) needs for an indefinite period. In other words, whether or not they are defined as refugees, they will have the needs and expenses associated with refugees.

IV. Crime and violence.

12. Streaming immigrant and refugee populations will generate issues of both opportunistic, individual crime, and organized crime. This includes slavery, sexual exploitation, and "employment" in chattel-like conditions. Migration itself may be one of the significant opportunities for the advancement of organized crime through the current century, providing slaves, forced military recruits,

and gang recruits a pipeline to move illicit goods through and a highly mobile population in which to hide.

13. Coastal areas of the major ports and megadeltas will provide opportunities for organized crime and for terrorism as they become increasingly unusable for commercial purposes due to sea-rise. These areas are at risk for becoming pipelines for crime, organized crime, and terrorism.

14. Storm intensification and eased access to civilian populations from sea-rise pose substantial threats to criminal justice infrastructure, capable of effectively shutting down local criminal justice systems. The lesson of Katrina was that these threats are immediate and substantial.

15. Violence crucibles in megacities and megadeltas represent Gordian knots of crime, gang activity, and social problems, in the absence of municipal infrastructure and security. Some of these crucibles may number in the millions of inhabitants. Controlling violence in crucibles may not be possible; containing it will become a major security issue.

V. State security.

16. Global warming presents an enormous security threat. It may be an existential security threat, in the sense that it will substantially disrupt the nation-state system globally. The pattern beginning to emerge is one in which states officially seek to work together while at the same time bolstering their own militaries against possible threats.

17. Global warming will tend to favor nonstate actors over states, especially those involved in international crime and the illicit marketplace. Nonstate actors are fluid and can adapt rapidly to changes in the environment. States are heavily tied to fixed elements of the physical infrastructure and lack fluidity when that infrastructure is damaged.

18. Changing disease vectors, increasing virulence of some strains, and the increasing ineffectiveness of antibiotics are capable of becoming a state threat. The lessons of AIDS in Africa include the finding that decimation of local populations leads to a wide variety of state-undermining security risks.

19. Based on our review of activities in the Arctic, the major powers will adapt to global warming by (1) attempting to

increase their access to resources that warming might make available and (2) bolstering their military regimes in response to perceived threats created by warming conditions.

20. Illicit markets, already representing about 10% of the total global market, appear poised to benefit from global warming. This is in part a consequence of their lack of vulnerable physical infrastructure, in part from their ability to globalize, and in part from their increasing contacts with gang activities and with insurgents and terrorists. They are effectively in control of some states today, which are criminalized states, and with the state vulnerabilities created by climate change they are likely to become a significant challenger to state authority.

VI. Recommendations for criminology and criminal justice.

21. The fields of criminology and criminal justice are inadequately involved in climate change. Given the enormous crime and security risks it poses, more research needs to be carried out. Our central challenge, beyond a need to focus resources in this direction, is to bolster our skill base so that we are up to the levels needed for this kind of work.

22. Strong quantitative methods are needed in this field, to engage in modeling work directly with earth science specialists. Some of our methods training needs to be adapted to the wide range of systems modeling techniques currently being used in climate change. Fortunately, some schools are already providing this level of training.

23. Criminology and criminal justice programs should participate in committees, research boards, multidisciplinary grants, and other interdisciplinary entities whose primary focus is climate change.

24. Though this might seem inconsistent with the call for methods skills, the field needs to develop a tolerance for big picture issues, even when the data do not fully enable adequate statistical resolution of a particular research outcome. Efforts to model the future will always have large uncertainties and, inevitably, errors built into them; in the field of climate change the problems are too important not to address.

25. The fields need a strong peer-reviewed journal whose purpose is the advancement of knowledge about crime and global warming.

26. Our major associations should set aside graduate scholarship money for training in this field. Our major universities need to create postdoctorates to develop the skills for this work.

Endnote

1. "World population estimates." Retrieved February 10, 2014 at http://en.wikipedia.org/wiki/World_population_estimates.

REFERENCES

Agnew, R. (2012). Dire forecast: A theoretical model of the impact of climate change on crime. *Theoretical Criminology, 16*(1), 21–42

Anderson, C. (1987). Temperature and aggression: Effects on quarterly, yearly, and city rates of violent and nonviolent crime. *Journal of Personality and Social Psychology, 52*(6), 1161–1173. Available at http://academic.research.microsoft.com/Paper/5977290.

Anderson, C. (1989). Temperature and aggression: The effects of heat on occurrence of human violence. *Psychological Bulletin, 106*(1), 74–96. http://www.psychology.iastate.edu/faculty/caa/abstracts/1985-1989/89A1.PDF.

Anderson, C. (2001). Heat and violence. *Current Directions in Psychological Science, 10*(1), 33–38.

Archer, D. (2009). *The long thaw: How humans are changing the next 100,000 years of Earth's climate.* Princeton, NJ: Princeton University Press.

Baron, R., & Ransberger, M. (1978). Ambient temperature and the occurrence of collective violence: The long hot supper revisited. *Journal of Personal and Social Psychology, 36*, 351–360.

Beck, V. (1992). *Risk society: Towards a new modernity.* London: Sage Publications Inc.

Bogen, K., Fischer, L., & Jones, E. (2010). *Hurricane intensity, sea surface temperature, and stochastic variation.* Croatia: InTech Open. http://www.studymode.com/essays/Hurrican-Intensity-403587.html.

Brauch, H. G. (2011). *Coping with global environmental change, disasters, and security: Threats, challenges, vulnerabilities, and risks.* Berlin: Springer.

Brennan-Galvin, E. (2002). Crime and violence in an urbanizing world. *Journal of International Affairs, 56*(1), 123–145.

Brower, J., & Chalk, P. (2003). *The global threat of new and reemerging infectious diseases: Reconciling U.S. national security and public health policy.* Santa Monica: RAND Corporation.

Brown, O., & McLeman, R. (2009). A recurring anarchy? The emergence of climate change as a threat to international peace and security. *Conflict, Security and Development, 9*(3), 289–305. http://www.humansecuritygateway.com/documents/CSD_RecurringAnarchy_EmergencyOfClimateChange_ThreatToInternationalPeaceSecurity.pdf.

Brulle, R. J. (2013). Institutionalizing delay: Foundation funding and the creation of U.S. climate change counter-movement organizations. *Climatic Change, 122* (4), 681–694. http://dx.doi.org/10.1007/s10584-013-1018-7.

Brzezinski, Z. (1993). *Out of control: Global turmoil on the eve of the twenty first century.* New York: Touchstone.

Burke, M., Miguel, E., Satyanath, S., Dykema, J. A., & Lobell, D. B. (2009). Warming increases the risk of civil war in Africa. *Proceedings from the National Academy of Sciences of the United States of America, 106*(49), 20670–20674.

Chacon, J. (2009). Managing migration through crime. *Columbia Law Review, 109*, 138–148. http://www.columbialawreview.org/articles/managing-migration-through-crime.

Chua, A. (2003). *World on fire.* New York: Doubleday.

Church, J., White, N. J., Aarup, T., Stanley Wilson, W., Woodworth, P. L., Domingues, C. M., et al. (2008). Understanding global sea levels: Past, present and future. *Sustainability Science, 3*, 9–22.

Carlsmith, J., & Anderson, C. (1979). Ambient temperature and the occurrence of collective violence: A new analysis. *Journal of Personality and Social Psychology, 37*, 337–344.

(The) CNA Corporation (2007). *National security and the threat of climate change.* p. 168. http://www.cna.org/sites/default/files/news/FlipBooks/Climate%20Change%20web/flipviewerxpress.html.

Cohen, L., & Felson, M. (1979). Social change and the crime rate: Towards a routine activity approach. *American Sociological Review, 44*, 588–608.

Cohn, E. G. (1990). Weather and crime. *British Journal of Criminology, 30*(1), 50–64.

Cohn, E. G., & Rotton, J. (2000). Weather, seasonal trends, and property crimes in Minneapolis, 1987-1988: A moderator-variable time-series analysis of routine activities. *Journal of Environmental Psychology, 20*, 257–272.

Cohn, E., & Rotton, J. (2012). The curve is still out there: A reply to Bushman, Wang, and Anderson's (2005) is the curve relating temperature to aggression linear or curvilinear? *Journal of Personality and Social Psychology - PSP, 89*(1), 67–70.

Corbyn, Z. (2011). Global warming wilts malaria. *Scientific American.* http://www.scientificamerican.com/article/global-warming-wilts-malaria/.

Crank, J. P. (2003). Crime and justice in the context of resource scarcity. *Crime, Law and Social Change, 39*(1), 39–67.

Crank, J., Murray, R., Sundermeier, M., & Irlbeck, D. (2011). *Mission-based policing.* New York: Taylor & Francis.

Curry, J. (2010). Hurricanes and global warming: 5 years post Katrina. *Climate.* http://judithcurry.com/2010/09/13/hurricanes-and-global-warming-5-years-post-katrina/.

Davis, M. (2006). *Planet of slums.* London: Verso.

Dean, J., Lovely, M., & Wang, H. (2004). *Foreign direct investment and pollution havens: Evaluating the evidence from China: Office of economics working paper.* Washington, DC: International Trade Commission. http://www.usitc.gov/publications/332/working_papers/ec200401b.pdf.

Decker, S., van Gemert, F., & Pyrooz, D. (2009). Gangs, migration, and crime: The changing landscape in Europe and the USA. *Journal of International Migration and Integration, 10*(4), 393–408. http://www.streetgangs.com/bibliography/2009/2009_decker_gemert_101509.pdf.

Desdemona Despair (2012). *Graph of the day: 2011–2012 ratio of U.S. heat to cold records.* http://www.desdemonadespair.net/2012/04/graph-of-day-2011-2012-ratio-of-us-heat.html.

Ding, D., Maibach, E. W., Zhao, X., Roser-Renouf, C., & Leiserowitz, A. (2011). Support for climate policy and societal action are linked to perceptions about scientific agreement. *Nature Climate Change, 1*, 462–466.

Duran, P. T., & Kendall Zimmerman, M. (2009). Examining the scientific consensus on climate change. *Eos, 90*(3), 22–23.

Erdoğan, A., Gedík, A., & Dǔzgǔn, H. Ş. (2010). Integrated analysis of crime incidents within a loosely-coupled GIS-based system: Case of Etlik Police Station. *Gazi University Journal of Science, 23*(4), 531–550.

Evans, A. (2010). *Resource scarcity, climate change, and the risk of violent conflict: World development report, 2011.* Washington, DC: U.S. Institute for Peace. http://siteresources.worldbank.org/EXTWDR2011/Resources/6406082-1283882418764/WDR_Background_Paper_Evans.pdf.

Fagan, B. (2004). *The long summer: How civilization changed climate.* New York: Basic Books.

Fajnzylber, P., Lederman, D., & Loayza, N. (Fall 2000). Crime and victimization: An economic perspective. *Economía, 1*(1), 219–302.

Farah, D. (2012). *Transnational organized crime, terrorism, and criminalized states in Latin America: An emerging tier-one national security priority.* Carlisle Barracks, PA: U.S. Army War College, Strategic Studies Institute. http://strategicstudiesinstitute.army.mil/pubs/display.cfm?pubID=1117.

Felson, M. (2002). *Crime in everyday life.* Thousand Oaks, CA: Pine Forge Press.

Foster, J. B. (1999). Marx's theory of metabolic rift: Classical foundations for environmental sociology. *American Journal of Sociology, 105*(2), 366–405.

Freedman, A. (2012). *How global warming made Hurricane Sandy worse.* Princeton, NJ: Climate Central. http://www.climatecentral.org/news/how-global-warming-made-hurricane-sandy-worse-15190.

Freudenburg, W. R. (1984). Boomtown's youth: The differential impacts of rapid community growth on adolescents and adults. *American Sociological Review, 49,* 697–705.

Garrett, L. (1994). *The coming plague. Newly emerging diseases in a world out of balance.* New York: Penguin Books.

Garrett, L. (2000). *Betrayal of trust: The collapse of global public health.* New York: Hyperion.

Garrett, L. (2005). *HIV and national security: Where are the links?* New York: Council on Foreign Relations. http://www.cfr.org/national-security-and-defense/hiv-national-security-links/p8256.

Garrett, B., & Tetlow, T. (2006). Criminal justice collapse: The Constitution after Hurricane Katrina. *Duke Law Journal, 56,* 127–178.

Gaviria, A., & Pages, C. (1999). *Patterns of crime victimization in Latin America.* IDB Working paper no. 339. Rochester, NY: Social Science Electronic Publishing, Inc. http://papers.ssrn.com/sol3/papers.cfm?abstract_id=1817205.

Hansen, J. (2009). *Storms of my grandchildren.* New York: Bloomsbury.

Harries, K. (2006). Property crimes and violence in United States: An analysis of the influence of population density. *International Journal of Criminal Justice Sciences, 1*(2), 24–34.

Heede, R. (2014). Tracing anthropogenic carbon dioxide and methane emissions to fossil fuel and cement producers, 1854–2010. *Climatic Change, 122,* 229–241.

Herrnstadt, E., & Muehlegger, E. (2013). *Weather, salience of climate change and congressional voting: Discussion paper 2013–48.* Cambridge, MA: Harvard Environmental Economics Program, June.

Hobsbawm, E. (1984). *The age of extremes: The short twentieth century, 1914-1991.* New York: Pantheon.

Homer-Dixon, T. (1999). *Environment, scarcity, and violence.* Princeton, NJ: Princeton University Press.

Homer-Dixon, T. (2002). *The ingenuity gap: Facing the economic, environmental, and other challenges of an increasingly complex and unpredictable future.* New York: Vintage Books.

Homer-Dixon, T. (2006). *The upside of down: Catastrophe, creativity, and the renewal of civilization.* Washington, DC: Island Press.

Homer-Dixon, T. (2013). *The upside of down.* Toronto: Random House of Canada.

Horton, B., Rahmstorf, S., Engelhart, S., & Kemp, A. (2014). Expert assessment of sea-level rise by AD 2100 and AD 2300. *Quaternary Science Reviews, 84,* 1–6.

Hossain, S. (2008). Rapid urban growth and poverty in Dhaka city. *Bangladesh e-Journal of Sociology, 5*(1), 57–80.

Hsiang, S. M., Burke, M., & Miguel, E. (2013). Quantifying the influence of climate on human conflict. *Science, 341*(6151), 1235367.

Hsiang, S. M., Meng, K. C., & Cane, M. A. (2011). Civil conflicts are associated with the global climate. *Nature, 476*(7361), 438–441. http://dx.doi.org/10.1038/nature10311.

Huebert, R., Exner-Pirot, H., Lajeunesse, A., & Gulledge, J. (2012). *Climate change & international security: The arctic as a bellwether.* Arlington, Virginia: Center for Climate and Energy Solutions. Available at http://www.c2es.org/publications/.

Huntington, S. (1996). *A clash of civilizations.* New York: Touchstone.

Hussey, A., Nikolsko-Rzhevskyy, A., & Pacurar, L. S. (2011). *Crime Spillovers and Hurricane Katrina.* http://umdrive.memphis.edu/ipacurar/public/Katrina 5 28.pdf Accessed December, 2013.

Immerzeel, W. W., van Beek, L. P. H., & Bierkens, M. F. P. (2010). Climate change will affect the Asian water towers. *Science, 328*(5984), 1382–1385, (as cited in Bostrom, D. (2010). Return to the Himalayas—fate of the glaciers. *Skeptical Science*, June 29, 201).

Johnson, M. H. (2006). *National policies and the rise of transnational gangs.* Washington, DC: Migration Policy Institute. http://migrationinformation.org/Feature/display.cfm?id=394.

Kaplan, R. (2004). The coming anarchy. *Atlantic Monthly*, (February). http://www.theatlantic.com/ideastour/archive/kaplan.html.

Kilcullen, D. (2012). *Out of the mountains: The coming age of the urban guerilla.* New York: Oxford University Press.

Kilcullen, D. (2013). *Nairobi foreshadows tomorrow's urban conflicts. The Financial Times.* London: Pearson PLC. http://www.ft.com/cms/s/0/17d09b3e-2606-11e3-8ef6-00144feab7de.html#ixzz2lmvwSq5o.

Klare, M. (2002). *Resource wars: The new landscape of global conflict.* New York: Henry Holt and Company.

Klare, M. (2012). *The race for what's left: The global scramble for the world's resources.* New York: Picador.

Kolbe, A., Puccio, M., & Muggah, R. (2012). *After the storm: Haiti's coming food crisis.* Strategic Note 6, December, Brazil: Igarape Institute.

Korteweg, R., & Ehrhardt, D. (2005). *Terrorist black holes: A study into terrorist sanctuaries and governmental weakness.* The Hague, The Netherlands: Clingendael Centre for Strategic Studies, p. 22.

Kramer, R., & Michalowski, R. (2012). Is global warming a state-corporate crime? In R. White, (Ed.), *Climate change from a criminological perspective* (pp. 71–88). New York: Springer.

Lee, M. (2003). *Crime on the border: Immigration and homicide in urban communities.* New York: LFB Scholarly Publishing.

Lee, M., Martinez, R., & Rosenfeld, R. (2001). Does immigration increase homicide? Negative evidence from three border cities. *The Sociological Quarterly, 42*, 559–580.

Leigh, P. (2012). US northeast coast is hotspot for rising sea levels. *Nature News*, (October). http://www.nature.com/news/us-northeast-coast-is-hotspot-for-rising-sea-levels-1.10880?WT.ec_id=NEWS-20120626.

Leiserowitz, A., Maibach, E., Roser-Renouf, C., Feinberg, G., Rosenthal, S., & Marlon, J. (2014). *Climate change in the American mind: Americans' global warming beliefs and attitudes in November, 2013.* New Haven, CT: Yale University and George Mason University, Yale Project on Climate Change Communication.

Leiserowitz, A., Maibach, E., Roser-Renouf, C., Smith, N., & Dawson, E. (2013). Climategate, public opinion, and the loss of trust. *American Behavioral Scientist, 57*(6), 818–837.

Lynas, M. (2008). *Six degrees: Our future on a hotter planet.* Washington, DC: National Geographic.

Manea, O. (2013). Gangs, slums, megacities and the utility of population-centric COIN. *Small Wars Journal*, http://smallwarsjournal.com/jrnl/art/gangs-slums-megacities-and-the-utility-of-population-centric-coin.

Marcott, S., Shakun, J., Clark, P., & Mix, A. (2013). A reconstruction of regional and global temperature for the past 11,300 years. *Science, 339*(6124), 1198–1201.

Marx, K. (1867). Capital: A critique of political economy, vol. I. The process of capitalist production (S. Moore, E. Aveling, trans. 1906). In F. Engels, & E. Untermann (Eds.), Indianapolis, IN: Liberty Inc.

McCright, A. M., & Dunlap, R. E. (2011). The politicization of climate change and polarization in the American public's views of global warming 2001-2010. *The Sociological Quarterly, 52*, 155–194.

McIbben, B. (2011). *Introduction: The global warming reader.* New York: Penguin.

Mervis, J. (2011). Ralph Hall speaks out on climate change. *ScienceInsider*, (December 14). Retrieved from http://news.sciencemag.org/2011/12/ralph-hall-speaks-out-climate-change.

Michael, R., & Zumpe, D. (1983). Annual rhythms in human violence and sexual aggression in the United States and the role of temperature. *Social Biology, 140*, 883–886.

Michael, R., & Zumpe, D. (1986). An annual rhythm in the battering of women. *American Journal of Psychiatry, 143*, 637–640.

Michalowski, R., & Kramer, R. (2006). *State-corporate crime: Wrongdoing at the intersection of business and government.* New Brunswick, NJ: Rutgers University Press.

Miller, T. (2005). Blurring the boundaries between immigration and crime control after September 11th. *Boston College Third World Law Journal, 25*, 81–123. http://lawdigitalcommons.bc.edu/twlj/vol25/iss1/4.

Miskel, J., & Liotta, P. (2006). *A fevered crescent: Security and insecurity in the greater near east.* Gainesville: University Press of Florida.

Myers, N. (2002). Environmental refugees: A growing phenomenon of the 21st century. *Philosophical Transactions of the Royal Society, 357*, 609–613.

Myers, N. (2005). Environmental refugees: An emergent security issue. *In: 13th economic forum, Sprague.* http://www.osce.org/eea/14851.

Naim, M. (2005). *Illicit: How smugglers, traffickers and copycats are hijacking the global economy.* New York: Vintage Books.

Naim, M. (2012). Mafia states: Organized crime takes office. *Foreign Affairs*, May/June, 100. See also http://www.foreignaffairs.com/articles/135279/moises-naim/mafia-states.

Nicholls, R., Marinova, N., Lowe, J. A., Brown, S., Vellinga, P., de Gusmão, D., et al. (2012). Sea-level rise and its possible impacts given a 'beyond 4°C world' in the twenty-first century. *Philosophical Transactions of the Royal Society, 369*(1934), 161–181.

Nisbett, M., & Myers, T. (2007). Twenty years of public opinion about global warming. *Public Opinion Quarterly, 71*(3), 444–470.

Norton, R. (2003). Feral cities. *Naval War College Review, 65*(4), 96–108. Newport, RI: U.S. Naval War College.

Ohmae, K. (1995). *The end of the nation state. The rise of regional economies.* New York: The Free Press.

Oreskes, N., & Conway, E. (2010). *Merchants of doubt: How a handful of scientists obscured the truth on issues from tobacco smoke to global warming.* New York: Bloomsbury Press.

Parenti, C. (2011). *Tropic of chaos: Climate change and the new geography of violence.* New York: Nation Books.

Pearce, F. (2007). *With speed and violence: Why scientists fear tipping points in climate change.* Boston: Beacon Press.

Perry, J., & Simpson, M. (1987). Violent crimes in a city: Environmental determinants. *Environment and Behavior, 19*, 77–90.

Peterson, S., & Shellman, S. (2006). *AIDS and violent conflict: The indirect effects of disease on national security.* Williamsburg, VA: College of William and Mary. http://web.wm.edu/irtheoryandpractice/security/papers/AIDS.pdf?svr=www.

Phillips, L. (2012). U.S. northeast coast is hotspot for rising sea levels. *Nature*, http://www.nature.com/news/us-northeast-coast-is-hotspot-for-rising-sea-levels-1.10880.

Pinker, S. (2011). *The better angels of our nature: Why violence has declined.* London: Penguin Books.

Podesta, J., & Ogden, P. (2007). The security implications of climate change. *The Washington Quarterly, 31*(1), 115–138. http://www2.dsi.gov.tr/iklim/dokumanlar/the_security_implications_of_climatechange.pdf.

Proctor, R. (1995). *The cancer wars: How politics shapes what we know and don't know about cancer.* New York: Basic Books.

Pumphrey, C. (2008). *Global climate change: National security implications* (pp. 1–446). Strategic Studies Institute. http://docs.lib.noaa.gov/noaa_documents/NOAA_related_docs/Pumphrey_global_climate_change_2008.pdf.

Purvis, N., & Busby, J. (2004). *The security implications of climate change for the UN system.* The United Nations and Environmental Security: Policy Brief. Washington, DC: The Wilson Center. http://www.wilsoncenter.org/sites/default/files/ecspr10_unf-purbus.pdf.

Ranson, M. (2012). *Crime, weather, and climate change: Working Paper 8.* Cambridge, MA: Harvard Kennedy School.

Reinert, S. (2004). Globalization, economic development and inequality: An alternative perspective. *New horizons in institutional and evolutionary economics series.* Northampton: Edward Elgar Publishing.

Reuveny, R. (2008). Ecomigration and violent conflict: Case studies and public policy implications. *Human Ecology, 36*(1), 1–13.

Robb, J. (2007). *Brave new war: The next state of terrorism and the end of globalization.* Hoboken, NJ: John Wiley & Sons.

Rollins, J., & Wyler, L. (2013). *Terrorism and transnational crime: Foreign policy issues for Congress.* Washington, DC: Congressional Research Service.

Romig, A., Backus, G., & Baker, A. (2010). *A deeper look at climate change and national security.* Albuquerque, NM: Sandia National Laboratories. http://prod.sandia.gov/techlib/access-control.cgi/2011/110039.pdf.

Rotton, J., & Cohn, E. G. (2000). Weather, disorderly conduct, and assaults: From social contact to social avoidance. *Environment and Behavior, 32*(5), 651–673. http://www.sagepub.com/lippmanccl2e/study/articles/Rotton.pdf.

Rotton, J., & Cohn, E. G. (2001). Temperature, routine activities, and domestic violence: A reanalysis. *Violence and Victims, 16*(2), 203–215.

Rotton, J., & Frey, J. (1985). Air pollution, weather, and violent crime: Concomitant time series analysis if archival data. *Journal of Personality and Social Psychology, 49*, 1207–1220.

Rousseau, J.-J. (1762). *The social contract.* Available at http://www.constitution.org/jjr/socon.htm.

Sartin, J. S. (1993). Infectious diseases during the Civil War: The triumph of the "Third Army." *Clinical Infectious Diseases, 16*(4), 580–584.

Shahbaza, M., Ozturkb, I., Afzac, T., & Alid, A. (2013). Revisiting the environmental Kuznets curve in a global economy. *Renewable and Sustainable Energy Reviews, 25*, 494–502.

Shaw, C., & McKay, H. (1942). *Crime and delinquency in urban areas.* Chicago: University of Chicago Press.

Smith, P. (2007a). Climate change, mass migration and the military response. *Orbis, 51*(4), 617–633.

Smith, P. (2007b). Climate change, weak states, and the war on terrorism in south and southeast Asia. *Contemporary Southeast Asia, 2*, 264–285. https://transnet.

act.nato.int/WISE/FSE/FuturesPap/ClimateCha/file/_WFS/climate%
20change%20weak%20states.pdf.

Smith, H. (2011). Sex trafficking: Trends, challenges, and the limits of international law. *Human Rights Review, 12,* 275–286.

Sullivan, J., & Elkus, A. (2011). Command of the cities: Towards a theory of urban strategy. *Small Wars Journal,* http://smallwarsjournal.com/jrnl/art/command-of-the-cities-towards-a-theory-of-urban-strategy.

Tanner, T., & Allouche, J. (2011). Towards a new political economy of climate change and development. *IDS Bulletin, 42*(3), 1–14.

Thomas, K., Melillo, J., & Peterson, T. (2009). *Global climate change impacts in the United States.* New York: Cambridge University Press. Available Online: http://downloads.globalchange.gov/usimpacts/pdfs/climate-impacts-report.pdf.

Tisdale, C. (2001). Globalisation and sustainability: Environmental Kuznets curve and the WTO. *Ecological Economics, 39*(2), 185–196.

Union of Concerned Scientists (2012). *A climate of corporate control.* Cambridge, MA: Center for Science and Democracy. http://www.ucsusa.org/scientific_integrity/abuses_of_science/a-climate-of-corporate-control.html.

Villarreal, A., & Silva, B. F. A. (2006). Social cohesion, criminal victimization and perceived risk of crime in Brazilian neighborhoods. *Social Forces, 84*(3), 1725–1753.

Walker, S. (1989). *Sense and nonsense about crime: A guide to policy.* Monterey, CA: Brooks/Cole.

Wallerstein, I. (1996). *Open the social sciences. Report of the Gulbenkian Commission on the restructuring of the social sciences.* Stanford, CA: Stanford University Press.

Warner, B. (1999). Whither poverty? Social disorganization theory in an era of urban transformation. *Sociological Focus, 32,* 99–113.

Weinstein, L. (2008). Mumbai's development mafias: Globalization, organized crime and land development. *International Journal of Urban and Regional Research, 32*(1), 23–39.

White, G. (2012). *Climate change and migration: Security and borders in a warming world.* New York: Oxford University Press.

Williams, P. (2008). *From the new middle ages to the new dark age: The decline of the state and U.S. strategy.* Carlisle Barracks, PA: U.S. Army War College, Strategic Studies Institute.

INDEX

Note: Page numbers followed by *b* indicate boxes, *f* indicate figures, and *t* indicate tables.